HOUGHTON MIFFLIN SOCIAL STUDIES

# From Sea to Shining Sea

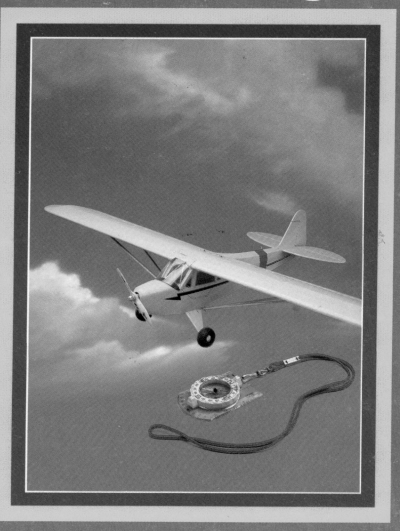

## TEACHER'S EDITION

Beverly J. Armento

Gary B. Nash

Christopher L. Salter

Karen K. Wixson

**Houghton Mifflin Company • Boston**

**Atlanta • Dallas • Geneva, Illinois • Princeton, New Jersey • Palo Alto • Toronto**

# Contents

## Acknowledgments

**Text**
(47A–47C) *The Mountain That Loved a Bird* by Alice McLerran. Copyright © 1985 by Alice McLerran. Reprinted by permission of Picture Book Studio, Saxonville, MA. (47D) From *Cowboys and Indians* by Kathryn & Byron Jackson. © 1968, 1948 by Western Publishing Company, Inc. Used by permission. (79A–79B) Reprinted with permission of Bradbury Press, an Affiliate of Macmillan, Inc. from *The Gift of the Sacred Dog* by Paul Goble. Copyright © 1980 by Paul Goble. (153A–153D) "Fresh Water to Drink" from *Little House on the Prairie* by Laura Ingalls Wilder. Text copyright 1935 by Laura Ingalls Wilder, copyright renewed 1963 by Roger L. MacBride. Reprinted by permission of Harper & Row, Publishers, Inc.

**Illustrations**
Jeanne Robertson 1B, 61B, 113B, 167B.

**Photographs**
T4 Ralph J. Brunke. T6–T15 All contemporary author, teacher, and student photographs by Jeff Schewe. T41 Peter Bosy. 25B © Pete Saloutos, Photographic Resources. 41B © Lawrence Migdale. 77B © Lawrence Migdale. 93B © Lawrence Migdale. 131B © Catherine Ursillo, Photo Researchers, Inc. 189B © Lawrence Migdale. 215B © Lawrence Migdale.

Printed in U.S.A.
ISBN 0-395-54024-0
ABCDEFGHIJ-B-99876543210

Development by Ligature, Inc.

T2

# Student Text with Teaching Notes

*The Houghton Mifflin Social Studies Teacher's Edition provides reduced Student Text pages with accompanying teacher's notes. Two pages of additional teacher information precede each chapter.*

## Openers

On unit and chapter openers, the teacher's margins present strategies where they are most useful—at the point of use.

The gray side margins offer suggestions for previewing the chapter to come and for discussing the images on the opener pages.

The bronze bottom margins contain a unit bibliography and chapter background information.

## Chapter Interleafs

Two pages immediately preceding each chapter provide a Chapter Organizer Chart, a Chapter Rationale, and chapter Activities and Projects.

## Lesson Pages

The design of the teacher's margins of all lesson pages continues the two distinct channels of information that were established on the opener pages.

The gray side margins present the three-part lesson plan: Introduce, Develop, Close. Again, critical teaching notes are located at point of use.

The bronze bottom margins offer long-range support, including lesson Objectives and additional Context information, plus a wealth of activities and extensions.

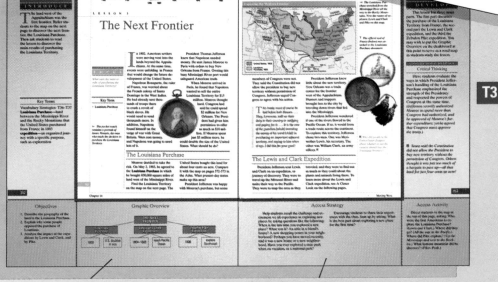

**The Graphic Overview** summarizes the major concepts of the lesson (see pages T36–T37).

**The Access Strategy** offers special tips for meeting the needs of LEP and other students (see pages T32–T33).

# Program Components

*Pictured here is a sampling of pages from Houghton Mifflin Social Studies. In addition to lesson pages and special features, the Student Text includes an array of appendices appropriate to each level. The Teacher's Edition provides instructional strategies and activities in the form of interleaf pages and point-of-use notes, as well as other features to support your teaching. Houghton Mifflin Social Studies also includes a wealth of Ancillaries to help you assess students' learning and enrich their social studies experience.*

**Big Book**

**Grade 6 Student Text**

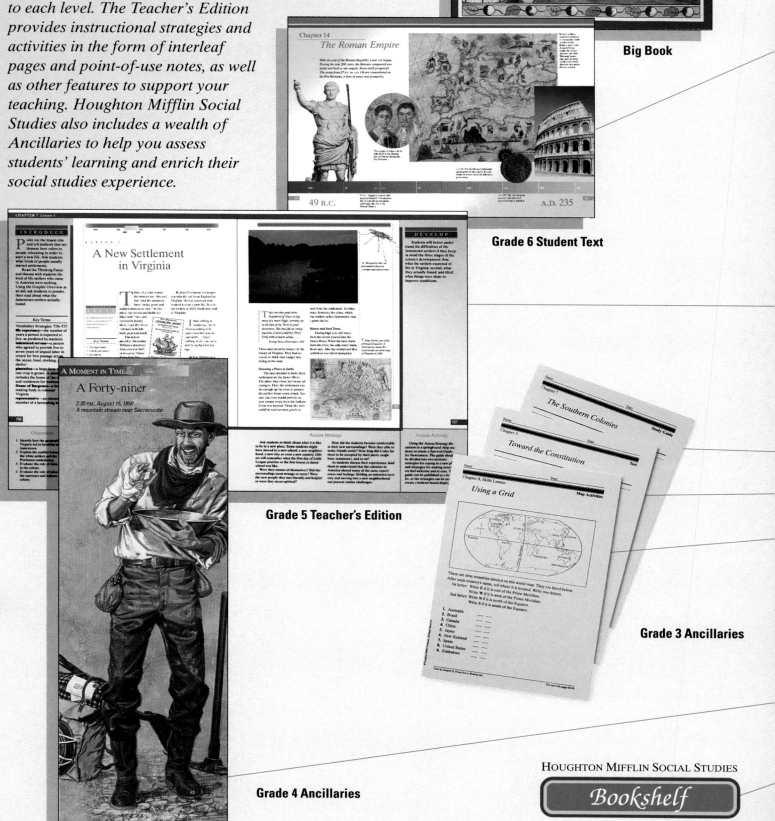

**Grade 5 Teacher's Edition**

**Grade 4 Ancillaries**

**Grade 3 Ancillaries**

HOUGHTON MIFFLIN SOCIAL STUDIES

*Bookshelf*

# PROGRAM COMPONENTS

| | Grade K | 1 | 2 | 3 | 4 | 5 | 6 | 7 | 8 |
|---|---|---|---|---|---|---|---|---|---|
| **BIG BOOK** | ■ | | | | | | | | |
| **STUDENT TEXT** | | ■ | ■ | ■ | ■ | ■ | ■ | ■ | ■ |
| Our Constitution Today | | | | | | | | | ■ |
| Constitution | | | | | | ■ | | | ■ |
| Declaration of Independence | | | | | | ■ | | | ■ |
| Additional Primary Sources | | | | | | | | | ■ |
| Minipedia | | | | | ■ | ■ | ■ | ■ | ■ |
| Atlas | | ■ | ■ | ■ | ■ | ■ | ■ | ■ | ■ |
| Geographic Glossary | | ■ | ■ | ■ | ■ | ■ | ■ | ■ | ■ |
| Gazetteer | | | | ■ | ■ | ■ | ■ | ■ | ■ |
| Biographical Dictionary | | | | | ■ | ■ | ■ | ■ | ■ |
| Glossary | | ■ | ■ | ■ | ■ | ■ | ■ | ■ | ■ |
| **TEACHER'S EDITION** | ■ | ■ | ■ | ■ | | ■ | ■ | ■ | ■ |
| Professional Handbook | ■ | ■ | ■ | ■ | ■ | ■ | ■ | ■ | ■ |
| Instructional Strategies | ■ | ■ | ■ | ■ | ■ | ■ | ■ | ■ | ■ |
| Additional Literature Selections | ■ | ■ | ■ | ■ | | | | | |
| **ANCILLARIES** | ■ | ■ | ■ | ■ | ■ | ■ | ■ | ■ | ■ |
| Study Guide | | ■ | ■ | ■ | ■ | ■ | ■ | ■ | ■ |
| Tests | | ■ | ■ | ■ | ■ | ■ | ■ | ■ | ■ |
| Map Masters | | ■ | ■ | ■ | ■ | ■ | ■ | ■ | ■ |
| Overhead Transparencies | | ■ | ■ | ■ | ■ | ■ | ■ | ■ | ■ |
| Home Involvement Booklet | | ■ | ■ | ■ | ■ | ■ | ■ | ■ | ■ |
| Study Prints | | ■ | ■ | ■ | ■ | ■ | ■ | ■ | ■ |
| Discovery Journal | | ■ | ■ | ■ | ■ | ■ | ■ | ■ | ■ |
| Posters | ■ | ■ | ■ | ■ | ■ | ■ | ■ | ■ | ■ |
| **BOOKSHELF** | ■ | ■ | ■ | ■ | ■ | ■ | ■ | ■ | ■ |

*Houghton Mifflin Social Studies:*

# Working With You to Develop Literate Citizens

*"All who have meditated
on the art of governing human beings
have been convinced that the fate of empires
depends on the education of youth."*

*Aristotle*

The goal of Houghton Mifflin Social Studies is the development of literate citizens—individuals with the knowledge, skills, and civic values they need to become active and reflective participants in the world of the twenty-first century. Our program weaves together knowledge, skills, and citizenship to form an integrated program. And because we focus on depth rather than breadth, our program helps you take the time to truly captivate, develop, question, and stretch your students. Take a moment and discover some of the ideas and people that make this program a powerful classroom tool.

T7

# A Program Based on In-Depth Learning

Whatever the task, we all know that doing something well takes time. Becoming a literate citizen is no exception. Students need time to explore topics, to practice skills in meaningful contexts, and to relate their learning to the world in which they live.

UNIT 4 *Lesson 2*
**From Here to There**

### LESSON 5
## One Little Kernel

**THINK**

Where does the corn that you eat come from?

**Key Word**

farmer

Here I am, one little kernel of corn.
The **farmer** calls me "seed corn."
Here I go into the planter.

### LESSON 6
## A Long Time Here

**THINK**

What traditions has Melanie learned from her family?

**Key Word**

weave

In beauty, I shall walk.
In beauty, you shall be my picture.
In beauty, you shall be my song.

*from the Navajo Nightway Ceremony*

This poem is about the land where Melanie Begaye (beh GAY) lives. Melanie is eight years old. She lives with her family near Round Rock, Arizona. Her ancestors have lived on this land for many years... United States became... her family are Navaj...

90

### LESSON 2
## Running Rivers

**THINKING FOCUS**

How do rivers affect the land?

**Key Terms**

- river
- lake
- flood

The river went on raising and raising for ten or twelve days, till at last it was over the banks. The water was three or four foot deep on the island in the low places and on the Illinois bottom. On that side it was a good many miles wide, but on the Missouri side it was the same old distance across—a half a mile—because the Missouri shore was just a wall of high bluffs.

Daytimes we paddled all over the island in the canoe.... Well, on every old broken-down tree you could see rabbits and snakes and such things; and when the island had been overflowed a day or two they got so tame, on account of being hungry, that you could paddle right up and put your hand on them if you wanted to; but not the snakes and turtles—they would slide off in the water.

*Mark Twain, from The Adventures of Huckleberry Finn*

The author who wrote these words lived along a river bank and often saw the water rise after a big rain. A **river** is a stream of water that flows across land. Rivers are different from oceans in two ways. First, oceans are much bigger than rivers are. Oceans cover most of the earth. Second, oceans are salty. Rivers are not. Water that comes from rivers is called fresh water.

18

### Early Grades

In the primary grades, students quickly move beyond their own areas to broaden their sense of place. This program gives students new insights into their communities and helps them make connections to the larger world. A variety of lesson formats invites students to explore the geographic, social, and economic aspects of their world. Literature, biographies, and lessons about real families introduce young learners to people and events in other times and places.

## Upper Grades

In the upper grades, students continue to study in depth. For example, in the fifth grade students study American history and geography from the first appearance of the American Indians to the Civil War era. In the eighth grade students focus on the period from the Constitutional Convention to the 1900s. In the sixth grade they study selected periods of ancient history. In the seventh grade they explore world civilizations and European history from the Fall of Rome to the Enlightenment. By narrowing the chronological focus, we give students time to take an in-depth, multi-perspective look at the world they live in.

LESSON 2

# The Railroad Is Born

Theodore Judah stood on a mountain peak, looking at the scene before him. At his feet, a rocky cliff dropped sharply into a valley 1,000 feet below. It was as if the mountains had put up a great stone stop sign in his path.

But Judah was not about to stop for the mountains. He was looking for a way to make his dream of a transcontinental railroad come true. Judah knew that building such a railroad meant crossing over the Sierra Nevada. So here he was, trying to find a way to lay . . . tracks from the top of this cliff down to the valley . . . imagine, it would not be easy for Judah . . .

**THINKING FOCUS**

What problems did Theodore Judah and the Big Four have to solve before they could build the transcontinental railroad?

**Key Terms**

* survey
* invest

➤ These are the mountains that Judah was hoping to build a railroad over. Does it surprise you that some people thought he was crazy?

168

LESSON 2

# Coming to America

It was not a pleasure trip, that 14-day . . . Crammed into a dark, stuffy cabin . . . the nights on sheetless bunks and no . . . for food that was ladled out to us as thou . . . Sheyna, and Zipke were seasick most o . . . remember staring at the sea for hours . . . be like.

Golda Meir, who later became prime minister of Israel, wrote words about her journey to . . . ica in 1906. She and her . . . and two sisters traveled from Russia to New York . . . re they continued to . . . where they joined . . .

. . . urage for Meir's . . . everything . . . move to a . . . ting to . . . almost . . .

**THINKING FOCUS**

What were the lives of immigrants like in the United States between 1870 and 1915 . . .

LESSON 1

# Exploring, Trading, and Converting

The seas rose towards the sky and fell back in heavy showers which flooded the ships. The storm raging thus violently, the danger was doubled, for suddenly the wind died out, so that the ships lay dead between the waves, lurching so heavily that they took in water on both sides; and the men made themselves fast not to fall from one side to the other; and everything . . . ng up . . . the ship was break- . . . ried to God for . . .

land for 96 days. The sailors thought they were lost. The crew was panic-stricken with fear, and murmurings of mutiny began.

But da Gama worried the captain. . . back, despite storms, sickness, and food shortages. He reached India in May 1498, after 14 months at sea. In 1499, when he finally re-turned to Portugal, only 44 of the . . . ginal 170 sailors still survived.

**THINKING FOCUS**

Why did explorers in the 1400s risk their lives to explore unknown parts of the world?

**Key Terms**

* monopoly
* balance of trad . . .
* bullion

Gaspar Correa, . . . of India, 1561

LESSON 3

# Daily Life in Ancient Rome

Before it is light I wake up, and, sitting on the edge of my bed, I put on my shoes and leg-wraps because it is cold. . . . Taking off my nightshirt I put on my tunic and belt; I put oil on my hair, comb it, wrap a scarf around my neck and put on my white cloak. Followed by my school attendant and my nurse I go to say good morning to daddy . . . them both, I find my writing things and exercise book and mumm . . . I followed by my school at-tendant . . .

I go in . . . me and . . . ing thing . . . ter to lea . . . white in . . . After b . . . says. . . .

As . . . my si . . . each c . . .

A b . . . family . . . of a ty . . .

**THINKING FOCUS**

How was daily life different for rich and poor Romans?

**Key Terms**

* rhetoric
* ritual

440                    Chapter 14

LESSON 3

# The Changing World of American Indians

The only way to check and stop this evil is for all the red men to unite in claiming a common and equal right in the land . . . for it never was divided, but belongs to all, for the use of each. . . . No part has a right to sell, even to each other, much less to strangers.

So spoke Shawnee chief Tecum-seh (ti KUM se) as he condemned and canceled the sale of Indian land to the U.S. government in 1809. Tecumseh had enlisted southern and northern warriors along the Mississippi Valley for a major united effort to recover lands lost to the white people. He was determined to hold the Ohio River as the boundary dividing the United States and Indian country.

As governor of the Indiana Territory, William Henry Harrison was also determined to defend white pioneers who invaded and settled in Indian territories. In 1810, Harrison met the Shawnee leader face to face at Vincennes, Indiana. As their talks began, Harrison's interpreter told Tecumseh "Your father requests . . .

He argued that the U.S. govern-ment had no real right to lands ceded, or transferred, to whites without the consent of all American Indians. Tecumseh shouted. "Sell a country! Why not sell the air, the clouds, and the great sea?"

The Great Spirit gave this great island to his red children. He placed the whites on the other side of the big water. They were not con-tented with their own, but came to take ours from us. They have driven us from the sea to the lakes—we can go no farther."

**THINKING FOCUS**

What were the different responses of the various American Indian peoples when their ancestral lands were threatened?

**Key Terms**

* revitalization
* cultural accommodation

➤ Tecumseh is shown here saving American prisoners during the War of 1812.

# A Team of Teachers and Authors

*Good ideas about effective instruction start with the reality of students in the classroom. Our authors have all brought their own expertise and classroom experience to Houghton Mifflin Social Studies, but they have also listened to what teachers like you have to say about improving social studies instruction. Listen to some of the suggestions teachers have made to our authors.*

**To Beverly Armento**

" I like history and culture as organizing concepts, but I want my students to be aware of the interaction of all human activities. I want a social studies curriculum that includes economics as well as the humanities. That's real social studies, and we've got to get it into the program."

**To Karen Wixson**

" Because social studies is an interweaving of many subjects, it's often difficult for my students to see how they all fit together. I'd like a textbook that is considerate of my students, one designed to help them make their way through the story and take responsibility for their own learning."

**To Gary Nash**

" My students are a very diverse group. I try my best to convince them that it took all kinds of people to build America. I want a book that addresses the historical presence of all those people. I want my students to identify with the many kinds of people who made this country great."

**To Kit Salter**

" My students have a hard time understanding that geography is more than just studying maps or memorizing the names of states and rivers. We need books that tell students the whole story of how people interact with the land."

# Beverly Armento on
# Integrating Social Studies

*"In this program we've enriched the content of social studies by drawing on knowledge from history, geography, and economics, as well as from the expressive arts and the humanities. Developing meaningful knowledge of the social world is a major goal of this program."*

In my daily life and in my work I use economics and the humanities as a way to step into social studies. But the goal of this program isn't simply to learn economics, or history, or geography. The goal is the development of an informed, active, caring decision maker who draws on meaningful knowledge, who has well-developed skills, who has a sense of what's important and what's not, and who is then able to take all of that and apply it to social issues."

**Beverly Jeanne Armento**
Professor of Social Studies Education
Director of the Center for Business and Economic Education
Georgia State University, Atlanta

## Graphs and Charts
" The visuals help us get a picture of how ideas relate to one another. The graphic aids are a way we can show these relationships."

**Cattle Driven from Texas to Abilene**

## Heading West

Since the early days of the colonies, Americans had been moving west. First, they moved into places like western Pennsylvania. Then they moved farther west into Kentucky and Missouri. The trail that Reggie saw was made by settlers moving as far west as Oregon. Many of ... ere the children, grandchildren, and ... ren of the earlier pioneers.

...rs went west to get away from crowded ... or to start farms on cheap land in the ...nt west to become miners. Miners are ... or gold, silver, and other valuable ...hers went west to buy and sell goods.

▼ Fast-moving water and rocks and holes along river bottoms made river crossings dangerous for pioneers.

...n the East to the far West was difficult. ...ad to cross the Great Plains. This huge ...pty and flat for hundreds of miles. ...inding food and drinking water was often a problem. S...me of the rivers they had to cross were dangerous. ...Pioneers going to the Pacific coast had to cross high mountains. These were steep and sometimes covered with ...ad to travel through

■ What were some of the reasons that pioneers traveled west, and why was the trip so difficult?

147

### DEVELOP

Preview the lesson headings and visuals. Then copy the Graphic Overview on the board and have students complete it as they read and discuss the lesson.

#### ECONOMICS
#### Critical Thinking

Discuss the basic wants and needs of the pioneers. Ask students what pushed the pioneers out of the East *(crowded cities),* and what pulled them west *(open space, farmland, gold, goods to trade).*

#### HISTORY
#### Visual Learning

Direct attention to the picture and ask why rivers were dangerous for wagon trains to cross. *(Wheels got stuck in holes; swift currents could upset wagons and wash away wagons, contents, and people.)*

Point out that the Indians of the time (shown smoking) did not know the dangers of smoking.

■ *Pioneers traveled west to find open space and good farmland or to become miners or traders. The trip was difficult because food and water were scarce, and pioneers had to cross dangerous rivers, steep mountains, and deserts.*

147

T13

## Literature and the Arts
" In my mind, literature, art, and music belong naturally in social studies. That's the way I've been teaching social studies for 26 years."

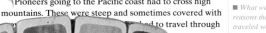

...ears ago, men, women, and children—young ...alike—went west to find a new land to settle. ...was not easy. Houses and food were hard to find. ...always, other people helped. Read this excerpt from ...ry about a pioneer family in Kansas.

LITERATURE

# WAGON WHEELS

**Written by Barbara Brenner**
**Illustrated by Don Bolognese**

## Chapter 1—THE DUGOUT

"T here it is, boys," Daddy said. "Across ... Nicodemus, Kansas. That is where ... build our house. There is fre... here in the West. All ...

# Gary Nash on
# Teaching History

*"Pick any movement you want in history, pick any great event, and as soon as you dig in you begin to see that the person in the street or the worker in the factory or the farmer in the field was involved in that movement."*

No one would think of writing a textbook without Abraham Lincoln or Julius Caesar. So it's not that we're completely changing the old vision in which famous people were carved in marble. I think for students we're making history more real, more accessible, more exciting, and more accurate by showing that great people were always interacting with ordinary people. History is the better for it. Women, minorities, and the working person can now find themselves in the historical pageant, the historical process."

T14

**Gary B. Nash**
Professor of History
UCLA

**Across Time and Space**

" Part of humanizing history is to show the connection of people in history to people today. Across Time and Space is a feature that makes those connections."

**Great People**

" Many famous people had grave doubts even in their twenties and thirties about what they were doing; they were still searching. In this program we try to make great people more human, so they're not cardboard heroes."

### Across Time & Space

*Many scientists believe that the earth was once one giant piece of land and one giant ocean. Look at the world map on pages 232-233. Imagine that Africa and South America are pieces of a puzzle. Fit them together.*

**All the People**

" My research and my writing have focused on people who have been left out of the history books: Native Americans, slaves, women, working people—people whose lives are another thread of the historical tapestry."

We the People

*Kit Salter on*

# Teaching Geographic Themes

*"Geography is essential to a good education because all of the human drama has been played out in an environmental setting, on an environmental stage. Climate, resources, the presence of some peoples, the absence of others are all elements of geography that give character to the events we're studying."*

In geography, we create an initial frame-work—the patterns of the human use of the earth—then we try to figure out how to study these patterns, and make sense of the landscape. The five fundamental themes of geography are tools we use to make sense of a place.

• Location: What are an area's absolute and relative locations?

• Place: What is its physical environ-ment and what are the patterns of its cultural landscape?

• Human-Environmental Interaction: How have people modified the landscape?

• Movement: What are the effects of the move-ment of goods, people, and ideas?

• Region: What are the knowable, regional segments of the land?"

**Christopher L. Salter**
Professor and Chair
Department of Geography
University of Missouri, Columbia

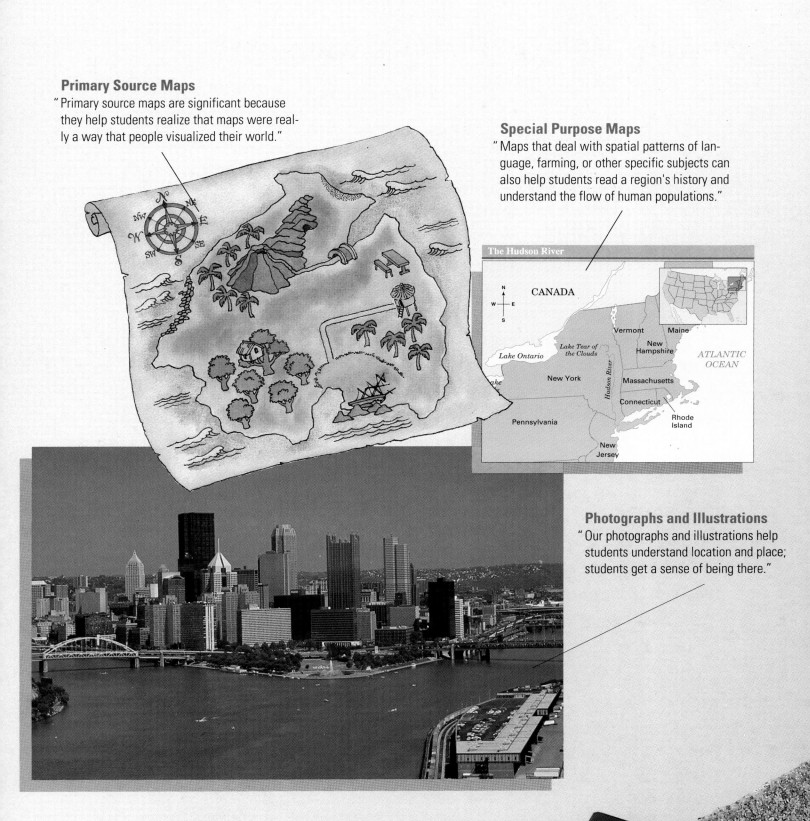

**Primary Source Maps**
" Primary source maps are significant because they help students realize that maps were really a way that people visualized their world."

**Special Purpose Maps**
" Maps that deal with spatial patterns of language, farming, or other specific subjects can also help students read a region's history and understand the flow of human populations."

**Photographs and Illustrations**
" Our photographs and illustrations help students understand location and place; students get a sense of being there."

**Geographic Tools**
" The wonder of geography is often captured in the thrill of exploration and discovery. Geographic artifacts can help bring an understanding of the human side of geography."

The Hudson River

CANADA

Lake Ontario

Lake Tear of the Clouds

Hudson River

Vermont
New Hampshire
Maine

New York

Massachusetts

Connecticut

Rhode Island

Pennsylvania

New Jersey

ATLANTIC OCEAN

*Karen Wixson on*
# Making Instruction Considerate

*"Instructional design really is a model of the thinking process that most of us learn to engage in through experience. Considerate instructional design makes the thinking process explicit. It helps the students become conscious of the thinking process."*

Being considerate of the student means working out an instructional design that helps the student learn. The text, for example, must have a logical flow of information, and the lessons, chapters, and units must be woven together by meaningful transitions. There must also be unity in the focus of the text so that the student stays with the big ideas. Instructional supports in the text, such as headings, graphics, and charts, have to relate to important information in a way that guides the learner through the text. Finally, the material has to be appropriate to the audience."

T18

**Karen K. Wixson**
Associate Professor of Education
University of Michigan, Ann Arbor

**Scholar's Margin**
" We designed an area outside the text body. We call it the Scholar's Margin. It was developed to guide student reading by focusing students on important ideas."

**Making Decisions**
" Our Making Decisions features give students a map of the process of decision making. Decisions made in history are connected with current concerns."

THINKING

FOCUS

What challenges did the Pilgrims face during their first year in the new homeland?

Key Terms

• colony
• survive

*Here's How*

Think about the things a pioneer family needed. Look at the items pictured on this page and on page 152 to get some ideas. What other things would you want to take in your wagon? Think about reasons for taking them.

*Try It*

Work with a partner. Make a list of all the things you would like to pack in your wagon. List those things that you must take. Also, list things that would be nice to take if there is room for them.

*Apply It*

If you had room in your wagon for only five items, which five would you choose to take? Tell why you would take each one.

153

the natural
the settlers
Indians ev
The Delaware also sh
herbs made the best medicines. ■

■ *How did the settlers adapt to the land?*

## R E V I E W

1. **FOCUS** What was life like for the people who moved from the coastal cities into the wilderness?
2. **CONNECT** Compare the way settlers and the Kwakiutl depended on forest goods.
3. **CRITICAL THINKING** Explain how you would feel about moving to the wilderness.
4. **ACTIVITY** Pretend you are a new settler traveling through the wilderness. Write a short description of what you are carrying and how you find food and shelter each day.

125

**Questions**
" The Scholar's Margin questions, preceded by a red box, and the Review questions were designed to help students check their understanding of important points in the lesson."

# A Program That Captivates

*Teachers and authors worked together to develop a program that reaches out and captivates a child. Together we developed books that students want to read, that capture student attention.*

## captivate

### A Moment in Time
A Pioneer on the Oregon Trail

4:50 P.M. May 7, 1843
On the banks of the Platte River
in central Nebraska

**Firewood**
Cottonwood branches make a great fire, and this woman plans to keep it going for several hours. After dinner, her new friends will join her family around the fire to talk about their plans to settle in Oregon.

**Shawl**
This woman's mother wore this colorful shawl when she traveled to America from Ireland. Now it is making another long journey as this pioneer crosses America.

**Flint**
Striking the rock in her pocket against a metal bar will make sparks to start a cooking fire. Tonight's dinner will be fresh fish from the Platte River.

**Dress**
Brand new at the start of the journey, this dress is now covered with prairie dust. The woman hopes that soon the wagon train will stop in one place long enough for her to wash it. The other dresses packed in her wagon are too fancy to wear on the trail.

**Shoes**
Before she left her farm in Ohio, this woman bought these tough leather shoes. The salesman who sold them to her said that they would hold up well on the rough, rocky trails of the mountains.

150

**A Moment in Time**
This feature allows students to get an in-depth look at people, objects, and places. History and geography come alive in the middle of everyday activities.

T20

## A Story Well Told

Each lesson begins with a hook—an engaging passage—sometimes taken from a primary source or a piece of literature. What follows is a well-told story, presented in a meaningful way.

LESSON 1

# Between Sea and Forest

THINKING
## FOCUS

*How did the Kwakiutl meet their basic need for food and shelter?*

### Key Terms

- salmon
- cedar
- long house

K wiskwis is very excited! Today her mother will show her how women make clothes out of tree bark.

"Where do we start?" asks Kwiskwis excitedly.

"With a cedar *(SEE dur)* tree," her mother says.

Kwiskwis and her mother pull long strips of bark off the trees. Then they pull the softer inner bark from these strips. When they collect as much of the softer bark as they can carry, they return to their big wooden house.

"First we pound the bark with this beater until it is not so stiff," says Mother. "Next, we will separate the bark into thin strips. We will weave these strips together on this frame to make a new cape for your grandmother."

Kwiskwis smiles, knowing the gift will keep her grandmother warm and dry.

► *This picture of a woman wearing a cedar bark blanket was taken long ago. Below is a wooden beater that women used to pound the bark before it could be woven into blankets or clothing.*

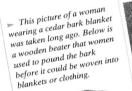

## Teacher's Edition Notes

Convenient teacher's notes, like the Understanding the Visuals feature, give you additional information to make your instruction relevant and engaging.

### Notes on the Photograph

This photograph was taken by David Muench, who has been fascinated with the wilderness of the United States since he was a child traveling with his famous photographer-father Josef Muench. David Muench is now himself a well-known Western landscape artist whose photographs appear in books and magazines. This picture shows a scene from the Grand Teton National Park in Wyoming.

## First Year in Plymouth, From Fall to Fall

┌ **Mayflower arrives**                          **Good harvest** ┐

| 1620 Nov. | Dec. | 1621 Jan. | Feb. | March | April | May | June | July | Aug. | Sept. | Oct. |
|---|---|---|---|---|---|---|---|---|---|---|---|

└ **Harsh Winter**        └ **Wampanaog help with crops**        **First Thanksgiving** ┘

## Timelines

Timelines draw students into the chronology of history. Timelines help students relate images, ideas, events, and places in temporal order.

# A Program That Develops

Developing and deepening student understanding of conceptual knowledge is a key part of forming literate citizens. Enriching student awareness of important ideas is one of the fundamental goals of this program. We include features that help you develop a deeper understanding of knowledge in your students.

**Understanding**
The Understanding feature takes an in-depth look at an important lesson concept. This feature allows students to relate concepts to ideas they already know.

### UNDERSTANDING NATURAL RESOURCES

## We Use Natural Resources

The Cheyenne used the buffalo to provide food, clothing, and shelter. The buffalo were a natural resource. A natural resource is anything found in nature that people can use.

Trees, soil, and water were also natural resources for the Cheyenne. The poles that dogs dragged behind them and that held up Cheyenne tipis came from trees. The Cheyenne raised crops in the soil and drank water from streams.

Today, we use many of the same natural resources. We use trees to make everything from houses to paper to clothing. We also use the soil to grow food. We drink water that comes from rivers, lakes, and underground wells.

Natural resources are also found inside the earth. Things like oil, coal, rocks, and metals are natural resources. Today, we use oil to make gasoline for cars. We burn coal in factories, and we use rocks to make cement sidewalks. We build many things, such as cars, with metals. These resources are as important to us as the buffalo were to the Cheyenne.

85

T22

## Graphic Overviews

Graphic Overviews in the Teacher's Edition give you a new way to organize knowledge. Each is a visual map to learning.

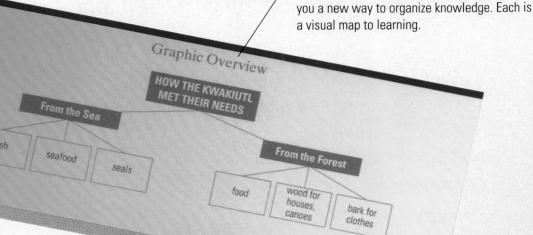

Graphic Overview

**HOW THE KWAKIUTL MET THEIR NEEDS**

From the Sea
- fish
- seafood
- seals

From the Forest
- food
- wood for houses, canoes
- bark for clothes

## Photographs and Illustrations

Visual learning is a special way to help students develop their knowledge. It also helps to reach students who might otherwise be unreachable.

## Teacher's Edition Notes

The Teacher's Edition point-of-use notes supply you with background knowledge and ideas to help you develop in students a deeper understanding of a subject.

**CHAPTER 7 Lesson 1**

### INTRODUCE

Discuss facing a situation for the first time, such as the first day of school or moving to a new neighborhood. Then read the lesson title, Thinking Focus, and introductory paragraphs, and ask how students would feel about moving under the circumstances described. Have students predict some problems that the Pilgrims might have faced when they landed at Plymouth. Have students read to confirm or reject their predictions.

LESSON 1

# Life in Plymout

Pretend you are living long in England. Your family has decided to make a new home away, so you leave your hon

**THINKING**
**FOCUS**

*What challenges did the*

# A Program That Questions

*H*elping students think about ideas and issues involves getting them to question and think in a critical way. We developed a program with solid critical thinking strategies and a thorough assessment component.

UNDERSTANDING MAIN IDEAS

## Finding Supporting Details

**Here's Why.** Writers often write about one main idea in each paragraph. Other sentences give details that support, or explain, the main idea. Knowing how to find main ideas and their supporting details will help you understand what you read.

**Here's How** Think of a chart such as the one below when you read a paragraph. The large box at the top has the main idea. The smaller boxes have the details. Read this paragraph:

The forest is home to many animals. Birds make their nests in tree branches. Hollowed-out tree stumps are homes for raccoons and other animals. Deer sleep and hide among the trees in forests.

The main idea of the paragraph is: *The forest is home to many animals.* The other sentences tell how the forest is home to the animals. They give the details that support the main idea.

**Main Idea:** The forest is home to many animals.

**Detail:** Birds make their nests in tree branches.

**Detail:** Hollowed-out tree stumps are homes for raccoons and other animals.

**Detail:** Deer sleep and hide among the trees in forests.

**Try It** Read the second paragraph on page 29 again. The main idea is stated in the first sentence. What details support the main idea?

**Apply It** Work with a partner. Write a paragraph about forests or forest animals. Make a chart of your main idea and supporting details.

**Understanding**
The Understanding feature helps integrate the development of skills with the learning of knowledge. In this program, Critical Thinking is one of the central skill strands.

## question

Remind students that in the last lesson they read about the Pilgrims in 1620. Now they are going to learn about a new group of settlers who lived in the early to middle 1700s. Write *wilderness* on the board. Point out the root *wild* and elicit a definition from students. Record their definitions on the board. Then have students look at the map on page 122. Point out the wilderness of eastern Pennsylvania and its proximity to Philadelphia. Then have students look at the pictures in the lesson and discuss what they notice about wilderness life from the pictures.

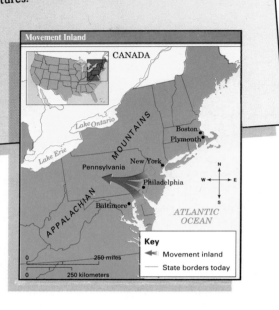

**Movement Inland**

CANADA

Lake Ontario

Lake Erie

MOUNTAINS

Boston
Plymouth

Pennsylvania

New York

Philadelphia

Baltimore

APPALACHIAN

ATLANTIC OCEAN

N W E S

**Key**
→ Movement inland
— State borders today

0 250 miles
0 250 kilometers

**Access Strategy**
Ideas to help you aid students with limited English proficiency and students with little prior knowledge of a subject are parts of the Access Strategy feature in the Teacher's Edition.

**Making Decisions**
Students are actively engaged in addressing important issues in this program. This feature helps students develop decision-making skills.

MAKING DECISIONS

Getting Farm Products to Stores

*You know that many different crops are grown in the San Joaquin Valley of California. You know why they grow so well there. You also know how they are harvested. But do you know how they get from a farm to stores across the country? Let's think about that a little bit.*

Here's Why

Suppose you grow almonds, tomatoes, and carrots on a farm in the San Joaquin Valley. You want to send them to cities in the United States and then to stores within the cities. You have to decide how to get your crops to the stores at the lowest cost before they spoil or rot. How will you send each of them?

Here's How

Your crops can be shipped by truck, airplane, or train. You may have to use more than one method of transportation. Use the chart below to help you decide how to ship your crops.

Comparing Ways of Moving Farm Products

**Airplane**
Travels faster than trucks or trains.
Costs more than trucks or trains.
Cannot carry products directly to stores.

**Truck**
Costs less than airplanes or trains.
Can carry products directly to stores.
Travels slower than airplanes and trains.

**Train**
Can carry more than airplanes or trucks.
Costs more than trucks.
Cannot carry products directly to stores.

LESSON 2

# Running Rivers

THINKING
**FOCUS**
How do rivers affect the land?

The river went on raising and raising for ten or twelve days, till at last it was over the banks. The water was three or four foot deep on the island in the low places and on the Illinois bottom. On that side it was a good many miles wide, but on the Missouri...

Key Terms
• river

**Thinking Focus**
The Thinking Focus question sets up a purpose for the lesson. It centers students' attention as they read.

T25

# A Program That Stretches

Effective instruction encourages students to go beyond the classroom to seek an understanding of the social world. You have asked us to come up with ideas that help you stretch student learning and to provide extra resources that enrich students' educational experience.

EXPLORE

## The Land Around You

What is the land like where you live? Are there rivers or lakes nearby? Is the land flat or is it hilly? Rivers, lakes, oceans, mountains, and hills are all physical features. You can explore the area where you live to find out more about its physical features.

**Get Ready** Begin by looking at the land near where you live. Then look at the land near your school and other places you visit close to home. Start a notebook of the physical features you see around you. Write about what you see. Draw pictures of the land you explore. You can also learn more about the land where you live by looking at maps and photographs.

**Find Out** Make a map of your area to show how the land looks. Use the notes and drawings in your notebook for help. You may also use photographs and maps from books and newspapers for help.

I see a river and a hill.

## stretch

### Explore

When students explore topics and ideas and try to find out new things for themselves, they are extending and stretching their knowledge. Our Explore feature provides opportunities for students to participate in the discovery process.

## Teacher's Information

In the Teacher's Edition page you will find special ideas for getting your students to try new things, to discover new ways of looking at the material found in the text. The entire Teacher's Guide is full of ideas for stretching student learning.

**Oregon Trail**

**Shawl**
This woman's mother wore this colorful shawl when she traveled to America from Ireland. Now it is making another long pioneer journey as this pioneer crosses America.

**Firewood**
Cottonwood branches make a great fire, and this woman plans to keep it going for several hours. After dinner, her new friends will join her family around the fire to talk about their plans to settle in Oregon.

**Flint**
Striking the rock in her pocket against a metal bar will make sparks to start a cooking fire. Tonight's dinner will be fresh fish from the Platte River.

**Shoes**
Before she left her farm in Ohio, this woman bought these tough leather shoes. The salesman who sold them to her said that they would hold up well on the rough, rocky trails of the mountains.

**Dress**
Brand new at the start of the journey, this dress is now covered with prairie dust. The woman hopes that soon the wagon train will stop in one place long enough for her to wash it. The other dresses packed in her wagon are too fancy to wear on the trail.

Read and discuss the captions. Ask students to use the information to infer what a typical day "on the road" would be like for pioneer children on the Oregon Trail. List some of the chores students mention on the board. (fishing, helping prepare meals, gathering fuel and tending fires, caring for livestock, etc.) Have students compare this list with a list of chores they do at home.

**More About Clothing** Clothing was hard to acquire on the frontier. Fabric for clothes was expensive, and spinning fabric was a long and difficult job. Shoes and boots were also a precious commodity. When the ones the pioneers brought with them wore out, they went barefoot or made shoepacks, which were similar to moccasins. Shoepacks covered the ankles and had heavy soles.

**Visual Learning**
Have students draw modern equivalents of the pioneer items shown on this page. Have students put the modern equivalents next to the items on the page and compare and contrast them.

**Role-Playing**
Have groups of about six students role-play the woman in the picture getting together with her friends that evening. Students can make up names for characters and improvise dialogue in which they talk about the day and their plans for settling in Oregon.

**Making a Model**
Students might work in small groups to make models of covered wagons. Have students bring shoeboxes, wheels from old toys, fabric, and wire or plastic straws. When the models are done, students might like to display them in the room... wagon train.

150

**GLOSSARY**

**GLOSSARY OF GEOGRAPHIC TERMS**

**GAZETTEER**

## Time/Space Databank

The appendix contains the most thorough supplement yet devised for a social studies program. There you will find geographical aids, additional maps that are referenced throughout the text, and other features to supplement learning.

T28

*" It is the supreme art*
*of the teacher to awaken joy*
*in creative expression and knowledge."*

*Albert Einstein*

By preparing your students to use their knowledge and skills to make the decisions that democracy will thrust upon them, you are developing caring, literate citizens. The formation of a nation of powerful decision makers begins in the classroom, and its ramifications will be felt by future generations. A future in which today's students have solid knowledge, know when and how to use skills, and possess an understanding of involved citizenship will be a future in which the principles of democracy will grow and flourish. All of us, working together, have developed a program aimed at that goal. Houghton Mifflin is proud to be a part of the process of creating literate citizens, of forming powerful decision makers who care both for our nation and for civilization itself.

# Social Studies and the Thinking Curriculum

The development of reflective and knowledge-able thinkers and decision makers is an important goal of instruction in social studies as well as in other curriculum areas. Many educators have traditionally approached thinking in terms of a hierarchy of skills in which young students master basic skills before progressing to "higher-order" skills such as analysis and interpretation. However, recent research indicates that these so-called higher-order skills are crucial to successful learning at even the earliest ages.

Another critical aspect of the new research on learning is that knowledge and skills must be developed together, and not as isolated elements. The dual agenda of knowledge and skills is an important part of the Houghton Mifflin program.

Instead of focusing on a rigid hierarchy of thinking skills, effective instruction takes into account many aspects of thinking. The following definitions describe four key aspects of thinking as they are used in Houghton Mifflin Social Studies.

**Metacognition:** Simply put, *metacognition* means being aware of our thinking as we perform tasks and using that awareness to monitor and direct what we are doing. This ability is exercised by all skilled readers and thinkers, and it is crucial to model metacognitive skills for students so that they can become independent learners.

**Critical Thinking:** Although *critical thinking* is a major focus in education today, the term is often ambiguously understood. Houghton Mifflin Social Studies adopts the widely used definition of critical thinking as reasonable, reflective thinking that is focused on deciding what to believe or what to do.

**Thinking Skills:** In Houghton Mifflin Social Studies, the term *thinking skills* refers to basic mental tasks such as observing, comparing, classifying, or predicting. These discrete skills can be learned and then used in metacognition, critical thinking, and other thinking processes.

**Thinking Processes:** The term *thinking processes* refers to goal-oriented processes such as problem solving and decision making that involve a variable but predictable sequence of thinking skills.

## Houghton Mifflin Social Studies Features That Promote Thinking

Because thinking is central to all instruction and learning, Houghton Mifflin Social Studies integrates metacognition, critical thinking, thinking skills and thinking processes throughout. However, several features are particularly effective devices for promoting the development of skilled thinkers.

### Scholar's Margin

In every lesson of Houghton Mifflin Social Studies, the outside margin of each page is a Scholar's Margin devoted to helping students take charge of their own learning. In other words, it is there to promote metacognition. Each lesson begins with a Thinking Focus question that alerts students to a key concept or idea they should keep in mind as they read. At the end of each major section of the lesson, they will also find a self-check question in the Scholar's Margin. By answering this question for themselves, students can monitor their own comprehension and determine for themselves when they need to reread. If students can answer each of these self-check questions, when they reach the end of the lesson they should be able to answer the Thinking Focus, which reappears as the first question in the lesson Review.

### Understanding Skills

Every chapter of Houghton Mifflin Social Studies contains one or more Understanding features that teach students skills in a carefully constructed context. The Here's How section of each feature carefully teaches students how to perform the skill—what is sometimes called procedural knowledge or "knowledge of how." In addition, however, each feature begins with a Here's Why section that addresses a critical but often overlooked aspect of thinking—conditional knowledge or "knowledge of why and when." This section helps students to understand the purposes for which they would use the skill and to identify conditions under which it would be useful. As a result, students learn not just how to use a skill but also how to determine for themselves when it would be useful to apply the skill.

Many of the Understanding Skills features focus on skills drawn from our Critical Thinking strand. Students have the opportunity to practice and apply skills of defining and clarifying problems and issues, evaluating and judging information, identifying alternative perspectives and solving problems and drawing conclusions. At every grade level, students work with these "higher-order" skills. What progresses from grade to grade is the difficulty of the information about which students are thinking and the sophistication of the context in which these skills are applied.

### Understanding Concepts

In most chapters another type of Understanding feature provides an in-depth look at a concept that is key to that chapter. These features provide support for students in the important thinking process of concept formation. They provide extended definitions and present examples and nonexamples of the concept. These features also help students identify the major attributes of the concept and relate it to other concepts they have learned previously.

### Making Decisions

Because a key goal of social studies instruction is the development of citizens who can make informed and responsible decisions, the process of decision making is a particularly appropriate thinking process to emphasize in social studies. The Making Decisions features in Houghton Mifflin Social Studies provide the opportunity for students to analyze important decisions in history and utilize the thinking skills that make up the decision-making process.

These features have been developed on the basis of a five-step model of decision making that maps out the sequence of critical thinking skills involved in making decisions:

1. Recognize the need for a decision.
2. Define the goals and values involved.
3. Acquire and evaluate necessary information.
4. Identify and analyze possible alternatives.
5. Choose the best alternative.

As this model demonstrates, the process of decision making involves all of the major strands of social studies instruction: knowledge, skills, and values. Thus these features provide a powerful tool for integrated learning and thinking.

## A Classroom Climate That Promotes Thinking

One thing that distinguishes proficient thinkers and decision makers from poorer ones is not so much the skills they possess as their motivation and tendency to use them. Because thinking is hard work, students need not only to know how to do it but also to have their own powerful reasons for wanting to think critically and reflectively. The role of the teacher is crucial in helping students become motivated and active thinkers. In particular, researchers point to the importance of modeling skillful thinking for students and of establishing a classroom environment that encourages and values thinking.

Modeling can take a variety of forms. For example, you as a teacher can model for students ways of becoming aware of your own thinking and using that awareness to control what you are doing. You may start by

verbalizing for students your internal thought processes as you process new information. This "thinking out loud" may include

- assessing your current knowledge ("Do I know the meaning of all the words in this text?" or "Do I understand the legend on this map?")
- setting goals ("What do I want to know or be able to do when I'm through?")
- checking your progress as you go along ("Do I understand what I just read?" or "Am I closer to my goal now than when I started?")

Teachers also play a vital role in modeling attitudes and dispositions that are essential to successful thinking and learning. Important first steps include modeling and reinforcing such basic attitudes as "hard work pays off" and "it's important to learn from mistakes." Teachers also provide a major service to students by exemplifying important dispositions of critical thinking, such as:

- seeking a clear statement of a question
- using and mentioning credible sources
- seeking reasons
- looking for alternatives and alternative viewpoints
- being open-minded
- changing one's position when the evidence merits

In addition to the teacher, student interaction can also play an important role in developing skilled thinkers. This is one reason why collaborative learning can be a powerful approach (see page T34). More capable students can model for peers effective ways of approaching problems, analyzing text, and organizing their work. Students in groups may also support each other in carrying out complicated tasks. By working collaboratively, the group can succeed at a task that individual students could not handle alone.

Finally, the social setting of the classroom can communicate to students that all aspects of thinking are valued. Through their behavior and interactions, teachers and students can convey the message that questioning, interpreting, and trying many possibilities are as important as "getting the right answer."

## For Further Reading

Laughlin, Margaret A., H. Michael Hartoonian, Norris M. Sanders, eds. *From Information to Decision Making: New Challenges for Effective Citizenship.* Washington, D.C.: National Council for the Social Studies (Bulletin No. 83), 1989.

Marzano, Robert J., et al. *Dimensions of Thinking: A Framework for Curriculum and Instruction.* Alexandria, Va.: Association for Supervision and Curriculum Development, 1988.

# Access to Social Studies for Limited English Proficient Students

Because of rapid demographic changes nationwide, many school districts now enroll a significant number of students whose first language is not English. In most cases, Limited English Proficient (LEP) students in a school have widely different educational backgrounds and function at a broad range of achievement levels. Some pupils may have had limited opportunities for formal education in their homeland and come to our schools preliterate. Others, while not proficient in English, have benefited from a high level of schooling in their first language and are highly literate in their mother tongue.

As a population, LEP students are diverse, yet they all share many identifiable instructional needs. Most LEP students are still in the process of developing English language fluency while trying to master new, academically demanding material. For these reasons, social studies instruction should be available to all pupils regardless of their language background. Furthermore, social studies should be presented in such a way that children can succeed in grade-level subject matter, and as a byproduct, expand their English language abilities.

Students who are completely non-English speaking may need to access social studies through their first language while acquiring English. As pupils reach intermediate-level fluency in English, they become less dependent on native language instruction to unlock new concepts. Intermediate speakers usually can comprehend content taught in the new language when teachers make effective use of context clues, such as facial expressions, gestures, and props.

## Features of Houghton Mifflin Social Studies That Promote Access

Houghton Mifflin Social Studies has been designed to facilitate maximum access to social studies concepts for students from a wide variety of cultural and linguistic backgrounds. No matter what their spoken language, all students have basically the same visual language. Thus the unique Visual Learning strand and prominent instructional visuals throughout the program provide a channel of access for LEP students. In addition, every chapter and lesson has many LEP-appropriate features built in. LEP-appropriate features are clearly identified for you in the Chapter Organizer chart that precedes each chapter. These features include the following:

- LEP Chapter Activities
- Access Strategies
- Access Activities
- Graphic Overviews
- Visual Learning Strategies

## Strategies for Accessible Instruction

Teachers of LEP students should consider the following suggestions when working with second language learners.

1. **Use language-sensitive techniques** to lower the language barrier for intermediate fluency LEP students. These techniques include:

   - using gestures and facial expressions
   - modeling the desired performance
   - using visuals and props
   - simplifying speech
   - showing a sample of the finished product
   - breaking down complicated tasks into smaller subtasks
   - checking frequently for understanding

   These strategies are, in fact, based on good teaching practices appropriate for all students. The integrity of high-level content is enhanced, not sacrificed, through such support.

2. **Build background knowledge** necessary to unlock key concepts in the lesson. For each lesson, the TE provides an Access Strategy specially designed to build requisite background to open a wider door to new concepts in the program. In addition, discussion of the Study Prints, Posters, and Overhead Transparencies all facilitate high-level comprehension of the material.

3. **Tap prior knowledge** by having pupils brainstorm what they already know about the topic. You can also focus prior knowledge through quickwrites (T39), which enable youngsters to write their thoughts in a free-form manner, and through using Venn diagrams (T36) to show similarities and differences among ideas or events.

4. **Preteach only essential vocabulary**—that is, the terms necessary for understanding the key concepts in a lesson. Where possible, introduce families of words in context with interactive activities (see T36–T37). You may also consider expanding vocabulary by using the room environment to chart new words centered around a theme. Paraphrasing, summarizing, reading key sections of the text aloud, and discussion of a visual in the text are also effective strategies for building vocabulary.

5. **Utilize collaborative learning** activities that enable pairs and small groups of students to read selected sections of text together to ensure comprehension. Collaborative learning enhances the language proficiency of LEP and native speakers of English alike (see T34–T35).

6. **Use oral and visual language** to focus learners. For example, you might talk through the Graphic Overview and Thinking Focus for each new lesson to help LEP students focus on key concepts. Some LEP pupils may lack the language skills key to reading comprehension. Asking questions orally can also help develop proficiency in the use of content-specific language. And use of the Graphic Overview for each lesson will help students visualize how ideas relate to one another. These visual images promote comprehension, retention, and recall.

## Social Studies and the Overall LEP Program

There is no simple way to eliminate completely the language barrier to social studies for LEP students. LEP youngsters are most successful when they have a program that enables them to achieve functional fluency in English quickly. Such a program begins with intensive English as a second language (ESL) lessons designed to teach the basics of English. Then an advanced ESL program might teach social studies vocabulary and build conceptual background to enable students to derive maximum benefit from the Houghton Mifflin Social Studies program.

In addition to a sequential English language development program, students who are in the initial phases of acquiring English may need primary language support to comprehend fully the key concepts in the program. To benefit all students, Houghton Mifflin Social Studies has been designed to facilitate access to grade-level social studies through instructional strategies that are grounded in language and learning theory as well as good teaching.

## For Further Reading

Cantoni-Harvey, G. *Content-Area Language Instruction: Approaches and Strategies.* Reading, Mass.: Addison-Wesley, 1987.

Crandall, J. A., D. Christian, and D. J. Short. *How to Integrate Language and Content Instruction: A Training Manual.* Berkeley, Cal.: Center for Language Education and Research, University of California, 1989.

Richard-Amato, P. A. *Making It Happen: Interaction in the Second Language Classroom from Theory to Practice.* New York: Longman, 1988.

# Using Collaborative Learning in Social Studies

Collaborative learning is a strategy or structure for learning that can be adapted to many lessons and activities. There are many models or approaches to collaborative learning (or cooperative learning), but all of these models share certain basic characteristics:

- Students work face to face in heterogeneous groups.
- Each member of the group has a clearly defined role and is individually accountable.
- Each member makes an important contribution to the success of the group's effort ("positive interdependence").

In addition to the advantages that it offers in all curriculum areas, collaborative learning is an especially appropriate strategy for social studies. Working together in collaborative groups is an excellent way to develop students' skills of social participation, always a key goal of the social studies curriculum.

As a teacher, you should feel free to take collaborative learning at your own pace. You may wish to begin with simple strategies in which students work in pairs. As both you and your students become comfortable with this approach to learning, you can tackle more elaborate activities involving groups of four or five.

## Your Role as Teacher

It is important to bear in mind that collaborative learning supplements direct instruction—it does not replace it. As always, the teacher provides the solid instruction that is the basis for learning. And simply putting students in groups and giving them an interesting assignment does not lead to successful collaborative learning. Instead, you as teacher play the key role of providing structure, guidance, and feedback. In a very real sense, your role becomes that of coach or facilitator.

An important ingredient in the success of collaborative groups is effective use of interpersonal skills. As facilitator, you can help groups identify ahead of time the kinds of interpersonal skills that will be important to the task they are undertaking. These skills may range from something as simple as speaking quietly to more complex skills such as encouraging participation and giving constructive criticism. Modeling these skills for students and helping students practice them are important parts of your role.

Another area in which student groups need support is in learning to manage the process of group interaction. It is usually easier for students to divide up tasks such as research and writing than it is for them to

make sure that someone keeps the group on target and monitors their progress. Supporting and guiding students in these process tasks can help assure the success of the group's efforts.

## Practical Tips

1. It takes times for group members to become comfortable with one another and work together effectively. You may want to begin by having groups engage in some simple brainstorming activities just to become acquainted and begin to develop trust. For the same reason, it is usually best to keep groups together for at least several weeks before regrouping.

2. To promote the development of interpersonal skills, you may wish to provide reinforcement to groups for exhibiting particular social skills in their work together.

3. Try to build in time for groups to evaluate their performance after completing an activity. How well did they do not only with the academic task but with their interpersonal and group processes? What lessons can they apply to future collaborative efforts?

## Strategies

The following strategies can be adapted to many lessons and activities in Houghton Mifflin Social Studies. For more information about these and other strategies, see For Further Reading on page T35.

### Three-Step Interview

**Procedures:** Students work in pairs to interview each other about an assigned topic.
1. One student interviews the other about the topic.
2. The students switch roles as interviewer and interviewee.
3. Each student then shares with the group what he or she learned during the interview.

**Uses:** The Three-Step Interview can be used effectively to build background knowledge in conjunction with the Introduce part of the Teacher's Edition lesson. You can use the notes under Introduce to formulate a question for the interview, such as "What do you know about [topic of lesson]?" As an option for the Close part of the lesson, occasionally you might also have students do a Three-Step Interview on a question such as "What's the most important thing you learned about [topic of lesson]?" or "What else would you like to know about [topic]?"

**Benefits:** Promotes participation, listening skills, divergent thinking

### Jigsaw

**Procedures:** In the Jigsaw strategy each member of the team becomes "expert" about a particular topic related to a larger team project. Team members then share information to prepare a presentation or solve a problem. Following are the main steps:
1. Identify several manageable topics related to a larger topic or concept.
2. Set up an "expert" group for each topic made up of one member from each team.
3. Have expert groups work together to research their topic.
4. Experts return to their original teams and share what they have learned.
5. You as teacher may assign the teams a particular format for presenting their findings, or you may let teams select for themselves the formats they wish to use.

**Uses:** The Jigsaw approach can be used with many of the Collaborative Learning activities in the Chapter Reviews. It is particularly effective in helping students to prepare for informed debate or to acquire and present new information.

**Benefits:** Promotes interdependence, helps students discover connections among concepts and bodies of information

### Group Investigation

**Procedures:** Students work in teams to prepare a presentation or project to share with the class. Students form teams based on a shared interest in the topic and divide the work so that each student on a team has a definite task to perform.

**Uses:** This strategy is helpful to students in synthesizing information from several sources, including interviews and library research. Many Chapter Review activities lend themselves to this approach.

**Benefits:** Promotes organizational and presentation skills; helps students direct their own learning

### Pair Debate

**Procedures:** Students debate an issue in pairs. First, each student defends one side of the issue; then pairs switch partners, and each student must defend the other side of the same issue.

**Uses:** Pair Debate can be used as an effective Close for many lessons, especially those that deal with conflict or controversy in history.

**Benefits:** Promotes role-taking, knowing, and respecting different points of view

## For Further Reading

Aronson, E., et al. *The Jigsaw Classroom.* Beverly Hills, Cal.: Sage Publications, 1978.

Johnson, D. W., R. T. Johnson, E. J. Holubec, and P. Roy. *Circles of Learning: Cooperation in the Classroom.* Alexandria, Va.: Association for Supervision and Curriculum Development, 1984.

Kagan, S. *Cooperative Learning: Resources for Teachers.* San Juan Capistrano, Cal.: Resources for Teachers, 1989.

Slavin, R. E., et al., eds. *Learning to Cooperate, Cooperating to Learn.* New York: Plenum Press, 1985.

# Developing Concepts and Vocabulary

Vocabulary instruction plays an important role in social studies, as it does in all content area reading. But teaching students a social studies term usually does not mean teaching them a new label for a concept that they already have. In most cases, it means teaching students an unfamiliar concept.

Houghton Mifflin Social Studies integrates vocabulary instruction with the teaching of other concepts and knowledge. Always the emphasis is on starting with what students already know and linking that prior knowledge to new concepts and information. This approach is solidly grounded in research that shows that knowledge is not just unrelated facts but sets of relationships. We learn new information by relating it to what we already know.

Many features of this Teacher's Edition will help you help your students activate their prior knowledge and link new concepts. The Unit Previews, the Chapter Overviews, and the Introduce portion of each lesson provide useful strategies. The Graphic Overviews can also help you show your students connections among the key ideas in each lesson. And in the students' own books, the Connect question in each lesson Review helps students link what they have learned in that lesson to previous learning.

## Effective Vocabulary Instruction

Much research has shown that some approaches to teaching vocabulary are far more effective than others. In general, approaches that involve just learning definitions or synonyms for new terms are not highly effective. The knowledge gained from definitions is too limited to provide mastery of new terms. In contrast, the most successful approaches to vocabulary expose students to in-depth knowledge and frequent opportunities to use new terms in meaningful contexts.

Houghton Mifflin Social Studies reflects these characteristics of effective vocabulary and concept instruction in its selection of Key Terms. The Key Terms listed for any lesson are terms that are related to an important idea in that lesson and are terms that students will encounter frequently in their social studies reading.

## Vocabulary Strategies

The strategies that follow present useful options for preteaching vocabulary for any lesson. There are, of course, many other effective strategies you may also choose to use, but these strategies will help your students develop the deep knowledge of new terms they will need to make the words part of their own social studies vocabulary.

### Semantic Feature Analysis

This strategy is particularly effective in helping students identify connections among related concepts. For this reason, it works best with terms that are closely related in meaning.

1. On the chalkboard or an overhead, write a list of words that share some properties.
2. Have students suggest features that at least one of the words possesses. List these features in a row across the top of the board or transparency.
3. Have students fill in the matrix with pluses (+) and minuses (−) to show whether or not a word has the given feature. (Depending on the set of words, you may need to use question marks or zeros for features that do not apply to some terms.)

**Example:**

|          | high | large | flat top | steep sides |
|----------|------|-------|----------|-------------|
| hill     | +    | −     | −        | +           |
| mountain | +    | +     | −        | +           |
| mesa     | +    | −     | +        | +           |
| butte    | +    | +     | +        | +           |

This activity can be made open-ended by having students add other related terms and features and continue filling in the matrix.

### Venn Diagram

A Venn diagram can also be used effectively for semantic feature analysis. Borrowed from the field of mathematics, a Venn diagram is a pictorial representation that uses intersecting circles to show features shared by two or more concepts and features peculiar to each concept.

**Example:**

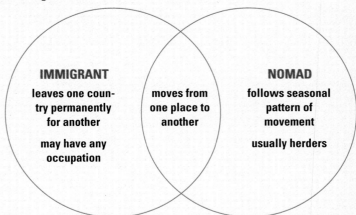

IMMIGRANT
leaves one country permanently for another

may have any occupation

moves from one place to another

NOMAD
follows seasonal pattern of movement

usually herders

## Graphic Overview

Graphic overviews like the ones provided in the Teacher's Edition for each lesson are visual representations of relationships among sets of ideas or events. You can use graphic overviews effectively in a wide variety of ways in the classroom:

1. Present the Graphic Overview before the lesson to provide an advance organizer for students.
2. Have students start a graphic overview for the lesson based on their prior knowledge and their preview of the lesson. As they read the lesson, students can add to, change, and refine their graphic overviews.
3. Have students complete a graphic overview to review and summarize a lesson or chapter.

## Contextual Redefinition

The strategy called contextual redefinition explicitly teaches students to use context as a clue to meaning. Because all Key Terms in Houghton Mifflin Social Studies are clearly defined in context, this strategy can be easily used with any lesson.

1. Present the words in isolation. Write each Key Term on the board or an overhead, and ask students to supply a meaning for each word. Students should defend their suggestions and come to consensus on the best definition.
2. Have students read the sentence from the lesson in which the term appears in boldface (dark type). Then students again suggest definitions and defend their suggestions. In this way, more skilled readers model for other students the thinking processes involved in formulating a definition from context.
3. Have students consult the Glossary, if appropriate, to confirm the definition.

## Prior Knowledge

This strategy, based on the Pre-Reading Plan (PReP) developed by Judith Langer, is useful for activating and assessing students' prior knowledge. It can be used effectively with Key Terms that are important concepts

in the lesson, but it may also be used with other concepts that are not being explicitly taught as vocabulary. This strategy works best when carried out with groups of about 10 students.

1. Preview the lesson and list key concepts important to understanding the text.
2. Use the following questions as the basis for a discussion about each concept:
   • What comes to mind when you hear ___? (Write the students' responses on the board.)
   • What made you think of ___? (responses to first question)
   • Given our discussion, what new ideas can you add about ___?
3. Have students work in groups of two or three to arrange words listed on the board into some sensible order.
4. Evaluate student responses as follows:
   • much prior knowledge: precise definitions, analogies, conceptual links among concepts
   • some prior knowledge: examples and characteristics but no connections or relations
   • little prior knowledge: sound alikes or look alikes, associated experiences, little or no meaning relations

After students have read the lesson, you may wish to follow up by

• Discussing how the text ideas relate to the ideas discussed prior to reading.
• Having students redo the organizing activity (number 3 above) and compare their results with what they did prior to reading. (This technique can serve as an informal learning assessment.)

## For Further Reading

Moore, David W., John E. Readence, and Robert J. Rickelman. *Prereading Activities for Content Area Reading and Learning.* Newark, Del.: International Reading Association, 1989.

Nagy, William E. *Teaching Vocabulary to Improve Reading Comprehension.* Urbana, Ill.: ERIC Clearinghouse on Reading and Communication Skills, 1988.

# The Role of Literature

In a well-designed social studies curriculum, young learners encounter many aspects of human experience, including social interaction, values and customs, geography, economics, as well as life in other times and places. To convey the richness of this experience, a textbook must employ a variety of modes of presentation: exposition, narration, description, and visual presentation. The inclusion of literature can enhance the effectiveness of any of these modes of presentation.

Good literature involves young children mentally and emotionally. It provides vicarious experiences with cultures they might not otherwise be exposed to. It also connects children emotionally to the universal feelings and needs that touch everyone's lives.

Houghton Mifflin Social Studies enriches the teaching and learning of social studies by integrating literature throughout the program. In Grades 1 through 3 of the program, you will find the following literature resources:

- at least one full-length literature selection in every unit of the Student Text
- poems or short excerpts from literature in Student Text lessons where literature can offer special insight into the lesson focus
- additional full-length selections to read aloud to students in the Teacher's Edition
- a bibliography of additional recommended literature on each unit opener in the Teacher's Edition
- an optional Social Studies Bookshelf that includes two books for each unit of the Student Text

## Using Literature

The major function of the literature in Houghton Mifflin Social Studies is to help students develop empathy for the experiences of people in other times and places. In the primary grades, this means that literature provides a way for students to reach out from their familiar everyday world to gain insight into life in other times and places. Through reading stories, legends, and poems, young students can begin to imagine what it was like to live in times past. By comparing the people and events in these stories with what they are learning about the world today, students also begin to recognize the elements of continuity and change that in later grades will become an important theme in their study of history. Similarly, literature provides opportunities for students to see how life in other parts of the world is both similar to and different from life in their own communities.

The full-length literature selections in Houghton Mifflin Social Studies are found before or after lessons at their most appropriate point of use. Sometimes literature provides an engaging point of entry for students into a new topic or theme. Other times it expands on or illustrates ideas that students have studied in a previous lesson. In either case, the use of the literature should be response centered. The goal is not to have students analyze the literature but rather to have them respond to it in ways that build a foundation for understanding their own social world and linking their experience with that of people in other times and places.

After you have read a literature selection, you will want to invite students' responses to the story. Discussions of why things happened as they did and how things might have been different stimulate a high level of thinking, reasoning, and evaluating. Responses through role playing and art can also help make social studies topics come alive in the classroom.

The Teacher's Edition notes with each literature selection provide suggested activities and strategies for student response to literature. In addition, each unit opener spread in the Teacher's Edition lists the titles from the Houghton Mifflin Social Studies Bookshelf that relate to that unit. On those same pages, you will also find a bibliography that includes other literature appropriate for use with the unit.

## For Further Information

A valuable source of information on recently published literature is the annual bibliography of outstanding children's trade books in the field of social studies that appears in the April/May issue of *Social Education*, published by the National Council for the Social Studies.

# Writing, Thinking, and Learning

Research has long supported the belief that writing fosters learning. In social studies, it is no surprise that a program rich in writing activities will provide a wide range of in-depth learning experiences.

Houghton Mifflin Social Studies gives students a multitude of writing opportunities that involve inquiry, discovery, and problem solving, as well as the integration of information. In this program, students use a variety of thinking skills and processes as they write: they identify, recall, define, explore, classify, order, select; they analyze content, synthesize choices, and evaluate conclusions. This process of learning through writing is both powerful and engaging.

## Integration of Writing

**Student Text:** An abundance of writing activities is included in the reviews in the students' books. Each activity challenges the student to apply the appropriate thinking skills to the content of the lesson in a meaningful way.

**Teacher's Edition:** Unit and Chapter Projects and Activities provide numerous writing opportunities:

- LEP activities that help bridge the language gap from visual to oral to written communication
- individual writing projects and activities covering a variety of formats, purposes, and points of view
- collaborative writing activities
- challenging longer-term writing projects that encourage more research and investigation

Writing activities in the side columns and bottom panel notes focus on skills, content, or values.

**Ancillaries:** The Discovery Journal is a thoughtful, balanced blend of structured and free-response writing activities correlated to the special features of the Student Text. The other ancillaries also provide many opportunities for writing.

## What Your Role Can Be

**As Facilitator:** You play a key role in providing structure, guidance, and feedback to any student writer. Younger writers need to be encouraged to use pictures and invented spellings to convey their ideas. All students need first to get their ideas down, massage them, and revise them. Then they can polish and refine the final expression and structure. Offer support and encouragement throughout this process.

**As Model:** Whenever feasible, participate in group or paired writing activities. Most of the Strategies for Accessible Instruction (T32–T33) are also excellent techniques for building students' confidence.

**As Evaluator:** Students need to know what is expected of them in any given writing situation. Provide constructive criticism; become the writing coach. Promote a mix of evaluation modes: self-evaluation, peer evaluation, group analysis, conferencing. You may want to have students keep long-term journals or writing "portfolios" that are evaluated in a holistic manner. If students feel that every written assignment is scrutinized and rigorously graded, they may be reluctant to explore and experiment. And without exploration, there is no discovery, no development of the writing craft.

## The Computer Connection

More and more elementary schools are providing students increased access to computers for a variety of learning experiences. In particular, word processing is playing a growing role in the composing process across the curriculum. Students of all ages compose on keyboards. Word processing makes the task of rethinking, revising, and recomposing a less tedious, less cumbersome operation. Using word processing for many writing activities in Houghton Mifflin Social Studies is an excellent way for students to explore and experiment as they think, learn, and write.

## For Further Reading

Holbrook, H. T. *Writing to Learn in the Social Studies.* Urbana, Ill.: ERIC Clearinghouse on Reading and Communication Skills, 1987.

Lake, D. T. "Teaching Writing in the 1990's." *English Journal* (November 1989): 73–74.

Langer, Judith A., and Arthur N. Applebee. *How Writing Shapes Thinking: A Study of Teaching and Learning.* Urbana, Ill.: National Council of Teachers of English (NCTE research report; no. 22), 1987.

Millett, Nancy Carlyon. *Teaching the Writing Process.* Boston, Mass.: Houghton Mifflin Company, 1990.

# The Role of Assessment in Houghton Mifflin Social Studies

Making assessment more authentic is a major theme in education today. Teachers and researchers alike have pointed to the need to broaden the range of assessment techniques we use to provide authentic measures of how well students are doing on the tasks and challenges that make up the core of each curriculum area. In social studies, that means not just recalling facts and performing isolated skills but rather understanding concepts, developing a rich and flexible repertoire of skills, and gaining insight into civic values and responsibilities.

Because the instructional goals of Houghton Mifflin Social Studies go beyond the learning of discrete facts and skills, a variety of assessment approaches are necessary to evaluate students' ability to relate ideas and concepts, to apply skills, and to think critically about what they are learning. Accordingly, Houghton Mifflin Social Studies provides a comprehensive assessment program that

- includes features of the Student Text, Teacher's Edition, and ancillaries as well as the separate Chapter Test component
- provides components for each of the three major strands in the curriculum: Knowledge, Skills, and Civic Values and Understanding (Citizenship)
- includes but is not limited to paper-and-pencil tests; other modes of assessment include teacher evaluation of student performance, student evaluation of personal progress, and peer evaluation
- provides opportunities for active student participation, including oral and written reports and stating and supporting positions

## Assessment Components

**Chapter Tests:** A four-page test in blackline master form is provided for each chapter. These tests assess each of the three strands and are structured as follows:

- Part I is three pages long and consists of a variety of short-answer formats. Subsections within this part address knowledge (including concepts and key terms), skills, and where possible citizenship.
- Part II consists of free-response questions, including at least one longer "essay" question. One question in this part will always assess citizenship; other questions will assess knowledge and skills through application. (You have the option of using Part II separately as part of a unit-level assessment.)

**Student Text Features:** Houghton Mifflin Social Studies has built into its Student Text many instructional features that can also be used to serve an assessment

function. These features are found within lessons, special feature pages, and the Chapter Review. The chart on this page identifies these features.

**Teacher's Edition Features:** You may also choose to use for assessment purposes many of the activities and strategies provided in the Chapter Organizers and lesson notes in the Teacher's Edition. These features are also identified in the chart.

**Discovery Journal:** The writing activities in this ancillary component provide ongoing opportunities for informal assessment of student progress.

**Profile Sheets:** In the Chapter Test booklet you will find a profile sheet that you can reproduce for each student to monitor progress and chart performance on the full range of assessment measures.

### Assessment Components in Houghton Mifflin Social Studies

This chart identifies the assessment components, the strands they assess (K=Knowledge, S=Skills, C=Citizenship), and the mode of evaluation in which they can be used (T=Teacher, S=Self, P=Peer).

| TEXT | STRANDS ASSESSED | | | EVALUATION MODE | | |
|---|---|---|---|---|---|---|
| | K | S | C | T | S | P |
| **Tests** | • | • | | | | |
| Part I | • | • | • | • | | |
| Part II | | | | • | | |
| **Student Text** | | | | | | |
| Chapter Review | | | | | | |
|   Reviewing Key Terms | • | | | • | | |
|   Exploring Concepts | • | | | • | | |
|   Reviewing Skills | | • | | • | | |
|   Using Critical Thinking | • | • | | • | | |
|   Preparing for Citizenship | • | | • | • | • | • |
| Lesson Items | | | | | | |
|   Focus Questions | • | | | • | | |
|   Review | • | • | • | • | | |
|   Self-check questions | • | | | | • | |
| Understanding Skills: Try It and Apply It | | • | | • | • | |
| Making Decisions | | • | • | • | • | • |
| Exploring | • | • | | • | • | • |
| **Teacher's Edition** | | | | | | |
| Chapter Activities | • | • | • | • | • | • |
| Collaborative Learning | • | • | • | | | • |
| Close (lesson part 3) | • | | | • | • | |
| Skill Activities | | • | | • | | |
| Discovery Journal | • | • | • | • | • | |

# SCOPE AND SEQUENCE

T his Scope and Sequence has been designed to provide students with the comprehensive knowledge, civic values, and intellectual skills they will need to meet the challenge of citizenship in the 21st century. The three strands of the program have been tightly integrated at all levels, so that skills are always taught in the context of the lesson content, and knowledge is enhanced by the application of sound values. The goals of each strand are listed on the following two pages. References in the Teachers' Edition key all learning objectives to these goals. Typically the student is introduced to a subject or skill at an early level, taught to actively use it at an intermediate level, and encouraged to analyze and critique it at an advanced level.

| Knowledge and Understanding | Civic Understanding and Values | Skills |
| --- | --- | --- |
| **History** | **National Identity** | **Study Skills** |
| **Geography** | **Constitutional Heritage** | **Visual Learning** |
| **Economics** | **Citizenship** | **Map and Globe Skills** |
| **Culture** | | **Critical Thinking** |
| **Ethics and Belief Systems** | | **Social Participation** |
| **Social and Political Systems** | | |

# ● KNOWLEDGE AND UNDERSTANDING

### HISTORY

1. Develop an understanding of the reasons for studying history and of the relationships between the past and the present
2. Develop an awareness of the ways in which we learn about the past and the methods and tools of the historian
3. Create a sense of empathy for the past
4. Understand the meaning of time and chronology
5. Analyze the sometimes complex cause-and-effect relationships of ideas and events, recognizing also the effects of the accidental and irrational on history
6. Understand the reasons for both continuity and change
7. Recognize the interrelatedness of geography, economics, culture, belief systems, and political systems within history
8. Comprehend the history of women, minorities, and the full range of social classes, not just the history of the elite or the notable individual

### GEOGRAPHY

1. Develop locational skills and understanding
2. Develop an awareness of place
3. Understand human and environmental interaction
4. Understand movement of people, goods, and ideas
5. Understand world regions and their historical, cultural, economic, and political characteristics

### ECONOMICS

1. Identify and apply basic concepts of economics (basic wants and needs, scarcity, choices, decision making, opportunity costs, resources, production, distribution, consumption, markets, labor, capital)
2. Develop an awareness of past and present exchange systems
3. Recognize and analyze the economic systems of various societies, including the United States, and their responses to the three basic economic questions: what to produce (value), how and how much to produce (allocation), and how to distribute (distribution)
4. Recognize the economic global interdependence of societies
5. Recognize the impact of technology on economics

# ▲ CIVIC UNDERSTANDING AND VALUES

### NATIONAL IDENTITY

1. Develop an appreciation for the multicultural, pluralistic nature of U.S. society
2. Understand the basic principles of democracy
3. Understand and appreciate American ideals, as expressed in historical documents, speeches, songs, art, and symbolic representations and activities
4. Recognize that the American patriotic ideals are not yet fully realized and that to be protected they must constantly be reaffirmed

### CONSTITUTIONAL HERITAGE

1. Develop an appreciation for the balance of power established by the Constitution between majority and minority, the individual and the state, and government by and for the people
2. Understand the historical origins of the Constitution and how it has been amended and changed over time
3. Recognize the Constitution as an expression of democratic ideals that is reinterpreted from time to time

### CITIZENSHIP

1. Recognize the reciprocal relationship between the individual and the state in a democracy
2. Understand and appreciate the kind of behavior necessary for the functioning and maintenance of our democratic society
3. Learn the duties and method of selection of our leaders
4. Develop a respect for human rights, including those of individuals and of minorities
5. Develop an understanding and appreciation for the rational settlement of disputes and for compromise
6. Recognize the special strategies required to allow the different elements within our pluralistic society to live together amicably
7. Develop an understanding of the processes that have led to the fall of democracies

# ■ SKILLS

### STUDY SKILLS

1. Locate, select, and collect information by interviewing or by using appropriate reference materials
2. Organize information from reference sources to address issues or problems
3. Present information convincingly in spoken or written forms

### VISUAL LEARNING

1. Develop careful and directed observation of images, objects, and the environment
2. Understand, use, and create graphic information (timelines, charts, tables, other graphic organizers, graphs, diagrams)
3. Interpret and respond to photographs, paintings, cartoons, and other illustrative materials
4. Understand and use symbols
5. Express meaning through sensory forms of representation

### MAP & GLOBE SKILLS

1. Identify and use map and globe symbols; identify and use different map projections
2. Understand and use locational terms; locate places and positions on a map or globe
3. Interpret and use directional terms and symbols on a map or globe
4. Understand and use terms to describe relative size and distance; identify and use map scales
5. Construct and use maps and geographic models

## CULTURE

1. Understand the concept of culture and how it is transmitted
2. Develop an appreciation for the rich complexity of a society's culture and an understanding of how the parts of a culture interrelate
3. Recognize and appreciate the multicultural and multiethnic dimensions of our society and the contributions made by various groups
4. Appreciate the cultural similarities and differences that exist among societies of different times and places
5. Recognize the special role literature and the arts play in reflecting the inner life of a people and in projecting a people's image of themselves to the world
6. Learn about the mythology, legends, myths of origin, and heroes and heroines of societies of different times and places

## ETHICS & BELIEF SYSTEMS

1. Recognize that all societies have ideals and standards of behavior
2. Understand that the ideas people profess affect their actions
3. Recognize the importance of religion in human society and its influence on history
4. Become familiar with the basic ideas of major religions and ethical traditions of other times and places
5. Develop an understanding of how different societies have tried to resolve ethical issues when conflicts occur between individuals, groups, and societies

## SOCIAL & POLITICAL SYSTEMS

1. Develop an awareness of the reciprocal relationship between the individual and various social and political groups: family, community, and nation
2. Understand the role of law and its relationship to social and political systems
3. Develop an appreciation for the tension between opposing ideals in human affairs
4. Develop an awareness of the structure of social classes and the changes in status of women and racial and ethnic minorities in U.S. society and other societies
5. Understand comparative political systems, past and present
6. Understand the complex relationship and interdependence that exists among the world's nations

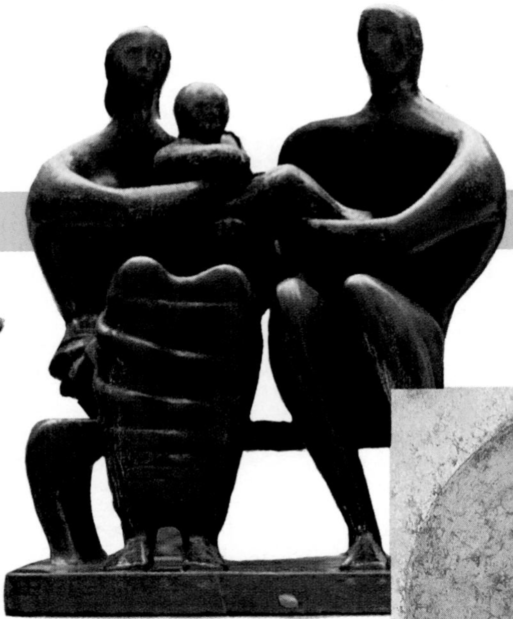

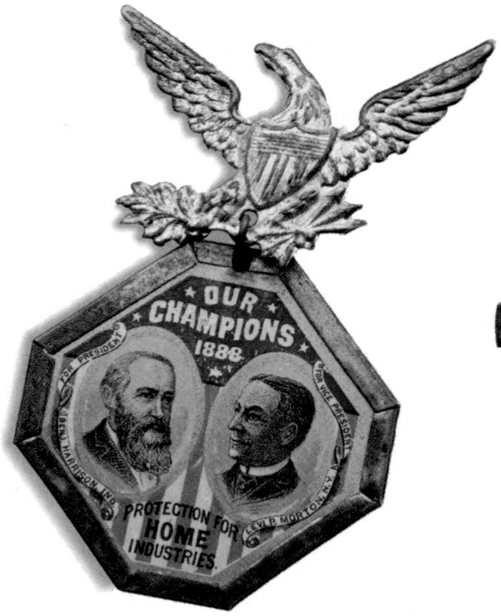


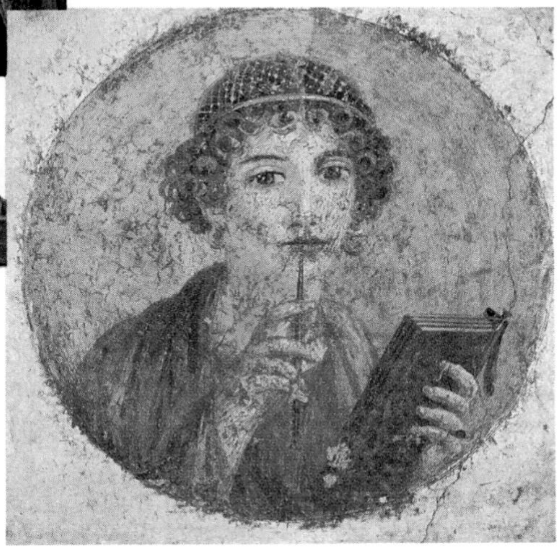



## CRITICAL THINKING

1. Define and clarify problems, issues, and ideas
2. Evaluate and judge information related to a problem, an issue, or an idea
3. Solve problems and draw conclusions related to an issue or idea*

*Critical thinking is taught both in a problem-solving and in a decision-making context.

## SOCIAL PARTICIPATION

1. Develop interpersonal skills
2. Work successfully in groups

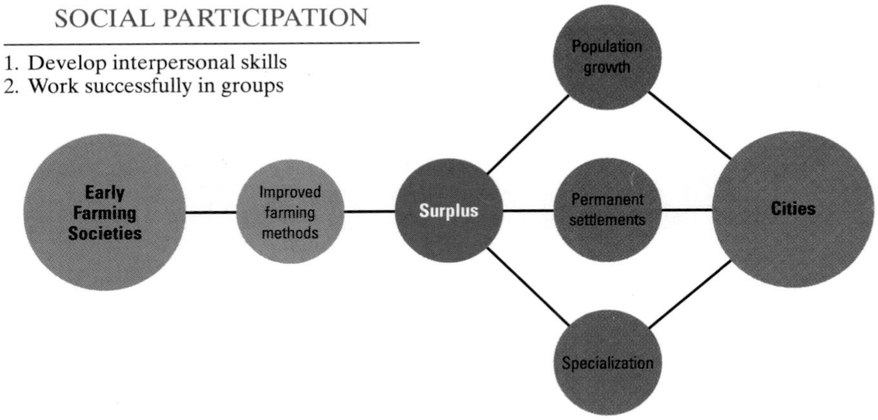

# ● KNOWLEDGE AND UNDERSTANDING

## HISTORY

| Grade | K | 1 | 2 | 3 |
|---|---|---|---|---|
| 1. Links to the past | Compare travel now and long ago | Parents and grandparents | Discuss traditions and their origins | |
| 2. How we know | – – | Family histories | | Physical evidence Journals of pioneers |
| 3. Empathy | Identification through literature | | Biographies | Real people of the past |
| 4. Time and chronology | Understand and use time sequence terms Identify seasons of the year | | | Read and use timelines |
| 5. Cause and effect | Introduce through group dynamics | Changes in community | Effects of war Inventions | Migration and settlement Conservation issues |
| 6. Continuity and change | In individuals, families | In community | Histories of families How basic needs were met, long ago and today | Bust of a boom town |
| 7. Interrelatedness | Of economics with history | Of geography with history | Origins of Thanksgiving | Of geography, economics with history |
| 8. Women, minorities | Through stories, illustrations | Diversity of people presented | | |

## GEOGRAPHY

| | K | 1 | 2 | 3 |
|---|---|---|---|---|
| 1. Location | The self in space | Home, school, community | Beyond the neighborhood | Relative location |
| 2. Place | Elementary land and water forms | Map locations Identify and analyze microenvironments | Global climates | Place characteristics |
| 3. Human-environment interaction | Adjustment of dress to climate | Environmental changes in area | | Environmental changes Community interactions |
| 4. Movement | Movement of goods and people | | | Historical movements of people |
| 5. Regions | – – | – – | Identify regions other than one's own | Regional characteristics |

## ECONOMICS

| | K | 1 | 2 | 3 |
|---|---|---|---|---|
| 1. Basic concepts | Differences between wants and needs | Discuss how needs are met Identify and discuss community jobs | | Compare how needs met over time, space |
| 2. Exchange systems | Role-playing (stores) | Trade of surpluses | How systems are learned (immigrants) | American Indian exchange systems |
| 3. Basic economic questions | Distribution of goods from production to market | | Production and distribution | |
| 4. Interdependence | – – | Interdependence of producers and consumers | Inventions | To and from community |
| 5. Technology | – – | – – | – – | Production and transportation |

## CULTURE

| | K | 1 | 2 | 3 |
|---|---|---|---|---|
| 1. Cultural understanding | Appreciation through participation | | Role of family | How transmitted |
| 2. Cultural complexity | Identify through literature | | Compare traditions | American Indians |
| 3. Multicultural society | – – | – – | Biographies | American Indians |
| 4. Similarities and differences | Compare through literature | | | American Indians |
| 5. Literature and the arts | Recognize and respond through examples | | | Of other times and places |
| 6. Myths and legends | Listen and respond to folk tales | | | Of American Indians, cowboys, settlers |

## ETHICS & BELIEF SYSTEMS

| | K | 1 | 2 | 3 |
|---|---|---|---|---|
| 1. Present in all societies | – – | – – | – – | In American Indian societies |
| 2. Ideas affect behavior | – – | – – | – – | In American Indian societies |

| 4 | 5 | 6 | 7 | 8 |
|---|---|---|---|---|
| State, region placenames<br>Family histories | Origins of today's institutions<br>Cultural heritage of self, others | | Global interaction today<br>Origins of law, gov't. | Personal, national identity<br>Redefinition of the past |
| Archaeological evidence<br>Primary sources, artifacts | Historian's techniques; archaeologist's<br>Limitations of information about the past | | | Historical record, newspapers, photos; points of view |
| Past settlers of the state, region | With pioneers, slaves, American Indians | With people of ancient times | Literature, art primary sources, artifacts | With pioneers, American Indians, slaves, immigrants |
| Read and use timelines | Use of B.C./A.D. | Developments in concurrent civilizations | | |
| Settlement, expansion<br>Cultural diversity | Analysis of settlement, expansion, wars | Of territorial expansion, cultural diffusion | Exploration, Reformation, technology | Of settlement, expansion, Industrial Revolution |
| Of region over time | Analyze reasons for | Steps to civilizations<br>Analysis of a civilization over time | | Regional development, urbanization |
| Of geography, economics, religion, culture | Of belief systems | Of trade and religion in the spread of ideas<br>Of class structure | | Of belief systems<br>Of class structure |
| Role of Amer. Indians, Hispanics, blacks, Asians, women in early U.S. society | Women, social classes, in ancient cultures, in past societies | | | Diverse groups in U.S. history |
| Factors that influence locations | Why different activities are in different locations | Evaluate reasons for a city's location | Historical significance of | Competition for locations |
| Rural/urban areas | Comparative historical analysis of places | Influences of physical, cultural geography on history | | Effect of place on population distribution |
| Environmental changes at different times | Use of natural resources<br>Effect on technology | Origin of the city<br>Environmental changes over time | Changes in cities | Use of natural resources<br>Effect on technology |
| Reasons for migrations | Migrations of people; movement of goods | Ancient migrations<br>Ancient trade routes | Global movements<br>Effect of technology | Migrations to America |
| Nature and characteristics of regions | Compare/contrast of regions over time | Identify and analyze criteria used to define regions | | |
| How wants met over time<br>History of businesses | Distribution of resources | How met long ago<br>Scarcity; specialization | In different societies<br>Rise of merchant class | Colonial markets/materials<br>Divisions of labor |
| Use of barter<br>Trace money flow | Early exchange systems<br>Role of trade routes | | Banking systems | Trade partnerships |
| Economic cycles | In early U.S. history<br>Role of government | In ancient times | At different times and places | Analyze econ. decisions<br>Roles of governments |
| Within, between regions<br>Effect of natural disasters | Between people, states, nations | Ancient global trade<br>Transportation changes | International trade routes | Debtor/lender nations<br>Imports/exports |
| Post World War II developments; pollution | Industrial Revolution | Effects of new technologies | Key inventions in world history | Industrial revolution; mass production |
| How transmitted | Role of education | Define culture<br>Analyze how culture is transmitted | Define and identify | |
| Recognize through state's, region's history | Identify in U.S. at different time periods | Analyze prehistoric, ancient cultures | Analyze other cultures | Analyze in U.S. historically |
| Contributions to local history | Contributions of Indians, blacks, immigrants | Identify origins of contemporary cultures | | Contributions of Indians, slaves, immigrants |
| American Indians<br>Other groups in region | Interactions and conflicts of cultures in U.S. | Analyze interaction and conflict in other cultures | | Among U.S. population<br>Interaction and conflict |
| Throughout area's history | Understand and appreciate cultural images presented | | | Analyze cultural images presented |
| American Indian, cowboy, settlers | Analyze heroes, heroines | Importance in ancient cultures | Analyze legends and tales of others | Analyze American legends, tall tales |
| In historical past in state, region, country | | Comparison of past societies | | Analyze ethical standards in past U.S. history |
| Role of missionaries<br>Beliefs of immigrants | Pilgrims, puritans, attitudes about slavery | Buddhist, Jewish, Christian examples | Crusades, from two points of view | The Great Awakening<br>Church and Abolitionists |

| ETHICS & BELIEF SYSTEMS | Grade K | 1 | 2 | 3 |
|---|---|---|---|---|
| 3. Influence of religion | – – | – – | – – | Among American Indians, Pilgrims |
| 4. Basic belief systems | – – | – – | – – | Of American Indians |
| 5. Resolution of ethical issues | Introduce through literature | | | Discuss examples in literature |

**SOCIAL & POLITICAL SYSTEMS**

| | K | 1 | 2 | 3 |
|---|---|---|---|---|
| 1. Belonging to groups | Recognize membership in groups Identify public/private sectors | | | Responsibilities of individual to group |
| 2. Law | Recognize and observe the need for rules | | | Rules among other societies |
| 3. Opposing ideals | – – | – – | – – | American Indians and settlers |
| 4. Social structure | – – | – – | – – | Social structure in other societies, times |
| 5. Comparative political systems | – – | – – | – – | Recognize not all political systems are alike |
| 6. Global interdependence | Recognize world neighbors | Recognize interdependence | Recognize other nations | International trade |

## ▲ CIVIC UNDERSTANDINGS AND VALUES

| | Grade K | 1 | 2 | 3 |
|---|---|---|---|---|
| **NATIONAL IDENTITY** | | | | |
| 1. Pluralism | Recognize national identity Recognize diversity of U.S. citizens | | | Through examples |
| 2. Democracy | Practice through classroom examples | | | Through historic, contemporary examples |
| 3. American ideals and symbols | Recognize flag, songs Role-play | Learn national symbols, Pledge of Allegiance, patriotic songs | | |
| 4. Reaffirmation of American ideals | – – | – – | – – | Conservation of resources |
| **CONSTITUTIONAL HERITAGE** | | | | |
| 1. Balance of power | Fair treatment of all in the classroom | | | In other societies |
| 2. Origin of Constitution | – – | – – | – – | – – |
| 3. Reinterpretation of ideals | – – | – – | – – | – – |
| **CITIZENSHIP** | | | | |
| 1. Individual and state | Through family, classroom examples | | | In conservation of natural resources |
| 2. Democratic behavior | Recognize problems that arise in groups | | | Develop awareness of need for rules |
| 3. Selection of leaders | – – | – – | Identify office of U.S. president | Awareness of Presidents' Day |
| 4. Human rights | Develop respect for others | | | Through examples in the past |
| 5. Settlement of disputes | Through classroom examples | | | Through group activities |
| 6. Strategies for pluralism | – – | Through classroom examples | | |
| 7. How democracies fail | – – | – – | – – | – – |

| 4 | 5 | 6 | 7 | 8 |
|---|---|---|---|---|
| Conflict between belief systems | Pilgrims, puritans, attitudes towards slavery | Spread through missionaries, diffusion | Split among Christians Islam; missionaries | Slavery; Manifest Destiny; 2nd Great Awakening |
| American Indians | Of American Indians, slaves, immigrants | Origins, early history of major world religions | Origins, history of Islam; Japanese Buddhism | Of Indians, slaves, early immigrants |
| Discuss examples in literature | Freedom to dissent; slavery; tolerance | Examples from ancient civilizations | Through religious wars | Attempts to resolve slavery issue |
| | | | | |
| Political sub-units | Early U.S. political units Origins of public/private | Identify social, political units in ancient times | Identify world social and political units | Conflicting group memberships in U.S. history |
| Who enforces laws | Reinterpretations of law over time | Identify origins of law | Recognize non-Roman systems of law | How law is enacted, changed; dissent |
| Conflicting goals in state, regional history | In early U.S. history | In and among prehistoric, ancient societies | In and among world societies, over time | At various times in U.S. history |
| Recognize differences in treatment over time | Analyze reasons for changes | Analyze social status in ancient times | Analyze changes over time | Analyze reasons for change |
| Recognize variety of political systems | Of American Indian, British, French, Spanish | Among ancient civilizations | Note changes over time | Among nations that have affected U.S. history |
| Trade, foriegn affairs | Identify relationships of U.S. with others | Analyze interdependence in ancient times | Identify and analyze interdependencies | History of U.S. relationship with other nations |

| 4 | 5 | 6 | 7 | 8 |
|---|---|---|---|---|
| Through examples | Origins of pluralism | Discuss identities of ancient civilizations | Discuss identities of other nations | Tensions of assimilation |
| Through historic, contemporary examples | History of, in U.S. | Origins of, in ancient times | Historical origins of democracy | History and development of U.S. democracy |
| Learn state symbols | As expressed in U.S. history | Ancient national symbols | Symbols of other nations and empires | As expressed in U.S.history |
| Focus on state's or region's future | Identify past crises in U.S. history | Compare and contrast examples from ancient, historical times, with U.S. | | Identify and discuss past crises in U.S. |
| | | | | |
| Examples in state, regional history | Checks and balances Historical examples | Balance of power in ancient civilizations | How balance of power achieved elsewhere | Checks and balances Historical examples |
| State constitutions | Writing of Constitution Passage of amendments | -- | Influence of Enlightenment ideas | Writing of Constitution Passage of amendments |
| Changes in state laws over time | Meaning then and now | -- | -- | Discuss reasons for reinterpretations |
| | | | | |
| Through examples in state history | Identify examples in U.S. history | Identify examples in ancient times | Identify examples in other societies | Analyze examples in U.S. history |
| Need for rules Violations in past | Discuss examples in U.S. history | Analyze behavior in ancient times | Analyze behavior in other societies | Discuss examples in U.S. history |
| Selection of state leaders | Analyze, using past U.S. examples | Compare selection process of long ago | Compare selection process of others | Analyze, using past U.S. examples |
| Through examples in state history | Evaluate cases from U.S. history | Discuss minority rights long ago | Discuss minority rights of others | Evaluate cases from U.S. history |
| Through examples in state history | Identify examples from U.S. history | Analyze disputes in ancient times | Analyze disputes in other societies | Analyze examples from U.S. history |
| Through examples in state history | Identify examples from U.S. history | Analuze pluralism in ancient times | Analyze pluralism in other societies | Analyze examples from U.S. history |
| -- | Identify crises in U.S. history | Analyze why past democracies failed | Analyze why past democracies failed | Analyze crises in U.S. history |

# ■ SKILLS

| | Grade K | 1 | 2 | 3 |
|---|---|---|---|---|
| **STUDY SKILLS** | | | | |
| 1. Collecting information | Interview others / Visit a library | Learn book parts / Picture dictionary | Use a library; reference materials / Interview for information | |
| 2. Organizing information | Listen to story and relate what happened | Identify and make categories | | Summarize a paragraph / Identify main ideas and details |
| 3. Presenting information | Tell events in sequence | | Tell events and ideas in sequence / Write simple paragraphs | |
| **VISUAL LEARNING** | | | | |
| 1. Observation | Classroom materials | School, neighborhood | Neighborhood, community features | |
| 2. Timelines | Know the seasons | Read and make simple timelines | | |
| Graphic organizers | Use a chart | Read charts, tables | | |
| Graphs | Use simple picture, bar graphs | Read and make picture, bar graphs | | Read line, circle graphs |
| Diagrams | | Read process and cut-away diagrams ; also, cross-section diagrams | | |
| 3. Interpretation | State main idea of illustrations | Gather information from and respond to photos, illustrations; also, fine art | | |
| 4. Symbols | Traffic signs; U.S. flag | National symbols; flag | | |
| 5. Visual self-expression | Drawings, constructions | Class activities | | |
| **MAP & GLOBE SKILLS** | | | | |
| 1. Symbols | Compare maps, photos, and real environments | | Color as symbol / Continents and oceans | Read a physical map / Use a map key, rose |
| 2. Location | Use simple locational terms | | Use grids to find locations / Relative location | Latitude, longtitude |
| 3. Direction | Orient self in space; use directional terms | | Cardinal directions / Describe routes | Intermediate directions / Follow routes on map |
| 4. Scale and distance | Use relative terms | Judge relative sizes, distances | | Use map scale / Time/distance |
| 5. Construction and use | Construct table or floor 3-D maps of community, neighborhood | | | |
| **CRITICAL THINKING** | | | | |
| 1. Define and clarify | Similarities and differences / Organize categories | Formulate questions | | Identify problems or central issues |
| 2. Evaluate and judge | Identify evidence | Sequence of events | | Evidence supporting main idea |
| 3. Solve and conclude | Identify cause and effect / Draw conclusions based on evidence | | | Cause and effect / Make "if...then" statements |
| **SOCIAL PARTICIPATION** | | | | |
| 1. Interpersonal | Develop self-respect and confidence; / Develop good listening skills | | | Others' points of view ; / Express one's own ideas |
| 2. Group work | Show willingness to participate in group activities | | Identify goal | |
| | | Accept group decisions | Practice collaborative learning roles | |

| 4 | 5 | 6 | 7 | 8 |
|---|---|---|---|---|
| Use a library catalog<br>Interview for information | | Use atlas; primary sources | Use Reader's Guide<br>Conduct interviews | Use special reference resources |
| Combine information<br>Give directions | Take notes, make outlines | Identify text patterns | Code notes<br>Interpret primary sources | Make bibliography cards |
| Develop oral discussion skills<br>Plan and write reports | | | Use a variety of oral and written genres, debates, skits, to present reports | |
| | | | | |
| Regional features | Apply to historical artifacts, photographs, fine art | | | |
| Read U.S. time zone maps; timelines | Understand B.C/A.D. | Read and make telescopic and parallel timelines | | |
| Read charts, tables | | Read and make cluster, cause-and-effect graphic organizers | | |
| Read bar, line, circle graphs | Make line graphs | Compare graphs | Choose, assess graphs | |
| Read and use variety of diagrams | | Analyze cross-section, process diagrams | | |
| Interpret illustrative materials; cartoons;<br>Compare media | | Identify limitations of illustrative materials | | |
| State symbols | Learn history of national symbols | Religious, historical symbols | | History of U.S. symbols |
| As class activities | | Making a mural, a Moment in Time | As class activities | |
| | | | | |
| Area characteristics<br>Making symbols | Parallels/meridians tied to earth/sun | Read cartograms<br>Draw inferences | Use topographical map | Make inferences<br>Relate routes/topography |
| Hemispheres<br>Global reference points | Use latitude/longitude to locate, specify places | | Earth/sun relationship and time of day | Analyze locations |
| Use directional terms to describe routes | Trace explorers' routes | Formulate hypotheses<br>Movement of people over time | | Cultural diffusion |
| Large and small-scale representations | Evaluate large and small-scale maps | Compute distances and travel time | Vertical profiles<br>Trace and analyze routes | |
| Make a map | Use landmarks to draw map | Make a map | Make a map, vertical profile | Design map based on information given |
| | | | | |
| Identify problems or central issues | Ask good questions | Interpret values and ideologies of individuals, groups<br>Identify central issues | | Analyze points of view |
| Facts and opinions<br>Evaluate information | Identify facts, opinions | Distinguish among facts, opinions, and reasoned judgements<br>Recognize bias | | Judge bias, propaganda<br>Analyze arguments |
| Cause and effect<br>Draw conclusions | Interpret cause and effect<br>Draw conclusions from evidence | | Make hypotheses<br>predict consequences | Compare causes/effects<br>Identify alternatives |
| | | | | |
| Listen to others<br>Express one's own ideas | Recognize the social needs of others<br>Provide positive feedback | | Overcome stereotypes<br>Recognize and respect others' points of view | |
| Participate in discussions | Participate in setting and planning goals<br>Develop collaborative learning roles | | Analyze and support group decisions | Appreciate and practice compromises |

*O* beautiful for spacious skies,
*For amber waves of grain,*
*For purple mountain majesties*
*Above the fruited plain.*
*America! America! God shed His grace on thee,*
*And crown thy good with brotherhood*
***From sea to shining sea.***


**Katharine Lee Bates**

Beverly J. Armento
Gary B. Nash
Christopher L. Salter
Karen K. Wixson

# From Sea to Shining Sea

Houghton Mifflin Company • Boston

Atlanta • Dallas • Geneva, Illinois • Princeton, New Jersey • Palo Alto • Toronto

## Consultants

*Program Consultants*

Edith M. Guyton
Associate Professor of Early
  Childhood Education
Georgia State University
Atlanta, Georgia

Gail Hobbs
Associate Professor of Geography
Pierce College
Woodland Hills, California

Charles Peters
Reading Consultant
Oakland Schools
Pontiac, Michigan

Cathy Riggs-Salter
Social Studies Consultant
Hartsburg, Missouri

Alfredo Schifini
Limited English Proficiency Consultant
Los Angeles, California

George Paul Schneider
Associate Director
  of General Programs
Department of Museum Education
Art Institute of Chicago
Chicago, Illinois

Twyla Stewart
Center for Academic Interinstitutional
  Programs
University of California—Los Angeles
Los Angeles, California

Scott Waugh
Associate Professor of History
University of California—Los Angeles
Los Angeles, California

## Teacher Reviewers

David E. Beer (Grade 5)
Weisser Park Elementary
Fort Wayne, Indiana

Jan Coleman (Grades 6–7)
Thornton Junior High
Fremont, California

Shawn Edwards
  (Grades 1–3)
Jackson Park Elementary
University City, Missouri

Barbara J. Fech (Grade 6)
Martha Ruggles School
Chicago, Illinois

Deborah M. Finkel
  (Grade 4)
Los Angeles Unified
  School District,
  Region G
South Pasadena,
California

Jim Fletcher (Grades 5, 8)
La Loma Junior High
Modesto, California

Susan M. Gilliam
  (Grade 1)
Roscoe Elementary
Los Angeles, California

Vicki Stroud Gonterman
  (Grade 2)
Gibbs International
  Studies Magnet School
Little Rock, Arkansas

Lorraine Hood (Grade 2)
Fresno Unified School
  District
Fresno, California

Jean Jamgochian
  (Grade 5)
Haycock Gifted and
  Talented Center
Fairfax County, Virginia

Susan Kirk-Davalt
  (Grade 5)
Crowfoot Elementary
Lebanon, Oregon

Mary Molyneaux-Leahy
  (Grade 3)
Bridgeport Elementary
Bridgeport, Pennsylvania

Sharon Oviatt
  (Grades 1–3)
Keysor Elementary
Kirkwood, Missouri

Jayne B. Perala (Grade 1)
Cave Spring Elementary
Roanoke, Virginia

Carol Siefkin (K)
Garfield Elementary
Sacramento, California

Norman N. Tanaka
  (Grade 3)
Martin Luther King Jr.
  Elementary
Sacramento, California

John Tyler (Grades 5, 8)
Groton School
Groton, Massachusetts

Portia W. Vaughn
  (Grades 1–3)
School District 11
Colorado Springs,
  Colorado

ISBN: 0-395-52726-0
ABCDEFGHIJ-VH-99876543210

Development by Ligature, Inc.

## Acknowledgments

Grateful acknowledgment is made for the use of the material listed below.
**10–17** *Where the River Begins* by Thomas Locker. Copyright © 1984 by Thomas Locker. Reprinted by permission of the publisher, Dial Books for Young Readers.

*–Continued on page 254.*

# From Your Authors

*B*lack Kettle licked buffalo grease from his lips and sighed happily. He looked at the other Cheyenne sitting around the campfire and knew they felt the same way. Their stomachs had not been full for a long time.

So begins the story of Black Kettle, a Cheyenne Indian boy about your age. In Chapter 5 of this book, you will have the chance to read more about Black Kettle and about those Indians who followed the buffalo.

Many of the people you will meet in this book lived long ago in places that may seem far away from your home. But they all had feelings just like yours. They had many of the same needs that you have today.

As you read about these people, places, and events, we hope you will ask many questions. Some questions may be about what things were like long ago. Other questions may be about the land. "What was it like in that place?" or "Why did those people choose to live there?" Still other questions may be about how they lived. "How did they get their food? or "What kind of houses did they live in?"

Most of all, we hope you continue to ask questions like these. We hope you enjoy asking questions and finding out answers, now and in the years to come.

Beverly J. Armento
Professor of Social Studies
Director, Center for Business and
Economic Education
Georgia State University

Christopher L. Salter
Professor and Chair
Department of Geography
University of Missouri

Gary B. Nash
Professor of History
University of California—Los Angeles

Karen K. Wixson
Associate Professor of Education
University of Michigan

# Contents

# Understanding Skills

*Each "Understanding Skills" feature gives you the chance to learn and practice a skill.*

# Understanding Concepts

*Each "Understanding Concepts" feature gives you information about an idea that is important to the lesson you have just read.*

# Making Decisions

*Much of history is made up of people's decisions. Here you see how people make decisions. Then you practice how to make good decisions for yourself.*

# Explore

*The story of the past is hidden in the world around you. "Explore" pages tell you the secrets of how to find it.*

# Literature

*Reading these stories will help you experience what life was like at other times and places.*

# Primary Sources

*Reading the exact words of people who lived long ago is a good way to learn about that time.*

## A Closer Look

*Take a closer look at the objects and pictures on these pages. With the clues you see, you'll become a detective.*

## A Moment in Time

*You can pretend to be there, at a moment in time. You'll get to know someone or something by the words and pictures on these pages.*

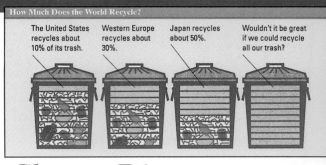

How Much Does the World Recycle?

The United States recycles about 10% of its trash.

Western Europe recycles about 30%.

Japan recycles about 50%.

Wouldn't it be great if we could recycle all our trash?

## Charts, Diagrams, and Timelines

*These pictures help give you a clearer idea of the people, places, and events you are studying.*

# Maps

*Often the land shapes the way things happen. Each map in this book tells a story about things that have happened and the places where they happened.*

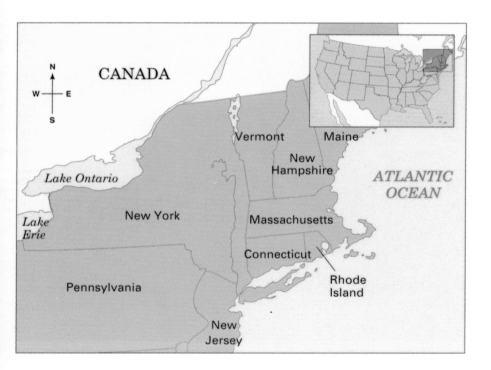

# Starting Out

*What makes this textbook so much more interesting than others you've used? Take some time, and look at each part of your book.*

**When and what?** This number tells you which lesson you are reading. The title tells you what the lesson is about.

**From unit to chapter to lesson—** the art and photos show you where events happened.

**Right from the beginning** the lesson opener pulls you into the sights, the sounds, the smells of life at another time, in another place.

LESSON 2

# Running Rivers

THINKING
**FOCUS**

*How do rivers affect the land?*

**Key Terms**

* river
* lake
* flood

*T*he river went on raising and raising for ten or t days, till at last it was over the banks. The water wa or four foot deep on the island in the low places an the Illinois bottom that side it was a many miles wide. the Missouri side the same old dist across—a half a n because the Misso shore was just a v high bluffs.
Daytimes we all over the island canoe. . . . Well, o old broken-down you could see rab snakes and such things; and when the island had b overflowed a day or two they got so tame, on acco being hungry, that you could paddle right up and your hand on them if you wanted to; but not the s and turtles—they would slide off in the water.

Mark Twain, from *The Adventures of Huckl*

The author who wrote these words lived alor bank and often saw the water rise after a big rair is a stream of water that flows across land. River different from oceans in two ways. First, oceans bigger than rivers are. Oceans cover most of the Second, oceans are salty. Rivers are not. Water t from rivers is called fresh water.

**Like a road sign,** the question that always appears here tells you what to think about while you read the lesson.

**Look for these key terms.** They are listed here so that you can watch for them. The first time they appear in the lesson they are shown in heavy black print and defined. Key terms are also defined in the Glossary.

**Every age has its great storytellers.** Each chapter includes short examples of fine writing from or about the period.

**Take a closer look,** in this case at the Grand Canyon. Look at the layers and layers of rock cut out by the river. Trace the route of the river on its way to Mexico.

### A CLOSER LOOK
# The Grand Canyon

The power of a river can change the earth. The Colorado River has formed a huge canyon by working its way through layers of rock. Every year, for millions of years, the canyon has become deeper and wider.

Millions of years ago, sand, gravel, and boulders were swept along by the river. These materials scraped away layers and layers of rock.

John Wesley Powell, standing on the right, explored the Grand Canyon by boat, in 1869. Few people knew about the canyon's beauty until Powell shared information he learned on his journey.

What was once a river bed is now the Grand Canyon. The Colorado River started out on flat land. Today it is a mile deep and almost 20 miles wide in some places.

**The Route of the Colorado River**

Nevada | Utah | Colorado River | Colorado
California | Grand Canyon National Park | Arizona | New Mexico

MEXICO

Trace the route of the Colorado River. It starts in Colorado and flows almost 1500 miles to Mexico. The gold area on this map shows Grand Canyon National Park. Each year, millions of people visit this park.

Fossils may be found where the Colorado River has cut down through layers of rock. Fossils are the remains or traces of past plants or animals. This fossil shows a fern that once grew in the canyon.

21

...e is a pool of water on land. Like rivers, most ...ve fresh water. One difference between rivers and ...hat rivers flow from place to place.

### ...nt Motion

...rs start in different ways. Some rivers begin in ...ook at the map. Where does the Hudson River ...other rivers start from underground streams. ...ins or melting snow can also cause rivers. Rivers ...ra water that the land can't soak up.

**...lson River**

CANADA

Lake Tear of the Clouds

...ntario

ATLANTIC OCEAN

New York | Vermont | Maine | New Hampshire | Massachusetts | Connecticut | Rhode Island

...nnsylvania

New Jersey

...they begin, rivers are always ...Most rivers run into another body ...Some rivers flow into other rivers. ...vers end in lakes or oceans. Others ...disappear underground.

...rs may be wide or narrow. They may be deep or ...But all river water moves because it flows ...If the land is flat, water runs slowly. If the land is ...ater runs quickly. The Colorado River often flows ...use it runs downhill through very steep land. ■

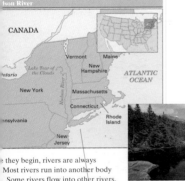
▲ *The Hudson River starts in Lake Tear-of-the-Clouds, which holds water from Mt. Marcy. Where does the river end?*

■ *How do rivers begin and end?*

19

**Pictured at a moment in time** is this cactus in an Arizona desert. Look at its blossoms and the birds and rabbit that come to visit it. You will learn what happens to the cactus after a spring rain.

**Every map tells a story.** The map on this page tells the story of where the Hudson River in New York State runs and what the land is like there.

### A MOMENT IN TIME
## The Saguaro Cactus

*10:32 A.M. May 5, 1991 After a spring rain in the Sonoran Desert in Arizona*

**Flowers**
Raindrops sparkle on these blossoms that opened during the cool night hours. The flowers will close again before the afternoon heat reaches 110°F.

**Elf Owl**
The unusual sound of falling rain woke this tiny owl from its daytime sleep. During the day, the owl hides in this hole made by a woodpecker months ago. At night, it leaves the nest to hunt.

**Arm**
Sharp thorns cover the arms that show that this cactus is very old. A saguaro doesn't grow arms until it's at least 75 years old. Some saguaros live 250 years. They may stand 50 feet tall and have 50 arms.

**Woodpecker**
A loud tap, tap, tap fills the desert air as this bird pecks a hole in the trunk of the cactus. Today, it will find plenty of water inside. Later, another bird will build a nest in this hole.

**Trunk**
Swollen to twice its normal size, the trunk is filled with hundreds of gallons of rain water. The saguaro's roots quickly soaked up the water from the desert sands.

**Jack Rabbit**
After nibbling tender young cactus sprouts in the early morning, this rabbit has hopped into the cool shade of the saguaro. There it can avoid the scorching sun until late afternoon.

# Continuing On

*As you read about your world and the people in it, you'll want ways of understanding and remembering them better. This book gives you some tools to use in learning about people and places and remembering what you've learned.*

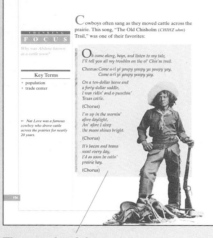

**The titles give the main points** of the lesson. On this page the red title tells you how rivers shape the land. On the next page the red title tells how rivers flood the land.

**The people of the past** speak directly to you in special parts of the text.

**You're in charge of your reading.** See the red square at the end of the text? Now find the red square over in the margin. If you can answer the question there, then you probably understood what you just read. If you can't, perhaps you'd better go back and read that part of the lesson again.

**Diagrams make clear** things that are hard to understand. Here the diagrams show the loops a river makes as it flows toward the sea.

xiv

**Some tools you'll always use.** The Understanding pages help you learn skills that you will use again and again. On this page you learn how to make a summary by listing the main ideas of what you've read.

**You get the inside story** when you read two special paragraphs. One, called How Do We Know?, tells you where information about the past comes from. Another, Across Time & Space, connects what you're reading to things that happpened long ago or far away. (See page 81 for an example.)

(See page 81 for an example.)

---

### UNDERSTANDING A SUMMARY

## Using Main Ideas

Look at what you've read

Main Idea
detail
detail
detail

Main Idea
detail
detail
detail

Remember main ideas

Main Idea
Main Idea

detail
detail
detail
detail

Main Idea
Main Idea

detail
detail
detail
detail

Retell main ideas in your own words

**Summary**

**Here's Why** Have you ever had to remember something you read? Maybe it was for a test. Or maybe you wanted to tell a friend. How do you go about remembering what you read? A good way to remembering what you read is to make a summary of it.

**Here's How** A summary is a few sentences that tell the main ideas of what you read. You should use as few words as possible in a summary. They should be your own words.

In the last lesson, you read about Arbor Day. What would you include in a summary about Arbor Day? Think about the main ideas. The meaning of Arbor Day is one important idea to remember. When we celebrate Arbor Day is another. The number of years that Johnny Appleseed planted trees is a detail. Details are not as important as main ideas. They are not part of a summary.

**Try It** Work with a partner. Write a summary of the information about Arbor Day on pages 219 and 220.

**Apply It** Write a summary of something you have read in a book or magazine. Read your summary to the class.

---

**A picture is worth a thousand words.** But just a few words in a caption can help you understand a picture, a map, or a photograph.

---

its banks and covers land that is Too much rain can cause a flood. the sudden melting of snow or d with water during a flood is

rmful. They damage homes and e floods are helpful. Sometimes a and leaves it behind when the water helps crops grow better. Rivers may y erosion, but they can also build up

#### How Do We Know?

Much of Louisiana was built up by the Mississippi River. We know this because Louisiana's soil is made up of river sand, gravel, and mud. Since the Mississippi ends in Louisiana, it drops these materials before joining the Atlantic Ocean.

◄ This whole area is a flood plain. You can see that the farmer's house barely missed going underwater too. Farms are often on flood plains because the soil is so good.

■ How can a flood bring good things to people?

#### R E V I E W

w do rivers affect the land? What are the differences oceans, rivers, and lakes? INKING We know that rivers er from the land. What do you uld happen if there were no carry off extra water?

**4. ACTIVITY** Take an imaginary trip on an ocean or a river. Write a short description of what you see, hear, and smell. Compare what you wrote with what your classmates wrote. How are river and ocean trips different? How are they the same?

23

---

**After you read the lesson,** stop and review what you've read. The questions and an activity help you think about the lesson. Chapter Review questions help you tie the lessons together. (See pages 24 and 25 for an example.)

(See pages 24 and 25 for an example.)

---

**A special kind of Understanding** page looks at the big ideas that help put all the pieces together. This section helps you understand ideas like how we use our natural resources—our water, land, and trees.

### UNDERSTANDING NATURAL RESOURCES

## We Use Natural Resources

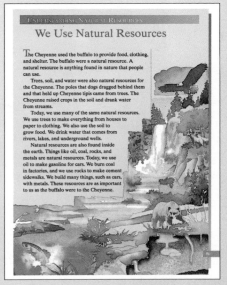

The Cheyenne used the buffalo to provide food, clothing, and shelter. The buffalo were a natural resource. A natural resource is anything found in nature that people can use.

Trees, soil, and water were also natural resources for the Cheyenne. The poles that dogs dragged behind them and that held up Cheyenne tipis came from trees. The Cheyenne raised crops in the soil and drank water from streams.

Today, we use many of the same natural resources. We use trees to make everything from houses to paper to clothing. We also use the soil to grow food. We drink water that comes from rivers, lakes, and underground wells.

Natural resources are also found inside the earth. Things like oil, coal, rocks, and metals are natural resources. Today, we use oil to make gasoline for cars. We burn coal in factories, and we use rocks to make cement sidewalks. We build many things, such as cars, with metals. These resources are as important to us as the buffalo were to the Cheyenne.

# Also Featuring

*Some special pages show up only once in every unit, not in every lesson in the book. These features continue the story by letting you explore an idea or activity, or read a story about another time and place. The Time/Space Databank in the back of the book brings together helpful pages you will use again and again.*

**What would you do?** The Making Decisions pages show you an important decision. Then you practice the steps that will help you to make a good choice.

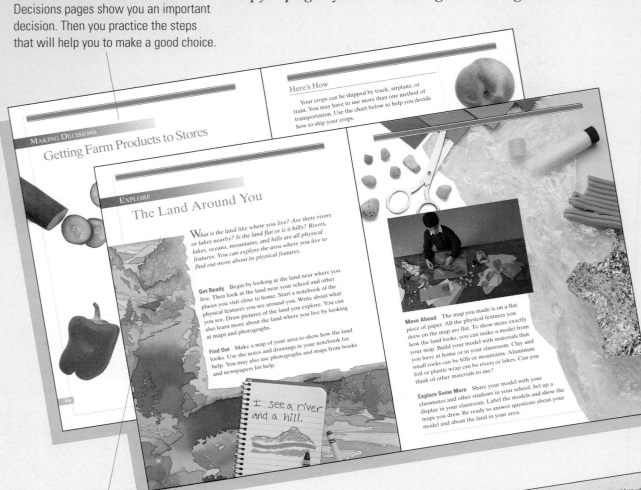

MAKING DECISIONS

Getting Farm Products to Stores

Here's How

Your crops can be shipped by truck, airplane, or train. You may have to use more than one method of transportation. Use the chart below to help you decide how to ship your crops.

EXPLORE

The Land Around You

What is the land like where you live? Are there rivers or lakes nearby? Is the land flat or is it hilly? Rivers, lakes, oceans, mountains, and hills are all physical features. You can explore the area where you live to find out more about its physical features.

**Get Ready** Begin by looking at the land near where you live. Then look at the land near your school and other places you visit close to home. Start a notebook of the physical features you see around you. Write about what you see. Draw pictures of the land you explore. You can also learn more about the land where you live by looking at maps and photographs.

**Find Out** Make a map of your area to show how the land looks. Use the notes and drawings in your notebook for help. You may also use photographs and maps from books and newspapers for help.

**Move Ahead** The map you made is on a flat piece of paper. All the physical features you drew on the map are flat. To show more exactly how the land looks, you can make a model from your map. Build your model with materials that you have at home or in your classroom. Clay and small rocks can be hills or mountains. Aluminum foil or plastic wrap can be rivers or lakes. Can you think of other materials to use?

**Explore Some More** Share your model with your classmates and other students in your school. Set up a display in your classroom. Label the models and show the maps you drew. Be ready to answer questions about your model and about the land in your area.

I see a river and a hill.

Many years ago, men, women, and children—young and old alike—went west to find a new land to settle. Travel was not easy. Houses and food were hard to find. But, always, other people helped. Read this excerpt from a story about a pioneer family in Kansas.

LITERATURE

WAGON WHEELS

Written by Barbara Brenner
Illustrated by Don Bolognese

Chapter 1—THE DUGOUT

There it is, boys," Daddy said. "Across this ri Nicodemus, Kansas. That is where we are goi build our house. There is free land for everyo here in the West. All we have to do is go and

**School isn't the only place** where you can learn social studies. This feature gives you a chance to explore people and places outside the classroom—at home or in your own neighborhood.

**Stories have always been important** parts of people's lives. Each unit in the book has at least one story about the time and place you're studying. In this case, it's a story about a pioneer family in Kansas.

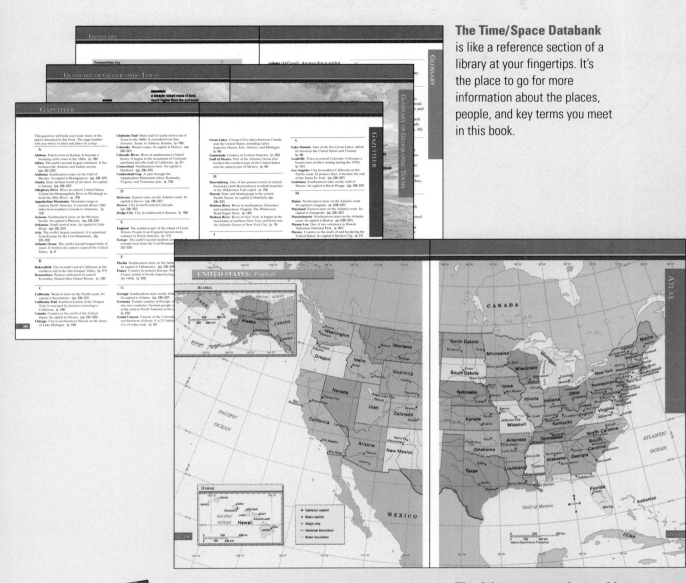

**The Time/Space Databank** is like a reference section of a library at your fingertips. It's the place to go for more information about the places, people, and key terms you meet in this book.

**The Atlas maps out the world.** Large maps show you the parts of your world and your country. One large map shows you the physical regions of the United States.

## UNIT OVERVIEW

Ask if students have ever heard a bird sing or leaves rustle in the wind. Explain to students that these are examples of the sounds of nature or the sounds of the land. Discuss with students other sounds they have heard when they listen to the land.

Then read aloud the unit title and the text. Have students look at the photograph and tell what sounds they might hear if they could listen to the land shown in this photograph. *(the sound of water flowing from mountain peaks, a moose call, water trickling through the beaver lodge, a beaver slapping its tail, a fish splashing in the water, leaves rustling in the wind)*

### Looking Forward

The land of the United States is the topic of the next three chapters:
Chapter 1: Mighty Waters
Chapter 2: Rustling Leaves and Grasses
Chapter 3: Majestic Peaks and Deserts

## Unit 1
## Listen to the Land

*Before people came to the land, only the sounds of nature could be heard. Water from melting snow rushed noisily down mountain peaks, and moose called in thick green forests. Today, roaring cars and planes can make them hard to hear, but—if you listen—you can still hear the beautiful sounds of the land.*

*David Muench. Beaver Lodge. Grand Teton National Park, Wyoming.*

## BIBLIOGRAPHY

**Books for Students**
Amos, William Hopkins. *Life in Ponds and Streams.* Washington, DC: National Geographic Society, 1981. A resource book on life in ponds and streams.

Carlisle, Norman and Madelyn. *Rivers.* Chicago: Children's Press, 1989. An account of how a river begins, grows, and affects the land.

Peters, Lisa Westberg. *The Sun, the Wind, and the Rain.* New York: Henry Holt, 1988. Readers learn how the elements affect mountains by examining a real mountain and one made by a young girl.

Williams, Vera B. *Stringbean's Trip to the Shining Sea.* New York: Greenwillow, 1988. Stringbean's postcards chronicle a cross-country trip with his older brother, Fred.

**Books to Read Aloud**
Baylor, Byrd. *Desert Voices.* New York: Charles Scribner's Sons, 1980. The desert creatures poetically speak of what it is like to live in the desert.

George, Jean C. *One Day in the Woods.* New York: Crowell Junior Books, 1988. A young girl discovers woodland wonders while searching the Teatown Woods of New York for the ovenbird.

## Notes on the Photograph

This photograph was taken by David Muench, who has been fascinated with the wilderness of the United States since he was a child traveling with his famous photographer-father Josef Muench. David Muench is now himself a well-known Western landscape artist whose photographs appear in books and magazines. This picture shows a scene from the Grand Teton National Park in Wyoming.

____. *One Day in the Prairie.* New York: Crowell Junior Books, 1986. The ecology of the prairie is explored on an Oklahoma wildlife refuge.

**Book for Teachers**
Attenborough, David. *The Living Planet: A Portrait of the Earth.* Boston: Little, Brown, 1984. Explores some of the factors that contribute to the formation of the earth's surface.

## Other Resources

**Computer Software**
*Beachcombing Treasures.* Lincoln, MA: Spectrum Software, 1987. Apple II family.

*Introduction to Geography, Maps and Globes.* Freeport, NY: Educational Activities, 1988. Apple II family.

### Bookshelf

Bowden, Joan Chase. *Why the Tides Ebb and Flow.* Boston: Houghton Mifflin, 1979. Folktale explaining why the sea has tides.

Carrick, Carol. *Lost in the Storm.* New York: Clarion, 1987. Christopher spends a fretful night before searching for his dog, who was lost in a storm.

**CHAPTER ORGANIZER**

# Chapter 1 *Mighty Waters*

## CHAPTER PLANNING CHART

| Pupil's Edition | Teacher's Edition | Ancillaries |
|---|---|---|
| **Lesson 1: Sand and Salt (3–4 days)**<br><br>Objective 1: Identify the oceans bordering the United States and their locations. (Geography 2)*<br>Objective 2: Describe ways oceans shape and reshape the land by eroding the land and by depositing soil. (Geography 2) | • Graphic Overview (4)<br>• Access Strategy (5)<br>• Access Activity (5)<br>Political Context (6)<br>Science Connection (6) | Home Involvement (1)<br>• Poster (1, 4)<br>Study Guide (1)<br>• Study Print (1, 2, 3) |
| **Understanding Map Directions: Using a Compass Rose**<br><br>Objective 1: Use a compass rose. (Map and Globe Skills 3)<br>Objective 2: Identify and use intermediate directions. (Map and Globe Skills 3) | | • Study Guide (2) |
| **Literature:** *Where the River Begins* | | Discovery Journal (1, 2) |
| **Lesson 2: Running Rivers (3–4 days)**<br><br>Objective 1: Define the characteristics of a river. (Geography 2)<br>Objective 2: Identify the differences between rivers and oceans, and between rivers and lakes. (Geography 2)<br>Objective 3: Describe ways rivers carve the land. (Geography 2)<br>Objective 4: Describe ways floods affect the land. (Geography 2) | • Graphic Overview (18)<br>• Access Strategy (19)<br>• Access Activity (19)<br>Science Connection (20)<br>Collaborative Learning (22) | Discovery Journal (3, 4)<br>Map Activity (2)<br>• Poster (2, 6)<br>Study Guide (3)<br>• Study Print (4)<br>• Transparency (1) |
| **Chapter Review** | Answers (24–25) | Chapter 1 Test |

\* Objectives are correlated to the strands and goals in the program scope and sequence on pages T41–T48.

• LEP appropriate resources. (For additional strategies, see pages T32–T33.)

This chapter is the first in a unit that examines the natural landscape of the United States. Chapter 1 focuses on how the two largest bodies of water—oceans and rivers—shape the land. Later chapters in this unit describe forests, prairies, mountains, and deserts—all of which are basic elements of the natural landscape of the United States.

The three chapters in this unit provide a foundation for later units that examine how people have interacted with the natural environment.

We first look closely at the natural landscape because the land has influenced our history and continues to affect our daily lives. After learning in this unit about the natural environment, students will later consider who settled the land, how people used natural resources, and how they changed the environment.

We chose to focus this chapter on oceans and rivers because they are major forces in shaping the land. **Lesson 1** describes how oceans both build up and erode coastal lands. This lesson uses photographs and diagrams to reinforce and supplement the text. We use literature to engage students in the topic of **Lesson 2**—rivers. This lesson emphasizes how rivers shape the land, both building it up and wearing it away. The feature A Closer Look: The Grand Canyon dramatizes how running water has, over time, eroded land to form the Grand Canyon.

We intend that this chapter and other chapters in this unit will help students look at continuity and change in their own communities, starting with the natural landscape.

## ACTIVITIES & PROJECTS

### Bulletin Board

Divide a bulletin board into six sections, with one of the following headings over each area: *Oceans, Rivers, Forests, Prairies, Mountains,* and *Deserts.* As students read and discuss Unit 1, have them bring in pictures from magazines and newspapers. Direct students to place their pictures under the appropriate headings on the bulletin board and tell the class what their pictures show.

### LEP: Investigation

After students read Lesson 2, bring in a cardboard box partially filled with dirt, a pail, and a large pitcher with a spout. Pack down the dirt so that it is significantly higher on the right side and carve a large groove in the dirt from right to left. Cut a hole in the box where the groove hits the left side of the box. Put the box on a table or desk so that the left side of the box is at the edge of the table. Then place the pail on the floor underneath the hole in the box and fill the pitcher with water. As other students observe, have a volunteer simulate the action of a river by slowly pouring the water into the groove on the higher right side so that it flows down the groove and out of the hole into the pail. Help students relate the changes in the dirt to the changes a river makes in land as it flows downhill.

### Challenge: Writing Ocean Imagery

After students read Lesson 1, have them work in small groups to create a poem of ocean imagery. Have each student think of three or four words that describe the ocean in its many moods. Remind students to use words that tell about the taste, touch, smell, sound, and sight of the ocean. Students who have never been to the ocean should use pictures of the ocean to spark ideas for words that describe what they think the ocean is like. Have the students in each group use their words to make a poem.

### Making a Map

At the conclusion of Lesson 1, have students use reference materials to find the names and locations of all five oceans on our planet. (*Pacific, Atlantic, Indian, Arctic, Antarctic*) Then supply students with outline maps of the world or have them trace a world map on their own paper. Have students label each of the world's oceans on the map to show its location.

1B

## Chapter 1

# Mighty Waters

*The story of this land begins with a look at its mighty waters. The United States is touched by two great oceans and crossed by many rivers and streams. Pounding ocean waves eat away at the shores and make sandy beaches. Powerful rivers and streams carry soil from one place to another. The United States is a land shaped by water.*

Oceans are filled with beautiful sea creatures. This animal is called a starfish, or a sea star. Starfish live in every ocean of the world.

Powerful waves have formed these cliffs along the Pacific Ocean.

The waters of the Atlantic Ocean broke up rocks and shells to form the sand on this beach.

### Oceans

Ocean waters cover approximately 70 per cent of the earth's surface. The Pacific Ocean is the largest ocean. It is twice as large as the Atlantic Ocean, which covers about 31,530,000 square miles. The Pacific Ocean is larger than the seven continents put together.

The oceans are really one large body of water that surrounds the continents. Included in the ocean are smaller bodies of water, like gulfs, seas, and bays.

The ocean reaches depths of more than six miles! If the highest mountain in the world, Mount Everest, were placed in the deepest part of the ocean, more than a mile of water would rise above the peak of the mountain.

It is easier to swim in an ocean than in a river or lake. The reason is that ocean water contains more than 3 per cent salt, and the salt helps keep a swimmer afloat.

### Rivers

The Nile, located in Africa, is the longest river in the world. It flows 4,187 miles. The longest river in the United States is the Missouri River, which flows 2,466 miles.

The photograph of the Mississippi River was taken near the Gulf of Mexico, which is the river's mouth or end point. Near the Gulf of Mexico, the Mississippi deposits huge amounts of silt, which has built up a large delta covering about 13,000 square miles.

The Earth is mostly covered with water. The United States lies between the Atlantic and Pacific oceans.

The Mississippi River, which winds through the middle of the United States, is the second longest river in North America. The Missouri River is the longest river in North America.

3

Both the Mississippi River and the Colorado River end their journeys at sea level as they flow into the ocean. The Mississippi River moves more slowly on its trip to the sea because it begins at an altitude of about 1,000 feet above sea level. The Colorado River, on the other hand, runs much faster because it begins at an altitude of over 14,000 feet above sea level.

4

# INTRODUCE

**P**oint out the lesson title and establish that the terms *sand* and *salt* describe an ocean. Ask if students have seen the ocean and briefly discuss any experiences they have had with the ocean. Have students read the Thinking Focus and create a word web of terms that are related to the land along the ocean, such as *beach, shore,* and *sand.* If necessary, elicit the terms *coast, coastal,* and *cliff.* Have students think of ways that oceans change the land. Have students read to check their answers.

### Key Terms

Vocabulary strategies: T36–T37
**ocean**—a large body of salt water
**coast**—land along the edge of an ocean
**erosion**—wearing away of land

LESSON 1

# Sand and Salt

### THINKING
## FOCUS

*How do oceans change the land?*

### Key Terms

- ocean
- coast
- erosion

**T**he sun was hot, but Matt didn't notice. He piled cool, damp sand onto his sand castle. The crashing waves of the ocean were so loud that he could barely hear the sea gulls calling. Matt picked up more sand and noticed something white, round, and flat. He carefully brushed off the sand. It was the first sand dollar Matt had ever found. He gently placed it next to the shells he had gathered.

Matt looked at the waves rolling toward him. He licked his lips, which tasted salty. Soon the waves would wash away his sand castle, but Matt didn't mind. He'd always have the sand dollar to remind him of the sea.

## Objectives

1. Identify the oceans bordering the United States and their locations.
2. Describe ways oceans shape and reshape the land by eroding the land and by depositing soil.

## Graphic Overview

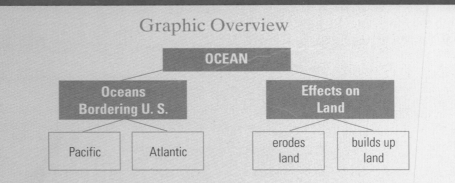

## Pacific and Atlantic

The waves that rolled toward Matt came from the Pacific Ocean. An **ocean** is a large body of salt water. Oceans cover more than half the earth's surface. The Pacific Ocean is the largest ocean. It borders the United States on the west. Hawaii is surrounded by the Pacific Ocean.

If Matt could see 3,000 miles across the United States, he would see another ocean! That one is the Atlantic Ocean, the second largest ocean in the world. Find the Pacific and Atlantic oceans on the picture of the globe. ■

## Coastal Land

Oceans constantly change the land. The land along the edge of an ocean is called the **coast.** Ocean waters act like a scraper on coastal land. Crashing waves slowly grind up the soil and rock and carry it away. This wearing away of land is called **erosion.**

### Across Time & Space

*Many scientists believe that the earth was once one giant piece of land and one giant ocean. Look at the world map on pages 232-233. Imagine that Africa and South America are pieces of a puzzle. Fit them together.*

■ *What oceans border the United States?*

◄ *Large ocean waves like these can change the shape of a coast.*

5

## DEVELOP

Read aloud the narrative under "Sand and Salt." Discuss what Matt sees, hears, feels, and tastes. Point out that these details reveal characteristics of the ocean.

Have students preview the text by finding the headings in the lesson. To help students grasp the main ideas, you may wish to begin the Graphic Overview on the board and complete it as you discuss the text.

■ *The Atlantic and Pacific oceans border the United States.*

### GEOGRAPHY
### Map and Globe Skills

Locate the Great Lakes and Mississippi River on a map or globe and ask students to explain how they differ from an ocean. Have students find their own locale on a map of the United States and identify the ocean nearest them and the direction they would travel to reach it.

### GEOGRAPHY
### Critical Thinking

Clarify the description comparing ocean waters to a scraper. Make sure students understand the term *scraper.* Relate it to a blade scraping ice from a window or to a nail file.

5

## Access Strategy

Preview the lesson by helping students read each heading aloud. Then have them explain what is shown in each photograph or drawing and how they think the photograph or drawing relates to the heading. Have students compare the coastal land shown on this page with that shown in the large photograph on page 7. Mention that both are coasts, but they are quite different from each other. Have students tell what these differences are, eliciting that one coast is rough and rocky, and the other is smooth, wide, and sandy. Explain that students will be finding out about these differences in the lesson.

Help students understand erosion by discussing the weight and power of water. Have them imagine picking up a large bucket of water to bring out the fact that water is heavy. Discuss being knocked over by a wave and explain that large, moving waves have much power.

## Access Activity

To show the erosive force of moving water and rocks, have students put pieces of red clay bricks in a can with a tight cover. Students should fill the can halfway with water and shake it vigorously for several minutes. When they pour the contents into a glass jar or bowl, the water should show small bits of clay material that were "eroded" off the brick.

## Visual Learning

To clarify how ocean waves create cliffs along the sea, have students use the diagram on this page to explain the process in their own words. Make sure they understand that "waves weaken the lower part of the hill" by beating against it and washing away some of the rock and sand that make up the hill.

Ocean waves are very powerful. Over hundreds of years, they can wear away even the hardest kinds of rock. In some places, crashing waves turn land along the coast into steep, rocky cliffs.

**How Sea Cliffs Are Formed**

**1.** A sea cliff starts out as a hill. Over many years, waves weaken the lower part of the hill.

**2.** Bit by bit, the earth and rock there begin to break into chunks and slide into the ocean.

**3.** Now the upper part of the hill hangs out over the water. When it becomes too heavy, that part begins to crumble and fall.

**4.** Finally, the side of the hill has become a steep cliff.

Ocean waves do not just cause erosion. They can also add to the land. When waves wash up on a shore, they may leave sand and mud behind. After years of sand and mud piling up this way, new beaches are formed.

6

## Visual Learning

Have students work in small groups. Provide each group with modeling clay and shallow boxes. Have students make clay models of a seacoast. Display the completed models and discuss the similarities and differences.

## Political Context

Mention to students that beach erosion is a serious problem for many seaside towns. Winter storms wash away sand, shortening the width of the beach. Seaside towns try to protect their beaches by preserving the sand dunes behind the beaches. The roots of dune grasses help hold the sand in place, preventing it from being easily washed or blown away. Many towns have laws against walking on sand dunes and dune grasses, since the dunes and plants are easily damaged.

## Science Connection

Ask students to describe the color of sand. Most will respond by describing sand as light brown or whitish. Tell students that some beaches in the world, especially on Pacific Islands, have black sand. Ask students for a reason for different colored sand. *(Sand takes its color from the material from which it eroded. The most common element in most sand is quartz, a light-colored or clear mineral. Black sand is created by the erosion of a black lava rock called basalt.)*

Where does sand come from? You may be surprised to learn that it was once rocks and shells. Rocks and shells are pounded by waves against other rocks and shells. This constant pounding breaks them down into small bits. Then the waves wash the small bits onto the shore.

Not all beaches are alike. In some places, rocks and shells are broken into tiny bits and become sand. In other places, rocks do not break into such small pieces. That is why some beaches are sandy and others are rocky. ■

■ *How does the ocean take away land and give land back?*

■ *The ocean takes away land when waves wear away rocks; it gives land back when waves wash sand and mud ashore.*

◄ *In some places, waves break rocks into very tiny pieces, and sandy beaches form. In other places, rocks are left in bigger pieces as on the rocky beach above.*

## C L O S E

Remind students of the focus question. Have them use the illustrations to discuss how oceans wear away coastal land and how oceans wash sand ashore to help build up beaches.

As an extension activity, encourage students who have seashell collections to share them with their classmates. If a seashell identification book is available, have children find shells from the collection in the book to see if any similar shells are found in different parts of the world.

If possible, bring in a jar full of beach sand for children to examine, perhaps under a microscope. Have them look for grains that seem to have come from rock and grains that seem to have come from shells.

## R E V I E W

1. **FOCUS** How do oceans change the land?
2. **CONNECT** Do you live closer to the Atlantic Ocean or the Pacific Ocean?
3. **CRITICAL THINKING** Is a sea cliff a safe place to build a house? Why?

4. **ACTIVITY** Draw a line down the middle of a piece of paper. On one side, draw a picture of things to do on a sandy beach. On the other side, draw a picture of things to do on a rocky beach.

## Answers to Review Questions

1. Oceans change the land by shaping the coast line. Ocean waves may wash away land; oceans may build up land by depositing sand and mud and forming new beaches. Ocean waters also break rocks and shells into sand.
2. Answer will vary according to location.
3. A sea cliff would not be a safe place to build a house because waves may begin to wear away the bottom of the cliff, eventually causing the cliff to crumble and fall into the ocean.
4. Sandy-beach activities might include digging in the sand, building sand castles, digging trenches into the water, looking for sand crabs, etc. Rocky-beach activities might include scrambling over the rocks, looking for sealife washed into the crevices between the rocks, watching crashing waves, etc.

## Homework Options

Provide students with outline maps of the United States. Have each student color and label the Pacific Ocean and the Atlantic Ocean.

**Study Guide:** page 1

This skills feature uses a compass rose to teach students to identify and use intermediate directions.

## GEOGRAPHY
### Map and Globe Skills

Give students time to study the map on page 9. Read aloud the material under "Here's How" and demonstrate how to find the answers to the questions.

## UNDERSTANDING MAP DIRECTIONS

# Using a Compass Rose

**Here's Why**   You know that the Pacific Ocean borders the United States on the west. The Atlantic Ocean is on the east. Canada is to the north. Mexico is to the south. North, south, east, and west are the main, or cardinal, directions.

Suppose you want to find a place between north and east, or between east and south. Then you need in-between directions. In-between directions are called intermediate directions. Knowing how to use intermediate directions will make it easier to locate places on a map.

**Here's How**   You will find a compass rose on many maps. A compass rose shows directions. Find the compass rose on the treasure map on the next page. North is at the top. South is at the bottom. East is to the right. Where is west?

Now find the direction halfway between north and east on the compass rose. Northeast is the intermediate direction between north and east. What two letters are used for this direction? Find the direction halfway between south and east on the compass rose. That direction is labeled SE. What does SE stand for? What is the intermediate direction halfway between south and west? What is the intermediate direction halfway between north and west?

**Try It**   Look at the treasure map again. Imagine that you are looking for hidden treasure. You walk north

## Objectives

1. Use a compass rose. (Map and Globe Skills 3)
2. Identify and use intermediate directions. (Map and Globe Skills 3)

## Giving Directions

Have the class use map directions on the playground. After identifying north, south, east, and west, call on volunteers to silently think of an object they can see, such as a particular tree or building. Then have them give cardinal and intermediate directions to help the other students find and name the object.

along the path and then turn east. You come to the hut, but the treasure isn't there. You decide to look under the table. In which direction is the table from the hut? Maybe the treasure is under the bridge. In which direction is the bridge from the table?

**Apply It** Now work with a partner. Plan your own treasure hunt. Use the map to decide where to hide your treasure. Give your partner a starting point and directions to find it. When your partner has found the treasure, it's your turn to search. Follow your partner's directions until you find the treasure.

9

## Answers to Try It

The table is north of the hut. The bridge is northwest of the table.

## Answers to Apply It

Monitor students as they give each other directions for finding treasure on the map. If any student is having trouble, check to be sure the partner is giving accurate directions.

## Map and Globe Skills

Help students identify where north, south, east, and west are in the classroom. Post signs with the letters *N, S, E,* and *W* at the appropriate locations. Then use cardinal and intermediate directions to describe the location of things in the classroom relative to one another.

## INTRODUCE

Point out that Thomas Locker both wrote and illustrated this story and is recognized as a painter as well as a writer. Mention that students will be reading about rivers in the next lesson and that they can discover some things about rivers in this story.

## READ AND RESPOND

You may wish to read this selection aloud with students. Before reading, ask if students have ever wondered where rivers begin. Suggest that they will learn about the source of one river.

*Two boys watched the river and wondered where it began. They asked their grandfather, who had lived near the river all his life. Together, they set out to find the beginning of the river. Read about their trip.*

LITERATURE

# WHERE THE RIVER BEGINS

**Written and Illustrated by Thomas Locker**

Once there were two boys named Josh and Aaron who lived with their family in a big yellow house. Nearby was a river that flowed gently into the sea. On summer evenings the boys liked to sit on their porch watching the river and making up stories about it. Where, they wondered, did the river begin.

10

## Thematic Connections

Social Studies: Rivers, characteristics of landscapes

Houghton Mifflin Literary Readers: Journeys

## Background

Thomas Locker, author and illustrator of *Where the River Begins*, is well known for his beautifully illustrated children's books dealing with themes in nature.

*Where the River Begins* was called "astonishing and haunting" by Christopher Lehmann-Haupt of *The New York Times*, and this critic named it one of ten outstanding illustrated books in 1984. It received the *Parents' Choice* Award for Illustration and was identified as one of the year's ten Best

Illustrated Books by *The New York Times Book Review*. *Booklist*, in a starred review, praised it as "A beautiful book . . . . Spectacular paintings are reminiscent of nineteenth-century art."

Other acclaimed books by Mr. Locker include *The Mare on the Hill* and *Sailing with the Wind*.

Their grandfather loved the river and had lived near it all his life. Perhaps he would know. One day Josh and Aaron asked their grandfather to take them on a camping trip to find the beginning of the river. When he agreed, they made plans and began to pack.

They started out early the next morning. For a time they walked along a familiar road past fields of golden wheat and sheep grazing in the sun. Nearby flowed the river—gentle, wide, and deep.

*foothills* low hills at the foot of a mountain

At last they reached the foothills of the mountains. The road had ended and now the river would be their only guide. It raced over rocks and boulders and had become so narrow that the boys and their grandfather could jump across.

In the late afternoon, while the sun was still hot, the river led them into a dark forest. They found a campsite and set up their tent. Then the boys went wading in the cold river water.

12

The first long day away from home was over. That night, around the flickering campfire, their grandfather told Josh and Aaron stories. Drifting off to sleep, they listened to the forest noises and were soothed by the sound of the river.

*soothed* calmed

*knoll* a small, rounded hill

*meandered* followed a winding course

Dawn seemed to come quickly and the sun glowed through a thick mist. The boys were eager to be off, but their grandfather was stiff from sleeping on the ground and was slower getting started.

The path they chose led them high above the river. On a grassy knoll they stopped to gaze around. The morning mist had risen and formed white clouds in the sky. In the distance the river meandered lazily. It was so narrow that it seemed almost to disappear. They all felt a great excitement, for they knew they were nearing the end of their journey.

Without a word the boys began to run. They followed the river for an hour or more until it trickled into a still pond, high in an upland meadow. In this small, peaceful place the river began. Finally their search was over.

As they started back, the sky suddenly darkened. Thunder crashed around them and lightning lit the sky. They pitched their tent and crawled inside just before the storm broke. Rain pounded on the roof of their small tent all night long, but they were warm and dry inside.

In the morning long before dawn they were awakened by a roaring, rushing sound. The river had swelled with the storm and was flooding its banks. They tried to take a shortcut across a field but were soon ankle deep in water. Grandfather explained that the river drew its waters from the rains high up in the mountains.

► Ask where the river began and where it got its water. *(It began in a pond in the mountains. It got its water from rains high up in the mountains.)*

16

They came down out of the foothills in the soft light of late afternoon. The boys recognized the cliffs along the river and knew they were close to home. Their weariness lifted and they began to move more quickly down the road.

*weariness* tiredness

At last they reached their house on the hill. The boys raced ahead to tell their mother and father about the place where the river began. But their grandfather paused for a moment and in the fading light he watched the river, which continued on as it always had, flowing gently into the sea.

## EXTEND

Have each student write a poem about a river. Suggest that students might make their poems meander on the page like a river does on land, or use words that describe how a river changes as it flows over different kinds of land.

## Making a Map

Have students work in groups to make maps showing the journey that Josh and Aaron took with their grandfather in search of the river's source. Suggest that group members begin by scanning the text and making a list of places to include on their maps. Possibilities would include the boys' home by the river, the fields of wheat and grazing sheep, the foothills of the mountains, the campsite in the forest, the upland meadow with the pond, the second campsite during the storm, the muddy field, and the road leading home.

Have students use their lists to create maps on large sheets of drawing paper. Display the maps so students can compare how they visualized the journey.

## Further Reading

You may want to have your students look for more books to read on this topic in the school or local library.

Have a volunteer read the lesson title aloud. Ask students to name a local river and, if possible, tell where it begins and ends. Then help students recall what they learned about rivers from reading *Where the River Begins.* Focus in particular on the way the river flowed and changed and how it flooded its banks after the rainstorm.

Remind students that the last lesson was about oceans. Then have students read the Thinking Focus and think about how rivers affect the land. Ask for their ideas on how oceans and rivers are alike and different. Have students read to check their answers.

### Key Terms

Vocabulary strategies: T36–T37
**river**—a stream of water that flows across land
**lake**—a pool of water on land
**flood**—water that overflows its banks and covers land that is normally dry

L E S S O N   2

# Running Rivers

## FOCUS

*How do rivers affect the land?*

### Key Terms

- river
- lake
- flood

*T*he river went on raising and raising for ten or twelve days, till at last it was over the banks. The water was three or four foot deep on the island in the low places and on the Illinois bottom. On that side it was a good many miles wide, but on the Missouri side it was the same old distance across—a half a mile—because the Missouri shore was just a wall of high bluffs.

Daytimes we paddled all over the island in the canoe. . . . Well, on every old broken-down tree you could see rabbits and snakes and such things; and when the island had been overflowed a day or two they got so tame, on account of being hungry, that you could paddle right up and put your hand on them if you wanted to; but not the snakes and turtles—they would slide off in the water.

Mark Twain, from *The Adventures of Huckleberry Finn*

The author who wrote these words lived along a river bank and often saw the water rise after a big rain. A **river** is a stream of water that flows across land. Rivers are different from oceans in two ways. First, oceans are much bigger than rivers are. Oceans cover most of the earth. Second, oceans are salty. Rivers are not. Water that comes from rivers is called fresh water.

## Objectives

1. Define the characteristics of a river.
2. Identify the differences between rivers and oceans, and between rivers and lakes.
3. Describe ways rivers carve the land.
4. Describe ways floods affect the land.

## Graphic Overview

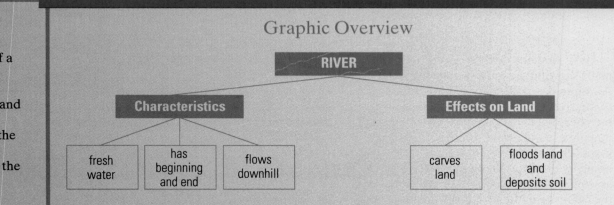

**RIVER**

**Characteristics**

| fresh water | has beginning and end | flows downhill |

**Effects on Land**

| carves land | floods land and deposits soil |

A **lake** is a pool of water on land. Like rivers, most lakes have fresh water. One difference between rivers and lakes is that rivers flow from place to place.

## Constant Motion

Rivers start in different ways. Some rivers begin in lakes. Look at the map. Where does the Hudson River begin? Other rivers start from underground streams. Heavy rains or melting snow can also cause rivers. Rivers carry extra water that the land can't soak up.

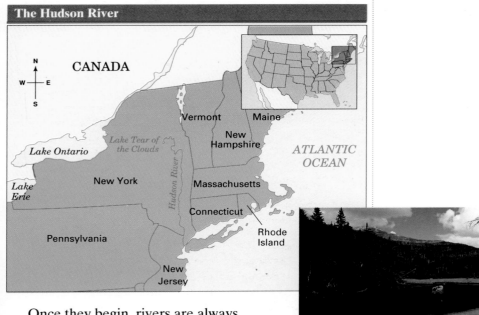

**The Hudson River**

CANADA

N W E S

Lake Ontario

Lake Tear of the Clouds

Vermont    Maine

New Hampshire

ATLANTIC OCEAN

Lake Erie

New York

Hudson River

Massachusetts

Connecticut

Rhode Island

Pennsylvania

New Jersey

Once they begin, rivers are always moving. Most rivers run into another body of water. Some rivers flow into other rivers. Some rivers end in lakes or oceans. Others may just disappear underground.

Rivers may be wide or narrow. They may be deep or shallow. But all river water moves because it flows downhill. If the land is flat, water runs slowly. If the land is steep, water runs quickly. The Colorado River often flows fast because it runs downhill through very steep land. ■

▲ *The Hudson River starts in Lake Tear-of-the-Clouds, which holds water from Mt. Marcy. Where does the river end?*

■ *How do rivers begin and end?*

19

## GEOGRAPHY
### Visual Learning

To help students understand the origin of the Grand Canyon, draw several cross-section illustrations on the board showing the gradual deepening of the valley that the Colorado River made as it cut through rock. Start with a straight line to represent the flat land over which the river once flowed. Show how the valley began and deepened in additional drawings until you show the steep, deep sides of the canyon with the riverbed at the bottom.

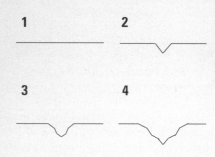

**More About Rock Layers** Part of the beauty of the Grand Canyon comes from the different kinds of rock that have been exposed over millions of years. The layers of granite, shale, limestone, and sandstone all vary in color and shade. As the intensity of sunlight changes throughout the day, different hues are highlighted.

20

## A CLOSER LOOK
# The Grand Canyon

*The power of a river can change the earth. The Colorado River has formed a huge canyon by working its way through layers of rock. Every year, for millions of years, the canyon has become deeper and wider.*

**Millions of years ago**, sand, gravel, and boulders were swept along by the river. These materials scraped away layers and layers of rock.

**What was once a river bed** is now the Grand Canyon. The Colorado River started out on flat land. Today it is a mile deep and almost 20 miles wide in some places.

20

### Study Skills

Challenge students to find out the two longest rivers in the world. Discuss how students would find this information, guiding them to such reference books as an encyclopedia or almanac. Have them report back what they find and where they found it. *(The Nile River is longest, with a length of 4,160 miles. The Amazon is next at 4,000 miles.)*

### Science Connection

Have students notice the horizontal lines along the canyon walls in the photographs on this page. Explain that these lines are layers of different kinds of rock that make up the earth's surface in this area. Have students pile several thin slabs of different colored clay on top of each other and then cut down through the pile to show a cross-section view. Ask which color of clay was the first they put down. *(the bottom layer)* Have students point to the oldest layer of rock in the picture of the Grand Canyon. *(the layer nearest the bottom of the canyon)*

**John Wesley Powell,** standing on the right, explored the Grand Canyon by boat, in 1869. Few people knew about the canyon's beauty until Powell shared information he learned on his journey.

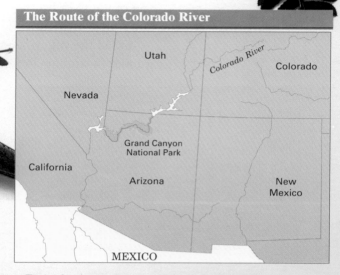

**The Route of the Colorado River**

Utah

Colorado River

Colorado

Nevada

Grand Canyon National Park

California

Arizona

New Mexico

MEXICO

**Trace the route** of the Colorado River. It starts in Colorado and flows almost 1500 miles to Mexico. The gold area on this map shows Grand Canyon National Park. Each year, millions of people visit this park.

**Fossils may be found** where the Colorado River has cut down through layers of rock. Fossils are the remains or traces of past plants or animals. This fossil shows a fern that once grew in the canyon.

21

### Visual Learning

To clarify the concept of a river valley, draw a *V* on the board and have students identify the place where the river flows, that is, at the bottommost point of the *V*. Clarify that the *valley* is the whole area that the river has cut out. For example, over time, the Mississippi River has carved the Mississippi River Valley.

■ *Rivers change the shape of a valley by constantly carving away at the land. Over the years, a steep, narrow valley will be carved away to become a deeper, wider valley.*

## Shaping the Land

You saw how the mighty Colorado River carved a deep canyon into the surface of the earth. Other rivers cut valleys into the land, too. At first a river valley is narrow with steep sides, like the letter V. Over many years, the flow of water wears away the soil and rock of the banks and of the river bottom. In time, the V becomes deeper and wider.

Often the valley becomes very wide. The river may wander in winding loops from side to side. A river may change directions. This makes the valley even wider. If a river changes directions many times, it starts to look like many winding loops. Sometimes a river cuts off one of these loops, forming a C-shaped lake. ■

▼ *Look at the winding loops of this big, old river.*

■ *How do rivers change the shape of a valley?*

**The Changing River**

A loop in a river is called a meander.

In time, the river may flow out of its banks, straight ahead. The loop it leaves behind is called an ox-bow lake.

### Critical Thinking

Ask students the following questions: Do you think meandering rivers flow mainly along flat lands or steep hilly lands? What reasons do you have for your answer? (*Meandering rivers are slow-moving rivers, so they flow along flat lands. A river flowing down steep hills would move too fast to meander.*)

### Collaborative Learning

Write *continental divide* on the board. Remind students that a continent is a large land area and that we live on the continent of North America. Tell students that continental divides affect rivers and that the continental divide in North America is known as the *Great Divide.* Have students work in small groups to use an encyclopedia to find out what a continental divide is. (*a line of peaks separating waters that flow to opposite sides of a continent*) Then have each group name two rivers east of the Great Divide and two west of the Great Divide and identify the source and end point of each river. Discuss what the groups learn about the divide and the rivers. Use a wall map of the United States to aid the discussion.

## Flooding the Land

Water that overflows its banks and covers land that is normally dry is a **flood.** Too much rain can cause a flood. Another cause might be the sudden melting of snow or ice. Land that is covered with water during a flood is called a flood plain.

Most floods are harmful. They damage homes and carry off soil. But some floods are helpful. Sometimes a flood brings new soil and leaves it behind when the water dries up. The new soil helps crops grow better. Rivers may take away the land by erosion, but they can also build up the land. ■

◄ *This whole area is a flood plain. You can see that the farmer's house barely missed going underwater too. Farms are often on flood plains because the soil is so good.*

■ *How can a flood bring good things to people?*

### R E V I E W

1. **FOCUS** How do rivers affect the land?
2. **CONNECT** What are the differences between oceans, rivers, and lakes?
3. **CRITICAL THINKING** We know that rivers drain water from the land. What do you think would happen if there were no rivers to carry off extra water?
4. **ACTIVITY** Take an imaginary trip on an ocean or a river. Write a short description of what you see, hear, and smell. Compare what you wrote with what your classmates wrote. How are river and ocean trips different? How are they the same?

23

### GEOGRAPHY
#### Critical Thinking

Remind students that a flood does two things—carries off soil and brings soil. Explain that when rivers flow rapidly, the waters can carry a great deal of soil. As a flooding river slows down, however, and flood waters recede, the soil that was carried in the river is deposited as "new soil" in a different place. Because the soil that was carried off was the upper, richest layer of soil, this "new" rich soil aids the area where it is deposited.

■ *A flood can bring rich soil into an area, which helps crops grow better.*

### C L O S E

Remind students of the focus question and have them answer it in their own words, referring back to the photographs in the lesson for help, if needed. If necessary, use the Graphic Overview to reteach the key concepts of the lesson.

23

### Answers to Review Questions

1. Rivers affect the land by carving out valleys and canyons as they pass over the land. Flooding rivers sometimes carry off soil from one area and deposit new soil in another area.
2. An ocean is a large body of salt water. A river is a stream of water that flows across land. A lake is a pool of water on land. Oceans are much bigger than rivers or lakes. Oceans are salty. Rivers are not salty. Lakes can have salt water or fresh water.
3. Some of the extra water would soak into the land eventually, but much land might become covered with water.
4. Students' writing should reflect some of the differences between oceans and rivers.

### Homework Options

John Wesley Powell was one of the first people to explore the Grand Canyon. Have students write a short diary entry that Powell might have written describing the Grand Canyon and its sights.

**Study Guide:** page 3

**Answers to Reviewing Key Terms**

| A. | B. |
|----|----|
| 1. lake | 1. ocean |
| 2. erosion | 2. erosion |
| 3. ocean | 3. lake |
| 4. coast | 4. river |
| | 5. flood |

**Answers to Exploring Concepts**

A. Rivers are fresh water. Oceans are bigger than rivers.

B. Sample answers:

1. Floods are helpful when they leave new, rich soil behind after the water dries up. They are harmful when they damage homes and carry off soil.
2. Some new beaches are formed by waves washing up on a shore and leaving sand and mud behind.
3. If the land is flat, river water runs slowly. If the land is steep, river water runs quickly.

# Chapter Review

## Reviewing Key Terms

coast (p. 5)    lake (p. 19)
erosion (p. 5)  ocean (p. 5)
flood (p. 23)   river (p. 18)

**A.** Write the key term for each meaning.

1. a pool of water on land
2. the wearing away of land
3. a large body of salt water
4. the land that is along the edge of an ocean

**B.** Write the correct key term for each numbered blank.

On his vacation, Jack saw big waves of salt water in the __1__. His mother told him that the waves caused __2__ of the land. Amy went to a __3__, which is a large pool of fresh water. From it, a __4__ began and flowed downhill between its banks. One day, too much rain caused a __5__.

## Exploring Concepts

**A.** Copy the chart below. Fill in the missing information in the two empty spaces. In the second column, fill in the kind of water that rivers have. In the last column, fill in the size of oceans. Your chart will show two ways in which rivers and oceans are different.

**B.** Write one or two sentences to answer each question.

1. How are floods helpful and how are they harmful?
2. How are some new beaches formed?
3. Explain why some river water runs slowly and some runs quickly.

| Bodies of water | Kinds of water | Size |
|----|----|----|
| Rivers | | Smaller than oceans |
| Oceans | Salty | |

## Reviewing Skills

1. Find Denver, Colorado, on the map on pages 234–235. Travel northwest from Denver to Canada. When you get near Canada, in what state will you be?
2. In what intermediate direction would you travel to go from Atlanta, Georgia, to the coast of Maine?
3. What state is next to and east of Mississippi? What two states are next to Mississippi on the west?

## Using Critical Thinking

1. You know that rivers change the land. How do you think the Colorado River will continue to change the Grand Canyon?
2. Suppose you take a boat trip down a long river. You go all the way to the end of the river. What might you see there?

## Preparing for Citizenship

1. **ART ACTIVITY** Look at the river pictures on the right. Then read Mark Twain's description of the river on page 18 again. Draw a picture that shows the scene described by Mark Twain. Color your picture if you want to.
2. **COLLABORATIVE LEARNING** Work with a partner. Have one person be a newspaper reporter who asks the other person questions about the effects of a flood on the land. Then switch roles so that the reporter becomes the person who answers questions. Finally, work together to write a newspaper story about the effects of the flood. Be sure to include some of the interview answers. If you can, read your story to your class.

25

**Answers to Reviewing Skills**
1. Washington (Idaho is also acceptable.)
2. northeast
3. Alabama; Arkansas and Louisiana

**Answers to Using Critical Thinking**
1. The Colorado River will probably make the Grand Canyon deeper and wider.
2. You might see an ocean, a lake, or another river. You might not see any of these if the river disappears underground.

**Answers to Preparing for Citizenship**
1. **ART ACTIVITY** Students' pictures might emphasize the wildlife stranded on the exposed branches, the vastness of the river, or the high bluffs of the Missouri shore.
2. **COLLABORATIVE LEARNING** Encourage students to ask who, what, where, why, when, and how. The picture and information on page 23 might be helpful.

## CHAPTER ORGANIZER

# Chapter 2 *Rustling Leaves and Grasses*

## CHAPTER PLANNING CHART

| | | |
|---|---|---|
| **Lesson 1: Wonderful Woodlands (3–4 days)**<br><br>Objective 1: Define a forest. (Geography 2)*<br>Objective 2: Identify the three types of forests. (Geography 2)<br>Objective 3: Describe the interdependence between trees and soil in a forest. (Geography 2)<br>Objective 4: Describe the interdependence between trees and animals in a forest. (Geography 2) | • Graphic Overview (28)<br>• Access Strategy (29)<br>• Access Activity (29)<br>  Collaborative Learning (30) | Study Guide (4) |
| **Understanding Main Ideas: Finding Supporting Details**<br><br>Objective: Identify the main idea and supporting details in paragraphs. (Critical Thinking 2) | | Study Guide (5) |
| **Lesson 2: A Sea of Grass (3–4 days)**<br><br>Objective 1: Define a prairie. (Geography 2)<br>Objective 2: Identify the kinds of animals that live in a prairie. (Geography 2)<br>Objective 3: Describe how prairie animals protect themselves from predators. (Geography 2) | • Graphic Overview (33)<br>• Access Activity (34)<br>• Access Strategy (34)<br>  Historical Context (35)<br>  Research (36) | Discovery Journal (5, 6)<br>Map Activity (3)<br>Study Guide (6) |
| **Understanding Graphs: Line Graphs and Circle Graphs**<br><br>Objective 1: Read a line graph. (Visual Learning 2)<br>Objective 2: Read a circle graph. (Visual Learning 2) | | Study Guide (7) |
| **Chapter Review** | Answers (40–41) | Chapter 2 Test |

* Objectives are correlated to the strands and goals in the program scope and sequence on pages T41–T48.

• LEP appropriate resources. (For additional strategies, see pages T32–T33.)

## CHAPTER RATIONALE

This chapter is the second of three chapters that focus on the natural landscape of the United States. In Chapter 1 students learned about the importance of oceans and rivers in shaping the land. Chapter 2 examines forests and prairies.

We chose to focus this chapter on forests and prairies because they make up a major part of our country's natural landscape. We look at the characteristics of forests and prairies and at their ecology—that is, how the land, plants, and animals are interdependent. We also discuss how the United States' forests and prairies have changed. Many forests have been cut down, and many prairies are now devoted to farming.

**Lesson 1** focuses on forests. It examines the relationship between the soil, trees, and animals of the forests. **Lesson 2** describes prairies. It tells how animals adapt to, and survive in, the prairie environment. The feature A Closer Look: A Prairie Dog Town highlights prairie dogs as an example of animal adaptation and details the life of these fascinating creatures. The lessons use photographs, diagrams, maps, and fine art to reinforce and extend the text.

This chapter includes two skill lessons that will aid students in reading and understanding the rest of the book. One skill lesson focuses on identifying main ideas and supporting details; the other explains how to read line and circle graphs.

This chapter lays the foundation for later chapters that examine how people adapted to and settled both forest and prairie lands. The theme of interaction with the land is woven throughout this book. In this unit it is animals who interact with the land; in later units it is people.

## ACTIVITIES & PROJECTS

### LEP: Investigation

After concluding Lesson 1, have each student "adopt a tree" near school or home. Tell students to draw pictures of their trees and to examine them closely to answer such questions as: What kind of leaves does it have? What does the bark feel like? Do any birds or insects live in the tree? If so, what kind? Does the tree lose its leaves in the winter? Students can also include information about how tall the tree is and how big around it is. You may wish to provide folders and have students do this activity as an ongoing project by drawing their trees in different seasons.

### Challenge: Research

After concluding Lesson 1, have students research and write reports on some of the forest animals they read about. Allow time for the reports to be presented orally in class. Then bind the pages together to make a classroom book: *Animals of the Forest*.

### Making a Model

After concluding Lesson 2, have students make a diorama of a forest or a prairie. Tell them to include plants and animals that would be found in each environment.

### Making a Map

At the conclusion of Lesson 2, supply students with outline maps of the United States. Have students do research and color in the areas of the United States that were formerly covered with forests. Then have students use another color to indicate the areas of the country that were formerly prairies.

# Chapter 2

# *Rustling Leaves and Grasses*

*Our mighty rivers flow across a huge land. Not all of this land looks the same. The rivers flow through great tree-covered lands called forests. They also cross huge grasslands called prairies. Forests and prairies are very different from each other, but they are both home to many kinds of animals.*

A sage grouse can hide from its enemies in the tall grasses of a prairie.

This is turkeyfoot prairie grass. The tops of the grass separate into many parts and look like turkeys' feet.

Forests grow in much of the eastern half of the country. Forests also grow in many mountains and along the coasts in the West. Prairies cover much of the middle part of our land.

26

tlers arrived in the 1600s, forests covered most of the land in the United States between the Atlantic Ocean and the Mississippi River as well as parts of the western United States. Today forests still cover about 750 million acres, or one-third of the land area of the continental United States.

Many prehistoric people depended on forests for wild plants they could gather and animals they could hunt and eat. People today do not depend on the forest for food, but forests remain important for many other reasons. Forests supply wood for many items,

including telephone poles, railroad ties, furniture, and paper products. Many plastic products, latex, and waxes come from trees.

Unlike some natural resources, such as coal and oil, trees are renewable. Trees are also important in the conservation of water and soil. Forest soil and tree roots soak up a great deal of water. This prevents water from running off too quickly and causing floods and erosion.

Forest trees—and all green plants—also help renew the air. When trees and green plants make food for themselves, they give

The photographs of the forest and the prairie demonstrate the main difference between the two. *(Forests are made up of trees; prairies are covered with grass.)* Prairies differ in the types of grass they have, and forests differ in the types of trees, depending on climate and soil.

The color of this gray fox's fur makes it hard to see against the greens and browns of the forest. This helps it sneak up on the animals that are its food.

Many of the trees in this forest are oaks and maples. Sugar maple trees grow from seeds like the ones at the top of this page.

off oxygen, and take carbon dioxide from the air. Almost all living things need oxygen. If trees and other green plants did not supply oxygen, almost all life would soon stop.

### Prairies

Prairies are flat or hilly areas covered with grasses. They extend from Texas into Canada, covering much of Oklahoma, Kansas, Nebraska, Iowa, Illinois, South Dakota, and North Dakota. When pioneers first saw grasses blowing on the prairie, they described the land as a "sea of grass." Today few prairies exist as they once did. Most prairies have been replaced by farms.

**INTRODUCE**

## INTRODUCE

Read the lesson title and have students use the picture clues to note that *woodlands* refers to forests. Ask students if there are any forests in their locale. Invite volunteers to share any experiences they may have had hiking through or playing in forests. Encourage students to name any animals they saw in the forest.

Have students read the Thinking Focus. Ask them to tell why they think forests are important. List some of their ideas on the board. Invite students to read to check their ideas.

### Key Terms

Vocabulary strategies: T36–T37
**forest**—a large area of land thickly covered with trees
**humus**—decayed material

**28**

---

LESSON 1

# Wonderful Woodlands

THINKING
## FOCUS

*Why are forests important?*

### Key Terms

- forest
- humus

Imagine being able to swing, hop, or fly from tree to tree all the way from the Atlantic Ocean to the Mississippi River without ever touching the ground! Long ago, the trees were so thick that a squirrel could have done just that. Most of the eastern half of our country was one big **forest,** a large area of land thickly covered with trees.

28

---

## Objectives

1. Define a forest.
2. Identify the three types of forests.
3. Describe the interdependence between trees and soil in a forest.
4. Describe the interdependence between trees and animals in a forest.

## Graphic Overview

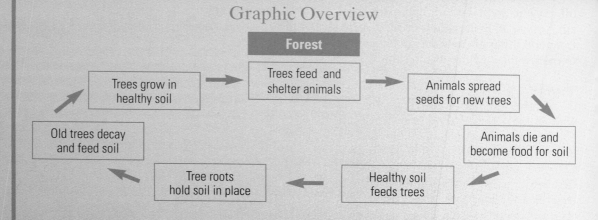

| Forest |
| --- |

Trees grow in healthy soil → Trees feed and shelter animals → Animals spread seeds for new trees → Animals die and become food for soil → Healthy soil feeds trees → Tree roots hold soil in place → Old trees decay and feed soil →

## United States Forests

Today, trees no longer cover so much area. About 100 years ago, most of those forests were gone. As our country grew, people cut down trees to make room for farmland and cities. Today, people plant new forests to help replace some of those that once covered much of America.

Three types of forests grow in the United States. One kind has trees that lose their leaves in the fall. Another type of forest has trees that stay green all year. The third kind is a mixed forest. It includes trees that stay green and trees that lose their leaves. What kinds of trees grow where you live? ■

### Types of United States Forests

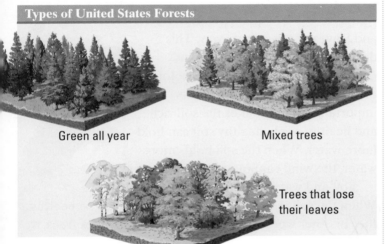

Green all year

Mixed trees

Trees that lose their leaves

## Trees and Soil Help Each Other

Trees are important because they help stop erosion. You have already seen how water in oceans and rivers wear away the land. Wind can cause erosion, too.

Trees help stop erosion in two ways. First, their roots hold the soil in place. The roots act like tiny fingers. When the wind blows, the "fingers" grab on to the soil and keep the wind from taking it away. Trees also stop erosion by "feeding" the land. When a tree dies, its branches, roots,

■ *What types of forests grow in the United States?*

◄ *Here are three types of forests in the fall. The trees that always stay green are called evergreens. The forest on the right is a mixed forest. Trees that lose their leaves have bare branches in the winter.*

### How Do We Know?

*Some trees can grow to be thousands of years old. Look at a round tree stump sometime. You can tell how old the tree was by counting the number of rings on the trunk. Each ring stands for one year.*

Read the first paragraph on page 28 aloud. Locate the Atlantic Ocean and Mississippi River on a map so students can see how large the forested area in the United States was. Then have students read the headings to preview the lesson. Point out that they will first read about different kinds of forests and then about how trees, soil, and animals depend on each other. As you discuss the lesson, use the Graphic Overview to help students visualize the interdependence of living things in a forest.

■ *Three types of forests: ones with trees that stay green all year; ones with trees that lose their leaves in the fall; and ones with both kinds of trees*

### GEOGRAPHY
#### Visual Learning

As students look at the types of forests in the United States, have them describe how the trees differ. Tell them that different types of forests grow in different regions.

## Access Strategy

To build background for this lesson, have available the following items: soil; weed with its roots intact; two leaves; an acorn and another kind of seed; and two pictures of forest animals, such as a bird and a squirrel, mounted on separate index cards. Arrange the objects on a table in this order: soil, weed, leaf, soil, acorn, animal card, seed, leaf, animal card, soil. Explain the cycle of interdependence of trees and soil: trees need soil to live; trees keep the soil from blowing away with their roots and by feeding it with their decayed leaves. Then explain the interdependence of animals and plants: animals get food and shelter from plants; in turn, animals help scatter seeds so new plants can grow and their decaying bodies help feed the soil.

## Access Activity

Bring in some dry soil and have students feel and describe it. Wet one half of the soil with water. Have students note the difference in texture. Demonstrate how much more easily the dry soil can be blown away. Explain this as an example of wind erosion. Then show some plant roots and discuss how they hold soil down so it isn't blown away.

GEOGRAPHY

## Critical Thinking

Clarify for students how moisture helps keep soil in place. Have them think about the land around their own locale after periods of much rain and no rain. Discuss how the rain helps hold the little bits of dirt together. When the soil dries out, the bits of dirt become loose particles that are easily blown away. Tree roots help by packing dirt together; this holds moisture in the soil longer.

■ *Trees help the land in two ways: their roots hold the soil in place, and they feed the soil when they decay.*

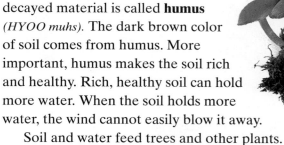

➤ *The green moss on this dead log makes a good place for mushrooms and insects to live.*

⋏ *Mushrooms get their food from dead plants. Mushrooms help break down dead trees into humus for rich new soil.*

■ *How do trees help the land?*

and leaves decay, or rot away. This decayed material is called **humus** *(HYOO muhs)*. The dark brown color of soil comes from humus. More important, humus makes the soil rich and healthy. Rich, healthy soil can hold more water. When the soil holds more water, the wind cannot easily blow it away.

Soil and water feed trees and other plants. When the soil is well-fed, trees and plants can be healthy, too. In other words, trees help soil and soil helps trees. ■

## Trees and Animals Need Each Other

Soil and trees are not the only things that depend on each other. Forest plants and animals need each other, too. The forest gives food and shelter to many animals. Squirrels and birds make their homes in tree branches. Raccoons live in holes in tree trunks. Insects live in tree bark. Many animals eat the seeds and nuts that grow on trees. Deer eat bark. Insects eat leaves, wood, and roots.

In return, the animals help more trees and plants

## Critical Thinking

Discuss the needs to preserve and to cut down forests. Divide students into groups and have each group fold a sheet of paper in half lengthwise to make two columns. One column should be headed *Reasons People Protect Forests;* the other, *Reasons People Cut Down Forests.* Ask each group to list three or four reasons in each column.

## Collaborative Learning

Have students work in small groups to collect leaves of trees in their area. Direct students to categorize the leaves as evergreen or deciduous, explaining the term *deciduous.* Have students mount the leaves on cardboard and label them.

◄ *Birds and squirrels help forests grow. By eating berries, this thrush scatters seeds on the ground from which new plants sprout. By burying an acorn, and then forgetting to dig it up later for lunch, this squirrel helps plant new oak trees.*

to grow. How? Trees and plants grow from seeds and nuts. Birds scatter seeds that allow new plants to grow. Have you ever seen a squirrel bury an acorn? Squirrels bury more nuts than they can eat. Each nut they bury has a chance to become a new tree.

Animals help the trees in another way. When they die, their bodies decay on the ground. The decaying bodies add to the humus in the soil that feeds the trees. The forest feeds its creatures, and the animals die and become food for the trees. In this way, forest life can go on and on.

So forest animals and plants depend on each other in many ways. If one living thing is damaged or destroyed, another may suffer, too. If whole forests are cut down, animals may lose their homes and die. Soil washes away and new plants cannot grow. If we learn how living things depend on each other, we can help forest life continue. ■

■ *How do trees and animals help each other?*

### R E V I E W

1. **FOCUS** Why are forests important?
2. **CONNECT** Would you rather visit a river or a forest? Why?
3. **CRITICAL THINKING** How might a forest be different if no animals lived in it?

4. **ACTIVITY** Draw a picture of a forest. In your picture, show how trees give shelter and food to animals.

31

UNDERSTANDING
MAIN IDEAS

This skills feature teaches students how to identify the main idea and supporting details of paragraphs.

## GEOGRAPHY

### Critical Thinking

Ask volunteers to give additional sentences about animals in the forest. Have the rest of the class determine whether or not each sentence supports the main idea. You might want to help them get started by supplying the following sentences.
Supporting:
• Squirrels live in trees.
Nonsupporting:
• Ferns grow under forest trees.
• Whales live in the sea.
• Squirrels eat acorns.

32

## UNDERSTANDING MAIN IDEAS

# Finding Supporting Details

**Here's Why**  Writers often write about one main idea in each paragraph. Other sentences give details that support, or explain, the main idea. Knowing how to find main ideas and their supporting details will help you understand what you read.

**Here's How**  Think of a chart such as the one below when you read a paragraph. The large box at the top has the main idea. The smaller boxes have the details. Read this paragraph:

> The forest is home to many animals. Birds make their nests in tree branches. Hollowed-out tree stumps are homes for raccoons and other animals. Deer sleep and hide among the trees in forests.

The main idea of the paragraph is: *The forest is home to many animals.* The other sentences tell how the forest is home to the animals. They give the details that support the main idea.

---

**Main Idea:  The forest is home to many animals.**

| **Detail:** Birds make their nests in tree branches. | **Detail:** Hollowed-out tree stumps are homes for raccoons and other animals. | **Detail:** Deer sleep and hide among the trees in forests. |
|---|---|---|

---

**Try It**  Read the second paragraph on page 29 again. The main idea is stated in the first sentence. What details support the main idea?

**Apply It**  Work with a partner. Write a paragraph about forests or forest animals. Make a chart of your main idea and supporting details.

---

## Objective

Identify the main idea and supporting details in paragraphs. (Critical Thinking 2)

## Collaborative Learning

Have students work in pairs. Ask each student to look through this book and find a paragraph that contains a main idea and at least two supporting details. Have students read their paragraphs to their partners and ask the partner to identify the main idea and the details.

## Answers to Try It

The main idea is: Three types of forests grow in the United States.
Details are: One kind has trees that lose their leaves in the fall. Another kind of forest has trees that stay green all year. The third kind is a mixed forest. It includes trees that stay green and trees that lose their leaves.

LESSON 2

# A Sea of Grass

Picture yourself standing in a field of grass. The grass is moving in the wind, like waves on the ocean. The land stretches out as far as you can see. Suddenly, the ground begins to shake. The land ahead looks dark and smoky. You begin to think the whole earth might be on fire! A rumbling sound grows louder and louder. Now you know that you are not looking at the smoke of a raging fire. What you see is the darkness of thousands of pawing and charging buffaloes coming toward you. A great cloud of dust blackens the sky for miles around.

### THINKING
# FOCUS

*How are prairies different from forests?*

### Key Terms

- prairie
- predator

◄ A Herd of Buffaloes on the Bed of the Missouri River *was painted by William Jacob Hays in 1860.*

## INTRODUCE

Have a volunteer read the lesson title aloud. Ask students to think of ways in which blowing grass reminds them of the sea.

Remind students that they read about forests in the last lesson. Have the Thinking Focus read aloud. Tell students that the photographs on this and the next page show prairies. Have students examine the pictures and note the lack of trees as one difference between forests and prairies. Then have students predict how the lack of trees could make other differences in the plant and animal life in prairies. Have students read to learn how prairies differ from forests.

### Key Terms

Vocabulary strategies: T36–T37
**prairie**—an area of flat or hilly land covered by grasses
**predator**—an animal that hunts other animals for food

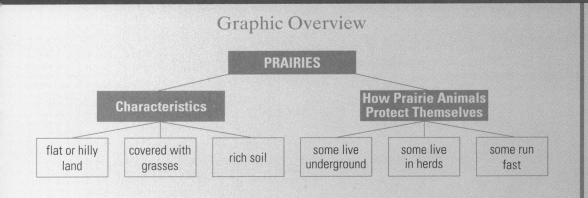

## Graphic Overview

**PRAIRIES**

**Characteristics**

flat or hilly land

covered with grasses

rich soil

**How Prairie Animals Protect Themselves**

some live underground

some live in herds

some run fast

## Objectives

1. Define a prairie.
2. Identify the kinds of animals that live in a prairie.
3. Describe how prairie animals protect themselves from predators.

Ask a volunteer to prepare a dramatic reading of the introductory paragraph on page 33. Have students identify the buffalo herd in the photograph on that page and tell how it might look like the smoke of a raging fire. Then have students look at the map of United States prairies on page 35. Ask them to identify the part of the country where prairies are found. *(middle)*

To help students focus on the main ideas of the lesson, you may wish to begin the Graphic Overview on the board and complete it as you discuss the lesson.

■ *You would see nothing but grass and sky. In the distance, there might be a hill. You would not see many trees.*

### GEOGRAPHY
### Visual Learning

Have students look at the photograph on this page. Have them identify it as a prairie from the caption. Then ask how students would know it was a prairie if there were no caption.

## What Is a Prairie?

**Across Time & Space**

*Two hundred years ago, millions of buffaloes roamed the U.S. prairies. Later, hunters killed all but about 500. Now buffaloes live in areas that are protected from hunters.*

■ *What would you see if you were standing on a prairie?*

▼ *This prairie in Nebraska grows short grass about two feet tall.*

People traveling across the United States long ago would often write about seeing these giant animals. During the fall, small groups, or herds, of buffaloes joined together to form larger herds. In the winter, these huge herds would move across the prairie to warmer areas. There they searched for food. A **prairie** is an area of flat or hilly land covered by grasses.

If you stood in the middle of a great prairie, you would see nothing but grass and sky. In the distance, you might notice a low hill. You would not see many trees.

The amount of rain that falls on prairies affects the height of the grass that can grow there. Eastern prairies get more rain than western prairies. Because of this, grass in the east can grow as tall as a person!

Prairie soil is very rich. Grasses and farm crops, such as wheat and oats, grow well in such soil. Because of this, much of the prairie land shown on the map on page 35 is now used for raising animals and crops. ■

## Access Activity

Have students create a mural of a prairie and include the animals that live there.

## Access Strategy

Remind students that in the last lesson they learned about forests—large areas of land thickly covered with trees. Explain that in this lesson they will learn about other large areas of land covered with a different kind of plant—grass. Read the lesson title aloud and ask students why they think a prairie is called a sea of grass. Compare the photographs of prairies with the photographs of forests in the previous lesson and help students describe in their own words how prairies are different from forests.

Have students look at the pictures of the animals that live in the prairies. Remind students that there are no trees for the animals to live in. Then ask students to think about the kinds of homes prairie animals might build and how they would be different from the homes of forest animals. Tell students that in this lesson, they will be learning more about prairies and the lives of some prairie animals.

## Original United States Prairies

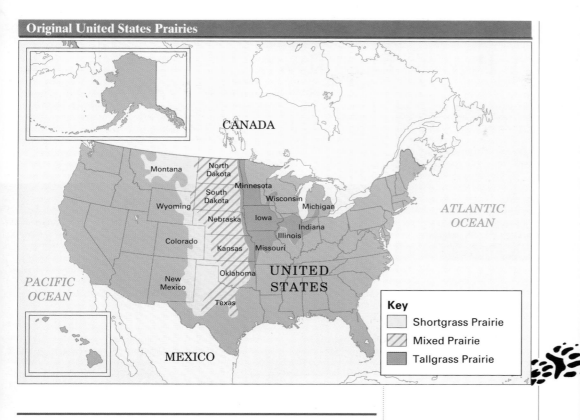

CANADA

Montana
North Dakota
Minnesota
South Dakota
Wisconsin
Wyoming
Michigan
Nebraska
Iowa
Indiana
Illinois
Colorado
Kansas
Missouri
New Mexico
Oklahoma

UNITED STATES

ATLANTIC OCEAN

PACIFIC OCEAN

Texas

MEXICO

**Key**
- Shortgrass Prairie
- Mixed Prairie
- Tallgrass Prairie

## Map and Globe Skills

As students look at the map, ask them to name the states that originally had each type of prairie. Note again that much of this land is now covered with farms and ranches.

## Prairie Life

Prairies are home to many creatures. The animals that live on prairies have special ways to protect themselves from predators. A **predator** is an animal that hunts other animals for food. Forest animals use the trees to hide from their enemies. Since few trees grow on prairies, the animals there have other ways to escape predators.

Some prairie animals, such as badgers and prairie dogs, dig underground tunnels, or burrows, to protect themselves from predators. If an enemy is near and there is no burrow around, a badger will quickly dig a new one to hide in. Prairie dogs nibble down the grass around their burrows. Doing so makes it easier for prairie dogs to see predators coming.

◄ *Badgers have large front paws with sharp claws. How does this help them in their prairie life?*

■ *The sharp claws on badgers' front paws help them to dig underground tunnels.*

35

35

## Historical Context

As students look at the map on this page, tell them that today many people live in this part of the country; but hundreds of years ago, early pioneers traveled across this sea of grass in covered wagons called prairie schooners. Explain that a schooner is the name of a ship, and from a distance these wagons with their white tops looked like sailing ships.

Tell students that by the middle 1800s more than 50,000 settlers a year traveled across the prairies. Some continued west to California, but many remained in the prairie states to build homes, farms, cattle ranches, cities, and towns. Since wood was scarce on a prairie, many early settlers built houses out of sod.

## Study Skills

Tell students that Argentina, a South American country, has prairie land called "pampas." Challenge students to find information about the pampas and to compare them to prairies. Discuss how students would locate information in an encyclopedia. Have them report on what they found and how they found it.

**GEOGRAPHY**

## Visual Learning

Have students use the pictures and captions to explain why the prairie is a perfect place for the prairie dog to live. Then closely examine with students the diagram of a burrow. Elicit why certain rooms and tunnels are located where they are. *(The nursery is deep in the ground, perhaps for safety or warmth; the listening room is close to the surface of the ground, which makes it easier to hear predators; the dry room has a tunnel that leads up, which prevents water from getting in; the emergency exit leads into grass, which provides cover.)*

**More About Prairie Dogs** The prairie dog is a type of rodent and is related to the squirrel family. The name *prairie dog* comes from a warning call that the animal makes, which sounds like a dog's bark. Prairie dogs grow to be 12 to 20 inches long, including the tail. Adult prairie dogs weigh between 1 and 2 pounds.

---

## A CLOSER LOOK

# A Prairie Dog Town

*If you were to visit a prairie, what animals do you think you'd see? Prairie dogs live on prairies in large groups called towns. A town may have 50 to 100 burrows.*

**Prairie grass for lunch?**
Sounds delicious! Prairie dogs eat mostly grasses and grain. They also eat small insects.

**Home means being together!**
Many prairie dogs live in one burrow. The entrance is called a mound.

**Let's take a tour** of a prairie dog burrow:
**a.** *emergency exit*—used to escape predators
**b.** *nursery or bedroom*—used to sleep or give birth
**c.** *bathroom*—used only during bad weather
**d.** *listening room*—used to listen for predators
**e.** *dry room*—used during floods

---

## Visual Learning

Have students look at the photographs on this page and speculate about why prairie dogs build their homes together rather than separately. Ask such questions as: Could a single prairie dog build the kind of home you see in the pictures? Would one prairie dog be as safe from predators as a group of prairie dogs? Elicit the benefits of living in a community.

## Research

Have students discuss the social nature of prairie dogs—how they live together to help and protect one another. Help students find analogies to the ways they and their families live together in communities.

Then have students work in small groups to investigate other animals that live in the prairies. Assign one of the following animals or birds to each group: jack rabbits, mice, foxes, skunks, hawks, and owls. The group should look up the name of their animal in an encyclopedia or nature book. Have students describe their animal and tell why the prairie is a good place for it to live. Then have groups present their findings to the class.

*◄ The pronghorn's long legs help make it one of the fastest animals in the world.*

*▼ The coyote can leap 14 feet. How does this help make it a good predator?*

Pronghorns protect themselves from predators by living in herds. When a predator is near, the animals warn each other. The animals in a herd also stay together. It is much harder for an enemy to attack a whole herd than to attack a single animal. If an animal gets separated from the herd, its best chance to escape is to outrun its enemy. Being able to run fast helps many animals stay alive on the prairie.

Who are these enemies? Coyotes *(ky OH teez)* are among the most feared predators. Coyotes hunt everything from the smallest prairie dog to the largest pronghorn. They are also very fast. Coyotes can outrun many small animals and are very good hunters. They have to be. After all, coyotes must stay alive in the sea of grass, too. ■

■ *How do prairie animals protect themselves from predators?*

## R E V I E W

1. **FOCUS** How are prairies different from forests?
2. **CONNECT** Compare the way forest and prairie animals escape from predators.
3. **CRITICAL THINKING** Tell how living in a burrow in a prairie dog town is like living in an apartment in a big apartment building. How is it different?
4. **ACTIVITY** Imagine you are a traveler long ago, seeing a prairie and its animals for the first time. Write a paragraph in your journal telling what you see.

37

## UNDERSTANDING GRAPHS

This skills feature shows students how to read line and circle graphs.

### Visual Learning

Work through the "Here's How" section with students, demonstrating how to read the line graph and the circle graph.

# Line Graphs and Circle Graphs

**Here's Why**   Have you ever heard the expression "a picture is worth a thousand words"? Line graphs are like pictures of number facts. Knowing how to read line graphs will help you see changes over a period of time.

Circle graphs compare the amount of things. Knowing how to read circle graphs will help you understand differences in amounts.

**Here's How**   As you know, line graphs deal with numbers. The dots on a line graph represent numbers. We use line graphs to see how something changes. Look at the line graph below. It shows the amount of rain that fell on a prairie for six months during one year.

The numbers down the left side of the line graph are inches of rain. For April, the dot is at three inches of rainfall. The dot for May is at a larger number. The June

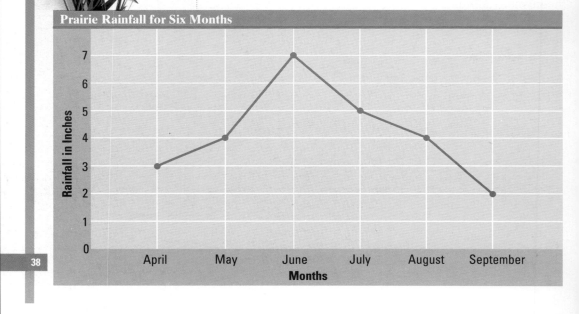

**Prairie Rainfall for Six Months**

## Objectives

1. Read a line graph. (Visual Learning 2)
2. Read a circle graph. (Visual Learning 2)

## Making Graphs

Write the following numbers of students in a school on the chalkboard:
1st grade — 20 students
2nd grade — 20 students
3rd grade — 40 students
4th grade — 20 students
Have students make a line graph with the grades listed in order across the bottom and the number of students in each grade up the side in increments of 10. (10, 20, 30, 40)

Then discuss with the students which slice of a circle graph giving the same information would be the largest. Then make a circle graph of the same information. *(1st grade 20%, 2nd grade 20%, 3rd grade 40%, 4th grade 20%)*

dot is at a still larger number. The dots are connected by lines to show the amount of change in rainfall during the six months. Which month had the most rainfall? Which had the least?

Circle graphs show parts of a whole. You have learned that different kinds of forests grow in the Northeast. The circle graph on this page shows how much of the Northeast is covered by each kind of forest. The key above the graph shows what the colors in the graph stand for. What color stands for mixed trees? You can see that most of the forest area is mixed trees, because that is the largest part of the circle.

**Try It** Look at the line graph again. How can you find the amount of rain that fell in July? How much rain fell in September? How much more rain fell in June than in September?

Now look at the circle graph again. What type of forest is shown by the smallest part of the graph? What does the graph tell you about the trees in that type of forest?

**Apply It** Look in books, magazines, or newspapers for graphs. Find one line graph and one circle graph. Tell how your graphs show change in amounts or compare amounts.

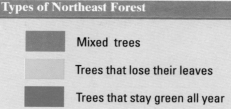

**Types of Northeast Forest**

- Mixed trees
- Trees that lose their leaves
- Trees that stay green all year

## Answers to Reviewing Key Terms
**A.**
1. prairie
2. humus
3. predator
4. forest

**B.**
1. False. Some trees lose their leaves in the fall.
2. False. Prairies in the United States are mainly in the Mid-west region.
3. True
4. False. There are fewer trees now than there were many years ago.

## Answers to Exploring Concepts
**A.** Squirrel—forest; nuts and seeds
Prairie dog—prairie; grasses, grain, insects
Coyote—prairie; other animals

**B.** Sample answers:
1. Trees and other plants grow from seeds and nuts that are scattered and buried by birds and squirrels. Also, when animals die, their decayed bodies add humus to the soil that feeds trees and plants.
2. Some prairie animals escape from predators by digging underground tunnels and hiding there. Other prairie animals protect themselves from predators by living in herds.

# Chapter Review

## Reviewing Key Terms

forest (p. 28)   prairie (p. 34)
humus (p. 30)   predator (p. 35)

**A.** Write the key term that best completes each sentence.
1. A large area of flat or hilly land covered with grasses is called a _____.
2. Decayed tree branches, roots, and leaves help make _____.
3. A _____ is an animal that hunts other animals for food.
4. A large area of land covered with trees is called a _____.

**B.** Write *true* or *false* for each sentence below. If a sentence is false, rewrite it to make it true.
1. All trees lose their leaves in the fall.
2. Prairies in the United States are mainly near the west coast.
3. Farm crops grow well in prairie soil.
4. There are more trees in forests now than there were many years ago.

## Exploring Concepts

**A.** The chart below shows three animals that live in the forest or the prairie. Copy the chart on a piece of paper. Fill in the second column to show where each animal lives. Fill in the third column to show what each animal eats.

**B.** Write one or two sentences to tell why each sentence below is true.
1. Forest animals help trees and other plants.
2. Prairie animals escape from predators in different ways.

| Animal | Where it lives | What it eats |
|---|---|---|
| Squirrel | | |
| Prairie dog | | |
| Coyote | | |

## Reviewing Skills

1. Write three supporting details for this main idea: *Many animals find food on the prairie.*
2. The line graph shows the number of people who visited Grand Teton National Park in seven months.

Which month had the fewest visitors? Which month had the most visitors?

3. Look again at the circle graph on page 39. How many kinds of forests are shown on the graph?

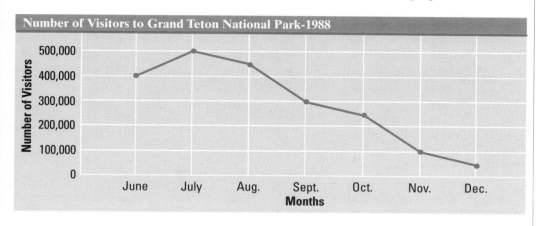

**Number of Visitors to Grand Teton National Park-1988**

Months

## Using Critical Thinking

1. If much of the eastern forest had not been cut down many years ago, how would our country be different today?
2. What happens to forest animals when trees are cut down or burned?

## Preparing for Citizenship

1. **ART ACTIVITY** Many grain crops, such as corn and wheat, are grown on the prairie. Find out what kinds of foods are made from wheat. Breakfast cereals and breads are two examples. Then cut out pictures from a magazine. Use your pictures to make a poster showing how wheat is used for foods.
2. **COLLABORATIVE LEARNING** Make a class book about what animals do in winter. Work in small groups. Each group should choose one kind of animal, such as birds, bears, deer, foxes, or rabbits. Make drawings and write a paragraph that tells what the animal does in winter. Put the work from all the groups into a class book.

## CHAPTER ORGANIZER

# Chapter 3 *Majestic Peaks and Deserts*

## CHAPTER PLANNING CHART

| Pupil's Edition | Teacher's Edition | Ancillaries |
|---|---|---|
| **Lesson 1: Touching the Clouds** (4–5 days)<br><br>Objective 1: Describe a mountain. (Geography 2)*<br>Objective 2: Describe how elevation affects plant and animal life on a mountain. (Geography 2)<br>Objective 3: Describe how a mountain affects the weather of regions on both of its sides. (Geography 2) | • Graphic Overview (44)<br>• Access Strategy (45)<br>• Access Activity (45)<br>Research (46)<br>Language Arts Connection (46) | Study Guide (8) |
| **Understanding Maps: Reading a Physical Map**<br><br>Objective: Read a physical map. (Map and Globe Skills 1) | | Map Activity (4)<br>Study Guide (9)<br>• Transparency (2, 8) |
| **Understanding Physical Features: Physical Features and People**<br><br>Objective 1: Identify several types of physical features. (Geography 2)<br>Objective 2: Explain how physical features affect where and how people live. (Geography 3) | | Study Guide (10)<br>• Transparency (7) |
| **Lesson 2: A Dry Place** (4–5 days)<br><br>Objective 1: Describe the characteristics of a desert. (Geography 2)<br>Objective 2: Identify ways that plants and animals survive in a desert. (Geography 2) | • Graphic Overview (51)<br>• Access Activity (52)<br>• Access Strategy (52)<br>Research (53)<br>Making a Model (53)<br>Economic Context (54)<br>Language Arts Connection (54) | Discovery Journal (7)<br>Study Guide (11) |
| **Explore: The Land Around You**<br><br>Objective 1: Identify physical features of your local community. (Geography 2)<br>Objective 2: Make a physical map of your local community. (Map and Globe Skills 5)<br>Objective 3: Make a model from the physical map of your local community. (Map and Globe Skills 5) | | Discovery Journal (8) |
| **Chapter Review** | Answers (58–59) | Chapter 3 Test |

\* Objectives are correlated to the strands and goals in the program scope and sequence on pages T41–T48.

• LEP appropriate resources. (For additional strategies, see pages T32–T33.)

This chapter is the final one in a unit that examines the landscape of the United States. Chapter 3 focuses on mountains and deserts, two major elements of the American landscape.

Like chapters 1 and 2, Chapter 3 helps build an understanding of the geographical setting of the United States. It takes a close look at the characteristics of mountains and deserts and the ways plants and animals adapt to these environments.

**Lesson 1** focuses on mountains. This lesson uses diagrams to clarify two difficult concepts: the effect of altitude on vegetation and the effects of mountains on the climate of the area around them. **Lesson 2** focuses on deserts. In this lesson, the feature A Moment in Time: The Saguaro Cactus highlights the saguaro cactus as a concrete example of the adaptation and interdependence of plants and animals in deserts.

Chapter 3 includes Understanding Physical Features, which explores how such physical features as mountains and oceans affect where and how people live. This chapter also includes Explore: The Land Around You, a feature that invites students to examine the landscape of the area in which they live.

The lessons and features of Chapter 3 help prepare students for Unit 2, which focuses on the early Native Americans and how they adapted to the lands in which they lived.

### LEP: Making a 3-Dimensional Model

After reading Lesson 1, have students make a mountain range with clay. Then have them color, cut out, and mount on toothpicks pictures of trees. Students can then designate a timberline on their mountains and stick the trees into the clay up to the timberline.

### Challenge: Research

After concluding Lesson 1, have students use encyclopedias and other reference books to find out about the four kinds of mountains and how they were formed: folded mountains, block mountains, dome mountains, and volcanic mountains. (See Background, page 42 of this Teacher's Edition.)

### Making a Terrarium

After concluding Lesson 2, have students make a desert terrarium. Provide milk cartons, plastic wrap, masking tape, scissors, gravel, a mixture of soil and sand, and cactus plants. Have students cut the top off the milk carton and cut a rectangular hole in each side panel of the carton. Have students cover the holes with plastic wrap, taping it in place. Then have students place two inches of gravel at the bottom of the carton and cover it with a two-inch layer of the soil and sand mixture. Add cactus plants and a little water. Cover the entire carton with plastic wrap and put it on a windowsill where it will get indirect sunlight.

### Conducting a Survey

After reading Lesson 2, have a group of students survey their classmates to find out which of the land regions they've read about—forests, prairies, mountains, or deserts—students would most like to live in. Their surveys should include questions about why students would prefer to live in the areas they chose. Have students graph the results of the survey and read some of the reasons that were given when they present the graph to the whole class.

## CHAPTER PREVIEW

Read aloud the chapter title and have students use the visuals to infer that *majestic peaks* refers to mountains. After students read the text and look at the visuals, ask what this chapter focuses on. (*plants and animals of mountains and deserts*)

### Looking Back

Remind students that they have studied plants and animals that live in forests and prairies. They will now look at the plants and animals of other kinds of land regions.

### Looking Forward

Mountains and deserts are the topics of the next two lessons: Touching the Clouds and A Dry Place.

## Chapter 3

# Majestic Peaks and Deserts

*Much of the land in the western United States is made up of towering mountains or dry deserts. Mountaintops can be very cold, and deserts are often very hot. The animals and plants that live on these kinds of land must have special ways of staying alive.*

Cactus plants have spines that protect them from animals that live in the desert. Without their spines, these plants would be eaten for the water inside.

This brightly colored lizard is a Gila (*HEE luh*) Monster. It is right at home in the blazing summer heat of an Arizona desert.

42

## BACKGROUND

Both mountains and deserts are more sparsely populated than other types of land regions. Few people live in mountains because of the difficult terrain and cold climate. The scarcity of water and the heat make many deserts difficult places to live.

### Mountains

Approximately one-fifth of the earth's land is covered with mountains. The highest mountain in the world is Mount Everest (29,028 feet) in Asia. The highest mountain in the United States is Mount McKinley (20,320 feet) in Alaska; it is also the highest mountain in all of North America.

Mountains are formed by movements in the earth's crust, and they are classified on the basis of how they are formed. One kind of mountain is a folded mountain, which is formed when the earth's crust folds into huge waves. Another kind of mountain is the block mountain. It is formed when the earth's crust breaks into giant blocks. Some blocks move upward and some move downward. Sometimes the earth's crust rises to form a dome. Mountains formed in this way are called domed mountains. The fourth kind of mountain is a volcanic mountain. Volcanic mountains are formed when volcanoes erupt and

The photographs on these pages illustrate that mountains and deserts are difficult environments in which to live. The plants and animals that live in these environments have adapted in various ways. The Gila Monster, for example, stores fat in its thick tail and can live on this fat for months.

Bighorn sheep move easily over jagged rocks in high mountains.

This is one of the Sawtooth Mountains in Idaho. Few plants grow at the top of this high peak, but below you can see evergreen forests.

spew out huge quantities of lava and ash. The lava and ash build one layer on top of another until a mountain is formed.

### Deserts

Roughly one-seventh of the earth's land surface is desert. The largest desert in the world is the Sahara in northern Africa. Covering more than 3 million square miles, it is about the size of the United States!

Most people think of deserts as hot, barren places, covered with sand and devoid of life. Although deserts cannot support abundant plant and animal life because they get so little rainfall, many kinds of plants and animals thrive in desert climates.

The mesquite tree is particularly well adapted to the desert. It has roots that extend 40 feet into the ground to absorb water when rain does fall. Other desert plants can store large amounts of water in their stems and leaves.

The desert is home to many kinds of spiders, insects, birds, reptiles, and mammals.

Such mammals as deer, foxes, and wolves visit the desert after a rainfall and hunt at night when it's not so hot. Other desert animals protect themselves by burrowing underground or by hibernating in the hottest summer months.

## INTRODUCE

**H**ave the lesson title read aloud and ask where students would need to be standing to "touch the clouds."(*on a mountain*) Allow time for students to discuss any experiences they have had with mountains.

Have students read the Thinking Focus. Discuss ways in which they think mountains could affect the land around them. Remind students that they have already looked at land and animals in forests and on prairies. Suggest that students read the lesson to find out about plants and animals that live on mountains.

### Key Terms

Vocabulary strategies: T36–T37
**mountain**—a piece of land that is higher than a hill and stands much higher than the land around it
**physical feature**—a natural part of the earth's surface
**temperature**—how hot or cold something is
**timberline**—the height at which trees can no longer grow

---

LESSON 1

# Touching the Clouds

THINKING
## FOCUS

*How do mountains affect the land around them?*

### Key Terms

- mountain
- physical feature
- temperature
- timberline

➤ *These are the beautiful Teton (TEE tahn) Mountains in northwestern Wyoming. Find the highest peak. It is called Grand Teton.*

**A**nn stood on the edge of a cliff and caught her breath. She had been mountain climbing for years, but this sport was new to her. She was almost ready to go. She thought about her teacher's directions.

One end of her rope was firmly attached to the mountain. Ann had hooked the rope to her body, and now she gripped it with both hands. She backed slowly over the edge of the cliff and pushed off into space!

Down, down, down she went. The wind whistled past her ears. Her hands fed out more and more rope. Her feet touched the cliff face again and again. Ann was rappelling *(ra PEHL ihng)* down a mountain for the first time, and she loved it!

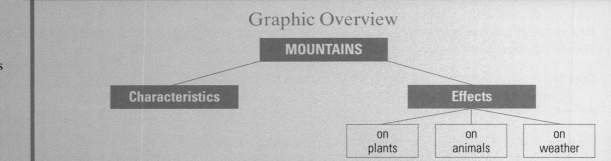

---

### Objectives

1. Describe a mountain.
2. Describe how elevation affects plant and animal life on a mountain.
3. Describe how a mountain affects the weather of regions on both of its sides.

### Graphic Overview

**MOUNTAINS**

**Characteristics**

**Effects**

| on plants | on animals | on weather |

## Height Makes a Difference

Mountain climbing, like rappelling, has many exciting moments. Climbing to the peak of a mountain is also hard work. And it's no wonder. A **mountain** is a piece of land that is higher than a hill and stands much higher than the land around it. This **physical feature,** or natural part of the earth's surface, is easy to see. A mountain has steep sides and a pointed or rounded top.

Air is cooler in high places than it is in low places. At the top of tall mountains, the temperature is very cold. The **temperature** of air is how hot or cold it is.

What does this colder air mean to plant life on mountains? Few plants are able to grow in the highest parts of tall mountains. The plants that do live there must be strong, indeed. They must be able to grow in very cold air and wind.

Different kinds of plants grow well at different heights. Oak and aspen trees grow well on the lower parts of a mountain. Only the very toughest trees, such as bristlecone pines, can grow at higher levels. No trees are able to grow at the highest levels. The height where trees can no longer grow is called the **timberline.** A few small plants can live above the timberline. Columbines and moss campions are wildflowers that can grow in this bitter cold.

▼ *The chart below shows two kinds of small flowers and two kinds of large trees that can grow at different heights on a mountain. When a person is standing far from a mountain, the wildflowers are too small to be seen.*

**Plant Life on a Mountain**

Timberline

Columbine

Moss Campion

Bristlecone Pine

Aspen

45

Invite a volunteer to read aloud the introductory description on page 44. Tell students to look at the picture of the rappeller at the top of page 44 and the picture of the Grand Tetons at the bottom. Ask students to imagine what Ann saw as she rappelled down the mountain. Tell students that they are going to learn more about mountains and the effects they have on the land around them in this lesson.

To help students grasp the main ideas of the lesson, you may wish to begin the Graphic Overview on the board. Have students complete it as they read the lesson.

**GEOGRAPHY**

### Visual Learning

Direct attention to the diagram. Ask students to run their fingers from the bottom of the mountain to the top. Have them use both the text and the diagram to describe the changes in temperature and plant and animal life. Then have students name the point at which they would see no more trees. (*timberline*)

### Access Strategy

Remind students that they have already read about plants and animals that live in forests and on prairies. Tell students that they are going to learn the same types of things in this lesson, which is about mountains. Have the lesson title read, and help students use the photograph of the Teton Mountains to see how mountains "touch the clouds." Use the snow-capped peaks in the photograph to explain that the air at the top of a mountain is much colder than the air at the bottom.

Point out that the temperature can vary about 30 degrees, and ask students to think about how they would dress when it's 30°F (just below freezing) and when it's 60°F.

### Access Activity

Have each student take a thin strip of paper and blow on it, noting what happens to the paper. Then have each student hold a hand between his or her mouth and the strip of paper and blow again. Tell students that their hands keep the air from reaching the paper much like a mountain keeps wind from reaching its eastern side.

## Critical Thinking

Have students describe the bighorn sheep pictured here. Discuss with students how the bighorns can live above the timberline in the spring and summer and why they go down the mountain for the fall and winter. Ask a volunteer to describe how a bighorn gets away from predators. *(Bighorns are able to easily escape predators by moving to steep areas. Their sure-footedness allows them to move up and down steep areas much more quickly than their predators.)*

■ *Only a few plants and animals can live in the higher parts of mountains. Plants must be strong to grow in the cold air. Some animals move down a mountain when fall comes.*

➤ *"Bighorn" is a good name for these animals. Some bighorns have horns that are over four feet long.*

■ *How does height affect the plant and animal life on a mountain?*

*Standing in the Rocky Mountains today, you'd never guess that this land was once under an ocean. Fossils of sea creatures are found in rocks all over these mountains.*

Because of the low temperatures, very few animals live above the timberline. Some animals, such as bighorn sheep, live there during late spring and summer. When fall comes, these wild sheep go down the mountain to avoid deep snow that will cover the grasses they feed on.

Bighorns have very little trouble traveling up and down the mountains. They are able to jump and climb quickly, even in very steep places. For this reason, bighorns can easily escape predators on rocky mountainsides. ■

## A Powerful Force

Mountains affect more than just the plants and animals that live on them. Mountains are a powerful force that can change the weather a long distance away.

In the United States, clouds usually move from west to east. They must rise to pass over mountains. Remember that air gets colder at higher levels. Cold air cannot hold as much water as warm air can. As clouds begin to rise, the damp air grows cooler, so the clouds cannot hold as much water. The water falls in the form of rain or snow.

## Critical Thinking

Lead a class discussion on why few people live on mountains. Have students discuss the logistics of building roads and large buildings on rocky, steep terrain. Encourage students to then research and report on the kinds of homes and towns that are found on mountains.

## Research

Have students work in small groups to research other animals, besides bighorn sheep, that live on mountains. Students can then draw mountains with appropriate animals and label the animals.

## Language Arts Connection

Suggest that students imagine that they have just completed a successful mountain-climbing expedition. Have each student write and illustrate a diary entry describing the experience. Remind students to use sensory words to express what they saw, heard, felt, smelled, and tasted.

## How Mountains Affect the Weather

West   East

◄ *How do you think the different amounts of rainfall on the east and west sides of a mountain affect the plant life on each side?*

As the clouds drift over mountains, they may drop more water. By the time the clouds have moved farther east, most of their water is gone. This means more rain falls on land west of mountains and less rain falls on land east of them.

In the same way, mountains usually protect land to the east of them from high winds and snowstorms. These storms move from west to east, just as rain clouds do. The west sides of mountains get most of the storms, while the land east of the mountains is protected. ■

■ *How does a mountain affect the weather in the area around it?*

### R E V I E W

1. **FOCUS** How do mountains affect the land around them?
2. **CONNECT** How does melting mountain snow affect some rivers?
3. **CRITICAL THINKING** How is plant and animal life on the highest parts of

mountains different in the summer than it is in the winter?

4. **WRITING ACTIVITY** Decide whether you would rather live on the east side or the west side of a mountain. Write a paragraph telling why.

---

◄ *Since more rain falls on the western side of a mountain, that side probably has more trees and plants than the eastern side.*

GEOGRAPHY
### Visual Learning

Have students trace the path of the clouds from west to east on the diagram. Remind students that the air at the top of the mountain is colder than the air at the bottom. Cold air holds less moisture, so clouds drop their water as they rise up the western side of a mountain.

Note that the west to east pattern of air movement is true for mountains in the United States, but not for *all* mountains. The pattern of air movement varies with latitude.

■ *Mountains force clouds to drop more of their water on the western side, and they protect the eastern side from high winds and snowstorms.*

### C L O S E

To check students' understanding of the lesson, have them answer the focus question. If necessary, use the Graphic Overview and visuals to reteach the lesson.

---

## Answers to Review Questions

1. Land west of a mountain gets more rain, snow, and wind than land east of a mountain.
2. When snow melts on mountains, some of the water runs down the sides to the nearest river. This can cause the rivers to flow very fast, and it may also cause floods.
3. More plants grow during the summer, and more animals live on a mountain during the summer.
4. Have students work in groups to compare

answers and living choices. Suggest that students add new information that comes out of their group discussions to their paragraphs.

## Homework Options

Have students pretend to be weather reporters. Have them write a short weather report for a city high on the western side of a mountain and a report for the same day in a city just east of the mountain.

**Study Guide:** page 8

# LITERATURE

# The Mountain That Loved a Bird

## by Alice McLerran

There was once a mountain made of bare stone. It stood alone in the middle of a desert plain. No plant grew on its hard slopes, nor could any animal, bird or insect live there. The sun warmed the mountain and the wind chilled it, but the only touch the mountain knew was the touch of rain or snow. There was nothing more to feel.

All day and all night the mountain looked only at the sky, watching for the movement of the billowing clouds. It knew the path of the sun that crossed the sky by day, and the course of the moon that crossed the sky by night. On clear nights, it watched the slow wheeling of the far-off stars. There was nothing more to see.

But then one day a small bird appeared. She flew in a circle above the mountain, then landed on a ledge to rest and preen her feathers. The mountain felt the dry grasp of her tiny claws on the ledge; it felt the softness of her feathered body as she sheltered herself against its side. The mountain was amazed, for nothing like this had ever come to it from the sky before.

"Who are you?" the mountain asked. "What is your name?"

"I am a bird," replied the other. "My name is Joy, and I come from distant lands, where everything is green. Every spring I fly high into the air, looking for the best place to build my nest and raise my children. As soon as I have rested I must continue my search."

"I have never seen anything like you before," said the mountain. "Must you go on? Couldn't you just stay here?"

Joy shook her head. "Birds are living things," she explained. "We must have food and water. Nothing grows here for me to eat; there are no streams from which I could drink."

"If you cannot stay here, will you come back again some day?" asked the mountain.

Joy thought for a while. "I fly long distances," she said, "and I have rested on many mountains. No other mountain has ever cared whether I came or went, and I should like to return to you. But I could only do so in the spring before I build my nest, and because you are so far from food and water I could only stay a few hours."

"I have never seen anything like you before," repeated the mountain. "Even if it were only a few hours, it would make me happy to see you again."

"There is one more thing you should know," said Joy. "Mountains last forever, but birds do not. Even if I were to visit you every spring of my life, there might be only a few visits. Birds do not live very many years."

"It will be very sad when your visits stop," said the mountain, "but it would be even sadder if you fly away now and never return."

Joy sat very still, nestled against the side of the mountain. Then she began to sing a gentle, bell-like song, the first music the mountain had ever heard. When she had finished her song, she said, "Because no mountain has ever before cared whether I came or went, I will make you a promise. Every spring of my life, I will return to greet you, and fly above you, and sing to you. And since my life will not last forever, I will give to one of my daughters my own name, Joy, and tell her how to find you. And she will name a daughter Joy also, and tell her how to find you. Each Joy will have a daughter Joy, so that no matter how many years pass, you will always have a friend to greet you and fly above you and sing to you."

The mountain was both happy and sad. "I still wish you could stay," it said, "but I am glad you will return."

"Now I must go," said Joy, "for it is a long way to the lands that have food and water for me. Goodbye until next year." She soared off, her wings like feathered fans against the sun. The mountain watched her until she disappeared into the distance.

Year after year, when every spring came, a small bird flew to the mountain, singing, "I am Joy, and I have come to greet you." And for a few hours, the bird would fly above the mountain, or nestle against its side, singing. At the end of each visit, the mountain always asked, "Isn't there some way you could stay?" And Joy always answered, "No, but I will return next year."

Each year the mountain looked forward more and more to Joy's visit; each year it grew harder and harder to watch her go. Ninety-nine springs came and went in this way. On the hundredth spring, when it was time for Joy to leave, the mountain asked once more, "Isn't there some way you could stay?" Joy answered, as she always did, "No, but I will return next year." The mountain watched as she disappeared into the sky, and suddenly its heart broke. The hard stone cracked, and from the deepest part of the mountain tears gushed forth and rolled down the mountainside in a stream.

The next spring a small bird appeared, singing, "I am Joy, and I have come to greet you." This time the mountain did not reply. It only wept, thinking of how soon she would have to leave, and of all the long months before she would come again. Joy rested on her ledge, and looked at the stream of tears. Then she flew above the mountain, and sang as she always had. When it was time for her to go, the mountain still wept. "I will return next year," said Joy softly, and she flew away.

When the next spring came, Joy returned, carrying in her beak a small seed. The mountain still wept a stream of tears. Joy carefully tucked the seed into a crack in the hard stone, close to the stream so that it would stay moist. Then she flew above the mountain, and sang to it. Seeing that the mountain was still unable to speak, she flew away once more.

During the weeks that followed, the seed in the crack of the rock began to send down tiny roots. The roots reached into the hard stone, little by little spreading into yet smaller cracks, breaking through the hardness. As the roots found water in the cracks, and drew food from the softening stone, a shoot rose from the seed into the sunlight and unfolded tiny green leaves. The mountain, however, was still deep in sorrow, blind with

## Background

*The Mountain That Loved a Bird* is an original story written by Alice McLerran. It has already been translated and published in both Japan and the Soviet Union and will soon be available in Germany. McLerran lives in Minneapolis, Minnesota, and has written a second book called *Roxen Boxen*.

tears. It did not notice a plant so small.

The next spring Joy brought another seed, and the spring after that another. She placed each one in a protected place near the stream of tears, and sang to the mountain. The mountain still only wept.

Years passed in this way, the roots of new plants softening the stone near the stream of tears. As softened stone turned to soil, moss began to grow in sheltered corners. Grasses and little flowering plants sprouted in hollows near the stream. Tiny insects, carried to the mountain by the winds, scurried among the leaves.

Meanwhile, the roots of the very first seed went deeper and deeper into the heart of the mountain. Above the ground, what had started as a tiny shoot was growing into the trunk of a young tree, its branches holding green leaves out to the sun. At last, the mountain felt the roots reaching down like gentle fingers, filling and healing the cracks in its heart. Sorrow faded away, and the mountain began to notice the changes that had been taking place. Seeing and feeling so many wonderful new things, the mountain's tears changed to tears of happiness.

Each year Joy returned, bringing another seed. Each year, more streams ran laughing down the mountain's sides, and the ground watered by the new streams grew green with trees and other plants.

Now that the mountain no longer wept with sorrow, it began to ask once more, "Isn't there some way you could stay?" But Joy still answered, "No, but I will return next year."

More years passed, and the streams carried life far out into the plain surrounding the mountain, until finally, as far as the mountain could see, everything was green. From lands beyond the horizon, small animals began to come to the mountain. Watching these living things find food and shelter on its slopes, the mountain suddenly felt a surge of hope. Opening its deepest heart to the roots of the trees, it offered them all its strength. The trees stretched their branches yet higher toward the sky, and hope ran like a song from the heart of the mountain into every tree leaf.

And sure enough, when the next spring came, Joy flew to the mountain carrying not a seed, but a slender twig. Straight to the tallest tree on the mountain she flew, to the tree that had grown from the very first seed. She placed the twig on the branch in which she would build her nest. "I am Joy," she sang, "and I have come to stay."

## Role-Playing

Have pairs of students role-play Joy telling her daughter about the mountain. Suggest that students include the history of how Joy and the mountain met and what has happened since, instructions about how to continue the relationship, and a personal description of Joy's special feelings for the mountain.

# Open Range

*by Kathryn and Byron Jackson*

Prairie goes to the mountain,
  Mountain goes to the sky.
The sky sweeps across to the distant hills
And here, in the middle,
  Am I.

Hills crowd down to the river,
  River runs by the tree.
Tree throws its shadow on sunburnt grass
And here, in the shadow,
  Is me.

Shadows creep up the mountain,
  Mountain goes black on the sky,
The sky bursts out with a million stars
And here, by the campfire,
  Am I.

## READ AND RESPOND

Tell students that the term *open range* in the title of the poem refers to the prairies. Suggest that, as they listen to you read, students try to visualize the scene and the location of the speaker.

◄ Ask students where the speaker is in each stanza. *(1—on prairie looking at mountain range; 2—in tree's shadow by river, watching sunset; 3—by campfire at night)*

## EXTEND

Suggest that students write a poem or draw a picture expressing special feelings they have for something or some spot in nature, such as a favorite tree, lake, or even vacant lot.

**47D**

## Making a Mural

Have students paint a mural showing from left to right how the mountain changed over time. Form groups of students and assign a panel for a particular time period to each group.

## UNDERSTANDING MAPS

This skills feature uses a diagram to help teach students how to read a physical map.

### GEOGRAPHY

## Visual Learning

Read each label on the diagram aloud and have students point to it. Be sure they understand that sea level refers to the surface of the ocean, not its depth. Have students name the physical features from highest to lowest. *(mountains, highlands, lowlands)* Then have them find mountains, highlands, and lowlands on the map on page 49.

48

## UNDERSTANDING MAPS

# Reading a Physical Map

**Here's Why** You know that mountains are one of the physical features of the earth's surface. Mountains and other physical features of an area can be shown on a physical map. There are many kinds of physical maps. One kind shows lowlands, highlands, and mountains. Lowlands are large areas of land that are at about the same level as the sea, or ocean. Highlands are high above sea level. Physical maps also show water features, such as oceans, lakes, and rivers.

**Land Above Sea Level**

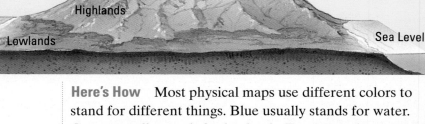

Highlands

Lowlands

Sea Level

**Here's How** Most physical maps use different colors to stand for different things. Blue usually stands for water. Green usually stands for lowlands. Every map has a map key that shows what the colors on the map stand for.

Look at the map key for the physical map on page 49. Notice the colors and what they stand for. What does yellow stand for? What does brown stand for?

Now look at the map itself. Find Lake Ontario. How does the map show that Lake Ontario is a body of water? Two rivers are also shown on the map. Trace the route of the Mississippi River with your finger. It begins in a northern state and ends at the Gulf of Mexico.

## Objective

Read a physical map. (Map and Globe Skills 1)

## Writing a Paragraph

Have students examine the physical map of the United States on pages 238–239. Direct them to write a paragraph describing what they notice about the physical features of the United States.

## Physical Features of the Eastern United States

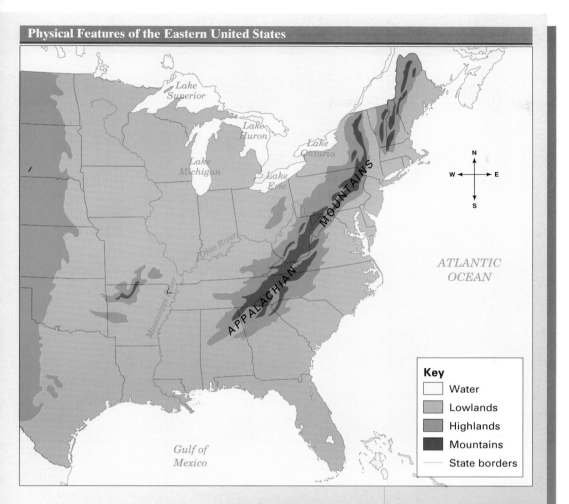

**Key**
- ☐ Water
- ☐ Lowlands
- ☐ Highlands
- ■ Mountains
- — State borders

The map shows a long range of mountains through the eastern states of our country. Can you name any of these mountain states?

**Try It**   Work with a partner. Ask each other questions about the physical map on this page. For example, what is the largest lake shown on the map?

**Apply It**   Look at the physical map of the United States in the Atlas on pages 238–239. How are mountains shown on the map? Name two rivers that flow into the Mississippi River. What physical features are in or near the state of Alaska?

## Map & Globe Skills

Have students use the map key to identify the physical feature that each color represents. Call on individuals to find an example of the feature on the map. Then ask students to trace the line of the Appalachian Mountains on the map. Note that the Appalachians include the White, Green, Catskill, Allegheny, Blue Ridge, and Cumberland mountains. Help students name the states the Appalachians go through. (*Maine, New Hampshire, Vermont, Massachusetts, New York, New Jersey, Pennsylvania, Maryland, Virginia, West Virginia, North Carolina, South Carolina, Georgia, Alabama, Tennessee, and Kentucky*)

## Answers to Try It

The largest lake shown on the map is Lake Superior.  Here are sample questions for students who need help getting started:
- What kinds of bodies of water are identified on the map? (*lake, river, ocean, gulf*)
- What is the land in Florida like? (*lowland*)

## Answers to Apply It

- Mountains are shown in brown and yellow.
- The Red, Des Moines, Missouri, Ohio, and Arkansas rivers flow into the Mississippi.
- Mountains, highlands, lowlands, rivers, and the ocean are in or near Alaska.

## Map and Globe Skills

Have students use clay to make a three-dimensional model of the diagram on page 48. Provide paint for students to color each area the same color as the physical features on the map on this page. Students could also make a label for each feature, tape it to a craft stick, and put it in the appropriate place on the model.

## UNDERSTANDING PHYSICAL FEATURES

This feature expands on what students have learned about physical features and explains how physical features affect where and how people live.

### GEOGRAPHY
### Critical Thinking

Have students give examples of things that are and things that are not physical features and explain their reasoning. Then ask students to help you list on the board ways these physical features affect where or how people live. For example, the diets of people living near oceans, rivers, and lakes contain much more fish than diets of people living inland, away from any fishing waters.

---

UNDERSTANDING PHYSICAL FEATURES

# Physical Features and People

You have learned that physical features are the natural parts of the surface of the earth. A physical feature may be part of the earth's land or water. For example, a mountain is a land feature and an ocean is a water feature. A town is not a physical feature because it is not a natural part of the earth. A town is made by people. A drawing of many physical features is shown on pages 244–245 of the Time/Space Databank.

St. Louis, Missouri

The earth's physical features have a lot to do with where people live and how people live. Many cities, for example, grew next to a river. Rivers have always provided transportation for people and the things people grow or make. Find some river cities on the map of the United States on pages 236–237 of the Atlas.

Cities have also grown on ocean coasts. These cities often started near a harbor, which is an area of the ocean that is partly surrounded by land. The harbor provides a safe place for ships. Find some ocean cities on the map of the United States on pages 236–237.

There are many ways that physical features affect our lives. We do different things on a mountain than we do in a

Boston, Massachusetts

lowland. We may even eat different foods. As you study about our country, you will learn more about the effects of physical features on the lives of people.

---

### Objectives

1. Identify several types of physical features. (Geography 2)
2. Explain how physical features affect where and how people live. (Geography 3)

### Collaborative Learning

Separate students into groups of four or five, and assign each group to study a different area of the United States on a physical map. Have each group discuss what kinds of effects the physical features might have on the people who live there. Include such categories as dress, recreation, occupations, and foods. Have each group report its conclusions to the class.

LESSON 2

# A Dry Place

Katie pressed her nose against the glass. Inside the clear case, the creature stared back. Its body was covered with tiny scales and it had a long, thin tail.

"Wow!" said Katie. "Look at that funny-looking animal. Maybe it's from another planet."

"Now, Katie," Mrs. King said, smiling. "That's not from another planet. It's an animal called an iguana *(ih GWAH nuh)*."

"Why are its toes so long?" Tony wanted to know.

"To help it walk," Mrs. King said. "It comes from a very dry and sandy place. When an iguana walks, it spreads its long toes. Doing this helps it stay on top of the sand instead of sinking into it."

"Are you sure it's an iguana?" Katie asked. "It sure looks like something from another planet to me!"

THINKING
## FOCUS

*How do plants and animals adjust to living in the desert?*

### Key Terms

- desert
- climate

## The Desert Land

A **desert** is an area where little rain falls and few kinds of plants grow. Katie's iguana, like the one shown here, can be found in the deserts of the southwestern United States. This area includes the states of Arizona, Texas, New Mexico, California, Nevada, Utah, and Colorado. Look for this area on the map on page 52.

51

## INTRODUCE

Have students recall that they have studied forests, prairies, and mountains. Read the lesson title and have students predict what kind of land "A Dry Place" refers to. (*desert*) Have students describe any experiences they have had with deserts.

Then ask students to read the Thinking Focus and discuss what plants and animals live in a desert. Ask students to predict how plants and animals adjust to living in a desert. Have students read to confirm or reject these predictions.

### Key Terms

Vocabulary strategies: T36–T37
**desert**—an area where little rain falls and few kinds of plants grow
**climate**—the usual weather of an area over a long time

## Graphic Overview

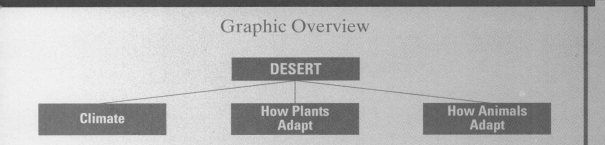

### Objectives

1. Describe the characteristics of a desert.
2. Identify ways that plants and animals survive in a desert.

# DEVELOP

Read, or have a student volunteer read, the introductory material under "A Dry Place" on page 51. Explain that the iguana is one of many animals that have developed special ways of living in desert conditions.

To help students focus on the main ideas of the lesson, you may wish to begin the Graphic Overview on the board. Have students complete it as they read the lesson.

### GEOGRAPHY
## Map and Globe Skills

Help students use the map key to identify the desert areas in the western part of the United States.

➤ *This desert contains plants that grow well in the dry, sandy soil there. Prairies are covered with grasses that grow well in rich prairie soil.*

■ *The desert soil is too dry and rocky or sandy for many plants to grow well.*

52

### United States Deserts

**Key**
▨ Desert

*CANADA*
*UNITED STATES*
Oregon, Idaho, Wyoming
Nevada, Utah, Colorado
California, Arizona, New Mexico, Texas
*PACIFIC OCEAN*
*ATLANTIC OCEAN*
*MEXICO*

N / S / W / E

▲ *How does this desert look different from prairies?*

52 ■ *Why don't many plants grow well in the desert?*

Most deserts are very hot, but not all deserts are the same. Some deserts are hot during the day but cool at night. Many deserts are hot in summer and cold in winter. Hot temperatures and changes from very hot to very cold make it hard for plants to live in deserts.

Temperatures are not the only problem for desert plant life. Little rain falls in deserts, so the soil is very dry. Desert soil is also rocky or sandy. Many plants do not grow well in such soil. Because there are not many plants in the desert, there are few decaying plants to form humus. Humus helps soil hold water. The sandy desert soil dries out quickly even after a hard rain.

Even though a desert is hot and dry and the soil is poor, some plants grow well there. You will see on the next page that the saguaro *(suh GWAHR oh)* cactus has special ways to live in the desert. ■

## Access Activity

Help students recall that rich soil in forests comes from decayed material called humus. Display a cup of soil and a cup of sand. Ask which would be found in a forest and which in a desert. Have students discuss how they are different. Explain that the dryness of the sand makes it difficult for plants and animals to live in deserts.

## Access Strategy

Read aloud the lesson title and tell students that the "dry place" referred to in the title is a desert. Identify the iguana in the photograph, explaining that it can spread its toes to keep from sinking in the desert sand. Have students read the head on page 51 and predict some characteristics of deserts. Then direct attention to the map on this page, and help students identify where deserts are found in the United States.

Read the head on page 54 and have students describe the desert landscape shown in each picture.

# The Saguaro Cactus

*10:32 A.M. May 5, 1991*
*After a spring rain in the*
*Sonoran Desert in Arizona*

**Flowers**
Raindrops sparkle on these blossoms that opened during the cool night hours. The flowers will close again before the afternoon heat reaches 110° F.

**Arm**
Sharp thorns cover the arms that show that this cactus is very old. A saguaro doesn't grow arms until it's at least 75 years old. Some saguaros live 250 years. They may stand 50 feet tall and have 50 arms.

**Trunk**
Swollen to twice its normal size, the trunk is filled with hundreds of gallons of rain water. The saguaro's roots quickly soaked up the water from the desert sands.

**Elf Owl**
The unusual sound of falling rain woke this tiny owl from its daytime sleep. During the day, the owl hides in this hole made by a woodpecker months ago. At night, it leaves the nest to hunt

**Woodpecker**
A loud tap, tap, tap fills the desert air as this bird pecks a hole in the trunk of the cactus. Today, it will find plenty of water inside. Later, another bird will build a nest in this hole.

**Jack Rabbit**
After nibbling tender young cactus sprouts in the early morning, this rabbit has hopped into the cool shade of the saguaro. There it can avoid the scorching sun until late afternoon.

53

**Note:** You may wish to use this Moment in Time after completing the rest of the lesson to expand students' understanding of ways that plants and animals adapt to desert life.

## GEOGRAPHY
### Visual Learning

Have students look at the diagram of the saguaro cactus. Point out that the captions on the left side of the diagram show how the saguaro cactus adapts to desert life and that the captions on the right explain how desert animals use the saguaro cactus to help them live in the desert. Call on volunteers to summarize the information in each caption.

**More About the Jack Rabbit** The jack rabbit is actually a large hare, not a rabbit. Most hares are larger and have longer ears and legs than rabbits. Jack rabbits grow to be about two feet in length. They have large eyes and brownish-gray fur. Most female hares produce two or three litters a year. Each litter consists of two to five young.

53

## Research

Tell students that the elf owl, woodpecker, and jack rabbit are only a few of the animals that live in deserts. Have students research and report orally on other desert animals, such as the scorpion, kangaroo rat, kit fox, pocket mouse, pallid bat, coyote, cactus wren, gila monster, and sidewinder. Encourage students to include visuals in their reports.

## Making a Model

Have students make a model of a desert. Provide a large box and sand. Have students find twigs and grasses to simulate desert plants and use clay to make models of desert animals.

## Visual Learning

Ask how the saguaro cactus differs in appearance from such plants as oak trees or lilac bushes. *(It lacks branches and leaves.)*

Help students summarize how plants and animals live in the harsh dry climate of the desert. *(A cactus gets water through its long roots, which are spread out and not very deep. These roots quickly draw up rain water, which is then stored in the cactus's trunk. The plants are also widely scattered, so there are not so many "competing" for the scarce water. Animals get water by eating seeds, plants, or other animals.)*

► *The saguaros in this picture, like the one on page 53, grow tall, thick, and straight. A few of the saguaros in this picture have grown arms.*

▲ *The desert above is full of different kinds of cactus. Can you find the saguaros?*

▼ *Sagebrush covers the desert below. Like a cactus, sagebrush grows well in very dry soil.*

54

## Life in the Desert

The dry desert climate presents problems for living things. **Climate** is the usual weather of an area over a long time. How do plants and animals live in such a dry climate?

The cactus has a special way of staying alive in the desert. Its long roots spread out around it and are not very deep in the soil. When rain comes, a cactus uses these roots to draw water up into its trunk. The cactus saves the water for use during dry weather.

Animals have their own ways of staying alive in the desert. Many desert animals get much of their water from their food. The little kangaroo rat, for example, gets most of its water from the seeds it eats. Meat also contains water, so predators get water from the animals they eat.

## Study Skills

Have students examine the sagebrush picture on this page. Have them use encyclopedias or other references to find out more about how sagebrush survives in dry, desert soil. Have them compare these methods of desert survival with those of cactus plants.

## Economic Context

Because deserts have such harsh climates, they are generally not heavily populated. People have to adapt to hot, dry conditions in order to live in desert areas. For example, some Native Americans live in adobe or mud houses that keep out the heat. Modern methods of irrigation have made it possible to farm some desert areas. Furthermore, air conditioning has made it possible for people to live comfortably and build cities in desert areas, such as Palm Springs and Phoenix.

## Language Arts Connection

Ask students to think about the different animals they read about and how those animals adapt to the desert climate. Then ask each student to write "A Day in the Life of a ___" account, describing what the animal does during the day and night. You may wish to provide reference books for students to do additional research before they begin writing.

Animals must also find a way to deal with hot desert temperatures. Kangaroo rats dig burrows. The earth is cooler under the desert soil. These animals nest in their burrows during the day. At night when it is cooler, they search for food.

Other animals have different ways of staying comfortable. An iguana crawls into the shade of a rock when it gets hot. When the iguana becomes cool, it covers its body with sand. The iguana leaves only its head showing. Snakes stay in underground holes or in the shade of rocks and bushes during hot daylight hours. They come out to hunt for food at night.

Desert life is not easy for plants or animals. However, with their special ways of staying alive, the desert is full of life. ■

▲ *This kangaroo rat never needs to drink water. It gets most of its water from seeds like the ones above.*

◄ *A rattlesnake gets its name from the rattle at the end of its tail. Poison shoots out of the snake's two long fangs when it bites.*

■ *Why is life in the desert hard?*

Ask students how they stay cool when it is very hot. Then discuss the ways animals stay cool in the hot desert. Review such ways as nesting in burrows, covering themselves with sand, and staying in the shade of a rock or bushes.

■ *Life in the desert is hard because it is dry and hot there.*

C L O S E

Help students summarize the lesson by first identifying the characteristics of a desert. Then have students answer the focus question, describing how plants and animals adapt to the desert climate.

As an extension activity, encourage each student to draw two pictures—one that shows how a specific animal adapts to the desert, and one that shows how a specific plant adapts to the desert.

## R E V I E W

1. **FOCUS** How do plants and animals adjust to living in the desert?
2. **CONNECT** How is desert soil different from forest and prairie soil?
3. **CRITICAL THINKING** How is desert life during the day different from desert life during the night?

4. **WRITING ACTIVITY** Pretend you have a friend who thinks that nothing grows in deserts. Write a paragraph that explains why the desert is full of life.

## Answers to Review Questions

1. Plants have long, shallow roots that draw up water when it rains. Plants store the water and so survive dry spells. Animals get moisture from the foods they eat. They stay underground or in the shade when it is hot and hunt for food when it is cooler.
2. Desert soil has less humus than forest and prairie soil. Because of this lack of humus, desert soil dries out quickly.

3. Answers should include the fact that many animals hunt at night because of cooler temperatures.
4. Students' writing should describe the various plants and animals that dwell in the desert.

## Homework Options

Have students draw an imaginary animal that could survive very well in a desert. Have them label and explain the body parts that help the animal to live comfortably.

**Study Guide:** page 11

## DISCOVERY PROCESS

Students will use the following steps in the discovery process to complete the activity:

**Get Ready** Make a notebook about physical features in your local area.

**Find Out** Make a map of your local area.

**Move Ahead** Build a model of your local area.

**Explore Some More** Exhibit and explain your model.

*Materials needed:* Notebook; maps and photographs of local area; cardboard or other sturdy material for model base; paste; clay; small rocks, aluminum foil, plastic wrap, and other materials to represent physical features

### GEOGRAPHY
Map and Globe Skills

Make this activity a class project. First help students decide on the size of the area they wish to explore and mark off this area on a community map. Divide the class into groups and assign a part of the area to each group. Guide the groups in working together to produce a composite physical map, and then a model, of the area.

**56**

---

# The Land Around You

**W**hat is the land like where you live? Are there rivers or lakes nearby? Is the land flat or is it hilly? Rivers, lakes, oceans, mountains, and hills are all physical features. You can explore the area where you live to find out more about its physical features.

**Get Ready** Begin by looking at the land near where you live. Then look at the land near your school and other places you visit close to home. Start a notebook of the physical features you see around you. Write about what you see. Draw pictures of the land you explore. You can also learn more about the land where you live by looking at maps and photographs.

**Find Out** Make a map of your area to show how the land looks. Use the notes and drawings in your notebook for help. You may also use photographs and maps from books and newspapers for help.

*I see a river and a hill.*

56

---

## Objectives

1. Identify physical features of your local community. (Geography 2)
2. Make a physical map of your local community. (Map and Globe Skills 5)
3. Make a model from the physical map of your local community. (Map and Globe Skills 5)

## Activity

Display a physical map of your state at the front of the classroom. Have students work together to make a model of the state.

**Move Ahead**   The map you made is on a flat piece of paper. All the physical features you drew on the map are flat. To show more exactly how the land looks, you can make a model from your map. Build your model with materials that you have at home or in your classroom. Clay and small rocks can be hills or mountains. Aluminum foil or plastic wrap can be rivers or lakes. Can you think of other materials to use?

**Explore Some More**   Share your model with your classmates and other students in your school. Set up a display in your classroom. Label the models and show the maps you drew. Be ready to answer questions about your model and about the land in your area.

57

Critical Thinking

Have students use the model to summarize the physical features of their local area. Ask about the highest and lowest points on the model and the relative size of various features.

57

Collaborative Strategy

For recommended strategies for collaborative learning, see pages T34–T35.

# Chapter Review

## Reviewing Key Terms

climate (p. 54)   physical feature (p. 45)
desert (p. 51)    temperature (p. 45)
mountain (p. 45)  timberline (p. 45)

**A.** Write the key term for each meaning.
1. how hot or cold something is
2. the place on a mountain above which trees do not grow
3. the usual weather of an area
4. a land feature that has steep sides and a peak
5. a natural part of the earth's surface
6. an area that gets very little rain

**B.** Write a complete sentence to answer each question.
1. How are bighorn sheep able to live so well on mountains?
2. What are some of the physical features of the area where you live?
3. What kind of plants grow above the timberline?
4. What is the climate where you live?

## Exploring Concepts

**A.** The chart to the right lists one plant and three animals that live in the desert. Copy the chart and fill in the second column. Your chart will show what the plant and the animals do to stay alive in the desert.

**B.** Write your answer to each question in one or two sentences.
1. How do high mountains affect the land east of them?
2. Why doesn't desert soil hold rain water well?

| Plant or Animal | How it lives in the desert |
| --- | --- |
| Cactus | |
| Kangaroo rat | |
| Iguana | |
| Elf owl | |

## Reviewing Skills

1. Copy the map of Wyoming shown below. Add the mountains, lakes, and rivers. Then make a physical features key for your map. Use the map on pages 238–239 for help.

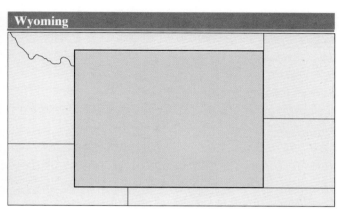

**Wyoming**

2. Locate your state on the map on pages 238–239. List the physical features that are in your state.

3. Look at the map on pages 236–237. Choose a state. Write three clues that will help a classmate guess the name of the state you choose. Include a cardinal or intermediate direction in each clue. For example, "To get to this state, you must travel northeast from Texas." Take turns trying to name each other's state.

## Using Critical Thinking

1. Air conditioning keeps people cool in hot weather. If there were no electricity, how could you stay comfortable in a very hot climate?

2. High mountains are cold and deserts are hot, but in some ways they are alike. Make a list of the ways they are alike.

3. Would you rather live on a mountain top or in a desert? Why?

## Preparing for Citizenship

1. **WRITING ACTIVITY** Pretend you and a partner climbed a high mountain. Tape record your reports about what you took with you and what you saw above the timberline.

2. **COLLABORATIVE LEARNING** Prepare a class bulletin board on desert animals. Work in groups and find books about life in the desert. Some group members can draw pictures of desert animals, such as the desert tortoise and the roadrunner. Some group members can write a sentence or two about each animal. Add your pictures and sentences to the bulletin board.

59

Tell students that the Native Americans were the first people to live in North America.

Read aloud the unit title and the text. Ask students to tell what they see in the design woven in this Indian cloth. *(three figures, one appears to be holding a bow and arrow)* Have students discuss what they know about early Native Americans.

## Looking Back

Remind students that in the last unit, they learned about the land of the United States. Ask what land regions they studied. *(forests, prairies, mountains, deserts)* Note that the Native Americans lived in or near these land regions.

## Looking Forward

The next three chapters focus on how the first American people lived from the land:
Chapter 4: By the Shining Sea
Chapter 5: Over Waves of Grass
Chapter 6: In Red Rock Country

60

# Unit 2

# The Land and the First Americans

The first Americans lived all across the land—by the sea, in the forests, on the prairies, and in the deserts. These Native Americans understood the land and lived from it. They chose their clothing, food, and homes from what nature offered them. Items used every day were not only made from natural materials, they were often colored with natural dyes and decorated with artwork that told stories about the land.

60

*Navajo sand painting blanket of the Nightway Chant, 1880.*
*Werner Forman Archive/Private Collection, New York.*

## BIBLIOGRAPHY

**Books for Students**
Baylor, Byrd. *When Clay Sings.* New York: Charles Scribner's Sons, 1972. Poetic text sings the praises of Indian pottery.

Blood, Charles L. and Martin Link. *The Goat in the Rug.* New York: Four Winds Press, 1980.

Geraldine, a goat, describes the steps in making a rug, beginning with the cutting of her own wool.

**Books to Read Aloud**
Connolly, James E. *Why the Possum's Tail Is Bare and Other North American Indian Nature Tales.* Owings Mills, Maryland: Stemmer House, 1985. Accompanying each legend is a brief history of the Native Americans in it and background information on the tale.

Goble, Paul. *Iktomi and the Boulder: A Plains Indian Story.* Shapleigh, ME: Orchard Press, 1988. This Plains Indian tale explains why the Great Plains are covered with small stones.

_____. *Buffalo Woman.* New York: Bradbury Press, 1984. In this legend, a young hunter sets out to pass the Buffalo Chiefs' tests to become a buffalo.

Levitt, Paul M. and Elissa S. Guralnick. *The Stolen Appaloosa and Other Indian Stories.*

## Notes on the Textile

This blanket is over a hundred years old. It was made by the Navajo, who live in the Southwestern deserts. The Navajo were famous for their sand paintings, which were designs made with powdered rock on the ground. This blanket has a sand painting design. The figures in the design are Navajo spirits, or gods.

Longmont, Colorado: Bookmakers Guild, 1988. Northwest Indian folktales.

McDermott, Gerald. *Arrow to the Sun*. New York: Penguin USA, 1974. A myth portraying the Pueblo's reverence for the source of life—the sun.

**Books for Teachers**
Bernstein, Bonnie and Leigh Blair. *Native American Crafts Workshop*. Belmont, CA: D. S. Lake, 1982. A book of Native American crafts, which includes a chapter on cooking.

Tunis, Edwin. *Indians*. New York: Harper and Row Junior Books, 1979. An account of early Indian life.

## Other Resources

**Visual Media**
*Along Sandy Trails*. Ancramdale, NY: Live Oak Media, 1989. Filmstrip, cassette.

*Hiawatha*. Weston, CT: Weston Woods, 1989. Filmstrip, cassette.

HOUGHTON MIFFLIN SOCIAL STUDIES

Batherman, Muriel. *Before Columbus*. Boston: Houghton Mifflin, 1981. A picture book of the life of early Native Americans.

Perrine, Mary. *Nannabah's Friend*. Boston: Houghton Mifflin, 1989. Nannabah bridges the gap between the security of her Indian home and the world outside.

## CHAPTER ORGANIZER

# Chapter 4 *By the Shining Sea*

## CHAPTER PLANNING CHART

| Pupil's Edition | Teacher's Edition | Ancillaries |
|---|---|---|
| **Lesson 1: Between Sea and Forest (4–5 days)** | • Graphic Overview (64) | Home Involvement (2) |
|  | • Access Strategy (65) | Map Activity (5) |
| Objective 1: Identify who the Kwakiutl were and where they lived. (History 3; Geography 1)* | • Access Activity (65) | • Poster (3) |
| Objective 2: Describe the way of life of the Kwakiutl. (Culture 2, 4) | Reader's Theater (66) | Study Guide (12) |
| Objective 3: Identify the natural resources used by the Kwakiutl. (Economics 1) | Collaborative Learning (66) | • Study Print (5, 6) |
| Objective 4: Describe the Kwakiutl's beliefs about nature. (Belief Systems 4) | | |
| **Understanding Time: Using Timelines** | | Study Guide (13) |
| Objective 1: Read a timeline. (History 4; Visual Learning 2) | | |
| Objective 2: Create a simple timeline. (History 4; Visual Learning 2) | | |
| **Lesson 2: Of Art and Wood (4–5 days)** | • Graphic Overview (70) | Discovery Journal (9) |
|  | • Access Strategy (71) | • Poster (9) |
| Objective 1: Identify the importance of woodcarving to the Kwakiutl. (Culture 2, 5; History 3) | • Access Activity (71) | Study Guide (14) |
| Objective 2: Describe Kwakiutl canoes and totem poles. (Culture 2) | Cultural Context (72) | |
| Objective 3: Explain how the Kwakiutl used woodcarvings in ceremonies. (Culture 2) | Language Arts Connection (73) | |
|  | Speaking and Listening (74) | |
| **Chapter Review** | Answers (76–77) | Chapter 4 Test |

\* Objectives are correlated to the strands and goals in the program scope and sequence on pages T41–T48.

• LEP appropriate resources. (For additional strategies, see pages T32–T33.)

This chapter is the first in a unit that focuses on North American Indians—the first inhabitants of our continent. Chapter 4 examines the Kwakiutl, who lived on the northwest coast of North America. Later chapters explore Native Americans who lived on the plains and those who lived in the desert. We chose these groups because of their adaptation to different environments.

Each chapter in this unit shows how geographic setting affected the lives of Native Americans. We begin with a look at how each group adapted to the land and used natural resources to meet basic needs. Next, we explore the values and belief systems of the people, which reflect their deep regard for the land.

We chose to focus Chapter 4 on the Kwakiutl because they are representative of Indians who lived along the coast in forested areas. **Lesson 1** describes how the Kwakiutl relied on the forests, the ocean, and rivers to meet their basic needs for food, cloth-

ing, and shelter. The lesson also discusses their respect for nature. **Lesson 2** examines the Kwakiutl art of woodcarving and their use of woodcarvings in ceremonies. The discussion of Kwakiutl art and ceremonies emphasizes the people's closeness to nature.

This chapter includes a skill lesson on using timelines, which will aid students as they begin this chronological look at the United States.

## ACTIVITIES & PROJECTS

### Bulletin Board

Use a physical map of North America as the center of the bulletin board display. As students learn about the Kwakiutl, the Cheyenne, and the Navajo in this unit, have them draw pictures of the homes of each group and of objects used by each group. Post the pictures around the map and connect them with yarn to the area of the country where the group lived.

### LEP: Making a Map

After concluding Lesson 1, tell students to imagine that they are birds flying north over a Kwakiutl village, with the ocean on the left (west), the mountains on the right (east), and the village along the coast. Have students draw picture maps of what the Kwakiutl village and the surrounding area look like from above. Remind them that the long houses were built close together facing the sea.

### Challenge: Research

After students read Lesson 2, tell them that the American Indians who lived in the woodlands of the Northeast developed many of the same ways of life as the Kwakiutl. Have students do research to find out more about the lives of some of these

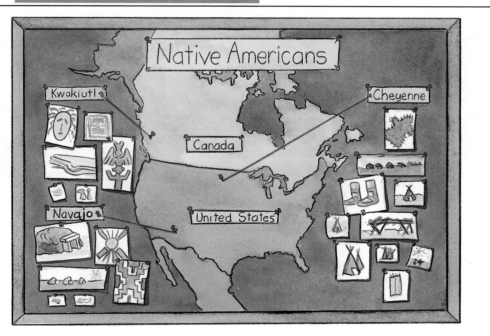

groups, such as the Chippewa, Delaware, Iroquois, and Mohegan. After students present their reports orally, have the class discuss similarities and differences in the lives of the northeast and northwest groups.

### Making a Mask

After concluding Lesson 2, have students design masks similar to those of the Kwakiutl. Provide paper plates, paint and brushes, construction paper, scissors, glue, and craft sticks. Have students cut out holes in the paper

plates for eyes, noses, and mouths. Then have them use construction paper and glue to create animal faces on the paper plates. They can add details with paint and brushes.

61B

### CHAPTER
## PREVIEW

**H**ave a volunteer read aloud the chapter title. Point out that *shining sea* refers to the ocean, and have students tell how an ocean could appear to shine. *(Light reflecting off the water could make it look shiny.)*

Read the introduction and have students look at the visuals and read the captions. Emphasize the fact that the Kwakiutl lived where natural resources from the sea and forests were plentiful.

## Looking Forward

The Kwakiutl way of life, including their woodcarvings and ceremonies, is the topic of the next two lessons: Between Sea and Forest and Of Art and Wood.

# Chapter 4

# *By the Shining Sea*

*Can you imagine eating fish and forest plants almost every day? These were the main foods of a group of people called the Kwakiutl* (kwah kee OO duhl). *They lived along the northwest coast of North America. The Kwakiutl depended on the land and sea for all of their needs. In return, these people held celebrations and created beautiful artwork to honor nature.*

Tall totem poles stood in front of many Kwakiutl homes. The Kwakiutl carved wood from the forest into works of art that were used to tell stories of a family's history.

This piece of clothing was worn as a skirt or a cape. It was made out of tree bark at least 100 years ago by Northwest Coast Indians.

62

### BACKGROUND

The Kwakiutl were just one of many native groups who inhabited the narrow strip of coastal land between the Pacific Ocean and the Coast Mountains. Some of the other groups were the Tlingit, Haida, Tsimshian, Bellacoola, Nootka, Salish, and Chinook. The mountains isolated these people of the Northwest from other native

groups. As a result, they developed a way of life that was quite different from other native groups.

**Bounty from the Sea**

Indians of the Northwest never went hungry because food from the sea was plentiful. The tide washed in crabs, clams, mussels, and edible seaweed and eelgrass. The Kwakiutl fished for other food, such as salmon, cod, herring, and halibut. They used many methods to catch fish, including huge basketlike traps and poles to guide the fish into the

traps. The Kwakiutl also used nets, spears, harpoons, rakes, and special hooks to catch fish.

The Kwakiutl were able to catch enough fish in the summer months to last them through the winter. They developed elaborate ways to dry and smoke fish, seaweed, and meat to make it last.

The sea also provided the Kwakiutl with sea otters, sea lions, seals, and porpoises. These animals were used both for food and for their furs.

The photographs on these pages demonstrate the rich culture of the Kwakiutl as well as their dependence on the sea and the forest. The Kwakiutl carved beautiful totem poles, canoes, and masks. They made almost everything they used from wood, including clothing. Fish was a major part of their diet.

The Kwakiutl made large wooden canoes for fishing and traveling. Sometimes they would dress in special costumes and masks to attend celebrations in nearby villages.

Kwakiutl masks showed the faces of creatures from ancient stories. Dancers sometimes acted out these stories during celebrations.

63

## Bounty from the Forest

The forest supplied the Kwakiutl and other Indians of the Northwest with some food and a seemingly inexhaustible supply of natural resources for their homes and crafts.

It is sometimes said that the lives of Northwest Coast Indians began and ended with cedar bark. They were diapered and wrapped in shredded cedar bark as babies, and their cradles were lined with the same material. As adolescents and adults, most of their clothing was made of cedar bark. They slept on mats woven from cedar bark and used tablecloths made from bark. When Indians of the Northwest died, they were often buried in cedar bark mats.

The Kwakiutl also used wood from the forest to build huge homes, giant totem poles, and large canoes.

The sea and the forest provided so well for the Indians of the Northwest that they are the only groups who became wealthy without relying on farming or pottery making.

64

## INTRODUCE

Have a volunteer read the lesson title and Thinking Focus aloud. Ask students to predict how the Kwakiutl met their basic needs for food and shelter. Have students locate the Kwakiutl's coastal home on the map on page 65. (Note that the Kwakiutl still live in this area.) Have students read to find out more about these people's daily lives.

### Key Terms

Vocabulary strategies: T36–T37
**salmon**—a large fish with silvery scales that lives in the Northern Pacific and Atlantic oceans
**cedar**—a type of evergreen tree
**long house**—long wooden house built by the Kwakiutl

---

LESSON 1

# Between Sea and Forest

### THINKING
### FOCUS

*How did the Kwakiutl meet their basic need for food and shelter?*

### Key Terms

• salmon
• cedar
• long house

➤ *This picture of a woman wearing a cedar bark blanket was taken long ago. Below is a wooden beater that women used to pound the bark before it could be woven into blankets or clothing.*

Kwiskwis is very excited! Today her mother will show her how women make clothes out of tree bark.

"Where do we start?" asks Kwiskwis excitedly.

"With a cedar *(SEE dur)* tree," her mother says.

Kwiskwis and her mother pull long strips of bark off the trees. Then they pull the softer inner bark from these strips. When they collect as much of the softer bark as they can carry, they return to their big wooden house.

"First we pound the bark with this beater until it is not so stiff," says Mother. "Next, we will separate the bark into thin strips. We will weave these strips together on this frame to make a new cape for your grandmother."

Kwiskwis smiles, knowing the gift will keep her grandmother warm and dry.

---

## Objectives

1. Identify who the Kwakiutl were and where they lived.
2. Describe the way of life of the Kwakiutl.
3. Identify the natural resources used by the Kwakiutl.
4. Describe the Kwakiutl's beliefs about nature.

## Graphic Overview

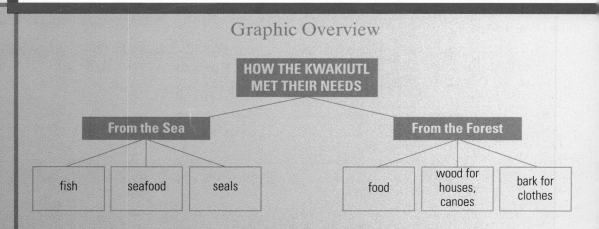

**HOW THE KWAKIUTL MET THEIR NEEDS**

**From the Sea**

| fish | seafood | seals |

**From the Forest**

| food | wood for houses, canoes | bark for clothes |

## Sea of Plenty

If you could have visited a Kwakiutl village one hundred or more years ago, you might have seen a girl like Kwiskwis and her mother making clothes from tree bark. The Kwakiutl were one of many Indian groups that lived along the northwest coast of North America. These northwest coast groups lived on a strip of land that stretches from the southern tip of Alaska all the way to northern California. Look at the map. Notice that the Kwakiutl lived in what is now Canada.

Remember what you learned about oceans and forests in Chapters 1 and 2? The Kwakiutl lived in thick forests between the ocean and the high mountains.

### Water Provides Food

Water played a large part in the way the Kwakiutl lived. The Pacific Ocean and nearby rivers provided plenty of fish to eat, such as trout, halibut, and **salmon** *(SA muhn)*. The Kwakiutl also ate small seafood, such as clams, and large sea animals, such as seals. However, salmon was their favorite food.

The Kwakiutl believed that all things in nature lived in order to help each other. Each year the salmon left the ocean and swam upstream past Kwakiutl villages to lay their eggs. The Kwakiutl thought these fish swam upstream to feed the villagers.

The Kwakiutl wanted to be sure that the salmon would come back each year. When they ate salmon, they always saved the bones. Then they would return the bones to the

▼ *Kwakiutl villages were near plentiful water resources—the water of rivers, streams, and the ocean.*

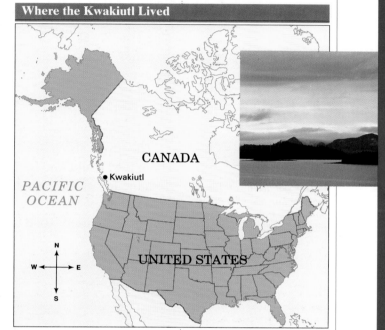

Where the Kwakiutl Lived

CANADA

Kwakiutl

PACIFIC OCEAN

UNITED STATES

N
W　E
S

Read aloud the narrative on page 64. Ask students where Kwiskwis and her mother probably went to get the cedar bark they were using to make the cape. *(forest)* Explain that the forest was one place that provided for the Kwakiutl's needs. Have students skim the lesson headings and illustrations to confirm this and to find the other place that provided for the Kwakiutl's needs. *(sea)* You may wish to start the Graphic Overview at this time.

### GEOGRAPHY
### Map & Globe Skills

Have students look at the map and locate where in North America the Kwakiutl lived.

## Access Strategy

Discuss and list on the board the three basic needs: food, shelter, and clothing. Ask students how they meet each of these needs, and list their responses next to the appropriate need.

Then erase the answers, and ask students to imagine that none of these sources were available. Ask students how they could meet their needs when the only resources available were the sea and the forest.

Then tell students that in this lesson, they will learn about the lives of the Kwakiutl and the ways in which they used the resources available to them.

## Access Activity

Provide each student with three sheets of paper. Tell students to draw a forest on one sheet, a sea on the second sheet, and two products from each place on the third sheet. Then have students tape the sheets together with the drawing of the products in the middle. Display the drawings, and discuss what life is like in lands that are near forests and seas.

## ECONOMICS
### Critical Thinking

Identify the resources provided by the sea and forest and the ways in which geography influenced the kinds of resources available. (*Sea provided food; forest provided food and trees for shelter and clothes.*) Discuss how the Kwakiutl's lives would have been different if they had lived inland on a plain, instead of on the coast near a forest. (*The Kwakiutl would not have eaten saltwater fish or have built wooden houses.*)

■ *The sea provided the Kwakiutl with food.*

## BELIEF SYSTEMS
### Critical Thinking

Ask how and why the Kwakiutl showed respect for their natural environment. (*They showed respect for the water by returning the salmon skeletons to it because they believed this would assure the return of the salmon the next year. They showed respect for the forest by not pulling too much bark from the cedar trees because they believed the cedar trees were there to help them.*)

➤ *The Kwakiutl made fish hooks from wood. First, they heated the wood with steam. Then they bent it to form a hook.*

■ *How did living near water affect Kwakiutl life?*

▼ *This wooden box is fitted together and tied with cedar bark rope. Boxes were used for seats and shelves. They were also used to hold food, water, and family treasures.*

66

water where the fish had been caught. They believed those fish would get new bodies and come again the next year.

The Kwakiutl ate fish more than any other food, and they became very good at fishing. The Kwakiutl caught fish with hooks made of wood, bone, or horn. They also used spears and nets. When the Kwakiutl caught more than they could eat, they would dry the extra fish. This gave them food for the winter. ■

## Forest Gifts

The forest also helped the Kwakiutl meet their needs. There they could find berries and animals to eat. Wood from the forest was even more important to them. They lived in houses made of wood and traveled in wooden canoes. They used wood to make chests, dishes, toys, bows, arrows, and more.

Cedar was the type of wood used most often by the Kwakiutl. A **cedar** is a type of evergreen tree. The Kwakiutl used cedar's soft inner bark to make rope, mats, and clothing. Sometimes they would weave cedar bark and mountain goat wool together to make warm blankets.

The Kwakiutl were careful not to pull too much bark from a cedar tree. They knew that this could kill the

### Visual Learning

Refer to the wooden beater photograph on page 64. Ask students to think of another thing from the Kwakiutl's environment that might be painted on the wooden beater. Then have students draw what that beater would look like. Have students share their drawings and explain why they chose to decorate them as they did.

### Reader's Theater

Have a group of students work together to perform a skit using the dialogue provided in the paragraphs on page 64 of this lesson. Assign students the roles of Narrator, Mother, and Kwiskwis. Suggest that the group write a short introduction to their skit that explains something about the Kwakiutl and the way that they lived. Also suggest that they act out collecting bark, pounding it, and cutting it into strips.

### Collaborative Learning

Remind students that the Kwakiutl took from nature only what they needed and were careful to give back what they could. Ask students to work in small groups to list what they take from nature and what they give or could give back. Have students share their lists.

tree. The Kwakiutl believed that cedar trees, like the salmon, were there to help them. Sometimes they sang a song to the cedar, asking it to clothe and shelter them. Then they thanked the tree for giving them so much.

Cedar was the Kwakiutl's favorite wood for building houses. These houses were called **long houses.** They were up to 60 feet long. The Kwakiutl split logs into thin boards to make the walls and roof. Some roof boards could be moved to let out smoke from the cooking fires.

◄ *The artist has drawn this so you can see the inside of a long house. How many different ways do they use wood in this picture?*

Three or four related families usually shared a long house. Each family had its own space and cooking fire in one corner of the house. Kwakiutl long houses were all built close together in a row, facing the sea.

The Kwakiutl cared about nature. They felt that the land and sea gave them many things. The Kwakiutl took only what they needed and gave back what they could. ■

■ *How did forests help the Kwakiutl?*

## REVIEW

1. **FOCUS** How did the Kwakiutl meet their basic need for food and shelter?
2. **CONNECT** From what you know about oceans and rivers, where did the Kwakiutl get their freshwater fish?
3. **CRITICAL THINKING** The Kwakiutl believed that all things in nature lived to help each other. How did this affect the way the Kwakiutl treated nature?
4. **ACTIVITY** Draw a picture that shows how the Kwakiutl used either the sea or the forest in their everyday lives.

## Critical Thinking

Direct attention to the illustration of the long house. Remind students that these houses were built close together, shared by several families, and faced the sea. Have students recall what they learned about the Kwakiutl way of life that would explain why they built their houses facing the sea. (*The sea was their major food source.*)

◄ *The long house is built of wood, firewood is burning, the canoe is wooden, and the carved figure in front of the house is of wood.*

■ *The Kwakiutl found food in the forest, used wood from trees to build houses and canoes, and used the bark of the trees for clothing.*

## CLOSE

Have students discuss answers to the focus question. Use the Graphic Overview to review and reteach the main concepts of the lesson.

## Answers to Review Questions

1. The Kwakiutl ate fish from the ocean and rivers as well as berries and animals from the forests. They used tree bark to make clothes. They used wood from trees to make houses, canoes, bows, toys, etc.
2. The Kwakiutl caught freshwater fish from rivers.
3. The Kwakiutl treated nature with respect. After they ate the salmon, they saved the bones and returned them to the water. They believed the fish would get new bodies and come back the next year. In addition, when the Kwakiutl used bark they were careful not to pull too much from the tree. Furthermore, they thanked the tree and sometimes sang a song to the cedar.
4. Students' drawings should include fish from the sea, and wood products or berries and animals from the forest.

## Homework Options

Have each student write a paragraph contrasting the Kwakiutl way of life with the student's own.

**Study Guide:** page 12

UNDERSTANDING
TIME

This skills feature uses important events in a person's life to teach students how to read and create timelines.

UNDERSTANDING TIME

# Using Timelines

**Here's Why**   It is not easy to keep track of all the events we read about. Timelines can help. A timeline shows events in the order in which they happened. Some timelines show events for a short period of time, such as a week. Many timelines, however, cover more than one year. Years are shown on those timelines. Suppose you wanted to show certain events in the life of a Kwakiutl boy named Weesa.

**Here's How**   You read most timelines from left to right. Events that took place earlier in time are shown on the left side of the timeline. Events that happened later are shown on the right.

**Events in Weesa's Life**

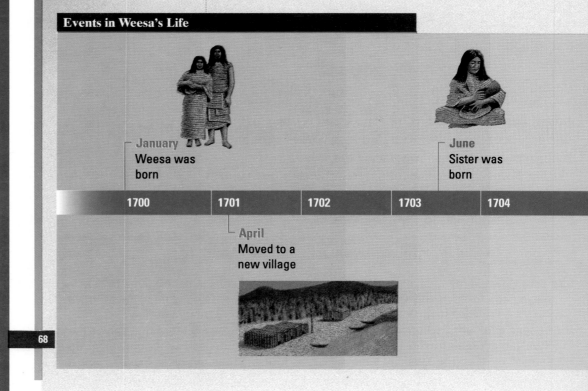

January
Weesa was born

June
Sister was born

| 1700 | 1701 | 1702 | 1703 | 1704 |

April
Moved to a new village

## Objectives

1. Read a timeline. (History 4; Visual Learning 2)
2. Create a simple timeline. (History 4; Visual Learning 2)

## Collaborative Learning

Divide the class into small groups. Ask the students in each group to share and discuss the timelines of their lives. Suggest that they ask each other questions about events on these timelines similar to those asked in this lesson about Weesa.

Look at the left side of the timeline below. What happened to Weesa in the year 1700? Notice that dates are shown by years on the timeline. What happened to Weesa in the year 1701? How old was he then? How old was he when his sister was born?

**Try It** You can learn many things about the Kwakiutl boy's life by looking at the timeline. In what year did Weesa help his father carve a mask? Was that before or after he went to the totem-pole raising? How old was Weesa when he helped his father carve a mask? What is the latest date that is shown on the timeline? What happened that year?

**Apply It** Make a timeline of your life. Start on the left with the year you were born. Then write the year it is now at the right. Show five or six events on your timeline in the order in which they happened. Draw pictures of some of the events on your timeline.

69

**September**
Helped father carve a mask

| 1705 | 1706 | 1707 | 1708 | 1709 |

**February**
Went to a totem-pole raising

**April**
Went on a fishing trip

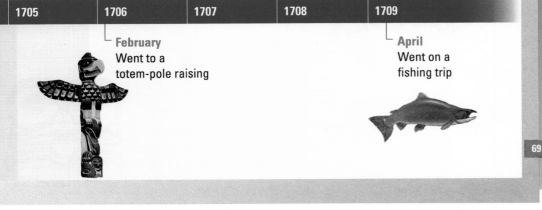

**INTRODUCE**

**INTRODUCE**

Help students recall that the Kwakiutl lived in a forested area near the sea. Ask students to name some products the Kwakiutl got from the forests and the sea. *(berries and wood products from forests; fish from the sea)* Then read aloud the lesson title and Thinking Focus. Elicit that this lesson focuses on the importance of wood to the Kwakiutl, and have students name two uses of wood that they already learned. *(clothing and housing)*

Direct attention to the illustrations on this page and tell students that they show woodcarvings. Guide students to understand that art is an important part of people's lives, too. Suggest that students read the lesson to learn more about how woodcarving was important to the Kwakiutl.

### Key Terms

Vocabulary strategies: T36–T37
**totem pole**—wooden pole decorated with figures
**ceremony**—the way people act during important events

70

---

LESSON 2

# Of Art and Wood

THINKING
**FOCUS**

*How was wood important to the Kwakiutl?*

### Key Terms

- totem pole
- ceremony

The Indians of the northwest coast were some of the best woodworkers in North America. They carved animals on many of the things they made. An artist chose certain parts of an animal to carve.

The large front teeth and the wide, flat tail show that this is a beaver.

Big claws help to show that this is a bear.

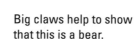

This animal has large teeth and fins. It also blows air through a hole on the top of its head. It is a killer whale.

What parts of this drawing help to show it is a frog?

70

---

Objectives

1. Identify the importance of woodcarving to the Kwakiutl.
2. Describe Kwakiutl canoes and totem poles.
3. Explain how the Kwakiutl used woodcarvings in ceremonies.

Graphic Overview

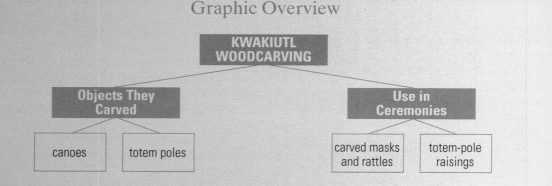

## Totem Poles and Canoes

Animals like the ones on page 70 were carved into many Kwakiutl objects. Almost everything the Kwakiutl used was made of wood. Carving was an important part of Kwakiutl life.

Remember that Kwakiutl women were weavers. Kwakiutl men were woodcarvers. They taught their sons this skill. If a boy grew up to be a good carver, he became an important person in a Kwakiutl village.

Kwakiutl woodcarvers made beautiful totem poles. A **totem pole** is a wooden pole decorated with figures that showed a family's history. A Kwakiutl totem pole could be 10 to 70 feet tall. Each figure on it stood for an animal, a person, or an event in a family's history.

One of the biggest jobs for a woodcarver was making a canoe like the one shown below. First, he cut down a tall cedar tree and chopped it into the shape of a canoe. Then he used hot stones to burn out the inside of the log. He chipped away the burned parts to form the inside of the canoe.

### Across Time & Space

*The Kwakiutl still carve totem poles today. In 1980, Kwakiutl carvers in Canada created a totem pole as tall as an eight-story building.*

▼ *This colorful Kwakiutl totem pole stands in Canada today. Can you name any of the figures on it?*

71

## DEVELOP

Have students preview the lesson by reading the headings and looking at the visuals. Point out that students will be reading about what the Kwakiutl carved from wood and how they used carvings in ceremonies. You may wish to start the Graphic Overview on the board, and have students complete it as they read the lesson.

◄ *The top figure is a bird, perhaps an eagle. Since the central figure has ears above its head, it is an animal—perhaps a bear because of its teeth. The bottom figure is a person being held, hugged, or protected by the animal. People are shown as having ears on the sides of their heads.*

### HISTORY
### Critical Thinking

Discuss with students the ways that wood was used by the Kwakiutl. Then ask students why they think that the woodcarver was a person of great importance in a Kwakiutl village.

71

## Critical Thinking

Have students describe the steps that were taken to build a canoe. Guide them to present the steps in sequential order. Then ask students to recall the geography of the Kwakiutl land and discuss why canoe making was such an important skill.

■ *Wood was used by the Kwakiutl to make canoes and totem poles.*

*■ How did the Kwakiutl use wood in everyday life?*

► *The Kwakiutl in this picture are wearing costumes that they wore during ceremonies. During these ceremonies, they might have used a rattle like the one pictured below.*

Next, the woodcarver put water into the canoe. He added very hot stones to make steam. The steam softened the wood. Once the sides were soft, they could be stretched. Bigger and bigger sticks were forced between the two sides until the opening was big enough to fit many people in the canoe. A finished canoe could be 50 feet long and hold 40 people.

Finally, like most Kwakiutl items, many canoes were carved and painted. Even Kwakiutl boats became works of art. ■

## Special Ceremonies

The Kwakiutl celebrated important events such as weddings or births. There were special words, actions, and songs for each event. The way people act during such important events is called a **ceremony.** Kwakiutl ceremonies were full of dancing, storytelling, and feasting.

The Kwakiutl used finely carved masks, rattles, and puppets during ceremonies. These pieces of art showed animals of the land, water, and air. They were used to tell stories about families and nature.

## Critical Thinking

Remind students that the costumes worn by the Kwakiutl at their ceremonies showed that nature was important to the Kwakiutl. Ask students to think about the things that are important to them and describe costumes that would represent those things.

## Cultural Context

The Kwakiutl celebrated ceremonies with songs and dancing. With their hands they manipulated masks or shook rattles. The rattle shown on this page tells a story. This rattle shows a Kwakiutl chief, named Wakiash, lying on the back of a great raven. (Wakiash's name is pronounced as spelled.) The raven flies Wakiash around the world in search of a new dance. On Wakiash's chest is a green frog. You can see the frog's tongue going into the man's mouth—signifying that the man

and frog can talk to each other. The frog helps the man get a dance, a long house, and a totem pole from the forest animals. The rattle represents a mythical time long ago when people and animals communicated with and helped each other.

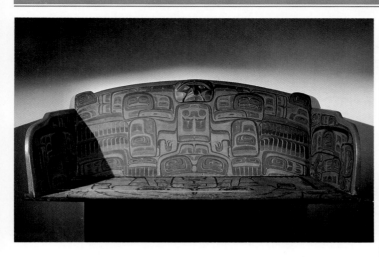

◄ *During Kwakiutl ceremonies, a chief would sit in a wooden seat like this one.*

One Kwakiutl ceremony was a totem-pole raising. A totem-pole raising was held on many special occasions, such as weddings and funerals. Sometimes a family raised a totem pole to call attention to something brave a family member had done.

Not all Kwakiutl families had totem poles. Totem poles showed a family's importance in the community. A family had to be important and rich enough to have one made.

A totem pole was usually set up in front of a house. During the totem-pole raising, a family would gather near the totem pole. In a loud voice, the head of the family would tell stories about his family's past.

The speechmaker used the figures on the totem pole to remind him of his family's story. For example, the carving of a sea lion on the pole might remind him of an important event that happened long ago.

A totem-pole raising was an important event. The speechmaker, like the one on the next page, wore special clothes to tell his family's story. People outside of the family were allowed to hear the story, but only a family member was allowed to tell it.

### How Do We Know?

*There are no old totem poles left today, since wood decays quickly in forests. We know that totem poles were carved by northwest coast groups as long as 200 years ago, because a French visitor described one in his journal.*

▲ *Even from far away, a Kwakiutl could tell who lived in this house. The totem pole is like a sign that tells which family lives there.*

73

**CULTURE**

Visual Learning

Direct attention to the photograph at the bottom of the page. Discuss how a Kwakiutl could know who lives in a house by looking at a totem pole. *(A totem pole was a recognizable sign of a family to a local villager, much as a family crest is a sign of a particular family.)*

73

---

## Language Arts Connection

Tell students that you are going to read a poem that honors the totem pole given to his people by Wakiash. Explain that Wakiash was first named after a river as generous with food as the chief was with his people. Further explain that the pole was called Kalakuyuwish, which means "the pole that holds up the sky." Wakiash then was also called Kalakuyuwish since he brought the pole. Read aloud this poem, which honors the pole and the chief.

**Song of the Totem-Pole**
Now doth it rise, our river;
Our river is Wakiash, good is he.
Now doth it creak, this totem pole;
    Clouds rest on its top.
Kalakuyuwish, great as the sky-pole is he!

Have students tell what the poem means. Then ask them to write their own poem about something that they think could "hold up the sky."

## Study Skills

Write *Ketchikan* on the chalkboard. Explain that this is a town in Alaska that has many totem poles. Locate the town on a map. Have students find pictures of totem poles in encyclopedias and reference books about Alaska and report on their findings in class.

**Note:** This Moment in Time may be used at this point, or as a summary of the lesson.

**CULTURE**

## Visual Learning

Ask students to name special occasions on which they get dressed up. Then point out that the Kwakiutl dressed in special clothing and used special objects in ceremonies such as totem-pole raisings. Point to each item called out in this Moment in Time. Have students read the captions and summarize the information in each.

**More About the Ceremony** The speechmaker's speech is filled with boastful tales of his family. He tells of certain animals that helped his ancestors long ago; some of the animals may be carved into the new totem pole. He also speaks of his family's power and wealth. After his speech, a potlatch (which means "giveaway") is held. A potlatch is an event where people gather to receive valuable gifts, such as blankets or canoes, that the family gives away. The more a family gives away, the greater the family's status in the community—and the more the recipients owe the giver. The only way the recipients can pay back the debt is by holding an even greater potlatch of their own.

74

**A MOMENT IN TIME**

# A Kwakiutl Speechmaker

*5:06 P.M., October 20, 1843
In front of a long house on
the northwest coast*

**Talking Stick**
A whale's tail is carved into this stick. The day the speechmaker was born, his mother saw a whale's tail flashing in the sea. Now it is a sign of his family's strength.

**Neck Ring**
The speechmaker wears this colorful ring made from red cedar bark. He last wore it at his daughter's wedding.

**Copper**
His thoughts are far from a fight, but the speechmaker is proudly holding a shield called a copper. It is so valuable that he could trade it for 2,500 blankets.

**Blanket**
The blanket that drapes the speechmaker's shoulders is made from cedar bark and the hair of a mountain goat.

74

## Visual Learning

Direct attention to the talking stick pictured on this page. Discuss the significance of the whale's tail. Then have students design their own talking sticks. Have students share their drawings and explain the special signs that they would have carved into their personal alking sticks.

## Speaking and Listening

Explain to students that when a person holds a talking stick it is a signal for the audience to be quiet and pay attention. In a gathering, only the person holding the talking stick is allowed to speak.

Designate a classroom object such as a yardstick or pointer to serve as a talking stick. Challenge students to think of an important event that has taken place in school. You may wish to provide examples, such as a special assembly, a school fair or

party, or an athletic event. Have students choose an event. Then ask volunteers to tell the story of the event. Pass the talking stick around the classroom and have students use it while they talk about the event.

◄ *This mask was worn during Kwakiutl ceremonies by a dancer who opened and closed the bird's mouth to make a loud snapping sound. The bird was an evil creature in Kwakiutl myths.*

Totem-pole raisings were not the only Kwakiutl ceremonies. The winter days in Kwakiutl villages were filled with the sounds of singing, dancing, speeches, and feasting. Often performers wearing large wooden masks acted out stories of spirits in nature. The masks were carved and painted to look like these spirits. They added to the excitement of Kwakiutl winter ceremonies.

The Kwakiutl had more time for ceremonies in the winter because they didn't spend as much time gathering food. During the warmer days, they caught more fish than they could use. They dried some of these fish to eat during the winter. This gave the Kwakiutl time during the winter for their ceremonies. ■

◄ *This mask shows the face of a feared giant in Kwakiutl myths. It is made from wood and human hair. At one time it had thick eyebrows and a mustache and beard made from bear fur.*

■ *How did the Kwakiutl use wood in their ceremonies?*

### R E V I E W

1. **FOCUS** How was wood important to the Kwakiutl?
2. **CONNECT** How would Kwakiutl life have been different if these people had lived in a desert?
3. **CRITICAL THINKING** How did the Kwakiutl's ideas about nature affect their art and ceremonies?
4. **WRITING ACTIVITY** Choose an animal from land, sea, or air. Make a drawing of it like the Kwakiutl figures on page 70. Write a short story that a speechmaker might tell about your animal.

**Answers to Reviewing Key Terms**
**A.**
1. totem pole
2. cedar
3. salmon
4. long house
**B.**
Change tent to long house
Change hamburgers to salmon
Change bamboo to cedar
Change flagpole to totem pole
Change game to ceremony

**Answers to Exploring Concepts**
**A.** Sample answers:
Forest—wood or cedar; houses, canoes, dishes, toys, clothing
River or ocean—fish or salmon; food
**B.** Sample answers:
1. The Kwakiutl did not waste fish. When they caught more than they could eat, they dried the extra fish and saved them for winter food. The Kwakiutl were careful not to pull too much bark from a cedar tree.
2. Kwakiutl woodcarvers made beautiful totem poles and canoes. The Kwakiutl carved and painted masks, rattles, and puppets to use in ceremonies.

# Chapter Review

## Reviewing Key Terms

cedar (p. 66)  salmon (p. 65)
ceremony (p. 72)  totem pole (p. 71)
long house (p. 67)

**A.** Write the key term for each meaning.
1. a carved, wooden pole owned by a family
2. a kind of evergreen tree
3. a fish that lives in the Pacific Ocean and swims up rivers to lay eggs
4. a wooden house up to 60 feet long

**B.** Copy the story below. Change one word in each sentence to make the sentences correct.

Long ago, a Kwakiutl girl lived in a tent with her family. They ate hamburgers for dinner. Her father took her for rides in a boat made of bamboo. Her family had their own flagpole. They celebrated important events with a game.

## Exploring Concepts

**A.** The chart below shows where the Kwakiutl found many useful things. Copy the chart. Fill in the last two columns to show what was used and how it was used.

**B.** Write two details to support each of the following main ideas.
1. The Kwakiutl took only what they needed from nature.
2. The Kwakiutl made beautiful things.

| Where | What was used | How it was used |
|---|---|---|
| Forest | | |
| River or ocean | | |

## Reviewing Skills

1. Copy the timeline of a week below. On your timeline, mark the days you go to school, the days you stay home, and the days you have something special planned.

2. Look at the map on page 65 again. What body of water lies west of where the Kwakiutl lived? What state lies north of where the Kwakiutl lived?

**Timeline for a Week**

┌School

| Monday | Tuesday | Wednesday | Thursday | Friday | Saturday | Sunday |
|--------|---------|-----------|----------|--------|----------|--------|
|        |         |           |          |        |          |        |

## Using Critical Thinking

1. The Kwakiutl used wood from the forest in many ways. How would a forest fire have changed their lives?

2. The Kwakiutl were fine artists and spent long hours making beautiful things. Name some types of art that people today spend a long time making.

3. Compare a Kwakiutl family's totem pole to a family's photo album today. How are they alike?

## Preparing for Citizenship

1. ART ACTIVITY Work with a partner. Write a story about a Kwakiutl family. Tell something they did or something that happened to them. Then, make a totem pole by rolling and pasting cardboard or heavy paper into a long tube. Decorate your totem pole to match your story.

2. COLLABORATIVE LEARNING With your class, have a totem-pole raising. Choose speechmakers to tell the family stories shown on the totem poles you made. Others in the class can make paper neck rings and talking sticks. Gather together to listen to the stories.

77

# Chapter 5 *Over Waves of Grass*

## CHAPTER PLANNING CHART

| Pupil's Edition | Teacher's Edition | Ancillaries |
|---|---|---|
| **Lesson 1: Following the Buffalo (4–5 days)**<br><br>Objective 1: Identify who the Cheyenne were and where they lived. (History 3, Geography 1)*<br>Objective 2: Describe the way of life of the Cheyenne. (Culture 2, 4)<br>Objective 3: Explain the importance of the buffalo to the Cheyenne. (Economics 1)<br>Objective 4: Describe how the horse changed the way of life for the Cheyenne. (History 5, 6) | • Graphic Overview (80)<br>• Access Strategy (81)<br>• Access Activity (81)<br>Research (82)<br>Role-Playing (83) | Discovery Journal (10)<br>Study Guide (15) |
| **Understanding Natural Resources: We Use Natural Resources**<br><br>Objective 1: Identify examples of natural resources. (Economics 1)<br>Objective 2: Describe uses of natural resources. (Economics 1) | | Study Guide (16) |
| **Lesson 2: The Medicine Dance (4–5 days)**<br><br>Objective 1: Identify what the Medicine Dance was. (Culture 2)<br>Objective 2: Explain the meaning and importance of the Medicine Dance. (Culture 2)<br>Objective 3: Describe how the Medicine Dance was celebrated. (Culture 2) | • Graphic Overview (86)<br>• Access Strategy (87)<br>• Access Activity (87)<br>Research (88) | Map Activity (6)<br>Study Guide (17) |
| **Explore: The First American People**<br><br>Objective 1: Identify the original Native American group or groups who lived in your local community. (Culture 3, 4)<br>Objective 2: Describe the way of life of the original Native American group or groups. (Culture 3, 4) | | Discovery Journal (11) |
| **Chapter Review** | Answers (92–93) | Chapter 5 Test |

\* Objectives are correlated to the strands and goals in the program scope and sequence on pages T41–T48.

• LEP appropriate resources. (For additional strategies, see pages T32–T33.)

## CHAPTER RATIONALE

This chapter is the second of three chapters on Native Americans. Chapter 5 examines the Cheyenne, a Plains Indian group. In this chapter we show how the geographic setting of the plains affected the lives of the Cheyenne.

We chose to focus on a Plains Indian group because of the importance of prairies in the natural landscape of the United States and because the way of life of Plains Indians was substantially different from those of other groups. We specifically chose the Cheyenne because they demonstrate how a new development may cause people to change their way of life even though their environment stays the same. In this instance, the cause of change was the introduction of the horse. After they obtained horses, the Cheyenne abandoned their agricultural lifestyle in favor of a nomadic one, hunting buffalo year round.

**Lesson 1** examines the problems that the Cheyenne had farming the prairie and how their lives changed after they obtained horses and started following the buffalo all year. The feature A Closer Look: The Great Provider demonstrates ways the Cheyenne used various parts of the buffalo.

**Lesson 2** takes a look at Cheyenne values and beliefs, particularly their respect for nature. The specific focus is a major religious ceremony, the Medicine Dance. We chose to examine the Medicine Dance (also called the Sun Dance) because of its importance in Cheyenne cultural and religious life. In fact, the Medicine Dance was practiced in some form by most Plains Indian groups as a way of continuing the cycle of life, death, and rebirth in nature.

Chapter 5 includes the features Understanding Natural Resources and Explore: The First American People. The first feature helps build students' understanding of how natural resources were used in the past and are used today. The use of natural resources is a major theme throughout this book. The other feature gives students an opportunity to learn more about the early Native Americans of their local area.

## ACTIVITIES & PROJECTS

### LEP: Making a Costume

After concluding Lesson 1, provide students with brown crepe paper or tissue paper to simulate buffalo hide, colored paper for designs, scissors, tape or glue, and a stapler. Have students make a Cheyenne girl's dress, cape, and moccasins from the crepe paper "buffalo hide" and decorate them with Cheyenne designs.

### Challenge: Research

After concluding Lesson 2, have students research and write reports on other Plains Indians, such as the Arapaho, the Blackfeet, the Comanche, the Kiowa, and the Sioux. Allow time for oral presentations of the reports and discussion of similarities and differences among the various Native American groups.

### Role-Playing

After reading Lesson 1, select two volunteers, one to play the part of Black Kettle as an old man after acquiring horses, and the other to be the interviewer. Have the interviewer prepare questions to ask Black Kettle about his life before and after obtaining horses. The student playing Black Kettle should have an opportunity to prepare answers to the questions. Ask the students to perform their interview for the class.

### Writing an Essay

After concluding Lesson 1, have students write essays describing what they think it would be like to be a Cheyenne youngster following the buffalo. Encourage students to include descriptions of what they would hear, see, taste, and smell inside a tipi, during a hunt, and during a buffalo feast.

### Collaborative Learning

After concluding Lesson 2, mark vertical divisions on a continuous sheet of shelf paper. Have students work in small groups to illustrate scenes from the myth on page 86. When the drawings are finished, cut a "screen" in a cardboard box that is large enough to accommodate each scene. Also cut slits in the sides of the box opposite the "screen." Have students slide their drawing through the slits and show one scene at a time on the screen. Students could also use a flashlight to light up the back of the picture as they show their "movie."

77B

## CHAPTER
# PREVIEW

Have students read the chapter title and introductory paragraph and look at the visuals. Ask students what kind of land *Waves of Grass* reminds them of. *(prairies, which they read about in Unit 1)* Have students name some ways in which prairies differ from forests. *(few trees, less rain)* Be sure students understand that native people long ago had no stores in which to buy food or clothing, so they had to rely completely on the resources where they lived to meet their needs.

## Looking Back

Have students describe the major difference between the Kwakiutl and the Cheyenne. *(The Kwakiutl had plenty of food from the sea, but the Cheyenne had to work hard to get food by farming or hunting the buffalo.)*

## Looking Forward

The Cheyenne's way of life is the topic of the next two lessons: Following the Buffalo and The Medicine Dance.

# Chapter 5

# Over Waves of Grass

*Finding food was not an easy task for the Cheyenne (shy AN) people. Unlike the Kwakiutl, who had plenty of fish nearby, the Cheyenne had to work hard for their food. Hundreds of years ago, they spent most of their time farming to grow food. Later they had horses and hunted buffalo for meat.*

The buffalo lived on the plains in huge herds. The Cheyenne depended on this great beast for food, clothing, and even shelter.

Buffalo hides had many uses. Sometimes the Cheyenne would decorate hides with drawings that told stories of important events, such as hunts or celebrations.

## BACKGROUND

In the 1500s the Cheyenne hunted and fished in the area around Lake Superior. They were gradually pushed out of that area and onto the plains by the Sioux and Ojibwa. There they lived in earthen lodges made of logs, dirt, and grass. They practiced farming all year round, with occasional hunting trips.

## Life on the Plains

Many factors contributed to making life on the plains difficult for the Cheyenne. They knew how to grow only a few crops, such as corn, squash, and beans. So, when one crop failed, the results were disastrous. Furthermore, crop failures were fairly common because the climate was harsh and rainfall was unpredictable.

Because they had to struggle to survive, the Cheyenne developed a very different culture from the Kwakiutl, who had much leisure time. The Cheyenne did not have elaborate woodcarvings, but they did have a wealth of myths, beliefs, and customs extolling virtues that were important to their way of life, such as bravery, strength, and faith.

## Hunting the Buffalo

The Cheyenne gradually depended more and more on the buffalo as a source of food. To follow the buffalo, they made portable homes called tipis, which were made from buffalo hides stretched over poles. Before they acquired the horse, the Cheyenne

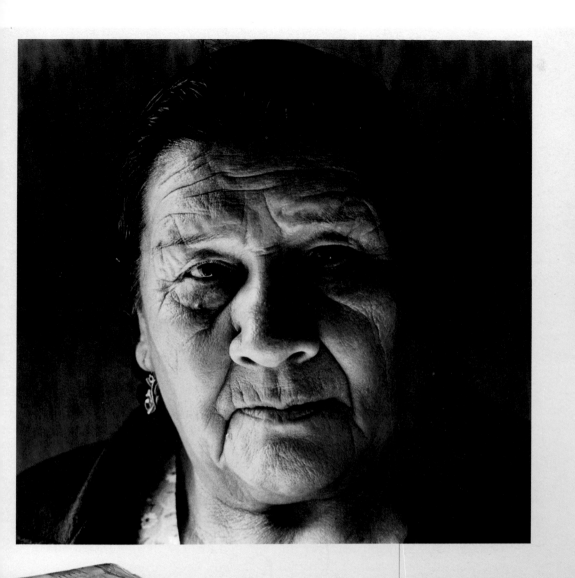

This Cheyenne woman
follows the ways of her
ancestors.

The Cheyenne used buffalo
leather bags to hold many
things. This bag is about
200 years old.

## Understanding the Visuals

As students look at the photograph of the Cheyenne woman, emphasize that the Cheyenne today no longer need to hunt buffalo for food and clothing, but many still celebrate ceremonies that have been handed down for generations. Many Cheyenne gather each summer on the plains to celebrate the Medicine Dance, a ceremony honoring nature. The Medicine Dance is described in Lesson 2.

hunted buffalo on foot. Travel was slow and laborious, and they covered only about 5 or 6 miles a day. Women carried heavy loads, and dogs pulled 40 to 60 pounds of equipment.

The hunt itself was even more difficult than the trip. Sometimes bands of Cheyenne would surround a part of a herd, close in, and shoot the buffalo with bows and arrows. Other times the Cheyenne would disguise themselves in the skins of animals the buffalo did not fear so that they could get close enough to shoot the animal. Another method the Cheyenne used was to flank a herd on three sides and drive them into a corral or over a ravine. The skin of the buffalo belonged to the man who killed it, but the meat belonged to everyone.

When the Cheyenne began to ride horses in the 1750s, hunting the buffalo became much easier. In the 1770s, the Cheyenne gave up their villages and started following the buffalo all year.

## INTRODUCE

Note that this chapter deals with the Cheyenne, a Plains Indian group who hunted buffalo. Tell students that you will read aloud *The Gift of the Sacred Dog*, an Indian myth retold by Paul Goble. Explain that this myth tells about an Indian tribe that could not find buffalo to hunt and how the Great Spirit (God) came to their aid.

## READ AND RESPOND

Suggest that, as they listen, students think about who the Sacred Dog was and how the Sacred Dog could help the people.

**79A**

## Thematic Connections

Social Studies: Native American culture

Houghton Mifflin Literary Readers: Changes

# LITERATURE

# *The Gift of the Sacred Dog*

## *by Paul Goble*

The people were hungry. They had walked many days looking for the buffalo herds. Each day they hoped to see the buffalo over the next ridge, but they were not to be found in that part of the country. Even the buzzards and crows circled looking for something to eat, and the wolves called out with hunger at night. The people wandered on until they were too tired and hungry to go any farther, and the dogs could no longer be urged to drag their heavy loads.

The wise men said that they must dance to bring back their relatives, the buffalo. Every man who had dreamed of the buffalo joined in the dance. The buffalo would surely know the people needed them. Young men went out searching in all directions but they did not see any buffalo herds.

There was a boy in the camp who was sad to hear his little brothers and sisters crying with hunger. He saw his mother and father eat nothing so that the children could have what little food there was.

He told his parents: "I am sad to see everyone suffering. The dogs are hungry too. I am going up into the hills to ask the Great Spirit to help us. Do not worry about me; I shall return in the morning."

He left the circle of tipis and walked toward the hills. He climbed higher and higher. The air was cool and smelled fresh with pine trees.

He reached the top of the highest hill as the sun was setting. He raised his arms and spoke: "Great Spirit, my people need your help. We follow the buffalo herds because you gave them to us. But we cannot find them and we can walk no farther. We are hungry. My little brothers and sisters are crying. Great Spirit, we need your help."

As he stood there on the hilltop, great clouds closed across the sky. Wind and hail came with sudden force, and behind them Thunderbirds swooped among the clouds. Lightning darted from their flashing eyes and thunder rumbled when they flapped their enormous wings. He felt afraid and wondered if the Great Spirit had answered him.

The clouds parted. Someone came riding toward the boy on the back of a beautiful animal. There was thunder in its nostrils and lightning in its legs; its eyes shone like stars and hair on its neck and tail trailed like clouds.

The boy had never seen any animal so magnificent.

The rider spoke: "I know your people are in need. They will receive this: he is called Sacred Dog because he can do many things your dogs can do, and also more. He will carry you far and will run faster than the buffalo. He comes from the sky. He is as the wind: gentle but sometimes frightening. Look after him always."

The clouds closed and the rider was not there. Suddenly the sky was filled with Sacred Dogs of all colors and the boy could never count their number. Their galloping was like the wind and the drumming of their hoof beats shook the hilltop on which he stood. They circled round and round and he did not know if he was standing or falling.

He did not remember going to sleep, but he awoke as the sun was rising. He knew it was something wonderful he had seen in the sky. He started down the hill back home again to ask the wise men what it meant. They would be able to tell him. The morning and everything around him was beautiful and good.

When the boy had reached the level plain he heard a sound like far-away thunder coming from the hill behind. Looking back he saw Sacred Dogs pouring out of a cave and coming down a ravine toward him. They were of all colors, just as he had seen in the sky, galloping down the slopes, neighing and kicking up their back legs with excitement.

The leading ones stopped when they were a short distance away. They stamped their feet and snorted, but their eyes were gentle too, like those of the deer. The boy knew they were what he had been promised on the hilltop. He turned and continued walking toward the camp and all the Sacred Dogs followed him.

The people were excited and came out from the camp circle when they saw the boy returning with so many strange and beautiful animals. He told them; "These are Sacred Dogs. They are a gift from the Great Spirit. They will help us to follow the buffalo and they will carry the hunters into the running herds. Now there will always be enough to eat. We must look after them well and they will be happy to live with us."

Life was good after that. The people lived as relatives with the Sacred Dogs, together with the buffalo and all other living things, as the Great Spirit wished them to live.

When the people passed the place where they had hunted the buffalo, they would gather up the bleached skulls in a circle and face them toward the sun. "Let us thank the spirits of the buffalo who died so that we could eat."

A Sioux song for the return of the buffalo:
*The whole world is coming,*
*A Nation is coming, a Nation is coming,*
*The Eagle has brought the message to the tribe,*
*The Father says so, the Father says so.*
*Over the whole earth they are coming,*
*The Buffalo are coming, the Buffalo are coming,*
*The Crow has brought the message to the tribe,*
*The Father says so, the Father says so.*

Sioux songs of horses:
*Friend*
*my horse*
*flies like a bird*
*as it runs.*

*The four winds are blowing;*
*some horses*
*are coming.*

*Daybreak*
*appears*
*when*
*a horse*
*neighs.*

*ravine* a deep, narrow crack in the earth

*bleached* whitened by the sun

◄ Ask students who the Sacred Dogs were and why they were so named. (*Horses. The Cheyenne used dogs to drag their loads as they followed the buffalo. The horses could carry more and travel faster than dogs. They could also carry riders.*)

### EXTEND

Have students imagine being the boy in this story. Have them make up diary entries for the day before the dream or vision and the day after. Suggest that students write about the hunger of the people as well as the coming of the Sacred Dogs. Urge students to include both feelings and events in their diary entries.

**79B**

### Background

Paul Goble has brought us many American Indian stories. Students might be directed to *Custer's Last Battle* (Red Hawk's account), *The Fetterman Fight* (Brave Eagle's account), *Lone Bull's Horse Raid*, *The Friendly Wolf*, and *The Girl Who Loved Wild Horses*, which won the 1979 Caldecott Medal.

80

## INTRODUCE

Read aloud the lesson title and remind students that buffaloes lived on the prairie. Help students recall what they learned about prairies in Unit 1. Discuss the fact that the Cheyenne people lived on the prairie. Point out that this land was very different from the Kwakiutl's forested land near the sea. The Cheyenne had to rely on different sources to meet their needs. Have students read the Thinking Focus and then read the lesson to learn more about how the buffalo helped the Cheyenne meet their needs.

### Key Terms

Vocabulary strategies: T36–T37
**tipi**—cone-shaped tent that can be put up and taken down quickly
**natural resource**—anything found in nature that helps people live

LESSON 1

# Following the Buffalo

**THINKING FOCUS**

*How did the Cheyenne depend on the buffalo?*

### Key Terms

- tipi
- natural resource

➤ *This is part of a painting called* Tall Tales on a Full Stomach. *It was painted in 1985 by Paladine Roye, a Native American artist.*

80

Black Kettle licked buffalo grease from his lips and sighed happily. He looked at the other Cheyenne sitting around the campfire and knew they felt the same way. Their stomachs had not been full for a long time.

Black Kettle knew how it felt to be hungry. The crops had failed to grow this summer. At night, he dreamed about food. Often, he listened to his uncles tell stories about hunger. He wondered how long it would be before they would have another buffalo feast. Hunting buffalo on foot was hard work. His people had followed one herd for almost a week before they got close enough to shoot this buffalo. Even then, the men had been almost too weak from hunger to lift their bows for the kill.

## Objectives

1. Identify who the Cheyenne were and where they lived.
2. Describe the way of life of the Cheyenne.
3. Explain the importance of the buffalo to the Cheyenne.
4. Describe how the horse changed the way of life for the Cheyenne.

## Graphic Overview

**HOW THE CHEYENNE MET THEIR NEEDS**

**Help from the Buffalo**

| food | clothing | shelter | tools |

**Help from the Horse**

| travel faster | hunt buffaloes more easily |

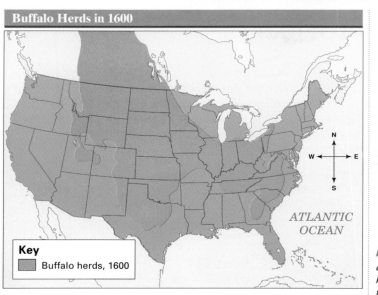

**Buffalo Herds in 1600**

ATLANTIC OCEAN

**Key**

Buffalo herds, 1600

▲ *The Plains Indians used arrowpoints like these to hunt buffalo as long as two thousand years ago. They were chipped into points with bone or stone tools.*

## The Great Provider

If you were a Cheyenne living about 400 years ago, you might have eaten a feast like the one Black Kettle ate. Your family would have farmed and often hunted buffalo in the vast area shown on the map above. The Cheyenne were one of many groups of Plains Indians.

Growing beans, corn, and squash on the plains was difficult. The earth was tough to dig into for planting, and was often dry. If it rained enough, and the Cheyenne had a good harvest, they would eat well. If harvests were small, the Cheyenne hunted whatever animals they could find, such as deer and rabbits. Even so, there often wasn't enough to eat.

Several times during the year, the Cheyenne would leave their homes to hunt buffalo. They camped along the way in tipis *(TEE peez)*. **Tipis** are cone-shaped tents that can be put up and taken down quickly.

To the Cheyenne, the buffalo was a great provider, an important **natural resource**. A natural resource is anything found in nature that helps people live. ■

**Across Time & Space**

*The Cheyenne moved about for a long time. Today, the Cheyenne people are divided into two groups and no longer move. The Northern Cheyenne live in Montana. The Southern Cheyenne live in Oklahoma. Find these states on the United States map on pages 234–235 in the Atlas.*

■ *Why was farming on the plains so difficult for the Cheyenne?*

81

Read aloud, or have a student volunteer prepare a dramatic reading of, the introductory narrative on page 80. Discuss the problem of hunger due to failed crops that Black Kettle and his people faced. Then have students preview the lesson heads to figure out how the Cheyenne tried to meet their needs. You may wish to start the Graphic Overview on the board and have students complete it as they read the lesson.

### GEOGRAPHY
### Map and Globe Skills

Use the map to help students understand the extent of the land where buffalo herds roamed in 1600. Point out that different herds migrated across different areas. Some herds migrated to the south when the northern plains were covered with snow.

Because the Cheyenne moved a great deal, it is difficult to say exactly where they lived. They lived in various places at different times, including present-day Minnesota, North Dakota, South Dakota, and Wyoming.

■ *The earth was tough to dig into for planting, and the land was often dry.*

## Access Strategy

Remind students that in the last chapter they learned about how the Kwakiutl used the resources around them to meet their needs. Explain that in this lesson students will learn how the Cheyenne used their most important resource—the buffalo. Read aloud the lesson title and direct attention to the map on this page. Point out the vast area over which buffaloes once roamed. Explain that buffaloes did not live in one place but traveled in many herds to different places on the prairies.

Tell students that the Cheyenne depended upon the buffalo for food, clothing, shelter, and tools. Help students understand that for these reasons the Cheyenne had to follow the buffalo. Have students speculate about ways in which these people who traveled all the time had to live. Tell students that they will learn more about the lives of the Cheyenne, their need for the buffalo, and the ways in which they used this resource.

## Access Activity

Ask students to think of ways we use animals, such as cows, to provide us with things we need. List the items on the board. After students have read the lesson, have them refer to the list and create a new list to show ways in which the Cheyenne used buffaloes. Then they can compare the two lists.

## ECONOMICS
### Visual Learning

Have students use the illustrations and captions to describe ways in which the Cheyenne used the buffalo. Stress that no part of the animal was wasted. Ask children to try to think of other ways the Cheyenne might have used parts of buffaloes. *(to make shields, rope, drums, cups, spoons, glue, soap, games, jewelry, and much more)*

**More About Tipis** About 15 to 30 buffalo hides were required to make one tipi cover. The average tipi was about 12 feet high and 15 feet across at the bottom. Poles were raised in the form of a cone. The ends of the poles crossed at the top and stuck out beyond the covering. At the top, flaps could either open to let out campfire smoke or close to keep out rain and snow. The tipi walls were pegged to the ground around the bottom. The front had a slit that could be partly closed with wooden pins and used as a doorway.

Women made and put up tipis. Two women could put up a tipi within 1/2 hour.

## A CLOSER LOOK
# The Great Provider

*The buffalo was an important source of food for the Cheyenne. A single buffalo could provide enough meat to feed a hundred people. Everything was used. Nothing was wasted. Today we use softened cowhide to make things we use every day, just as the Cheyenne used buffalo hide.*

**Tipi walls were hides** sewn together with a buffalo-bone needle, and thread that was also made from part of the buffalo. The hides were stretched over wooden poles.

**Rib bones were tied** together with buffalo-hide string to make sleds for moving camp in the snow, or for some winter fun!

### Visual Learning

Write the following headings on the chalkboard: *Food, Clothing, Shelter, Tools.* Have students work in small groups to list how the buffalo was used to provide each of these things for the Cheyenne. Then have students list their own sources of food, clothing, shelter, and tools. Have students contrast the lists.

### Research

Challenge students to find out the height and weight of a buffalo. Discuss how students would find out this information, guiding them to reference books such as an encyclopedia or a nature book. Have them report back on what they found and where they found it. *(A buffalo measures from 5 1/2 to 6 feet at the shoulders, and it usually weighs between 1,600 and 2,000 pounds.)*

**Buffalo fat was mixed** with dried meat, acorns, pine nuts, chokecherries, and honey to make pemmican *(PEHM ih kuhn)*. Pemmican was a healthy food they could eat anytime.

**Cheyenne women stretched** and dried buffalo hides before using them. Look at the buffalo meat drying on racks in the sun. Dried meat could be kept and eaten during the winter.

**Shoes became works of art** when leather moccasins were decorated with beads. The Cheyenne also made dresses, capes, shirts, and warm robes from buffalo hides.

83

## Visual Learning

Direct attention to the tipi. Discuss with students why this form of shelter was particularly well suited to the Cheyenne's way of life. *(It could be taken down and put up quickly, so the Cheyenne could follow the buffalo.)*

**More About Buffalo Robes** Buffalo robes were made from hides. Women skinned the buffalo after the kill; then the long tanning process began. Hides were repeatedly rubbed and stretched. Buffalo brains, liver, fat, and water were used to treat the leather to make it durable and soft.

The buffalo robe was an important piece of winter clothing because winters on the plains could be fiercely cold. The robe was made from one large piece of skin with the fur left on. The side without the fur was usually decorated with designs that were painted onto the skin.

83

## Role-Playing

Have students work in small groups to prepare skits in which they role-play different aspects of the Cheyenne way of life, such as hunting buffaloes, putting up a tipi, preparing food such as pemmican, curing buffalo hides, and drying buffalo meat. Encourage students to use the information in the Closer Look and additional research to make their skits as accurate as possible. Allow time for students to prepare and present their skits.

## Critical Thinking

Tell students that great herds of buffaloes no longer exist in the United States. Today small herds live on government preserves; if they were not protected, the buffalo would probably die out. Have students discuss this question: Why should buffaloes be protected?

## CULTURE

### Critical Thinking

Have students speculate about what the Cheyenne carried from place to place. Then discuss that the Cheyenne used dogs to carry these things before they had horses. Talk about why dogs were less reliable than horses. *(They got into fights and chased other animals.)* Have students contrast Cheyenne life before and after the horse. Discuss how having horses made life easier for the Cheyenne. *(They could travel faster and farther.)*

■ *Hunters could keep up with the herds; horses could pull heavier loads and travel faster than dogs.*

### CLOSE

Have students answer the focus question, referring back to the visuals in the lesson for help, if needed. If necessary, use the Graphic Overview to reteach the lesson.

## Help from the Horse

Picture loading all your belongings onto your back! That's what the Cheyenne did when they hunted buffalo. Everyone went on the hunt—grandparents, parents, and children. Women carried the babies and heavy loads. Men carried bows and arrows, in case an animal might run by. Families tied their bundles onto poles pulled by dogs.

Using dogs to travel wasn't easy. They chased rabbits, got into fights, even took naps! Traveling was so slow the Cheyenne moved only five or six miles a day. It was hard to chase buffalo at that speed!

Then the life of the Cheyenne became easier. About 250 years ago, they got horses from their Spanish and Indian neighbors to the south. As the Cheyenne learned to raise their own horses, they became skillful riders. Now hunters could keep up with the herds. Also, horses could pull heavier loads and travel faster than dogs.

Thanks to the horse, the Cheyenne stopped farming. They moved about freely, setting up new camps along the way as they followed the buffalo all year long. The Cheyenne were rarely hungry again. ■

▼ *Cheyenne men pose with their horses that brought them, their tipis, and their families to a summer celebration on the plains.*

■ *Find details to support this statement: The horse made life easier for the Cheyenne.*

### R E V I E W

1. **FOCUS** How did the Cheyenne depend on the buffalo?
2. **CONNECT** Remember what you learned about prairies. Do you think the Cheyenne had trouble finding wooden poles to put up the tipi? Why?
3. **CRITICAL THINKING** If you had to move around all the time to search for food, do you think you would keep a lot of things? Why?
4. **ACTIVITY** Imagine that you are a Cheyenne. Tear a piece of brown craft paper so that it looks like a buffalo hide. Draw an important scene from your life.

84

## Homework Options

Have each student write a paragraph comparing and contrasting the Kwakiutl's way of life with the Cheyenne's way of life.

**Study Guide:** page 15

## Answers to Review Questions

1. The buffalo provided the Cheyenne with food, clothing, and other useful items. Buffalo hide was used to make tipis, moccasins, shirts, capes, dresses, and robes. Buffalo rib bones were made into sleds.
2. The Cheyenne had trouble finding wooden poles because few trees grew on the prairies.
3. No. It would be best to have only a few belongings. You or your dogs or horses would have to carry your things when you move.
4. Invite students to explain their drawings.

# UNDERSTANDING NATURAL RESOURCES

# We Use Natural Resources

The Cheyenne used the buffalo to provide food, clothing, and shelter. The buffalo were a natural resource. A natural resource is anything found in nature that people can use.

Trees, soil, and water were also natural resources for the Cheyenne. The poles that dogs dragged behind them and that held up Cheyenne tipis came from trees. The Cheyenne raised crops in the soil and drank water from streams.

Today, we use many of the same natural resources. We use trees to make everything from houses to paper to clothing. We also use the soil to grow food. We drink water that comes from rivers, lakes, and underground wells.

Natural resources are also found inside the earth. Things like oil, coal, rocks, and metals are natural resources. Today, we use oil to make gasoline for cars. We burn coal in factories, and we use rocks to make cement sidewalks. We build many things, such as cars, with metals. These resources are as important to us as the buffalo were to the Cheyenne.

85

## UNDERSTANDING NATURAL RESOURCES

This feature identifies early and current examples and uses of natural resources.

### ECONOMICS
### Visual Learning

Call on a volunteer to define natural resources. Have students identify examples of natural resources in the illustration and describe uses for each natural resource. *(Animals: food, clothing. Trees: shelter, paper, boxes. Water: for drinking, for bathing, for washing things. Soil: to grow food. Rocks: to make fences, sidewalks.)*
Be sure students understand that metals include such materials as gold, silver, aluminum, and copper.

85

## Collaborative Learning

Have students work in small groups. Ask each group to rank the natural resources they read about in order of importance—from most important to least important. Advise students to discuss how people use each resource to help them determine where to rank it. Select a volunteer from each group to read its list. Compare the rankings.

## Research

Divide the class into three groups. Assign each group one of these resources: soil, coal, or a metal such as aluminum or copper. Have each group report on how people use the resource.

## Objectives

1. Identify examples of natural resources. (Economics 1)
2. Describe uses of natural resources. (Economics 1)

INTRODUCE

Ask students what medicine is and what it is used for. Then, select a student to read aloud the lesson title and Thinking Focus. Have students discuss what a medicine dance might be used for. Suggest that students read the lesson to find out what *medicine* meant to the Cheyenne and why the Medicine Dance was important to them.

### Key Terms

Vocabulary strategies: T36–T37
**myth**—a story about gods that explains something in nature
**symbol**—something that stands for something else

---

LESSON 2

# The Medicine Dance

### THINKING
# FOCUS

*Why was the Medicine Dance important to the Cheyenne?*

### Key Terms

- myth
- symbol

➤ *This Indian drum shows the Thunderbird. Many groups of Plains Indians believed that the Thunderbird controlled wind, rain, and snow.*

L̲ong ago, no rain had fallen on the land for many days. Grass died and animals starved. There was nothing to eat.

One day, a Cheyenne man and woman set out on a journey. They traveled for many days until they came to a tree-covered mountain. They pushed aside a rock that hid a cave. Inside, they saw an amazing room! Above and around them were wooden poles covered with buffalo robes. In the center stood a tree trunk with a nest of the magical Thunderbird at its top.

Then they heard the deep voice of the spirit Roaring Thunder. Roaring Thunder told the man and woman how to perform a dance. The dance would bring life back to the grasses of the earth and would bring herds of buffalo back to the people.

*Cheyenne myth, retold*

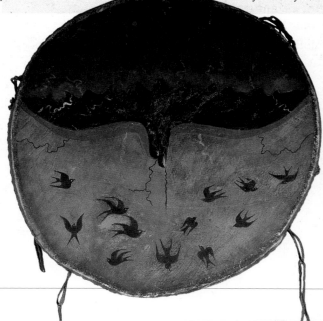

---

## Objectives

1. Identify what the Medicine Dance was.
2. Explain the meaning and importance of the Medicine Dance.
3. Describe how the Medicine Dance was celebrated.

## Graphic Overview

**MEDICINE DANCE**

**What It Meant**

| the cycle of nature | new life comes again |
| --- | --- |

**How It Was Celebrated**

| arranged tipis in circle | built Medicine Dance Tent | feasting and dancing |
| --- | --- | --- |

## The Cycle of Nature

This myth tells how the Cheyenne ceremony called the Medicine Dance began. A **myth** is a story that explains something in nature. This myth was the Cheyenne's way of explaining nature as changes that repeat over and over. We call this repeating pattern the cycle of nature.

To understand this cycle, think about a tree. In the spring, green leaves sprout. The tree grows all summer. In the fall, its leaves turn colors and fall off. During the winter, the tree looks almost dead. When spring comes, new buds appear. Then the cycle begins again.

The Cheyenne saw this cycle all around them. Each year the prairie grass grew and died, the buffalo came and went. The Cheyenne believed there were great powers in nature. They thought of these powers as medicine that could help people. The Cheyenne held a Medicine Dance to get help from these powers.

▼ *Scientists think that Indians from the plains may have held Medicine Dances on this circle called a medicine wheel. It is in Medicine Mountain, Wyoming.*

All the Cheyenne people would arrange their tipis in a huge circle for the eight-day ceremony. A Cheyenne couple took the part of the man and woman in the myth on page 86. The man was a medicine man. The Cheyenne

Read aloud the myth on page 86, explaining that it tells the origin of the Medicine Dance. Then start the Graphic Overview to help students focus on the main ideas of the lesson. Have them fill in the details as they read.

### CULTURE
### Visual Learning

Help students visualize the cycle of nature by drawing the following graphic on the board.

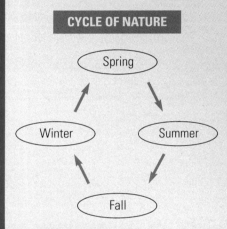

**CYCLE OF NATURE**

Spring
Winter   Summer
Fall

Invite volunteers to point to each season and describe a tree in that season. Clarify for students that buffaloes came and went like the leaves of a tree. When winter came and snow covered the northern plains, the buffaloes left to go farther south where they could find grasses to eat; when spring came, the buffaloes returned.

## Access Strategy

Ask students to name the four seasons and write the names on the chalkboard. Review each season with students and have them describe its weather and how the weather affects plants, animals, and even people. Some students may want to describe the outdoor activities they do for each season.

Then have students describe how a plant, such as a tree, changes as the seasons change. Explain that these changes are part of the cycle of nature. This cycle of nature was very important to the Cheyenne and they honored it with a very important celebration. Tell students they will learn more about the celebration as they read this lesson.

## Access Activity

Have students work in small groups to build models of a Medicine Dance tent. Students may use small sticks and twigs for the poles, and pieces of brown paper bag for the buffalo robes. Sticks may be placed in a clay base. Brown paper may be glued in place.

### Critical Thinking

Have students identify Roaring Thunder as one of the powers of nature. Ask what kind of weather usually comes with thunder. *(rain)* Remind students that rain is needed to grow crops and the grass that attracts buffaloes. Elicit that thunder was important to the Cheyenne because it signaled the onset of life-giving rain.

■ *The Cheyenne believed that because of the cycle of nature, grasses became green again and buffaloes returned to the prairies. This was important because the Cheyenne depended on the buffalo to live.*

### Critical Thinking

Discuss symbols and the fact that the tree was an important symbol in the Medicine Dance. Have students think of symbols that they use in their own celebrations, such as the number of candles on a birthday cake.

**88**

■ *Why was the cycle of nature important to the Cheyenne?*

➤ *These Cheyenne are ready for a Medicine Dance.*

➤ *This leather rattle was used during Medicine Dance ceremonies. It may have been used by the Cheyenne to make a sound like running buffalo.*

88

believed that a medicine man could talk with the powers of nature, such as Roaring Thunder.

The Cheyenne saw everything around them as part of the cycle of nature. All living things begin, grow, and die, but new ones take their place. When the Cheyenne celebrated the Medicine Dance, they were trying to make sure that the cycle of nature would continue. They believed that acting out this myth would help bring new life to the grasses, and would bring herds of buffalo back to the people. ■

## The Medicine Dance Tent

During the Medicine Dance celebration, the Cheyenne made a tent that looked like the mountain room in the myth. In it, they put up a tree like the tree in that room. The tree was the most important symbol in the Medicine Dance. A **symbol** is something that stands for something else. The tree was a symbol of the way life changes and begins again.

The Cheyenne would pick out a special cottonwood tree. Before cutting it down, the chief gave a speech, saying that the tree was a symbol of nature.

## Visual Learning

Have students look at the illustrations of the building of a Medicine Dance tent on page 89. Challenge students to think of additional steps that might be added, such as gathering poles, collecting buffalo robes, and sewing the robes in place.

## Research

Have students find and read other American Indian myths. Students can summarize the stories for the class.

After the Cheyenne cut down the tree and removed its branches, they decorated the top of it with branches and leaves. Women placed bits of brightly colored cloth on the branches. The tree then looked like the nest of the mighty Thunderbird. The nest reminded the Cheyenne of Roaring Thunder because they believed that this spirit flew through the sky in the shape of the Thunderbird.

Next, the Cheyenne put up the decorated tree in the middle of a round tent they had built. The tent was made of a circle of poles tied together. Buffalo robes covered the sides and part of the roof. Standing out from the top of the finished tent was the tree with its nest.

Finally, the dancing began. For the last two days of the ceremony, the Cheyenne would feast and dance around the pole. They celebrated the cycle of nature. ■

■ *How did the Cheyenne use symbols in their celebration of the Medicine Dance?*

## Building a Medicine Dance Tent

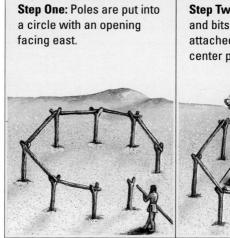

**Step One:** Poles are put into a circle with an opening facing east.

**Step Two:** Leaves, branches, and bits of cloth are attached to a tree trunk. This center pole is raised.

**Step Three:** Buffalo robes are attached to the sides and part of the roof. Now the dance begins.

## R E V I E W

1. **FOCUS** Why was the Medicine Dance important to the Cheyenne?
2. **CONNECT** How are Cheyenne ideas about nature like Kwakiutl ideas about nature?
3. **CRITICAL THINKING** Use an acorn to describe the cycle of nature.
4. **ACTIVITY** Create your own tree from a cardboard tube. Decorate it and add paper branches and leaves to make a Thunderbird nest. Add bits of colored paper to decorate its branches.

89

**CULTURE**
### Critical Thinking

Ask students to think about some of their important holidays and how they are celebrated. Note that the Medicine Dance was an eight-day celebration. Ask students to describe the celebration, comparing and contrasting it to their own celebrations.

■ *The center tree pole was a symbol of the cycle of nature. The Medicine Dance tent was a symbol of the mountain room in the myth.*

**CULTURE**
### Visual Learning

Have students use the diagram on this page to summarize the steps involved in building a Medicine Dance tent. Note that the opening faces east toward the rising sun.

## C L O S E

Have students answer the focus question in their own words. If necessary, use the Graphic Overview to reteach the main ideas of the lesson.

89

### Answers to Review Questions

1. The Cheyenne held a Medicine Dance when they needed help from the powers of nature. They celebrated the Medicine Dance to make sure the cycle of nature would continue.
2. Both the Cheyenne and the Kwakiutl respected nature.
3. Students might say that an acorn represents new life. The acorn grows into a tree, which eventually grows old and dies. But the tree produces other acorns, which continue the cycle of nature.
4. Display students' trees in the classroom.

### Homework Options

Have students draw a picture to illustrate part of the Cheyenne myth that explains the cycle of nature.

**Study Guide:** page 17

## DISCOVERY PROCESS

Students will use the following steps in the discovery process to complete the activity:

**Get Ready** List sources of information about original Native Americans in your local area.

**Find Out** Get information from books and maps and write it in a notebook.

**Move Ahead** Give a report that includes photographs and pictures.

**Explore Some More** Set up a history center with reports, pictures, posters, and models.

*Materials needed:* Encyclopedias, books, and magazine articles about original Native Americans in local area; notebook; drawing materials for pictures and posters; materials to make models

### CULTURE
#### Study Skills

Suggest that students use encyclopedias to begin the search for the names of the groups of people who first lived in the region. Ask students to record the information they find. Suggest that the main headings of their notes include *Houses, Food, Clothing,* and *Way of Life.* You may wish to talk to the school librarian beforehand to make sure that the appropriate reference books are available.

90

EXPLORE

# The First American People

*Try to imagine what your neighborhood was like a long, long time ago. There were no large houses, or wide streets, or busy highways. There were hundreds of different groups of Indian people who first lived in North America. These groups had different names and their own ways of living. Some of them lived where you live today.*

**Get Ready**   In a few places, Native Americans still live where they always did. In other places, you can see what's left of Indian homes. In most places, though, little is left to tell about these early people. How can you learn about the Indians who lived in your area?

**Find Out**   Begin by looking at books and maps to find the names of the Indians who lived in

▲ *Cliff Palace in Mesa Verde National Park, Colorado.*

➤ *Wichita Indian lodges made of logs and earth.*

90

## Objectives

1. Identify the original Native American group or groups who lived in your local community. (Culture 3, 4)
2. Describe the way of life of the original Native American group or groups. (Culture 3, 4)

## Activity

If there are any Native Americans in your class or in your community, invite them to speak on their heritage and their pride in it. If not, ask students who have seen Native American exhibits to share their experiences with the class. If possible, arrange a class trip to a museum exhibit of Native American cultures.

your area. Then read about how they lived, what they ate, what clothes they wore, and what their homes looked like. Write what you learn in a notebook.

**Move Ahead**   Give a report to your classmates. Tell the most interesting facts you discovered about the Indians in your area. Draw pictures to show how they lived. Show photos from the books you looked at.

**Explore Some More**   Set up a history center about the Indians who lived in your area. Display your reports and the pictures you drew. Make a poster with a list of places in your area that have names from these people. Make a model of their homes or make something they used, like a basket or a mask. Invite other students in your school to visit your history center.

Cherokee Indians

The Ingenious Hunting Tactics of Southeastern Indians

*Blowgun at his lips*, a modern Cherokee demonstrates an ancient hunting device made of hollowed-out cane. A dart like the one at his hand can kill a small animal at 60 feet

**Sequoyah** (c. 1773-1843), shown at left with his syllabary of the Cherokee

104

Map of the Original Habitats of the Important Indian Tribes of the United States

HUDSON BAY

The Cherokee lived near us in Georgia

These are masks. They are used in a special dance to help make sick people feel better This one is like a buffalo head.

↑ This is Sequoyah He invented the Cherokee alphabet

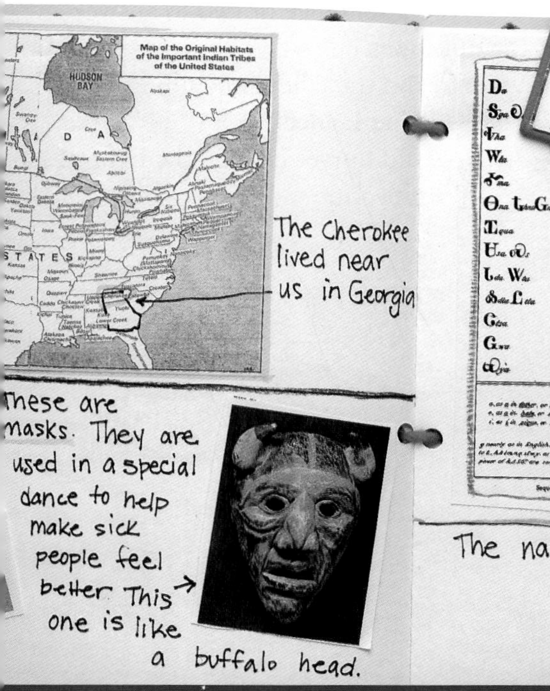

The name Cherokee means "real people."

91

**HISTORY**
## Visual Learning

Explain that a caption is a brief description or explanation of a picture or photograph and often appears just below the picture. Ask students to write captions for the pictures they draw. Point out that the captions will be helpful for visitors to the history center.

## Activity

Make available to students a book of Native American myths and folktales, preferably including some from the local area. Ask volunteers to prepare oral readings of selected tales. Or, have groups of students prepare dramatic enactments of myths or folktales.

## Collaborative Strategy

For recommended strategies for collaborative learning, see pages T34–T35.

**Answers to Reviewing Key Terms**
**A.**
1. natural resource
2. tipi
3. symbol
4. myth
**B.**
1. True
2. True
3. True
4. False. Natural resources are found above and below the ground.

**Answers to Exploring Concepts**
**A.** Food—dried meat and pemmican
   Clothing—dresses, capes, shirts, robes, and shoes
**B.** Sample answers:
1. The Cheyenne held Medicine Dances to get help from the great powers in nature and to ensure that the cycle of nature would continue.
2. Horses helped the Cheyenne become better hunters and helped them move about more easily.

# Chapter Review

## Reviewing Key Terms

myth (p. 87)          symbol (p. 88)
natural resource (p. 81)   tipi (p. 81)

**A.** Write the key term that best completes each sentence.
1. Something found in nature that people can use is a _____.
2. A _____ is a cone-shaped tent.
3. Something that stands for something else is a _____.
4. A _____ is a story that explains something in nature.

**B.** Write *true* or *false* for each sentence below. If a sentence is false, rewrite it to make it true.
1. Myths were important in the life of the Cheyenne.
2. To the Cheyenne, a tree was a symbol of the way life changes.
3. Tipis can be put up and taken down quickly.
4. All natural resources are found above ground.

## Exploring Concepts

**A.** The buffalo was very important to the Cheyenne. It supplied food and was used to make clothing and homes. Copy the cluster diagram below. Fill in the empty spaces. Your diagram will show how the Cheyenne used the buffalo.

**B.** Write a sentence or two to answer the questions below.
1. Why did the Cheyenne hold the Medicine Dances?
2. How did horses change the lives of the Cheyenne?

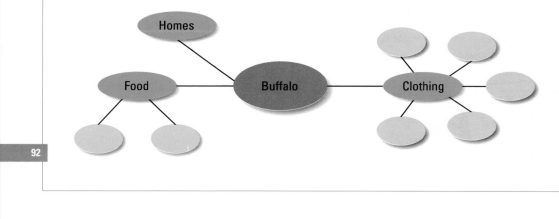

## Reviewing Skills

1. The line graph at the right shows how much water was used in a town during a six-month period. In which of the six months was the most water used? In which month was the least used? How many thousand gallons of water were used in July?

2. Look at the map on page 81. Then look at the map on pages 238–239. What physical features are part of the land where the Cheyenne hunted buffalo?

**Water Used for Six Months**

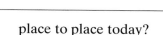

Thousands of Gallons

900
800
700
600
500
400

May  June  July  Aug.  Sept.  Oct.

**Months**

## Using Critical Thinking

1. When the Cheyenne moved from place to place, they tied their belongings to poles which were pulled by dogs or horses. How do we move our belongings from place to place today?

2. The Cheyenne were not able to grow as many crops as they needed. How might they have improved their farming?

## Preparing for Citizenship

1. **ART ACTIVITY** Draw and color pictures to show the cycle of nature. You should have one picture for each of the four seasons.

2. **COLLABORATIVE LEARNING** As a class project, make a model of the Cheyenne gathering for a Medicine Dance ceremony. Your model should have tipis in a large circle around the Medicine Dance tent. Use straws, clay, colored paper, and other materials you can find.

**CHAPTER ORGANIZER**

# Chapter 6 *In Red Rock Country*

## CHAPTER PLANNING CHART

| Pupil's Edition | Teacher's Edition | Ancillaries |
|---|---|---|
| **Literature Selection: *The Desert Is Theirs*** | | Discovery Journal (12, 13) |
| **Lesson 1: A Desert Homeland (4–5 days)** | • Graphic Overview (98) | Study Guide (18) |
| | • Access Strategy (99) | |
| Objective 1: Identify who the Navajo were and where they lived. (History 3, Geography 1)* | • Access Activity (99) Language Arts Connection (100) | |
| Objective 2: Describe the Navajo way of life. (Culture 2, 4) | Religious Context (100) | |
| Objective 3: Identify the natural resources used by the Navajo. (Economics 1) | | |
| Objective 4: Identify skills the Navajo learned from their neighbors. (History 6, Culture 1) | | |
| **Understanding Human Adaptation: We Adapt to Our Surroundings** | | Study Guide (19) |
| Objective 1: Define adaptation. (Geography 3) | | |
| Objective 2: Identify examples of human adaptation. (Geography 3) | | |
| **Lesson 2: Sand Painting (4–5 days)** | • Graphic Overview (103) | Discovery Journal (14) |
| | • Access Activity (104) | Study Guide (20) |
| Objective 1: Describe a sand painting. (Culture 2, 5) | • Access Strategy (104) | • Study Print (7) |
| Objective 2: Explain how the Navajo used sand paintings. (Belief Systems 4) | Historical Context (105) Music Connection (106) | |
| Objective 3: Identify the meanings of symbols used in sand paintings. (Culture 6) | Research (106) | |
| **Understanding Maps: Using Scale** | | Map Activity (7) |
| | | Study Guide (21) |
| Objective 1: Use a map scale to determine actual distances. (Map and Globe Skills 4) | | |
| Objective 2: Draw a map to scale. (Map and Globe Skills 5) | | |
| **Chapter Review** | Answers (110–111) | Chapter 6 Test |

\* Objectives are correlated to the strands and goals in the program scope and sequence on pages T41–T48.

• LEP appropriate resources. (For additional strategies, see pages T32–T33.)

This chapter is the last in a unit on the first American people. In chapters 4 and 5, students learned about Indian groups who used the natural resources of oceans, rivers, forests, and prairies. Chapter 6 examines a desert people, the Navajo. In Chapter 3, students learned about the characteristics of deserts and how plants and animals adapt to desert conditions. This knowledge will help them appreciate how the Navajo have adapted to the deserts of the Southwest.

Chapter 6 begins with a literature selection, an excerpt from a book called *The Desert Is Theirs*. The selection describes an Indian group's close relationship with the land. It also depicts desert plant and animal life.

**Lesson 1** examines how the Navajo used the natural resources of the desert. The lesson points out that the Navajo borrowed ideas and acquired certain skills from neighboring groups. Students will also add to their knowledge of the belief systems of Indian groups as they read about Navajo myths.

**Lesson 2** focuses on sand painting, one of the ways that the Navajo expressed their reverence for nature and the land. The feature A Closer Look: Reading a Sand Painting explains the symbols in a specific sand painting.

Chapter 6 includes the feature Understanding Human Adaptation, which expands students' understanding of the meaning of adaptation. In this chapter and throughout this book, adaptation to the land is a major theme.

### LEP: Telling Myths and Legends

After concluding Lesson 2, ask students to think about myths and legends in their own cultures. Have volunteers choose a myth or legend and tell it to the rest of the class. Ask the volunteer to explain the myth or legend and allow time for class discussion.

### Basic: Making Natural Dyes

After reading Lesson 2, have students make their own natural dyes. Provide dry onion skins and purple grapes (or bottled grape juice), bowls, and pieces of white cotton fabric. Have students pour boiling water over the onion skins to make light brown dye and crush the grapes, adding water as needed, to make purple dye. Students can then add small pieces of white cotton cloth to each mixture. Suggest that students let some pieces remain in each mixture longer than others. Dry the cloth on old newspapers and compare the intensity of the colors.

### Research

After concluding Lesson 1, have students do research to find out more about the Navajo or other Native Americans of the Southwest today, such as the Papago, the Apache, the Hopi, the Zuni, and the Yuma. Allow time for students to present their findings orally in class and discuss similarities and differences.

### Reader's Theater

After students have read Lesson 2, make available Navajo legends from such sources as Edward and M. P. Dolch's *Navajo Stories*, Garrard Publishing Co., and Richard Redhawk's *Grandfather Stories: Navajo Indian Children's Tales*, Sierra Oaks Publishing Co. Call on volunteers to give dramatic readings of some Navajo legends.

**93B**

CHAPTER
# PREVIEW

sk a volunteer to read aloud the chapter title and introductory paragraph. Tell students that the name *Red Rock Country* refers to the deserts in the southwestern United States. The name comes from the color of the earth in much of the area. Locate this area on a classroom map of the United States.

Have students look at the visuals and read the captions to predict what the chapter will be about. *(the way of life and the art of the Navajo)*

## Looking Back

Have students discuss why meeting basic needs might have been more difficult for the Navajo than for the Kwakiutl or Cheyenne. *(The Kwakiutl had fish from the sea, and the Cheyenne had buffalo from the plains; neither of these resources was available to the Navajo in the desert.)*

## Looking Forward

The Navajo culture is the topic of the next two lessons: A Desert Homeland and Sand Painting.

**94**

## Chapter 6

# In Red Rock Country

*The southwestern deserts do not have oceans alive with fish, or prairies covered with thundering herds of buffalo. The deserts are hot, dry lands where it is difficult to find the resources needed to live. The Navajo (NAV uh hoh) people, however, discovered many ways to find the food, clothing, and shelter they needed from their red rock country.*

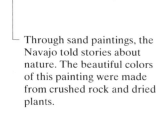

Through sand paintings, the Navajo told stories about nature. The beautiful colors of this painting were made from crushed rock and dried plants.

The mud that covers the outside of Navajo homes has always helped protect the people from winter cold and summer heat.

94

## BACKGROUND

The Navajo and Cheyenne cultures evolved in opposite directions. The Cheyenne stayed in one place to farm until they acquired horses. Then they became nomadic hunters. The Navajo started out as nomadic hunters and gatherers who gradually settled down and became farmers and shepherds.

**Life in the Desert**

Ancestors of the Navajo migrated from northern Canada and Alaska to the Southwest. They led nomadic lives as hunters and gatherers and raided nearby villages until they learned to farm and raise sheep in the 1600s.

The Navajo were an extremely adaptable people. They borrowed from other cultures to live better on the land. They most likely learned to farm from their neighbors the Pueblo, and they acquired sheep from Spaniards, who first brought these animals to

the country.

Of the crops the Navajo raised, corn was the most important. Men tended the corn, and women ground it into flour and cooked it in many ways. Corn also played an important part in the spiritual lives of the Navajo. They used corn pollen and corn meal in blessings to restore health and life.

The Navajo also learned loom weaving and metalworking from their neighbors and quickly improved on these skills. By 1700 the Navajo were well known for the fine quality of their woven goods. In the 1800s the

*Navajo Weavers* was painted by Harrison Begay, a Navajo artist. Note that the women in the painting are wearing the same type of clothing as the women in the photograph on page 94. Many Navajo still follow old ways of life on a reservation in Arizona, New Mexico, and Utah.

The Navajo still raise sheep for their wool today, just as they did long ago.

This painting, called *Navajo Weavers,* shows how women have woven wool rugs and blankets for hundreds of years.

Navajo began to outdo their Mexican teachers by making masterful silver and turquoise jewelry.

### The Navajo Today

The Navajo today still live in the Southwest. They are the largest group of Native Americans left in the United States. The Navajo reservation covers 14 million acres in the states of New Mexico, Arizona, and Utah. The Navajo still raise sheep, and skilled craftworkers still weave beautiful wool blankets and make turquoise jewelry.

However, most of the Navajo's wealth now comes from mining rich coal and uranium deposits found on their reservation.

## INTRODUCE

## INTRODUCE

Explain that the author, Byrd Baylor, spent much of her childhood in the southwestern part of the United States. Many of her books are story poems about the land and the people of the Southwest. Point out that in this selection, students will read about Indians who live in the desert and how they feel about their desert home.

## READ AND RESPOND

Have students read the selection with partners. Before students read, ask how they think people might feel about living in a desert. Suggest that they read to check their predictions.

*You have read how the desert can be a harsh place to live. How do the people who live there feel about it? Read this excerpt from a book-length poem to find out who calls the desert theirs.*

LITERATURE

# THE DESERT IS THEIRS

**Written by Byrd Baylor**

**Illustrated by Peter Parnall**

This is no place
for anyone
who wants
soft hills
and meadows
and everything
green
green
green . . .

This is for hawks
that like only
the loneliest canyons
and lizards
that run
in the hottest sand
and
coyotes
that choose
the rockiest trails.

It's for them.

And for
birds
that nest
in cactus
and sing out over
a thousand thorns
because
they're where
they want to be.

96

## Thematic Connections

Social Studies: Deserts, culture

Houghton Mifflin Literary Readers: Changes

## Background

The desert people described in *The Desert Is Theirs* are Papago Indians whose original home was southern Arizona near the Mexican border. Because of the extremely dry conditions, the Papago moved between two areas. They spent the summers in their villages deep in the desert. Water from heavy rainstorms was collected in ditches and used to irrigate their crops of pumpkins, beans, and corn. In the winter months, the Papago moved to their villages near streams in the mountains. During these months, they relied on game for food.

It's for them.

And for
hard skinny plants
that do without water
for months
at a time.

And it's for
strong brown Desert People
who call the earth
their mother.

They *have* to see
mountains
and *have* to see
deserts
every day . . .
or they don't feel right.

They wouldn't leave
even for rivers
or flowers
or bending grass.
They'd miss
the sand too much.
They'd miss
the sun.

So
it's for them.

Talk to Papago Indians.
They're
Desert People.

They know
desert secrets
that no one else
knows.

Ask
how they live
in a place
so harsh and dry.

They'll say
they *like*
the land they live on
so they treat it well—
the way you'd treat
an old friend.
They sing it songs.
They never hurt it.

And the land knows.

◄ Ask students why the Papago Indians call the earth their mother. *(They feel they are part of the land. They get food, water, and other necessities from the land.)*

## EXTEND

Have students draw a desert scene on one side of an index card to make a postcard. On the other side, have them write a brief message about their impressions of the desert and its dwellers based on reading *The Desert Is Theirs*.

## Reader's Theater

Divide the class into two groups. Have each group perform a choral reading of the poem while the other group listens, so that each student has the chance to both perform and be in the audience.

## Further Reading

You may want to have your students look for more books to read on this topic in the school or local library.

# INTRODUCE

Ask how the Papago Indians in *The Desert Is Theirs* felt about the desert. *(They considered it a friend.)* Have a volunteer read aloud the lesson title and Thinking Focus. Invite students to speculate about how the Navajo regarded their desert home. Have students read the lesson to check their predictions.

## Key Terms

Vocabulary strategies: T36–T37
**hogan**—one-room house built with mud and logs by the Navajo
**livestock**—farm animals, such as cows, horses, and sheep, raised to be used or sold
**adaptation**—a change in the way of life of people, animals, or plants in order to fit their surroundings.

---

LESSON 1

# A Desert Homeland

## THINKING
## FOCUS

*How did the Navajo use the natural resources of the land?*

### Key Terms

- hogan
- livestock
- adaptation

*I* see the Earth.
I am looking at Her and smile
Because She makes me happy.
The Earth, looking back at me
is smiling too.
May I walk happily
And lightly
on Her.

Ancient Navajo prayer

This prayer is one of many Navajo prayers about the earth. The Navajo called the earth Changing Woman. Changing Woman was one of the most important spirits in Navajo myths. The Navajo believed that she took care of them in many ways.

➤ *This Navajo is riding through Valley of the Gods in Utah. This area is called red rock country because of the color of the earth.*

---

## Objectives

1. Identify who the Navajo were and where they lived.
2. Describe the Navajo way of life.
3. Identify the natural resources used by the Navajo.
4. Identify skills the Navajo learned from their neighbors.

## Graphic Overview

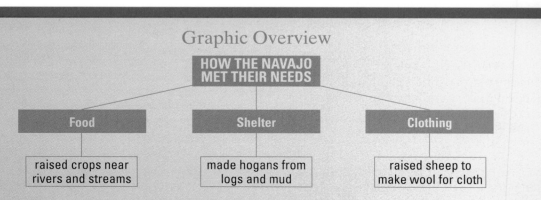

**HOW THE NAVAJO MET THEIR NEEDS**

| Food | Shelter | Clothing |
|------|---------|----------|
| raised crops near rivers and streams | made hogans from logs and mud | raised sheep to make wool for cloth |

## Living Close to the Earth

One of the ways the Navajo believed Changing Woman helped them was by giving them the first hogan. A **hogan** is a one-room house. Navajo have lived in hogans for hundreds of years. In Navajo myths, Changing Woman's hogan was made of shells and turquoise *(TUR kwoyz)*, a blue-green stone. When the Navajo made hogans, they made them from mud and logs.

The Navajo lived in the deserts of the southwestern United States. Hogans were good houses for desert living. The mud walls and roofs kept hogans cool in summer and warm in winter. A hogan did not have windows, and the doorway faced east toward the rising sun.

▼ *This Navajo family is standing in front of a hogan in Monument Valley, Utah.*

One family lived in each hogan. Women sat on the north side of a hogan. Men sat on the south side. The west side, the side that faced the doorway, was saved for guests.

In the center of the hogan was a fire that was used for cooking. There was a hole in the roof above the fire to let out smoke. At night a family slept on sheepskins around the fire. ■

■ *How did hogans help the Navajo stay comfortable in the desert?*

## Borrowing from Others

The Navajo had many myths to explain changes in their lives. For example, the Navajo believed that Changing Woman, the spirit who gave them hogans, also taught them how to grow corn. Actually, hundreds of years ago, the Navajo learned how to grow corn from another group of Indians. They probably also learned how to grow beans and squash from these people.

How did the Navajo raise corn and other crops in the dry deserts of the Southwest? They learned to farm near

99

**DEVELOP**

Read aloud the ancient Navajo prayer on page 98, and discuss the reverence for the land that it evokes. Point out that this is a reoccurring theme in everything students have read about the Americans who inhabited this country originally. You may wish to start the Graphic Overview to help students focus on how the Navajo used the land to meet their basic needs.

**CULTURE**
Visual Learning

Direct attention to the photograph of the hogan and have students describe it. Be sure students note that the hogan is windowless and has a rounded roof and thick walls. Point out that these features kept the hogan cool in summer and warm in winter.

■ *The mud walls and roof kept hogans cool in summer and warm in winter.*

99

### Access Strategy

Write *Kwakiutl* and *Cheyenne* on the board or on chart paper. Help students recall how these two native groups used available resources to meet their basic needs for food, shelter, and clothing. *(Kwakiutl got fish from the sea, and used trees from the forests to build homes and make clothing; the Cheyenne hunted buffalo on the plains for food, and they used its hide for clothing and shelter.)*

Suggest that students read to find out the same kind of information about the Navajo.

### Access Activity

Make a simple loom by cutting slits about 1/4 inch apart at the top and bottom of a piece of cardboard. Thread yarn vertically between slits until the cardboard is full. Provide students with extra pieces of yarn. Have them experiment with weaving designs by pulling their pieces of yarn over and under the yarn on the cardboard.

### Across Time & Space

*The Navajo are known for their fine weaving. Early Navajo left a hole in each blanket they wove to thank Spider Woman for the gift of weaving. They quit making these holes when they began selling blankets to traders.*

▼ *The Navajo still live in the Southwest today. They are the largest group of Native Americans.*

**The Navajo Today**

Utah

Colorado

Navajo

Arizona

Rio Grande

New Mexico

Oklahoma

Texas

MEXICO

**Key**
☐ Navajo land today

100

streams so that they would have water for their plants.

Corn became very important to the Navajo. They used it in many of their ceremonies because they believed it brought good luck and a long and healthy life.

### The Gift of Weaving

The Navajo also believed that weaving was a gift from a spirit. Their myths said Spider Woman taught them to weave. She lived in a tall, thin rock called Spider Rock. This rock still stands in what is now Arizona.

Neighboring Indians that had taught the Navajo to grow crops also taught them to weave cotton. The Navajo quickly improved on this way of weaving. They discovered that wool was even better than cotton for weaving. Wool was stronger and easier to dye, or color.

The Navajo were well known for their beautiful weaving. They began making wool cloth by shearing, or shaving, the wool from the sheep they had raised. Then they spun this wool into yarn. They used natural resources of the earth, such as plants and berries, to dye the wool. Then they wove the wool on a wooden loom. Before long, they had a beautiful piece of cloth to make into clothing or blankets.

### Raising Animals

Soon after the Navajo learned to weave, they learned how to raise livestock. Animals, such as sheep or horses, that are raised to be used or traded are called **livestock.** The

---

### GEOGRAPHY
## Map and Globe Skills

Point to the inset map of the United States and help students locate the part of the country shown on the larger map. Explain that most Navajo now live on reservations, areas set aside for use by Native Americans. Have students identify the states where the Navajo live today.

## Critical Thinking

Have students list Navajo gods and their gifts. *(Changing Woman, corn and hogan; Spider Woman, weaving)* Help students see that these gifts were basic to life: food, shelter, and clothing. Ask students how Navajo gods are like teachers and parents. *(They teach skills and take care of people.)*

## Language Arts Connection

Have students work in small groups of three for this activity. Direct students to the poem on page 98. Have each group present an oral reading of the poem. Students may choose to recite the poem chorally or to have each student recite one or two lines. Have each group present its reading to the class. If possible, have students find other Navajo poems that they can recite for the class.

## Religious Context

The religion of certain cultures is based on the belief in many gods, or spirits. Some of these gods have power over many forces in nature and others are less powerful. Such religions have existed from the beginning of our history to the present day and are found in cultures around the world.

**Making a Blanket**

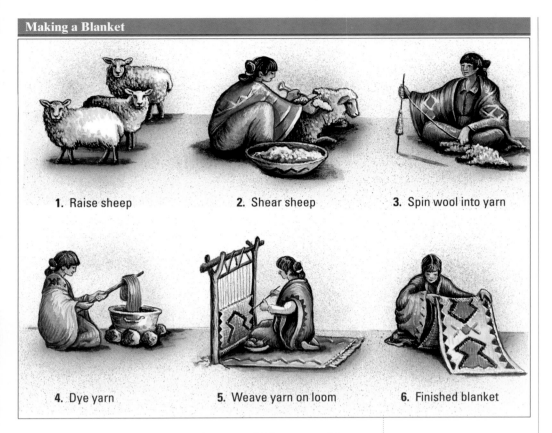

1. Raise sheep
2. Shear sheep
3. Spin wool into yarn
4. Dye yarn
5. Weave yarn on loom
6. Finished blanket

Navajo needed sheep so that they would have wool for weaving. They also raised goats and horses.

The way in which the Navajo learned to live in the desert is an example of adaptation. When people change the way they live to fit their surroundings, it is called **adaptation.** The Navajo used natural resources and ideas from others to live well in the desert. ■

■ *What skills did the Navajo learn from their neighbors?*

---

## R E V I E W

1. **FOCUS** How did the Navajo use the natural resources of the land?
2. **CONNECT** How are Navajo hogans different from Kwakiutl long houses and Cheyenne tipis?
3. **CRITICAL THINKING** Why did the Navajo use the name Spider Woman for the spirit who taught them to weave?
4. **WRITING ACTIVITY** Pretend you are sitting inside a Navajo hogan. Write a description of the hogan. Describe its shape and where people are sitting. Draw a picture to go with your description.

101

**CULTURE**

**Visual Learning**

Explain that weaving a blanket required many steps. Direct attention to the process diagram at the top of the page. Explain that wool had to be twisted, pulled, and spun over a long stick many times before it was strong enough and fine enough to be woven on a loom. Point out that a loom is a wooden frame that is threaded with the vertical yarn first. Weaving is done by passing a second piece of yarn horizontally, in and out of the yarn already on the loom. Have students speculate about how the Navajo got ideas for the designs they created. *(things from nature, such as plants or stars, or shapes, such as a circle or a diamond)*

■ *From their neighbors, the Navajo learned how to plant corn, beans, and squash; how to raise livestock; and how to weave.*

**C L O S E**

Have students answer the focus question in their own words. If necessary, use the Graphic Overview to stress the ways in which the Navajo used available resources to meet their basic needs.

---

## Answers to Review Questions

1. The Navajo made hogans out of logs covered with mud. They grew corn, beans, and squash near streams, and they raised livestock. They got wool from sheep to weave cloth for clothing and blankets.
2. Hogans are made of mud and logs, long houses are made of wood, and tipis are made of buffalo hides. Hogans and tipis are round; long houses are rectangular. Hogans are smaller than long houses.
3. The Navajo probably thought of weaving as being similar to a spider spinning a web.
4. Students' writing should include features of a hogan; that is, a round, windowless house with the women sitting on the north side and the men on the south side. A cooking fire is in the center.

## Homework Options

Have students find out more about other Southwestern Indian groups, such as the ancient Anasazi. Students can report their findings orally in class.

**Study Guide:** page 18

## UNDERSTANDING HUMAN ADAPTATION

This feature expands the definition of adaptation introduced in the previous lesson and teaches students to identify examples of human adaptation.

### Visual Learning

Ask what *adaptation* means. Make sure students understand that adaptation can occur in two ways—people might change their behavior to adapt to their environment (by wearing more clothes in cold weather, for example) or they may change the environment (by using irrigation to bring water to dry land, for instance). Call on volunteers to describe ways that people in their area have adapted to the place where they live.

## UNDERSTANDING HUMAN ADAPTATION

# We Adapt to Our Surroundings

At one time, the Navajo hunted animals for food. They made clothes from the skins of those animals. When they moved to the hot and dry desert, the Navajo could not find enough wild animals for food and clothing. They had to learn to raise their own animals. They learned how to weave animal hair to make clothing. They also learned how to grow crops, such as corn, beans, and squash. Changing the way we live to fit our surroundings, as the Navajo did, is called adaptation.

Adaptation still takes place today. For example, if you move from Florida to Alaska, you will have to change the way you dress. You will need warmer clothing in Alaska.

Adaptation also happens when people change their surroundings. For example, many people who live in hot climates keep cool by using air conditioning. Farmers in dry climates give their crops water to help them grow, as in the picture below of round corn fields in Kansas.

People often adapt to their surroundings. They change the way they live or they change the area around them.

## Objectives

1. Define adaptation. (Geography 3)
2. Identify examples of human adaptation. (Geography 3)

## Art Connection

Help students name various places in the United States that differ in climate and landscape from the area where they live by listing the Rocky Mountains, Kansas plains, Arizona desert, Maine coastline, and New York City on the chalkboard. Encourage students to extend the list. Then assign each student to select two of the listed locations. Have students draw pictures of themselves as though they lived in each location. Suggest that they consider clothing, housing, food, and recreation. Display the pictures and discuss with students how they changed to adapt to their surroundings.

LESSON 2

# Sand Painting

A pink sunrise colored the sky as we reached the hogan. My teacher, the medicine man, was quiet. He was thinking about the sick girl he had come to help. The girl's worried family and friends waited outside as we entered. Kneeling beside her, he closed his eyes. Then he began to sing the words of a ceremony used to treat her sickness. The words retold a myth of our people.

Years before, my teacher was a helper like me. He had learned the words from his teacher, a great medicine man who knew hundreds of **chants,** or prayers that are sung. I knew that, in a while, he would finish singing and make pictures of nature. Every chant and picture must be correct so that the girl would get well. I watched him and sighed. How would I ever learn all that I would need to know to become a medicine man myself someday?

**THINKING**
**FOCUS**

*Why was sand painting important to the Navajo?*

### Key Terms

- chant
- sand painting

◄ *Today, Navajo medicine men still make sand paintings. This medicine man takes a pinch of color from one of the bowls and sprinkles it in a design to make a beautiful work of art.*

103

**INTRODUCE**

Select a volunteer to read the lesson title. Discuss the kinds of activities students have done with sand. Remind students of the Cheyenne Medicine Dance they read about in the last chapter. Note that the Navajo also had many ceremonies, one of which was often used to heal the sick. Have students read the Thinking Focus. Suggest that they read the lesson to find out why sand paintings were important to the Navajo.

### Key Terms

Vocabulary strategies: T36–T37
**chant**—prayer that is sung
**sand painting**—picture made from crushed rock, plants, and other dry materials

Graphic Overview

**SAND PAINTING**

| **Description** | **Uses** | **Meaning** |

### Objectives

1. Describe a sand painting.
2. Explain how the Navajo used sand paintings.
3. Identify the meanings of symbols used in sand paintings.

## D E V E L O P

Read aloud the first-person narrative on page 103. Discuss the role of the medicine man in making a sand painting and his reasons for doing it. Then have students preview the lesson by reading the headings and looking at the illustrations. You may wish to copy the Graphic Overview on the board and have students add details to it as they study the lesson.

### BELIEF SYSTEMS
#### Critical Thinking

Discuss why the spirits told the Navajo to paint their pictures on the ground. *(because people might fight to get them)* Note that the sand paintings were believed to contain the power of nature and so were very valuable.

## Close to Nature

The medicine man's young helper that you just read about believed that the chants and sand paintings had been given to the Navajo by the spirits of nature. **Sand paintings** are pictures made with bits of crushed rock, plants, and other dry materials. The paintings tell stories about nature and Navajo spirits.

The Navajo believed that, long ago, the spirits told them to paint pictures on the ground with colors of the earth. The spirits warned the Navajo not to save the paintings because people might fight to get them. So the Navajo made sand paintings on the earth floors of their hogans and swept them up after 12 hours. In that time, the power of the painting would have helped those who needed it.

▼ *Here is a finished sand painting. It shows the four Wind People spirits. Each spirit rules the wind from one of the four directions of the earth. In one hand they hold clouds, in the other they hold a feather used to make the winds blow.*

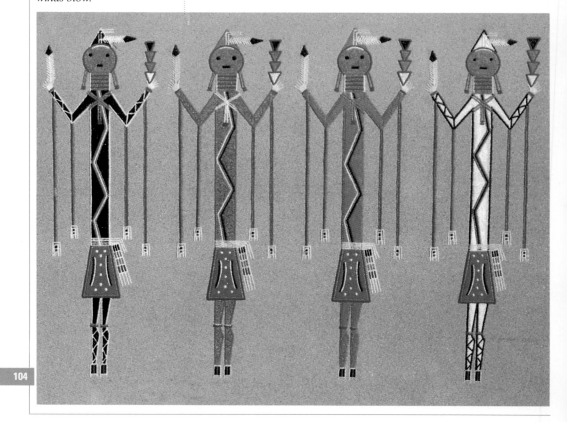

## Access Activity

Provide students with shallow boxes and sand of different colors. *(You can make colored sand by mixing powdered tempera paints with sand.)* Have students try to create designs by sprinkling sand into their boxes. Discuss the results and the difficulty of achieving good designs with such a medium.

## Access Strategy

Remind students that in the last chapter they read about how the Cheyenne lived and about a special celebration the Cheyenne had, the Medicine Dance. Explain that this lesson describes a ceremony of the Navajo, sand painting. Point out the photographs in the lesson and help students verbalize what they notice about the paintings.

Then discuss with students what happens when they are sick. *(They might need to go to a doctor and take medicine.)* Point out that the Navajo also had a way to help sick people become well again. The Navajo believed that sand paintings, together with chants and herbal medicines, brought a sick person closer to nature and gave the person strength.

The Navajo first learned sand painting from other Indians who lived nearby. But in Navajo myths, the Wind People taught the Navajo how to make sand paintings. The Wind People are the spirits of nature whom you just saw in the sand painting on page 104.

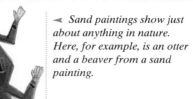

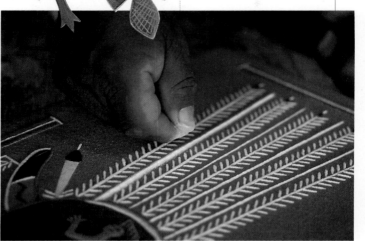

◄ *Sand paintings show just about anything in nature. Here, for example, is an otter and a beaver from a sand painting.*

The Navajo believed that living happily with the land, the air, and all living things was the only way to stay healthy. If someone got sick, they thought that using the art of the Wind People in ceremonies would make the person well.

A ceremony to help someone get well often included many chants and several sand paintings. A medicine man would sing the chants and create the paintings. Each painting told a story about people and spirits in Navajo myth. The Navajo believed that when a sick person sat inside the painting, its power would help that person get well. ■

▲ *The Navajo used 500 different sand paintings. A medicine man had to remember each line, since pictures of the paintings were not kept in any book.*

■ *How did the Navajo use sand paintings?*

## A Story to Tell

The Navajo wondered how and why things in nature came to be. Why do big rocks exist? Where do mountains come from? What makes the wind blow and the rain fall? The Navajo told myths to answer these questions.

In myths, things in nature often became spirits who explained why things happened. For example, real rainbows in the sky became the Rainbow People in stories and sand paintings. Let's look at a sand painting of the Rainbow People and the story it tells about nature.

## Critical Thinking

Write *close to nature* on the chalkboard. Discuss with students that the Navajo believed being close to nature was important to their health and happiness. Explain that being close to nature involves the understanding that people are a part of nature, just as animals, clouds, and plants are a part of nature. All things in nature, including people, depend on other parts of nature to stay alive and to be healthy and happy.

Ask students to describe how a sand painting helped a sick person get better. *(When the sick person sat inside the painting, the strength of the spirit or person in the myth would enter the sick person's body and help that person get well.)*

■ *The Navajo used sand painting to help sick people get well.*

105

## Historical Context

The ancient ancestors of the Navajo migrated from the north, from Alaska and Canada, and may not have settled in the Southwest until A.D. 1000 or later. Many people think that the Navajo learned various skills from the Pueblo, including agriculture, weaving, and sand painting. In the 1800s, the Navajo learned metalworking from the Mexicans. The Navajo are famous for their silverwork and for their intricate weaving.

## Study Skills

Have students do research to find out more about the Navajo or sand paintings and the stories behind the figures and designs used in them. Discuss how students might find the answers to these questions, guiding them to reference books like an encyclopedia or books about Indians. Have students report their findings to the class.

CULTURE

## Visual Learning

Direct attention to the sand painting. Call on volunteers to read each section aloud. Ask students to identify the colors used and what each color represented. Have students locate the Rainbow People and the black hole in the center of the sand painting. Have students locate the four clouds from each of the four directions; they are inside the inner square formed by the bars the spirits are standing on. Each cloud shows a dragonfly—a messenger of the sun and sunlight. Discuss the significance of each symbol. *(The Rainbow People were Navajo gods; the hole represents the source of all water on earth, clouds and sunlight mix to form rainbows.)*

### More About Protection Bands

Each sand painting has an opening, and three sides that are closed off and protected by a protection band. The opening faces east, a direction from which evil cannot enter easily. The other three sides must be protected. To do this, a continuous design is usually made to encircle the vulnerable southern, western, and northern sides. The most frequently used design is the Rainbow Spirit pictured here.

# Reading a Sand Painting

*This Rainbow People sand painting tells part of a Navajo myth that explains that water is a source of life. The circle in the center of the sand painting is a symbol for the source of all water on earth.*

**Look at the colors!** The Navajo use white to show east, black for north, blue for south, and yellow for west. These colors come from crushed rocks and plants.

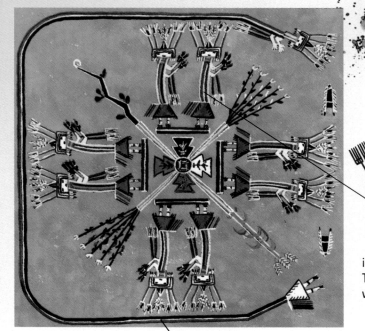

**Navajo spirits with long bodies** are shown on most sand paintings. The spirits in this painting are Rainbow People. They are wearing tall hats topped with feathers.

**To protect the painting's power,** another rainbow spirit wraps her extra-long body around three sides of the sand painting. Most sand paintings have protection bands like this.

106

---

## Visual Learning

Have students work in small groups. Discuss the symbols that the Navajo had. Ask each group to think of one or two symbols that could be associated with the society we live in today. Have each group draw pictures of the symbols and explain them.

## Music Connection

Obtain a recording from your public library of Native American chants and play it for the students. Choose one of the chants and write the "words" on the chalkboard. Help students learn the chant and perform it together.

## Research

Have students work in small groups to research other skills the Navajo had, such as metalworking, pottery, and rugmaking. Have each group choose one area to report on to the rest of the class.

Why do you think the Navajo told myths about the Rainbow People? Suppose you lived in a hot, dry desert. What would your most important resource be? If you said "water," you would be right. That's why you would always be happy to see a rainbow. It is a sign that rain has come.

Rainbow People were often used to protect three sides of sand paintings. That is because the Navajo felt safe when they saw a rainbow. It was a sign that life-giving rain had brought water to their crops.

Look at the Rainbow People sand painting on page 106. You can see four plants watered by rain. Beans, squash, tobacco, and corn grow between the pairs of Rainbow People. In the center box of the sand painting are symbols for clouds, water, and sunshine. Water and sunshine bring life to the earth because they help plants grow. Water and sunshine also create real rainbows in the sky. That is how this sand painting, and the story it tells, celebrate the beauty of nature. ■

◄ *The Navajo used tools like these to grind up rocks and plants to make the colors for their sand paintings. Many of the colors came from the colorful cliffs where they lived.*

◄ *Jet, which is a type of coal found in the Southwest, was often used for the color black in Navajo sand paintings.*

■ *Describe some of the things the Rainbow People sand painting tells us about nature.*

CULTURE

## Visual Learning

Direct attention to the picture of the mortar and pestle. Have students read the caption. Discuss how using colors from nearby cliffs brought the Navajo closer to nature and made the paintings more powerful.

■ *The four plants symbolized beans, squash, tobacco, and corn. The circle is the symbol of the source of all water. The color white stood for east, black for north, blue for south, and yellow for west. It also tells us that rainbows are a combination of water and sunlight.*

### CLOSE

Have students answer the focus question in their own words. Then use the Graphic Overview to review or reteach the lesson.

107

## R E V I E W

1. **FOCUS** Why was sand painting important to the Navajo?
2. **CONNECT** Compare the way the Navajo saw nature with the way the Cheyenne saw nature. How are they alike?
3. **CRITICAL THINKING** What skills did a medicine man need to create sand paintings?
4. **ACTIVITY** Draw a picture of a sand painting you would like to make. You might include something from the sky or from the earth, such as the moon, lightning, animals, people, trees, or a river. Make up a story that your sand painting tells.

107

## Answers to Review Questions

1. The Navajo used sand paintings to help heal sick people.
2. Both the Cheyenne and Navajo thought that nature had powers or spirits, which they honored. They both saw themselves as part of nature.
3. A medicine man needed a good memory, artistic skill, and great hand skill.
4. Students' stories should correlate with their sand paintings.

## Homework Options

Have each student make a list of some symbols and colors used in Navajo sand paintings. Have the student write what each represents.

**Study Guide:** page 20

## UNDERSTANDING MAPS

This skills feature uses a map of an area surrounding an Indian village to teach students to use a map scale to determine actual distances.

### GEOGRAPHY

## Map and Globe Skills

Read aloud the material under "Here's How" and demonstrate how to find distances on the map. Help students figure out how long it will take Bright Star to walk two miles.

- *Village to B—2 inches; 2 miles*
- *If she can walk one mile in 1/2 hour, it will take her twice as long to walk two miles; two halves are a whole, so it will take Bright Star one hour to walk two miles to the cliffs at B.*
- *A to B—2 inches; 2 miles*

# Using Scale

**Here's Why**   You can use a map to help you get from one place to another. The scale on a map will help you figure out how far it is from one place to another.

**Here's How**   Maps are drawn to scale. A scale is a way to show how far apart things are on the real earth. A certain distance on the map is equal to a larger distance on the real earth. Look at the map of the area around Bright Star's village on the next page. Find the scale. It shows that one inch on the map stands for one mile in real distance.

Now take your ruler and measure the distance between Bright Star's village and the place marked *A* on the stream. The two places are about two inches apart on the map. So, they are about two miles apart in real distance.

Measure the distance between Bright Star's village and the place marked *B* on the cliffs. About how far apart are the two places on the map? About how far apart are they in real distance? Bright Star can walk one mile in one-half hour. How long will it take her to walk from her village to place *B* on the cliffs?

Measure the distance between *A* and *B* on the map. About how far apart are the two places on the map? How many miles is that in real distance?

**Try It**   Measure the distance between other points on the map. About how far away from each other are they in real distance? Use your ruler and the map scale to find out.

## Objective

1. Use a map scale to determine actual distances. (Map and Globe Skills 4)
2. Draw a map to scale. (Map and Globe Skills 5)

## Making a Scale Drawing

Have students measure their rooms at home and the objects in them. Provide students with large-square graph paper and have them draw the outlines of their rooms on the graph paper, with each square representing one foot. Then have students make scale drawings of the furniture in their room. Show them how to move the furniture around to arrange their rooms in different ways. If students would prefer, they could work with fantasy or ideal rooms.

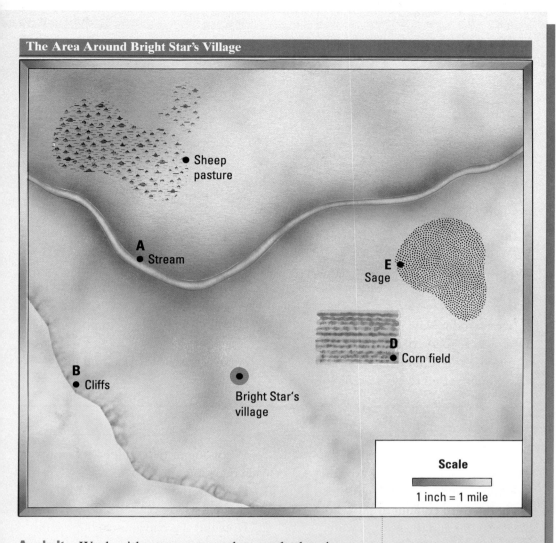

**The Area Around Bright Star's Village**

Sheep pasture

A
Stream

E
Sage

D
Corn field

B
Cliffs

Bright Star's village

**Scale**

1 inch = 1 mile

**Apply It** Work with a group to make a scale drawing of your classroom. You will need a measuring tape and a large piece of drawing paper. Use the measuring tape to measure the length of each wall. Draw a scale outline of the room on the drawing paper. One inch on your outline should stand for one foot of real distance in your classroom.

Then draw shapes to stand for large objects in your classroom, such as students' desks, teacher's desk, and bookcases. Try to put the objects in your drawing about where they are in your classroom.

## Answers to Try It

(Answers are approximate.)
- D to village — 2 miles
- D to A — 3 1/2 miles
- D to B — 4 miles
- D to E — 1 1/4 miles
- E to village — 2 1/2 miles
- E to A — 3 1/4 miles
- E to B — 4 1/2 miles

## Map and Globe Skills

Ask students to look at the world map on pages 232–233. Tell them that one inch on the map equals 2,000 miles. Have them find the approximate distance between Hawaii and Southern California. *(about 1 1/2 inches = 3,000 miles)*

**Answers to Reviewing Key Terms**
A.
1. chant
2. hogan
3. sand painting
4. livestock
5. adaptation
B. Sample answers:
1. The mud walls and roofs kept hogans cool in summer and warm in winter.
2. The Navajo raised sheep so that they would have wool for weaving.
3. Medicine men sang chants as part of the ceremony to help a sick person get well.

**Answers to Exploring Concepts**
A. The Kwakiutl and the Navajo both used the natural resources around them in their everyday lives and in their ceremonies. The Kwakiutl had a comparatively easy lifestyle in the forest by the ocean while the Navajo had to learn to adapt to the hard life in the desert.
B. Sample answers:
1. The Navajo adapted to the desert by learning to raise their own livestock, grow crops, and weave.
2. Sand paintings were used in ceremonies to help a sick person get well. Sand paintings were also used to tell stories.

# Chapter Review

## Reviewing Key Terms

adaptation (p. 101)　　livestock (p. 100)
chant (p. 103)　　　　sand painting (p. 104)
hogan (p. 99)

A. Write the key term for each meaning.
1. a song sung on a few notes, often as a prayer
2. a one-room Navajo house
3. a picture made of crushed rock, plants, and other dried materials
4. animals raised to be used or sold
5. a change in the way of life to fit the surroundings

B. Write one or two sentences telling why each of the following sentences is true.
1. A hogan was a very good house for desert living.
2. Raising livestock was important to the Navajo.
3. A Navajo chant was a kind of medicine.

## Exploring Concepts

A. Copy the chart below. Fill in the second column to show how the Kwakiutl and the Navajo were alike. Fill in the third column to show how the Kwakiutl and the Navajo were different.

B. Write one or two sentences to answer each question.
1. How did the Navajo adapt to the desert?
2. How did the Navajo use their sand paintings?

| Indian people | How they were alike | How they were different |
|---|---|---|
| Kwakiutl and Navajo | | |

## Reviewing Skills

**A.** Use a ruler and the map on the right.

1. About how many miles is it from Sam's house to the school? Use Second Street.

2. About how many miles is it from the school to the library? Use both Maryland Avenue and Third Street.

**B.** Write a sentence that tells what direction Sam's house is from the library.

**Sam's Neighborhood**

Maryland Avenue

School

Second Street

Third Street

Library

House

Washington Avenue

Scale
1 inch = 1 mile

## Using Critical Thinking

1. The Navajo learned from their neighbors how to raise livestock and crops. If they had not learned, how would their life have been different?

2. The Navajo made blankets and clothing from wool. Why do you think they used wool?

## Preparing for Citizenship

1. **WRITING ACTIVITY** Pretend you live in a Navajo hogan with your family long ago. Write a story about one day in your life. Use your imagination, but include some of the facts about Navajo life that you have learned. Read your story to your class. Listen while other students read their stories. Put all of your stories together into one class book.

2. **COLLABORATIVE LEARNING** Make a mural of a sand painting. First, class members can decide what pictures to include. Some class members can draw the design. Other class members can paint. Choose one person to tell about your sand painting to another class in your school.

111

**Answers to Reviewing Skills**
**A.**
1. 2 1/2 miles
2. 3 miles
**B.** Sam's house is southwest of the library.

**Answers to Using Critical Thinking**
1. The Navajo would not have had enough food or clothing because they would not have found enough animals to hunt. They might have moved to another area.
2. They used wool because it was stronger than cotton and they had sheep available to supply wool. Wool also protects from heat and cold.

**Answers to Preparing for Citizenship**
1. **WRITING ACTIVITY** Encourage students to imagine what life in a hogan in the desert felt like, smelled like, looked like, and sounded like.
2. **COLLABORATIVE LEARNING** You may wish to find additional resources that show sand paintings to give students more ideas. Help students to understand the meanings of the symbols they choose.

## UNIT
## OVERVIEW

Ask students how many ways they can think of to use the word *settle* and have them provide contexts. *(settle an argument, settle down, settle in a new town, settle in a comfortable chair)* Read the unit title and tell students what *settling the land* means. *(building homes in a place where no one has lived before)*

Ask a volunteer to read the introductory paragraph. Stress that the land that is now the United States was inhabited for thousands of years before settlers from Europe started coming here. However, the Native Americans did not greatly change the land. European settlers did.

### Looking Back

Help students recall some of the ways in which the Kwakiutl, the Cheyenne, and the Navajo lived from the land.

### Looking Forward

The next two chapters focus on how early settlers lived from the land and how they changed the land:
Chapter 7: Settling the
            Northeast
Chapter 8: Beyond the
            Appalachians

112

# Unit 3

# Settling the Land

American Indians lived on the land for thousands of years before settlers arrived from Europe. The settlers first built homes along the northeastern coast. As more people arrived, cities sprang up all along the Atlantic coast. Settlers looking for more space moved west. They traveled through thick forests, climbed great mountains, and crossed prairies and deserts on trails leading west. Some people went as far as the Pacific Ocean. Whether they were crossing the ocean or following trails to the Pacific, early settlers hoped that at the end of their journey they would find land to call their own.

112

*Moses Speese Family. Custer County, Nebraska. 1888.*
*Solomon D. Butcher Collection. Nebraska State Historical Society.*

## BIBLIOGRAPHY

**Books for Students**
Purdy, Carol. *Iva Dunnit and the Big Wind.* New York: Dial Books, 1985. Iva Dunnit and her six children brave the prairie's big wind.

Shub, Elizabeth. *The White Stallion.* New York: Bantam Books, 1982. Gretchen is saved by a white stallion on the trail west in 1845.

Turner, Ann. *Dakota Dugout.* New York: Macmillan, 1989. A grandmother tells about living in a sod house on the Dakota plains.

Whelan, Gloria. *Next Spring an Oriole.* New York: Random House, 1987. Libby, traveling by wagon to the Michigan frontier, becomes friends with a Native American girl.

**Books to Read Aloud**
Harvey, Brett. *Cassie's Journey: Going West in the 1860's.* New York: Holiday House, 1987. Cassie relates the hardships and dangers of moving to California by covered wagon.

____. *My Prairie Year.* Based on the diary of Elenore Plaisted. New York: Holiday House, 1986. Elenore, who moved from Maine to the Dakota Territory in 1889, narrates her prairie experiences.

Wilder, Laura Ingalls. *Little House in the Big Woods.* New York: Harper and Row Junior Books, 1953. An account of pioneer life in Wisconsin in the 1870s.

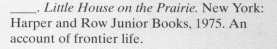

This photograph of the Speese family was taken in 1888 near Westerville, Nebraska, on the plains. Note that the sod house is made from bricks of grass and dirt. Because few trees grew on the prairies, settlers had to use what was available to build their homes. By frontier standards, the Speese family was prosperous, as evidenced by the large house, the windmill, and the horses and carriages. Settlers wore their best clothes when posing for photographs like this one.

113

____. *Little House on the Prairie.* New York: Harper and Row Junior Books, 1975. An account of frontier life.

**Book for Teachers**

Tunis, Edwin. *Frontier Living.* New York: Harper and Row Junior Books, 1976. An account of the life of frontier families.

## Other Resources

**Visual Media**

*Obadiah the Bold.* Ancramdale, NY: Live Oak Media, 1989. Filmstrip, cassette.

*Ox-cart Man.* Ancramdale, NY: Live Oak Media, 1989. Filmstrip, cassette.

*Thanksgiving Day.* Ancramdale, NY: Live Oak Media, 1989. Filmstrip, cassette.

**Computer Software**

*Voyages of Discovery: Lewis and Clark.* Fairfield, CT: HRM Software, div. Queue, Inc., 1985. Apple II family.

HOUGHTON MIFFLIN SOCIAL STUDIES

Anderson, Joan. *The First Thanksgiving Feast.* New York: Clarion, 1984.

Giblin, James Cross. *Fireworks, Picnics, and Flags.* New York: Clarion, 1983.

Edwards, Cecile Pepin. *John Alden Steadfast Pilgrim.* Boston: Houghton Mifflin, 1965.

## CHAPTER ORGANIZER

# Chapter 7 *Settling the Northeast*

## CHAPTER PLANNING CHART

| Pupil's Edition | Teacher's Edition | Ancillaries |
|---|---|---|
| **Lesson 1: Life in Plymouth (4–5 days)**<br><br>Objective 1: Identify who the Pilgrims were and locate the site of Plymouth Colony. (History 5; Geography 1, 4)*<br>Objective 2: Describe the hardships of the Pilgrims' first winter. (History 3)<br>Objective 3: Explain how the Wampanoag helped the Pilgrims. (Culture 3) | • Graphic Overview (116)<br>• Access Strategy (117)<br>• Access Activity (117)<br>Historical Context (118)<br>Writing a Journal Entry (118) | Home Involvement (3)<br>Map Activity (8)<br>• Poster (5)<br>Study Guide (22)<br>• Study Print (8)<br>• Transparency (3) |
| **Understanding Colonies: Why Countries Had Colonies**<br><br>Objective: Explain the relationship between colonies and their ruling countries. (History 5) | | Study Guide (23) |
| **Lesson 2: Life in the Eastern Forest (4–5 days)**<br><br>Objective 1: Locate the Pennsylvania wilderness of the early 1700s. (Geography 1, 2)<br>Objective 2: Explain why settlers moved into the wilderness. (History 5; Geography 4)<br>Objective 3: Describe the lives of settlers in the Pennsylvania wilderness. (Culture 4) | • Graphic Overview (121)<br>• Access Activity (122)<br>• Access Strategy (122)<br>Historical Context (123)<br>Research (124)<br>Math Connection (124) | Discovery Journal (15)<br>Study Guide (24)<br>• Study Print (9) |
| **Understanding Cause and Effect: "If . . . Then" Statements**<br><br>Objective 1: Identify causes and effects. (Critical Thinking 3)<br>Objective 2: Write "If . . . then" statements. (Critical Thinking 3) | | Study Guide (25) |
| **Explore: Early Settlers**<br><br>Objective 1: Identify early settlers of your community. (History 1, 2, 3; Geography 5)<br>Objective 2: Describe the way of life of the early settlers of your community. (History 1, 2, 3; Geography 5) | | Discovery Journal (16) |
| **Chapter Review** | Answers (130–131) | Chapter 7 Test |

\* Objectives are correlated to the strands and goals in the program scope and sequence on pages T41–T48.

• LEP appropriate resources. (For additional strategies, see pages T32–T33.)

T his chapter is the first of two chapters in a unit on the European settlement of the United States. Chapter 7 focuses on the European settlement of the northeastern coast and of the inland forests east of the Appalachians. Chapter 8 explores the pioneer movement westward. Thus, we begin this chapter with the first settlers of the northeastern seaboard and then proceed chronologically and physically westward.

**Lesson 1** discusses the Pilgrims at Plymouth, focusing on their first year. The Pilgrims are perhaps the best known of the first Europeans to settle in North America. The challenges and difficulties they faced are representative of those faced by many other early settlers.

**Lesson 2** looks at the next wave of settlers—specifically those who moved to the eastern forests of Pennsylvania, known as the Piedmont Plateau. These German and Scots-Irish immigrants typified the general movement inward from coastal cities in the early and middle 1700s. Lesson 2 vividly portrays everyday pioneer life. For example, the feature A Closer Look: A Log Raising details the process of building a log cabin. The feature Explore: Early Settlers

gives students an opportunity to learn about the early settlement of their local area.

In examining how the early settlers adapted to the land, students will make connections with earlier chapters and draw comparisons with the ways Native Americans adapted. In fact, many of the early settlers were aided by the Indians, who taught them where to hunt and fish and how to raise crops. Again in this chapter, as in earlier chapters, students will explore how people used natural resources to meet their needs.

### Bulletin Board

Make a large outline map of the United States and entitle it *Settling The Land*. Include the four compass points and the two bordering oceans and countries. As students read chapters 7 and 8, have them track the westward movement by labeling each area they read about with a banner. The banner should include relevant information about the date of the settlement, the people who settled there, the geography, and paper figures or symbols such as pioneers, log cabins, cowboys, or wagon trains. The banners can be made by taping a piece of paper to a straw and tacking the straw to the bulletin board. After completing each lesson, have students post the information.

### LEP: Making a Graphic Chart

After concluding Lesson 2, suggest that students make a graphic chart entitled *How the Pioneers Lived*. The chart might include such categories as food, shelter, clothing, and tools. Students should illustrate appropriate items under each category.

### Basic: Interviewing

After reading Lesson 1, help students create a form that includes name, ancestors' country or countries of origin, and date and place of settlement. Have students interview a relative or another willing adult and complete the form. Students may then work together to make a master list and discuss the results.

### Role-Playing

After concluding Lesson 1, divide students into small groups. Have each student assume a name and the role of either a Wampanoag or a Pilgrim man or woman planning the first Thanksgiving feast. Suggest that students discuss the place, date, time, food, activities, and preparation tasks. Have students perform their skits for the whole class.(See Background, pages 114–115 in this Teacher's Edition).

**113B**

## CHAPTER PREVIEW

Read the chapter title, and have students read the text and look at the visuals. Locate England on a classroom map of the world and have students note the distance the Pilgrims had to travel to get to the northeast coast of North America.

### Looking Forward

The lives of the early settlers is the topic of the next two lessons: Life in Plymouth and Life in the Eastern Forests.

# Chapter 7

# Settling the Northeast

*In 1620, the Pilgrims started out on a long journey from England and landed on the northeast coast of North America. Indians helped the Pilgrims learn how to adapt to the land. As more settlers came and cities grew, people moved away from the coast and cleared land for homes and farms in eastern forests.*

Before Pilgrims settled in Plymouth, they landed near Cape Cod. The only other English settlement then was in Virginia.

*Thanksgiving with Indians* is an unfinished painting from the 1940s by N. C. Wyeth. It shows Pilgrims sharing their first harvest with their Indian friends.

114

## BACKGROUND

After a winter during which half of the Pilgrims died (most probably of pneumonia or tuberculosis, complicated by scurvy), the Pilgrims were finally able to enjoy the New England seasons of plenty—summer and fall. Their first crop of Indian corn ripened in the sun, and their grapes were crushed and made into wine.

Because the Pilgrims were so thankful for their survival and plentiful first harvest, they set aside a harvest festival.

William Bradford, the governor of the Plymouth Colony, probably named a day in October for the first Thanksgiving celebration. (Today we celebrate Thanksgiving in November because President Abraham Lincoln made it a national holiday occurring in November in 1863.) Bradford sent an invitation to the Wampanoag men to come celebrate the harvest with the settlers. Four Pilgrims were sent out to shoot forest game

for the occasion. Everyone contributed their efforts to prepare for the feast, especially the four Englishwomen and two teenage girls who did all the cooking!

When the day arrived, so did a huge number of Wampanoag men—90 to be exact. The Wampanoag chief, Massasoit, sent some of his men to the forest, from which they soon returned with five deer to share with the rest of the company.

The harvest festival lasted for three days. Some of the foods that were most probably consumed were deer meat, pumpkins, corn

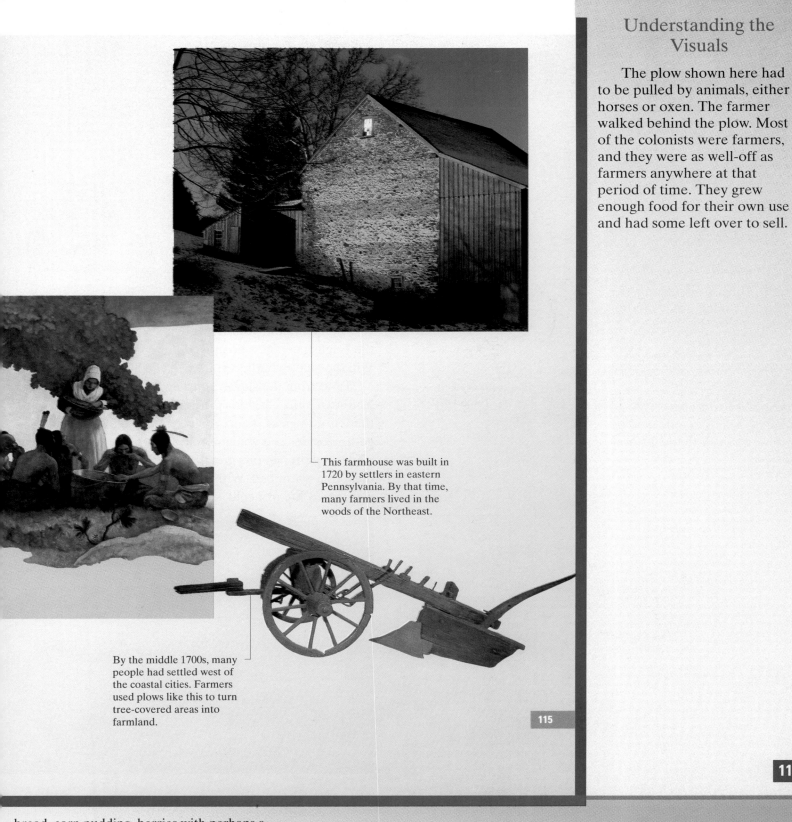

The plow shown here had
to be pulled by animals, either
horses or oxen. The farmer
walked behind the plow. Most
of the colonists were farmers,
and they were as well-off as
farmers anywhere at that
period of time. They grew
enough food for their own use
and had some left over to sell.

This farmhouse was built in
1720 by settlers in eastern
Pennsylvania. By that time,
many farmers lived in the
woods of the Northeast.

By the middle 1700s, many
people had settled west of
the coastal cities. Farmers
used plows like this to turn
tree-covered areas into
farmland.

115

bread, corn pudding, berries with perhaps a
bit of wild honey to sweeten them, eel pie,
salad greens, red and white wines, wild
plums, partridges, wild turkeys, ducks, geese,
and a variety of seafood and fish. They did
*not* have apple cider, milk, cheese, or bread,
since no orchards were available, and no
cows or wheat flour had been brought over
on the *Mayflower*.

## INTRODUCE

Discuss facing a situation for the first time, such as the first day of school or moving to a new neighborhood. Then read the lesson title, Thinking Focus, and introductory paragraphs, and ask how students would feel about moving under the circumstances described. Have students predict some problems that the Pilgrims might have faced when they landed at Plymouth. Have students read to confirm or reject their predictions.

### Key Terms

Vocabulary strategies: T36–T37
**colony**—a settlement ruled by a home country that is located far away
**survive**—live through

LESSON 1

# Life in Plymouth

*What challenges did the Pilgrims face during their first year in the new homeland?*

### Key Terms

- colony
- survive

Pretend you are living long ago in England. Your family has decided to make a new home far away, so you leave your home and friends. For 65 days you sail across the ocean. All the way, you wonder about your new home. Will it be cozy? Will the English people who moved there first be friendly? Will they have children your own age?

Tired from the stormy journey, you finally spot land. You search the coast for the neighbors you expected, but there is no sign of them. You can't keep looking. It is getting colder and you must choose a place to stay. As you wade to shore, no one greets you. No one offers you a hot meal or a warm bed. With only a few belongings, you must start a new life in a cold, strange land.

➤ Landing of the Pilgrims *was painted in the early 1800s. Pilgrims did row ashore in small boats, but the painting is incorrect in showing the Indians waiting on shore. The Pilgrims didn't meet the Indians until the following spring.*

116

## Objectives

1. Identify who the Pilgrims were and locate the site of Plymouth Colony.
2. Describe the hardships of the Pilgrims' first winter.
3. Explain how the Wampanoag helped the Pilgrims.

## Graphic Overview

**PLYMOUTH COLONY**

**Problems during the First Winter**

**How the Wampanoag Helped**

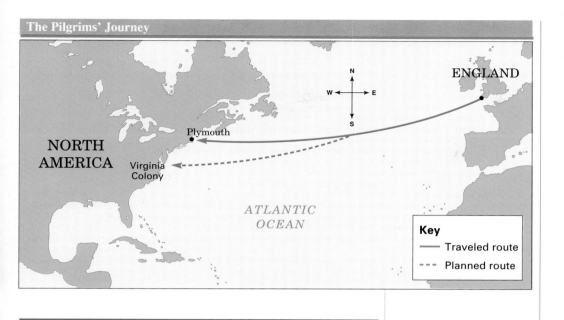

**The Pilgrims' Journey**

ENGLAND

NORTH AMERICA

Plymouth

Virginia Colony

ATLANTIC OCEAN

**Key**
— Traveled route
--- Planned route

## The Pilgrims' First Winter

That's how many Pilgrims felt who sailed from England on a ship called the *Mayflower* in the summer of 1620. The Pilgrims were a religious group who disagreed with the church in England. They decided to raise their children in a whole new place.

The Pilgrims had planned to join a colony already started in Virginia. A **colony** is a settlement ruled by a distant country. However, the *Mayflower* did not follow the route to Virginia. Instead, it landed in late November on what is now the coast of Massachusetts.

Not finding the neighbors they expected, the Pilgrims looked for a place to begin their own colony. Four weeks later, in late December, they chose a spot and named it Plymouth after a town in England. Notice how far Virginia Colony is from Plymouth on the map above.

Plymouth was rich in natural resources. It had good farmland and many streams. Forests were a source for wood and animal meat. From the sea they got lobster, clams, and fish. Still, the Pilgrims barely **survived,** or lived through, that first winter. They had not brought enough extra food with them to last until spring, and there were

**Across Time & Space**

*Historians are not sure what happened to the* Mayflower *after the crew returned it to England in the spring of 1621. Some believe that an English farmer bought the* Mayflower *and used part of it as a barn roof. The barn still stands in a village outside London.*

117

117

## Critical Thinking

Remind students that the Pilgrims' first winter was difficult due to a scarcity of food. Lack of variety was another problem. Without fresh fruits and vegetables, many Pilgrims died from scurvy, a disease caused by lack of Vitamin C. Ask students to explain how the winter made it harder for the Pilgrims to get food. (*The settlers could not plant until the spring, and many of the animals they could have hunted were hibernating.*) Remind students that the land was undeveloped—with no houses or stores.

■ *The Pilgrims lacked stored food and could not plant until the spring. Animals that might have provided meat were scarce in the winter. Winter began before the Pilgrims had time to build comfortable shelters. Many Pilgrims got sick.*

few animals around to be hunted in the wintertime.

During their voyage, the Pilgrims had not eaten any fresh foods. The winter cold destroyed any green vegetables and berries that grew in Plymouth. Without these foods, many Pilgrims got sick. Two or three people died almost every week. To add to their worries, the Pilgrims didn't know if the Indians who lived nearby were going to be friendly.

To make matters even worse, the Pilgrims settled in Plymouth at the beginning of the cold New England winter. They needed to find shelter right away. All winter, the women stayed on board the *Mayflower* to take care of the children. The men rowed ashore to hunt, living in caves or holes dug into the sides of hills. They built rough roofs and doorways out of logs and mud mixed with stones and sticks. These shelters were all that protected the men from the icy weather. ■

■ *Find facts to support this statement: The first winter the Pilgrims spent in America was very difficult.*

## Help from the Wampanoag

When spring finally arrived, only half of the 102 people that sailed from England were still alive. Women and children who had survived the winter joined the others on shore. The Pilgrims were determined to build a new English colony at Plymouth. Soon after, the Pilgrims met their Indian neighbors, the Wampanoag *(wahm puh NOH uhg)*.

Without help from the Wampanoag, the Pilgrims may never have been able to survive another winter. They taught the Pilgrims how to grow beans and pumpkins, and corn like that shown here. They also showed the Pilgrims that burying fish makes the soil richer for growing crops. The Wampanoag taught the colonists where and how to hunt and catch fish. The Pilgrims no

## Study Skills

Remind students that after their first harvest, the Pilgrims were able to store enough food for the entire winter. Ask students to research ways the Pilgrims did this without refrigeration. (*They salted or smoked meats and dried or pickled vegetables. Potatoes, apples, and pears kept well in cool cellars. Corn could be ground into meal.*)

## Historical Context

In November of 1621, the ship *Fortune* brought 35 new colonists to Plymouth. Though more settlers arrived at Plymouth over the next few years, only 300 people lived there in 1631. Some colonists left Plymouth in search of more suitable land. Some went north; others went east to settle Cape Cod. In 1643, Plymouth Colony formed the New England Confederation along with the Massachusetts Bay, Connecticut, and New Haven colonies.

## Writing a Journal Entry

Have each student write three brief journal entries from the point of view of a Pilgrim child. Have students write a few sentences about the day they landed at Plymouth; a day in May when they planted corn; a day when they prepared for the first Thanksgiving feast. Make sure students include the appropriate dates. Suggest that they describe the weather, their surroundings, their tasks, and so on.

longer feared that these people might be unfriendly. In fact, the Wampanoag proved to be great friends.

Thanks to the Wampanoag and lots of hard work, the Pilgrims adapted to their new land. That fall, they had a plentiful harvest. The Pilgrims were able to store enough food to last through the winter. They held a feast to give thanks to God. They invited the Wampanoag to share the foods the Wampanoag had made possible. This feast was the first Thanksgiving. ■

■ *How did the Wampanoag help the Pilgrims?*

## First Year in Plymouth, From Fall to Fall

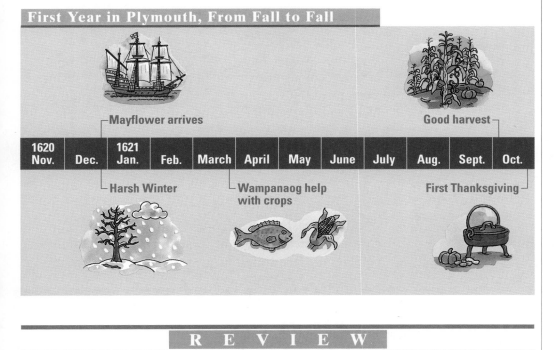

Mayflower arrives

Good harvest

| 1620 Nov. | Dec. | 1621 Jan. | Feb. | March | April | May | June | July | Aug. | Sept. | Oct. |
|---|---|---|---|---|---|---|---|---|---|---|---|

Harsh Winter

Wampanaog help with crops

First Thanksgiving

## R E V I E W

1. **FOCUS** What challenges did the Pilgrims face during their first year in the new homeland?
2. **CONNECT** Compare the materials the Navajo used to build hogans with the materials the Pilgrims used to build shelters that first year at Plymouth.
3. **CRITICAL THINKING** How did the Pilgrims' arrival in winter make their first few months harder than if they had arrived in the spring?
4. **ACTIVITY** Look at the timeline on this page. It shows the Pilgrims' first year at Plymouth. Think about a typical year in your own life. When do you start school? When do you celebrate the New Year? When is your birthday? Make up a timeline for yourself. Draw pictures to show what events you celebrate.

119

## Visual Learning

Have students use the timeline to summarize the Pilgrims' experiences in the first year in Plymouth. Emphasize that without the help of the Wampanoag, the Pilgrims may not have survived another winter.

■ *The Wampanoag shared their knowledge of how to fertilize the soil with nutrient-rich fish. They showed the Pilgrims how to cultivate fruits and vegetables and how and where to hunt and fish.*

## C L O S E

To check students' understanding of the lesson, have them answer the focus question. If necessary, use the Graphic Overview and the timeline to reteach important points.

119

## UNDERSTANDING COLONIES

This feature builds on the definition of a colony presented in Chapter 7, Lesson 1. It focuses on the relationship between colonies and the countries that rule them.

### Map and Globe Skills

Focus attention on the illustration. Help students identify England, Spain, and France and their flags. Have them find the corresponding flag on the ships crossing the ocean. Explain that each of these European countries owned colonies in the land that became the United States. Have students help you list on the board the advantages of having colonies, such as providing

- land to grow crops
- natural resources
- new markets for products made in the ruling country
- new products that the ruling country could sell elsewhere

---

UNDERSTANDING COLONIES

# Why Countries Had Colonies

When the Pilgrims began the Plymouth settlement, they were not planning to start a new country with new rulers. Instead, they claimed the land as a part of England. The Pilgrims remained citizens of England, and they were still ruled by English laws. Settlements like theirs, ruled by a country far away, are called colonies.

Having a colony helped a country in several ways. A colony gave its home country new lands for growing crops. A colony also provided natural resources, such as timber, gold, silver, oil, and coal. A colony was another place where the ruling country could sell its products. Finally, a colony made products that the ruling country could sell to other countries. Countries that had colonies often became richer and more powerful than other countries.

England was just one of many countries that ruled over colonies. France and Spain also had colonies in North America and in other places. Today, most of the colonies are free countries.

---

## Objective

Explain the relationship between colonies and their ruling countries. (History 5)

## Research

Have students use reference books to learn about American colonies held by various European countries. Direct students to find out what parts of the new land each European country controlled.

## Language Arts Connection

Ask students to imagine that they live in a colony like the one the Pilgrims established at Plymouth. Have each student write a letter to an imaginary friend in England, telling what is good and bad about living in a colony.

LESSON 2

# Life in the Eastern Forest

A dim lantern glow lit up the log cabin. It was 8:00 P.M., time for Maddie to go to bed. Pulling her nightcap down over her ears, she crawled in beside her sleeping sister. The wooden planks of the bed creaked. Each time Maddie moved, the dry leaves and cornhusks crackled inside the bed padding. During the summer, the deerhide covers felt itchy, and there were often bedbugs in it. But on this cold winter night, the bed felt cozy. Maddie snuggled under the hide, listened for a moment to the trees howling in the wind, then fell fast asleep.

## Moving Inland

Soon after the Pilgrims and other early settlers came to this country, cities began to grow along the Atlantic coast. By the early 1700s, there were several big cities with many people. People began to move **inland,** or away from the coast. Many families like Maddie's moved into the Pennsylvania forests. There they would build a log cabin and rough cornhusk beds and start farming.

### THINKING FOCUS

*What was life like for the people who moved from the coastal cities into the wilderness?*

### Key Terms

- inland
- goods
- wilderness

121

---

## Graphic Overview

**SETTLERS OF PENNSYLVANIA FORESTS**

| Reasons for Moving | How They Settled the Land | How They Met Their Needs |

---

## DEVELOP

Read aloud the narrative on page 121, explaining that it describes nighttime in a log cabin in the eastern forest. You may wish to start the Graphic Overview on the board to help students focus on the main ideas of the lesson. Students can fill in the details as they read.

### GEOGRAPHY

Map and Globe Skills

Have students read the title of the map on this page. Ask in which direction settlers would be going if they left Philadelphia and settled before crossing the Appalachian Mountains. *(west)* If settlers brought their crops to Philadelphia to sell, in what direction would they head? *(east)*

■ *Some settlers moved inland because they wanted to own land. Farmers could grow food for sale in the coastal cities. Trappers and hunters moved west to get animal furs and hides to sell.*

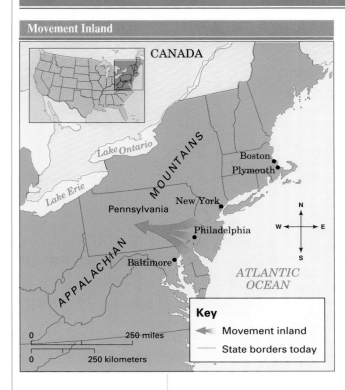

■ *What were some of the reasons settlers moved inland?*

### How Do We Know?

*Wilderness settlers were very busy, but they still found time to write. They wrote letters to friends and sometimes kept diaries. These writings help us know what life was like for those settlers.*

122

Many of these settlers came from Germany, Ireland, and Scotland. They moved to Pennsylvania for many reasons. Some, like Maddie's family, wanted to own their own land.

These farmers grew food to sell to the big eastern cities like Philadelphia. These cities were growing very quickly. The people in them needed more **goods,** or supplies, in order to live. Find Philadelphia on the map. What are some of the other cities near the Atlantic coast where farmers might have sold their food?

Trappers and hunters also moved inland. They provided city people with goods from the forest. Forest goods included animal hides and furs, and special plants called herbs. Colonists used hides and furs for clothing and blankets. They used herbs to make medicines. ■

## Clearing the Land

Land west of Philadelphia was mostly wilderness. A **wilderness** is land that has not been changed by farms or buildings. Indians living in these forests had built villages and cleared some land for crops. However, most of the land was still covered by thick forests.

Farmers needed open space to build homes and plant crops. When they found a flat place near fresh water, they cleared the wilderness by cutting down trees. Then they built cabins from logs from the trees. Settlers needed a one-room log cabin and a corn crop to survive the winter.

### Access Activity

Have each student draw two pictures of the wilderness: one showing the best part of a settler's life and the other showing the worst part. When students finish, display and discuss their impressions of wilderness life.

### Access Strategy

Remind students that in the last lesson they read about the Pilgrims in 1620. Now they are going to learn about a new group of settlers who lived in the early to middle 1700s.

Write *wilderness* on the board. Point out the root *wild* and elicit a definition from students. Record their definitions on the board.

Then have students look at the map on this page. Point out the wilderness of eastern Pennsylvania and its proximity to Philadelphia. Have students look at the pictures in the lesson and discuss what they notice about wilderness life from the pictures.

Settlers could not survive without two important tools—an ax and rifle. They used axes to clear land, chop firewood, and cut logs for the cabin. Settlers used rifles to kill deer, bears, squirrels, and turkey. Without rifles, settlers would not have eaten much meat. ■

■ *Why were axes and rifles so important to settlers in the wilderness?*

## Everyday Life

To survive, settlers had to make almost everything they needed themselves. In cities, people could buy goods from stores. There were no stores deep in the wilderness.

Wood was the most important resource in the settlers' everyday lives. Settlers used wood to build their cabins, and nearly everything that went inside. They used wood to make wagons, tools, cradles, benches, and bowls.

Wilderness settlers often lived far apart, but they would gather from miles around to help a new neighbor raise logs for a new cabin. Settlers turned these "log raisings" into a chance to visit. You'll read more about building a log cabin on the next page.

◄ *This settler is cooking supper in her fireplace. How many things can you see in her cabin that are made of wood?*

123

ECONOMICS
## Critical Thinking

Explain to students that both farmers and hunters moved west and that they had different needs. The hunters would build a rough shelter and clear only a small piece of land. Farmers, on the other hand, built log houses and cleared areas of forest for planting crops. Ask students why the farmers built sturdy log houses, and why the hunters built more temporary houses. (*Because they moved a lot, hunters didn't need permanent homes; farmers needed homes in which to live all the time.*)

■ *Axes were used to clear land, to chop firewood, and to cut logs for cabins. Rifles were used to kill deer, bear, squirrel, and turkey.*

◄ *The floor, cradle, bench, mantlepiece, picture frame, and the bracket that the pot hook hangs from are all made of wood.*

123

## Historical Context

Log cabins were constructed of notched logs laid one upon the other. Mud, dried manure, plaster, moss, or mortar filled the spaces between the logs. Generally, the interior consisted of one room, sometimes partitioned with a loft overhead. There were usually two windows, a door, a chimney, and a sloping roof.

Abraham Lincoln (President: 1861-1865) is probably the most famous American log cabin dweller. He was raised in one that was constructed in the early 1800s in Knob Creek, Kentucky.

Log cabins were built only in forested regions. Pioneer homes reflected not only the climate but also available materials.

## Critical Thinking

Point out to students that there were no schools in the wilderness in the early 1700s. If parents were literate, they taught their children how to read. The children of settlers learned other things by helping their parents run the family farm. Ask students what these children learned. (*to plant and harvest crops; boys to hunt; girls to cook and make clothing*)

### Visual Learning

Direct attention to the four-step process diagram. Have students identify the step that a settler might do alone. *(cut down trees)* Then have students describe how the people worked together to complete the other steps. Point out that there were no "blueprints" for building a log cabin. The boys helped the men, observed, and learned how to do it. The "plans" were then carried in their heads. Discuss why the settlers were happy to help each other. *(They needed one another's help, and it was an opportunity to get together with other people.)*

**More About Chimneys** The chimney was added after the cabin was built. A hole was cut in one of the walls, and a crib, or frame, was built out from the cabin and made to interlock with the logs of the cabin. The sides of the crib were lined with mud and flat stones. Flat stones were also used to make the hearth. The chimney was usually built about a foot away from the house on to the crib. Because it was an independent structure, it reduced the risk of fires.

124

# A Log Raising

*Think about your home. Can you imagine building it? What a job! To build their houses, settlers used axes to cut down trees and to make the logs fit together.*

**U-shaped cuts** were chopped into the ends of the logs. The cuts helped the logs fit together.

**Helping hands** from neighbors made the four main steps in building a log cabin go quickly.
1. Logs were dragged to the spot where the cabin would be built.
2. Bottom logs were put in place.
3. Ropes were used to pull wall logs up poles.
4. Roof and chimney were put up.

**Mud, moss, and stones** were mixed to fill the chinks, or holes, between the logs.

124

---

### Visual Learning

Have students work with partners to make models of the inside of a log cabin. Provide shoeboxes and have students cut out pieces of construction paper or make drawings of different pieces of furniture the settlers might have had. Tell students to move the pieces of furniture around until they have designed a functional living space.

### Research

Have small groups of students work together to investigate other aspects of the early settlers' lives, such as what foods they ate, how they preserved food for winter, how they spun yarn and used animal hides to make clothes, how they made medicine, what games the children played, etc. Allow time for groups to present their findings in class. Encourage them to include visuals whenever possible.

### Mathematics Connection

Help students use the picture to roughly estimate the number of logs needed to build a log cabin. *(9 logs x 4 walls = 36 logs; about 5 logs to build 2 sides to roof point, 5 x 2 = 10; 10 logs for roof rafters; 10 logs for roof shingles; 36 + 10 + 10 + 10 = 66 logs)*

◄ *In this 1796 sketch, a settler takes a break from her chores to look at her surroundings.*

▼ *Sometimes settlers used axes to plant seeds if they didn't have proper farming tools.*

After all the hard work of putting up a cabin, settlers enjoyed music, feasting, and storytelling. A finished log cabin might have looked like the one above.

Like the Pilgrims, the Pennsylvania settlers learned many of the skills they needed from their Indian neighbors. In the Pennsylvania forests, these were the Delaware Indians.

Like the Wampanoag, the Delaware knew how to use the natural resources of the land. The Delaware taught the settlers how to grow corn, beans, and squash. The Indians even shared recipes for cooking these foods. The Delaware also showed the settlers which wild herbs made the best medicines. ■

■ *How did the settlers adapt to the land?*

## R E V I E W

1. **FOCUS** What was life like for the people who moved from the coastal cities into the wilderness?
2. **CONNECT** Compare the way settlers and the Kwakiutl depended on forest goods.
3. **CRITICAL THINKING** Explain how you would feel about moving to the wilderness.

4. **ACTIVITY** Pretend you are a new settler traveling through the wilderness. Write a short description of what you are carrying and how you find food and shelter each day.

125

UNDERSTANDING
CAUSE AND EFFECT

This skills feature teaches
students to identify causes and
effects by writing "If...then"
statements.

## Critical Thinking

Point out the relationship
between "If...then" statements
and causes and effects. Copy
the diagrams from the page
onto the board. Write *Cause*
above the circles and *Effect*
above the rectangles. Stress
that one cause can have
different effects.

126

## UNDERSTANDING CAUSE AND EFFECT

# "If . . . Then" Statements

**Here's Why**   You have learned that many settlers moved
inland to the wilderness. They must have thought
carefully about the move before they made it. They may
have thought of many reasons to move and many reasons
not to move. They could have used "If . . . then"
statements to help them decide.

**Here's How**   An "If . . . then" statement is a way of
thinking about or talking about the results of doing
something. Some results may be good. Some may not
be so good.
     For example, suppose a family were thinking of
moving to the wilderness. Here are two possible results:

If we move to the wilderness, ➡ then we will have more land.

If we move to the wilderness, ➡ then we will leave our friends.

126

Objectives

1.  Identify causes and effects.
    (Critical Thinking 3)
2.  Write "If...then" statements.
    (Critical Thinking 3)

Perhaps some families moved because having more land was more important than living near old friends. Why do you think some families decided not to move?

"If . . . then" statements can help us make a decision. They help us see that most things we do have results.

**Try It**  Think of two other possible results of a family's move to the wilderness. Write each result as an "If . . . then" statement. Share your statements with your class.

**Apply It**  Suppose your family is thinking of getting a new puppy. Think of some possible results. Then write "If . . . then" statements that tell what might happen.

### Answers to Try It

Sample "If...then" statements:
If we move to the wilderness, then we will be freer to do as we please.
If we move to the wilderness, then we will have to build a new house.

### Answers to Apply It

Sample "If...then" statements:
If we get a new puppy, then we will have lots of fun playing with it.
If we get a new puppy, then we will have to train it.

### Critical Thinking

Ask students to think of real situations or make up situations in which they have had to make a choice about what to do. Have each student write a paragraph about the possible actions and the result of each action. Tell students to include in their paragraphs at least two "If...then" statements about the possible results of their actions.

## DISCOVERY PROCESS

Students will use the following steps in the discovery process to complete the activity:

**Get Ready** Find clues about early settlers in your community from building and street names.

**Find Out** Get information from books.

**Move Ahead** Write a report and include pictures.

**Explore Some More** Make a class scrapbook.

*Materials needed:* Street map of local area, books, drawing materials, scrapbook

---

### HISTORY
### Visual Learning

Use a map of your community to help students make a list of place names that might be clues to the identity of early settlers in the community. Point out that the names of towns, main roads, mountains, lakes, etc., are often the last names of early settlers.

Arrange with the school librarian to have books and other research material available. You might also want to ask the librarian to get additional information from local historical groups.

---

### EXPLORE

# Early Settlers

*P*retend you are a detective. You have been asked to discover who started your community and what it was like long ago. How would you get this information?

**Get Ready** Every detective looks for clues to find information. You can find clues about the beginning of your community by looking at the names of streets and buildings. Some of them are named for people who started your community.

**Find Out** Look through books to find out more about these early settlers. You can also find old pictures or photographs in books. You may even find old maps of your community.

LaClede Landing at Present site of St.Louis

---

## Objectives

1. Identify early settlers of your community. (History 1, 2, 3; Geography 5)
2. Describe the way of life of the early settlers of your community. (History 1, 2, 3; Geography 5)

## Activity

Encourage students to interview local senior citizens—grandparents, neighbors, shopkeepers—who know about the history of the community. These residents might provide interesting anecdotes about both the early and recent history of the area. Students might tape record their interviews and play them for the class.

**Move Ahead**   Write a report on what you discovered about the people who started your community and about its early years. Draw some pictures to go with your report.

**Explore Some More**   Make a class scrapbook of the early years of your community. Put your written report and pictures in the scrapbook. Include a list of streets and buildings that were named for people who started your community. Add any pictures and maps from the past that you can find. You may want to give your class scrapbook to your school or community library.

Joseph Morgan founded Morgantown in 1949

This is when he was a baby. He was born in 1904.

He grew up above his father's dry goods store in Pottersville.

his grandparents

He married Charl...

## Visual Learning

You might suggest that a few pages of the class scrapbook be a photographic essay or a collection of student drawings showing the culture and everyday life of the early community. Students could photograph or draw old buildings or historical markers if they exist. Drawings of early settlers in typical activities could also be included.

## Activity

If possible, have the class visit the headquarters of the historical society or a local history museum to see exhibits about the early days of the community.

## Collaborative Strategy

For recommended strategies for collaborative learning, see pages T34–T35.

# Chapter Review

## Reviewing Key Terms

colony (p. 117)     survive (p. 117)
goods (p. 122)      wilderness (p. 122)
inland (p. 121)

**A.** Write the key term that best completes each sentence.
1. During their first winter, the Pilgrims were barely able to _____.
2. A _____ is land that has not been changed by people.
3. A settlement ruled by a country far away is called a _____.
4. People buy _____, or supplies.
5. We move _____ when we move away from the coast.

**B.** Write *true* or *false* for each sentence below. If a sentence is false, rewrite it to make it true.
1. The Wampanoag helped the Pilgrims survive their second winter in Plymouth.
2. Hunters and farmers sold goods to people in cities.
3. In the colonies, the settlers had an easy life.
4. A colony belongs to another country.
5. Wilderness families lived far apart from one another.

## Exploring Concepts

**A.** The Pilgrims and the Navajo learned from other people. Copy the chart below and fill in the last two columns. Your chart will show what the Pilgrims and the Navajo learned and from whom they learned.

**B.** Answer the questions in one or two sentences.
1. Why were colonies important to their home countries?
2. Why did people move to the wilderness where life was hard?

| People | What they learned | From whom |
|---|---|---|
| The Navajo | | |
| The Pilgrims | | |

## Reviewing Skills

1. Write two "If . . . then" statements to tell what might happen if you move to a new city.
2. What physical features are shown on the map at the right?
3. Look at the map on the right again. What direction is Philadelphia from New York City? Is the distance between the two cities less than or more than 250 miles?

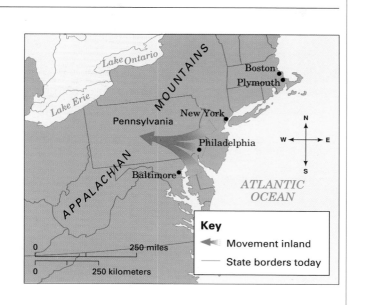

Lake Ontario

Lake Erie

MOUNTAINS

Boston
Plymouth

APPALACHIAN

Pennsylvania

New York

Philadelphia

Baltimore

ATLANTIC
OCEAN

N
W E
S

0        250 miles

0        250 kilometers

**Key**

Movement inland

State borders today

## Using Critical Thinking

1. If the Pilgrims had arrived at a desert in the summer, would more people have survived the first six months? Why?
2. When settlers in the forests built their own homes, other people came to help. What can we do today to help people who have no homes?
3. Rifles and axes were important tools for settlers. What are our most important tools today?

## Preparing for Citizenship

1. **WRITING ACTIVITY** Pretend you are a settler in the wilderness. Write a letter to a friend in England. Tell what you usually do during the day.
2. **COLLABORATIVE LEARNING** Work with other students in a group. Choose an event in the lives of the Pilgrims or the Pennsylvania settlers. Help your group act out your event for the rest of the class. The landing of the Pilgrims at Plymouth is one event that you could act out. A log raising by the settlers is another. After your group is finished, the rest of the class should try to guess the event you acted out. Try to guess the events acted out by other groups.

## CHAPTER ORGANIZER

# Chapter 8 *Beyond the Appalachians*

## CHAPTER PLANNING CHART

| Pupil's Edition | Teacher's Edition | Ancillaries |
|---|---|---|
| **Lesson 1: The Wilderness Road (4–5 days)**<br><br>Objective 1: Locate the Appalachian Mountains and the Wilderness Road. (Geography 1, 2)*<br>Objective 2: Explain the need for a route through the Appalachian Mountains to Kentucky. (History 5)<br>Objective 3: Describe Daniel Boone's role in building the Wilderness Road. (History 3)<br>Objective 4: Describe the travel conditions on the Wilderness Road. (History 3) | • Graphic Overview (134)<br>• Access Strategy (135)<br>• Access Activity (135)<br>Historical Context (136)<br>Role-Playing (136) | Study Guide (26)<br>• Study Print (10) |
| **Literature Selection:** *Wagon Wheels* | | Discovery Journal (17, 18) |
| **Lesson 2: Passages to the West (4–5 days)**<br><br>Objective 1: Identify the reasons that pioneers moved to the West in the early 1800s. (History 5; Geography 4)<br>Objective 2: Locate the Santa Fe Trail and the Oregon Trail and tell who traveled on each. (Geography 1, 4; History 5)<br>Objective 3: Describe the travel conditions on the Oregon Trail. (History 3) | • Graphic Overview (146)<br>• Access Strategy (147)<br>• Access Activity (147)<br>Historical Context (148)<br>Health Connection (149)<br>Science Connection (149)<br>Role-Playing (150)<br>Making a Model (150) | Discovery Journal (19, 20)<br>Study Guide (27)<br>• Transparency (4) |
| **Making Decisions: Packing Your Wagon for Oregon**<br><br>Objective 1: Analyze essential and nonessential items to take in a covered wagon. (History 3; Critical Thinking 1, 2)<br>Objective 2: Choose essential items to take in a covered wagon. (History 3; Critical Thinking 3) | | Discovery Journal (21, 22)<br>• Poster (8)<br>• Study Print (11) |
| **Lesson 3: An Early Prairie Town (4–5 days)**<br><br>Objective 1: Identify reasons for the growth of prairie towns. (History 5; Economics 1, 2)<br>Objective 2: Explain why Abilene, Kansas, grew into a busy trade center. (Geography 4; Economics 1, 2)<br>Objective 3: List reasons for Abilene's decline as a cattle town. (Economics 1, 2) | • Graphic Overview (154)<br>• Access Strategy (155)<br>• Access Activity (155)<br>Cultural Context (156) | Study Guide (28) |
| **Understanding Maps: Using Grids**<br><br>Objective 1: Use a map grid. (Map and Globe Skills 2)<br>Objective 2: Identify the equator and the prime meridian on a map and a globe. (Map and Globe Skills 2)<br>Objective 3: Locate places relative to the equator and to the prime meridian. (Map and Globe Skills 2) | | Map Activity (9)<br>Study Guide (29)<br>• Transparency (5) |
| **Lesson 4: Life in a Mining Community (4–5 days)**<br><br>Objective 1: Identify reasons for the growth of towns in the Rocky Mountain region. (History 5; Economics 1, 2)<br>Objective 2: Describe Leadville, Colorado, as a boom town. (Geography 4; Economics 1, 2)<br>Objective 3: List the reasons for Leadville's decline. (Economics 1, 2) | • Graphic Overview (160)<br>• Access Strategy (161)<br>• Access Activity (161)<br>Historical Context (162) | Study Guide (30) |
| **Chapter Review** | Answers (164–165) | Chapter 8 Test |

* Objectives are correlated to the strands and goals in the program scope and sequence on pages T41–T48.

• LEP appropriate resources. (For additional strategies, see pages T32–T33.)

Chapter 8 continues the story of the settlement of the United States. In Chapter 7, students read about the Pilgrims at Plymouth and the settlement of the Piedmont Plateau region of Pennsylvania. Chapter 8 focuses on the movement of settlers from the eastern seaboard to the Midwest and the West. The chapter spans the period from the late 1700s to the early 1900s.

**Lesson 1** describes how pioneers overcame a great barrier to westward movement—the Appalachian Mountains. The lesson explains how Daniel Boone helped blaze the Wilderness Road to enable people to cross the Appalachians and settle in Kentucky.

**Lesson 2** is introduced by a literature selection, an excerpt from the book *Wagon Wheels*. This excerpt tells of the experiences of a pioneer family in Kansas. Through this litera-

ture, students experience the thoughts and feelings of people who chose to move away from land they knew to settle in unknown territory. Lesson 2 explores the reasons people moved west and describes conditions on the Oregon Trail and the Santa Fe Trail. In particular, the lesson portrays the landscape of each trail and the difficulties of crossing the land by wagon. The feature A Moment in Time: A Pioneer on the Oregon Trail focuses on a pioneer woman gathering firewood.

Following Lesson 2 is a feature called Making Decisions: Packing Your Wagon for Oregon. This feature requires students to apply what they have learned about westward travel to choose items they would take if they planned to travel west in 1840. This exercise helps students personalize what they have learned.

**Lesson 3** focuses on Abilene, Kansas, during its heyday as a cattle town. We chose to focus on Abilene because the city demonstrates how the railroad and trade with the East helped western cities grow. Abilene is also an example of a boom town that declined as rapidly as it grew.

**Lesson 4** focuses on Leadville, Colorado, in the late 1800s. The city demonstrates another reason for a large wave of westward movement and the sudden growth of some western cities—the discovery of valuable minerals.

Chapter 8 concludes our look at our country's past and prepares students for Unit 4, in which we look at our country as it is today. By the end of Chapter 8, students will have looked broadly at the land, the original inhabitants, and the settlement of the United States.

**Reader's Theater**

After concluding Lesson 2, have students read books from the Unit 3 bibliography on pages 112–113 of this Teacher's Edition. Help groups of students select appropriate excerpts from the books and prepare dramatic readings for the class.

**Writing a Dialogue**

After reading Lesson 4, have pairs of students reread the account on page 160 of the two miners who struck it rich. Ask students to write a page of dialogue in which the two miners describe their next venture and/or how they plan to use their money.

131B

**LEP: Illustrating**

After reading Lesson 3, direct students' attention to the information in Across Time and Space on page 156. Have students make two drawings that compare a cowboy's life in 1867 and a cowhand's life in 1990.

**Challenge: Research**

After concluding Lesson 3, have students research the building of the transcontinental railroad and present oral reports to the entire class.

CHAPTER
**PREVIEW**

Read aloud the chapter title and introductory paragraph, and locate the Appalachian Mountains on a large map of the United States. Explain that these mountains prevented settlers from moving farther west for a while. Note that students will read about how this barrier was overcome. Suggest that students try to imagine themselves as pioneers as they look at the visuals and read the captions.

### Looking Back

Ask students to recall the pioneer spirit that brought the Pilgrims to Plymouth and later settlers to the forests of eastern Pennsylvania. Suggest to students that this same spirit encouraged people to forge their way even farther west.

### Looking Forward

Westward expansion and life in two kinds of western communities are the topics of the next four lessons: The Wilderness Road, Passages to the West, An Early Prairie Town, and Life in a Mining Community.

Chapter 8

# Beyond the Appalachians

*As more and more cities grew in the East, many settlers packed all that they owned to journey to new land in the West. First, they had to cross the Appalachian* (ap uh LAY chee uhn) *Mountains to settle in Kentucky. Later, wagons followed trails that led as far west as Oregon and California. It took about a hundred years, from the end of the 1700s to the end of the 1800s, to settle the West. During this time, the West became a land of growth and change.*

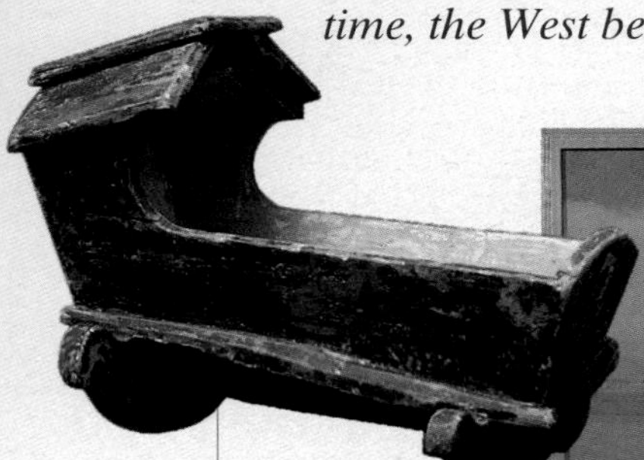

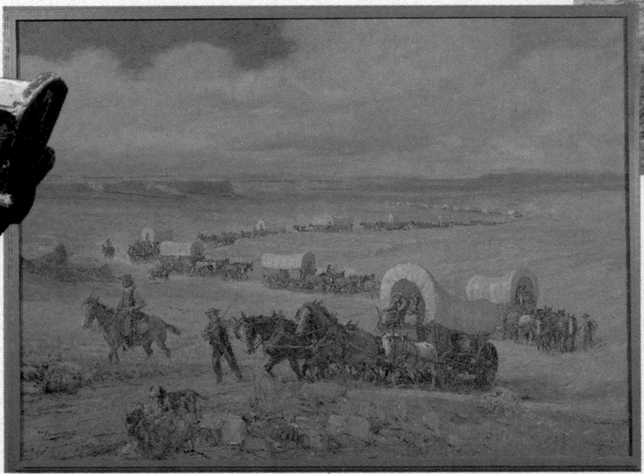

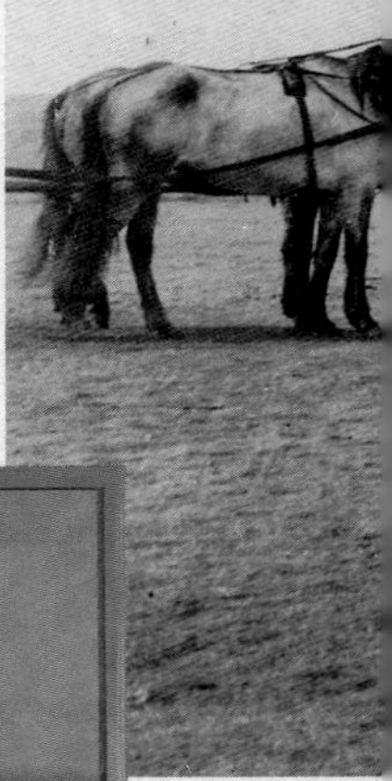

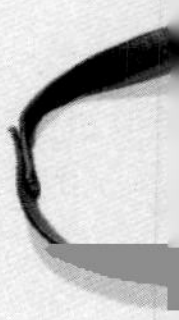

This child's cradle was made during the middle 1800s. Babies born along the western trails slept in cradles like this.

Oscar Berninghaus painted *Oregon Trail* in 1951. It shows families making the long trip across the United States.





## BACKGROUND

Westward expansion was hampered by a natural barrier—the Appalachian Mountains. Once trails were blazed to allow settlers to cross these mountains, many people headed west. The clearing of other trails and the development of railroads led to the settlement of many new towns in the Midwest and the West.

**Traders Lead the Way**

Over the years the frontier moved farther and farther west until it hit the Great Plains, the vast grassland with no forests to provide timber for homes and with a dry climate that made farming difficult. Despite some limited westward exploration, pioneer families might have stayed put for several more years had it not been for the traders and fur trappers. It was the traders who mapped out the Santa Fe Trail in 1821. And, when the trappers went after beaver and other animals in the middle 1820s, they had to scout out good trapping grounds ahead. By the 1840s, trappers had covered almost every corner of new territory in the West. They brought back word of this new, rich land to the restless pioneers—word that encouraged westward migration over the Great Plains.

In schools like the one pictured here, students learned how to read, write, and do arithmetic. Most settlement schools had no blackboards and very few books. Students learned by memorizing, and discipline was strict.

Some settlers' children attended schools like this one in Kansas. Children of all ages were taught by the same teacher. This one-room schoolhouse was made of big blocks of grass-covered earth.

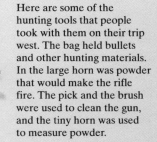

Here are some of the hunting tools that people took with them on their trip west. The bag held bullets and other hunting materials. In the large horn was powder that would make the rifle fire. The pick and the brush were used to clean the gun, and the tiny horn was used to measure powder.

133

### The Building of the Railroads

Railroads were vital to western expansion, bringing goods to and from frontier markets. In 1850, Congress started a grant program that aided construction of western railroads. The federal government gave parcels of land to railroad companies, who built railroads on some of the land and sold the rest to get money to pay construction costs. In return, the federal government got rail discounts on transporting government troops and carrying the mail (a price reduction that lasted until the 1940s).

In the 1860s the government proposed that the railroad should continue all the way to California. Two mountain ranges—the Rockies and the Sierra Nevadas—stood in the way of a transcontinental line. But the labor of thousands of immigrants from China and Europe and of Civil War veterans finally accomplished the task in 1869.

## INTRODUCE

Remind students that they have been learning about how our country was settled, beginning with the Plymouth colony in 1620 and moving on to the forests of eastern Pennsylvania in the early to middle 1700s. Read the lesson title and explain that the Wilderness Road was an important route through the Appalachian Mountains. Then have students read the Thinking Focus and make predictions about the importance of the Wilderness Road. Suggest that students read to confirm or reject their predictions.

### Key Terms

Vocabulary strategies: T36–T37
**pioneer**—a person who leaves a settled place and moves into the wilderness to make a new home
**blaze**—mark a trail and clear the way

**Translation of Journal Entry** Saturday, April 8th. We all packed up and started across Cumberland Gap. About one o'clock this day, we met a great many people turned back for fear of the Indians. But our company goes on, still with good courage. We come to a very ugly creek with steep banks and have to cross it several times....

134

---

LESSON 1

# The Wilderness Road

THINKING
FOCUS

*Why was the Wilderness Road important for the people who wanted to settle in Kentucky?*

### Key Terms

- pioneer
- blaze

➤ *The Cumberland Gap is a natural passageway through the Appalachian Mountains. Thousands of settlers traveled through this gap on their way to Kentucky.*

134

*S atrd April 8th—We all pact up and started crost Cumberland gap about one oclock this Day We Met a great maney peopel turned Back for fear of the indians but our Company goes on Still with good courage we come to a very ugly Creek with steep Banks and have it to cross several times. . . .*

William Calk, from his journal, 1775

William Calk may not have spelled very well, but he had many adventures along the Wilderness Road. Despite the dangers of travel, Calk was determined to reach Kentucky. It was a beautiful land with lots of open space.

---

## Objectives

1. Locate the Appalachian Mountains and the Wilderness Road.
2. Explain the need for a route through the Appalachian Mountains to Kentucky.
3. Describe Daniel Boone's role in building the Wilderness Road.
4. Describe the travel conditions on the Wilderness Road.

## Graphic Overview

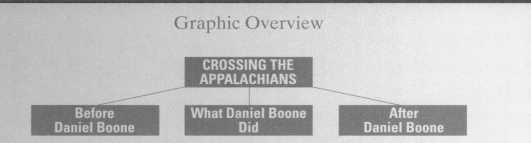

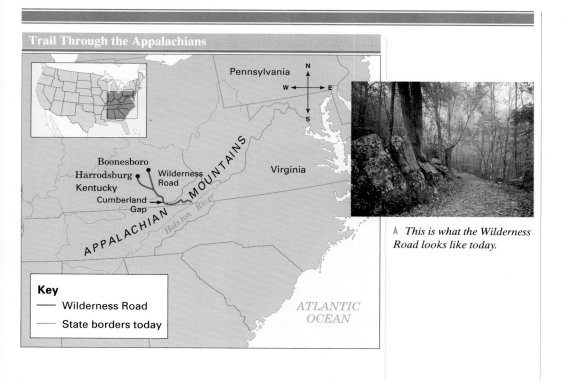

**Trail Through the Appalachians**

Pennsylvania

Virginia

Boonesboro
Harrodsburg
Kentucky
Cumberland Gap

Wilderness Road

APPALACHIAN MOUNTAINS

Holston River

ATLANTIC OCEAN

**Key**
— Wilderness Road
— State borders today

▲ *This is what the Wilderness Road looks like today.*

## A Difficult Crossing

William Calk was a **pioneer,** which is a person who leaves a settled place and moves into the wilderness to make a new home. In the late 1700s and early 1800s, thousands of pioneers like Calk moved to Kentucky. Why did they move to Kentucky? For one thing, land cost less there than along the east coast. For another, Kentucky had rich soil for farming. Herds of buffalo and other wild animals roamed there. People said there were so many birds in Kentucky that they could block out the sun.

Kentucky offered much, but getting there was difficult and dangerous. Notice on the map how the Appalachian Mountains blocked all travel west. If people wanted to reach Kentucky, they first had to haul everything they owned over these rugged mountains.

Narrow Indian or buffalo paths crossed some of these mountains. Pioneers had to follow these paths on foot or by horse. The paths were far too narrow for wagons. ■

■ *Why did the Appalachian Mountains present problems to pioneers who wanted to move west?*

135

## DEVELOP

Direct attention to the map on this page. Have students trace the length of the Appalachian Mountains with their fingers. Read aloud the first lesson heading, and explain that these mountains prevented many people in the east from moving farther west to places like Kentucky. You may wish to start the Graphic Organizer at this time and have students fill in the details as they read the lesson.

### GEOGRAPHY
Map and Globe Skills

Point to Virginia on the map on this page. Ask which direction students would travel to reach Kentucky. *(west)* Ask in what two states the Wilderness Road is located. *(Virginia and Kentucky)* Have students locate the Cumberland Gap. Explain that it is a natural passageway through the Appalachian Mountains.

■ *The Appalachian Mountains blocked travel west. Only narrow paths led through the mountains. Any travel had to be done on foot or horseback.*

135

## Access Strategy

Write the word *pioneers* on the board. Tell students that pioneers are like settlers in that they are the first group of people to move to a new place. Explain that there were several generations of pioneers in the development of our country as people kept moving farther west.

Locate Plymouth, Massachusetts, and eastern Pennsylvania on a wall map of the United States. Remind students that they have already read about the pioneers who settled these areas. Then locate the Appalachian Mountains on the map, and tell students that these mountains made it very difficult for people to move farther west into areas like Kentucky. Tell students that they are going to read about how people were able to cross these mountains.

## Access Activity

Have each student draw a close-up sketch of the Wilderness Road that includes blazed trees, tree stumps, wagon wheel tracks, and thick vegetation. Students could also draw commemorative signs that tell the name of the road, its completion date *(1774),* its length *(700 miles);* and the fact that it was cleared by Daniel Boone and his crew.

## Study Skills

Ask students to summarize why the Wilderness Road was needed and to describe what Daniel Boone did to help establish the Wilderness Road. (*The Wilderness Road was needed so that people could cross the Appalachian Mountains in wagons. Daniel Boone and his men built it.*) Then tell students that the carving on the bark on this page reads:

*D. Boon*
*Kilt a bar*
*1775*

The carving probably means that Daniel Boone killed a bear near the tree in 1775. The carving is believed to be authentic.

■ *Daniel Boone blazed the Wilderness Road, which allowed settlers to travel west by wagon over the Appalachian Mountains.*

▼ *Many believe that this piece of tree bark was carved by Daniel Boone in his travels through the Appalachians. It is dated 1775.*

■ *How did Daniel Boone help settle the land west of the Appalachian Mountains?*

## Daniel Boone Leads the Way

To help people settle in Kentucky, pioneers needed a better way to get there. Some people bought Kentucky land from the Cherokee (*CHAIR uh kee*) Indians in order to sell it to new settlers. Then these same people hired Daniel Boone to **blaze,** or mark, a trail for the settlers.

To build the Wilderness Road, Daniel Boone gathered a crew of 30 men. Their job was to clear the way from Virginia to Kentucky. The crew had to widen the trails that were already there. Sometimes they made new trails and connected them to the old ones.

Boone led the way, blazing trees to mark the route of the trail. His crew followed, clearing away underbrush and chopping down trees. Look at the map on page 135 again. Trace the Wilderness Road from the Holston River to the Cumberland Gap. At which two Kentucky towns did parts of the road end? ■

## Traveling the Wilderness Road

In 1774, Boone's Wilderness Road was finally ready. The road made travel easier, but it was still a difficult trip. Pioneers had to carry everything on horseback or in wagons. Storms caused serious delays. Flooded streams and rivers were hard to cross. Wagon wheels often got stuck in the mud after a heavy rain. Repairing broken wagons was difficult because pioneers had few tools or parts.

Sometimes pioneers were turned back by Cherokee attacks. Kentucky had been Cherokee hunting ground for

136

## Visual Learning

Tell students that while Daniel Boone was blazing the Wilderness Road, George Washington was fighting the American Revolution. Have groups of students research these two historical figures and make timelines showing important events in their lives. Display the timelines and have students compare them.

## Historical Context

The legendary hero and American frontiersman, Daniel Boone, was born in 1734 in Pennsylvania. Like many of his contemporaries, Boone had very little formal education, but he learned to read and write. After blazing the Wilderness Road, he made the first permanent settlement in Boonesborough, Kentucky, in August of 1775. Boone's wife and daughter were among the first white women to inhabit Kentucky. In 1778 Boone was captured by the Shawnee and made an adopted son of Chief Blackfish. After months of captivity, he escaped and resumed his life of adventure. Boone died in 1820 in Missouri.

## Role-Playing

Have students study the sketch of a pioneer family crossing the Appalachians on page 137. Have groups of three students write dialogue for and role-play the characters in the sketch.

hundreds of years. The Cherokee had sold part of the land, but people were settling in places that had never been sold. Also, there were more settlers than the Cherokee had expected. The Cherokee were being forced to live in lands farther to the west. Their people were losing the ways that they had lived for hundreds of years.

Until 1818, when other roads opened up for use, thousands of settlers used the Wilderness Road. Many of these first pioneers were the children and grandchildren of the German and other pioneer families who had settled the eastern Pennsylvania forest years before. ■

■ *What made a trip on the Wilderness Road so difficult?*

◄ *This sketch of a pioneer family crossing the Appalachians was drawn by someone who was actually there, Joshua Shaw.*

137

## R E V I E W

1. **FOCUS** Why was the Wilderness Road important to the people who wanted to settle in Kentucky?
2. **CONNECT** Compare problems that Plymouth colonists had with problems that Kentucky pioneers had. What were some of the differences?
3. **CRITICAL THINKING** If you were a Cherokee, how might you feel about settlers moving into your hunting grounds?
4. **WRITING ACTIVITY** Write a journal entry for a day on the Wilderness Road. You have to cross several deep streams with steep banks with your wagon and horses. Describe what you did to get across.

HISTORY

Critical Thinking

Summarize the difficulties the pioneers encountered on the Wilderness Road. Discuss the fact that these pioneers were the children of earlier pioneers. They knew about the difficulties, but the promise of open land was more important to them.

■ *A trip on the Wilderness Road was difficult because of Indian attacks, severe storms that flooded streams, and wagons that often got stuck in the mud or broke down.*

## C L O S E

Discuss answers to the focus question and have students describe Daniel Boone's role in building the Wilderness Road. You may wish to use the Graphic Overview to reteach the lesson if necessary.

Answers to Review Questions

1. The Wilderness Road made it possible to use wagons for traveling. With wagons, families could move to Kentucky and take the things they needed for settling in a new land.
2. Unlike the Plymouth colonists, the Kentucky pioneers could plan their trips so that they did not arrive in winter. Still, Kentucky pioneers were sometimes delayed by storms. The Kentucky pioneers were sometimes attacked by the Indians; whereas, the Plymouth colonists were helped by the Indians.
3. Students' answers should show an understanding of the Cherokee viewpoint.
4. Students' entries should indicate that the pioneers had to rely on their wits and materials at hand to deal with such problems.

Homework Options

Have each student list the good and not-so-good points about moving to Kentucky in the late 1700s. Tell students to then decide whether or not they would make the move and to explain the reasons for their choices.

**Study Guide:** page 26

## INTRODUCE

Students have just read about pioneers traveling on the Wilderness Road to Kentucky. Explain that people later moved farther west. Tell students that this selection is about a family that decides to move from Kentucky to Kansas.

## READ AND RESPOND

Ask students to read *Wagon Wheels* independently to find out how this pioneer family overcame hardships in their new community.

138

*Many years ago, men, women, and children—young and old alike—went west to find a new land to settle. Travel was not easy. Houses and food were hard to find. But, always, other people helped. Read this excerpt from a story about a pioneer family in Kansas.*

LITERATURE

# WAGON WHEELS

**Written by Barbara Brenner**

**Illustrated by Don Bolognese**

## Chapter 1—THE DUGOUT

There it is, boys," Daddy said. "Across this river is Nicodemus, Kansas. That is where we are going to build our house. There is free land for everyone here in the West. All we have to do is go and get it."

138

## Thematic Connections

Social Studies: Pioneer life

Houghton Mifflin Literary Readers: Special Friends

## Background

Barbara Brenner has written more than forty books for children, including two American Library Association Notables. *School Library Journal* selected *Wagon Wheels* as "the best of the best" books for children.

Mrs. Brenner has been a consulting editor for the Children's Television Workshop and has worked for the publications division of the Bank Street College of Education. Other books by Barbara Brenner include *On the*

*Frontier with Mr. Audubon, A Snake-Lover's Diary, A Year in the Life of Rosie Bernard, The Prince and the Pink Blanket, A Dog I Know,* and *The Snow Parade.*

We had come a long way to get to Kansas. All
the way from Kentucky. It had been a hard trip,
and a sad one. Mama died on the way. Now there
were just the four of us—Daddy, Willie, Little
Brother, and me. "Come on, boys," Daddy called.
"Let's put our feet on free dirt." We crossed the
river, wagon and all.

139

A man was waiting for us on the other side. "I am Sam Hickman," he said. "Welcome to the town of Nicodemus."

"Why, thank you, Brother," Daddy said. "But where *is* your town?"

"Right here," Mr. Hickman said. We did not see any houses. But we saw smoke coming out of holes in the prairie.

"Shucks!" my Daddy said. "Holes in the ground are for rabbits and snakes, not for free black people. I am a carpenter. I can build fine wood houses for this town."

➤ Pronounce the name of the town, Nicodemus (nik uh DEE muhs), for students. Then help them locate the present-day town of Nicodemus on a map of Kansas. (It is in the northwest corner of the state.) Using the map, have students identify the river that the boys and their father had to cross. *(South Fork of the Solomon River)* Discuss why settlers might establish a town near a river. *(transportation, fishing, supply of fresh water for household use and for irrigation)*

140

"No time to build wood houses now," Mr. Hickman told my Daddy. "Winter is coming. And winter in Kansas is *mean*. Better get yourself a dugout before the ground freezes." Daddy knew Sam Hickman was right. We got our shovels and we dug us a dugout.

It wasn't much of a place—dirt floor, dirt walls, no windows. And the roof was just grass and branches. But we were glad to have that dugout when the wind began to whistle across the prairie.

◄ Remind students that pioneers who settled in the forests of Pennsylvania and Kentucky built log cabins for shelter. Have students use what they know about prairies to explain why people there lived in dugouts or houses made of sod. *(There were few trees on the prairies, so wood was scarce.)*

Every night Willie lit the lamp and made a fire. I cooked a rabbit stew or fried a pan of fish fresh from the river. After supper Daddy would always say, "How about a song or two?" He would take out his banjo and *Plink-a-plunk! Plink-a-plunk!* Pretty soon that dugout felt like home.

## Chapter II—INDIANS

Winter came. And that Kansas winter *was* mean. It snowed day after day. We could not hunt or fish. We had no more rabbit stew. No more fish fresh from the river. All we had was cornmeal mush to eat.

142

Then one day there was no more cornmeal. There was not a lick of food in the whole town of Nicodemus. And nothing left to burn for firewood. Little Brother cried all the time—he was so cold and hungry. Daddy wrapped blankets around him. "Hush, baby son," he said to him. "Try to sleep. Supply train will be coming soon." But the supply train did not come. Not that day or the next.

On the third day we heard the sound of horses. Daddy looked out to see who it was. "Oh Lord!" he said. "Indians!" We were *so* scared. We had all heard stories about Indians. I tried to be brave.

"I will get my gun, Daddy," I said.

But Daddy said, "Hold on, Johnny. Wait and see what they do." We watched from the dugout.

◄ Point out that some of the Plains Indians were angry about being driven off their homelands by settlers and so were hostile toward the settlers.

143

Everyone in Nicodemus was watching the Indians. First they made a circle. Then each Indian took something from his saddlebag and dropped it on the ground. The Indians turned and rode straight toward the dugouts. "Now they are coming for us!" Willie cried.

We raised our guns. But the Indians rode right past us and kept on going. We waited a long time to be sure they were gone. Then everyone ran out into the snow to see what the Indians had left. It was FOOD! Everyone talked at once. "Look!" "Fresh deer meat!" "Fish!" "Dried beans and squash!" "And bundles of sticks to keep our fires burning."

144

## Making Cornmeal Mush

Have students recall that when winter storms made it impossible for the family to hunt and fish, they lived on cornmeal mush. Display the following traditional recipe for cornmeal mush. If possible, you may wish to supervise a small group as they prepare the mush for a class snack. Explain that in some parts of the country, cornmeal mush is enjoyed as a breakfast food or as a side dish to accompany chicken or pork.

**Cornmeal Mush**

1 cup cornmeal
1 1/2 teaspoons salt
4 cups water

Mix the cornmeal with 1 cup cold water. In a saucepan, bring 3 cups of water to a boil. Add the salt. Pour the cornmeal mixture into the boiling water and cook, stirring often over medium heat for 7 minutes or until thick. (Serves 6)

There was a feast in Nicodemus that night. But before we ate, Daddy said to us, "Johnny. Willie. Little Brother. I want you to remember this day. When someone says bad things about Indians, tell them the Osage Indians saved our lives in Nicodemus."

145

## EXTEND

Ask students to pretend they are Osage Indians and to retell this story from the Indians' point of view. Suggest that students describe reactions to the new settlement at Nicodemus and explain how they helped the newcomers survive.

## Reader's Theater

Have students work in small groups to write short scripts dramatizing either the family's arrival in Nicodemus and the building of the dugout or the winter in which the starving townspeople were rescued by the Osage. Encourage students to add characters and to make up dialogue between the family and the townspeople. Students who dramatize the second chapter may wish to arrange a meeting between the townspeople and the Osage in which the Indians are thanked for their generosity.

When the scripts have been revised, have students work cooperatively to assign roles and to practice reading their parts. Invite students to share their work with the rest of the class in a Reader's Theater presentation.

## Further Reading

You may want to have your students look for more books to read on this topic in the school or local library.

## INTRODUCE

Review where the family in *Wagon Wheels* moved from and to. *(Kentucky to Kansas)* Have students locate these two states on the map on page 149. Point out the two trails that start in Missouri and lead west, and have students name them. *(Oregon Trail, Santa Fe Trail)* Have students read the lesson title and Thinking Focus and predict why pioneers were moving even farther west. Tell students to read to confirm or reject their predictions.

### Key Terms

Vocabulary strategies: T36–T37
**pass**—a low point in the mountains
**wagon train**—a long line of wagons pulled by oxen or mules

LESSON 2

# Passages to the West

*Why did people travel on the Oregon Trail and the Santa Fe Trail?*

### Key Terms

- pass
- wagon train

Reggie walks along the trail in Scotts Bluff National Monument in western Nebraska. He tries to imagine the thousands of wagons that traveled this trail over a hundred years ago. He thinks about how excited the pioneers must have been when they reached Scotts Bluff.

The pioneers spent weeks crossing the Great Plains. The grassy land looked the same mile after mile. The pioneers could not tell how far they had come or how far they had to go. Scotts Bluff was the first sign these tired travelers had that their long prairie crossing was nearing an end. It also meant that their trip through the Rocky Mountains was about to begin.

## Objectives

1. Identify the reasons that pioneers moved to the West in the early 1800s.
2. Locate the Santa Fe Trail and the Oregon Trail and tell who traveled on each.
3. Describe the travel conditions on the Oregon Trail.

## Graphic Overview

**MOVING TO THE WEST**

**Reasons**  **Routes**  **Travel Conditions**

## Heading West

Since the early days of the colonies, Americans had been moving west. First, they moved into places like western Pennsylvania. Then they moved farther west into Kentucky and Missouri. The trail that Reggie saw was made by settlers moving as far west as Oregon. Many of these pioneers were the children, grandchildren, and great-grandchildren of the earlier pioneers.

Many pioneers went west to get away from crowded areas of the East or to start farms on cheap land in the West. Others went west to become miners. Miners are people who dig for gold, silver, and other valuable materials. Still others went west to buy and sell goods.

▼ *Fast-moving water and rocks and holes along river bottoms made river crossings dangerous for pioneers.*

The trip from the East to the far West was difficult. First, pioneers had to cross the Great Plains. This huge grassland lay empty and flat for hundreds of miles. Finding food and drinking water was often a problem. Some of the rivers they had to cross were dangerous.

Pioneers going to the Pacific coast had to cross high mountains. These were steep and sometimes covered with snow. Those going to the Southwest had to travel through a desert where there was little food or water. ■

■ *What were some of the reasons that pioneers traveled west, and why was the trip so difficult?*

147

## DEVELOP

Preview the lesson headings and visuals. Then copy the Graphic Overview on the board and have students complete it as they read and discuss the lesson.

### ECONOMICS
### Critical Thinking

Discuss the basic wants and needs of the pioneers. Ask students what pushed the pioneers out of the East *(crowded cities)*, and what pulled them west *(open space, farmland, gold, goods to trade)*.

### HISTORY
### Visual Learning

Direct attention to the picture and ask why rivers were dangerous for wagon trains to cross. *(Wheels got stuck in holes; swift currents could upset wagons and wash away wagons, contents, and people.)*

Point out that the Indians of the time (shown smoking) did not know the dangers of smoking.

■ *Pioneers traveled west to find open space and good farmland or to become miners or traders. The trip was difficult because food and water were scarce, and pioneers had to cross dangerous rivers, steep*

147

### Access Strategy

Using a wall map to demonstrate, remind students that the United States was settled in stages, from east to west by several generations of pioneers. Students have read about the colonists who settled the Eastern coast and the pioneers who moved across the Appalachian Mountains to Kentucky. Point out on the map the Great Plains, the Rocky Mountains, the Southwest, and the Western coast. Note that this lesson will describe trails leading across the plains to the West. Then have students turn to the map on page 149. Ask which trail is longest. *(Oregon Trail)* Explain that the Oregon Trail crossed the Rocky Mountains, while the much shorter Santa Fe Trail crossed a desert.

### Access Activity

Make labels of products made in the East and sold in the West (cloth, farm tools) and products from the West that were taken east (furs, gold, silver). Draw the Santa Fe Trail on a large sheet of paper. Have students load Eastern goods in a "wagon," drive the wagon over the trail, trade those Eastern goods for the Western goods, reload the wagon, and drive back.

## Critical Thinking

Remind students that the Santa Fe Trail and the Oregon Trail were traveled for different reasons by different groups of pioneers. Ask students to name the groups. *(Traders traveled the Santa Fe Trail; families who wanted to start farms traveled the Oregon Trail.)*

■ *Traders traveled the Santa Fe Trail to bring Eastern goods to Westerners and Western goods to Easterners.*

## The Sante Fe Trail

There were several trails that people could use to go west. Most travelers used either the Santa Fe (SAN tuh FAY) Trail or the Oregon Trail.

The Santa Fe Trail, which opened in 1821, was 780 miles long. It began in Independence, Missouri, and crossed the Great Plains. Then, instead of going over the Rocky Mountains, the trail dipped southwest. It went through the Cimarron Desert and ended in Santa Fe, New Mexico. Later the trail also went from Santa Fe to Los Angeles, California. Trace the route of the Sante Fe Trail on the map on page 149.

Most travelers on the Santa Fe Trail were traders. They went west with cloth, farm tools, and other goods from the East. They sold these goods in the West, where they bought furs, gold, silver, and more. Then they returned to the East for more selling and buying. ■

■ *Why did traders travel the Sante Fe Trail?*

▼ *These wagons may have been fuller when they reached the mountains. As pioneers crossed mountains, they often had to dump items to make their wagons easier to pull.*

148

## The Oregon Trail

Unlike the Santa Fe Trail, the Oregon Trail was used by families. Most of them were heading west to set up farms and build homes.

Look again at the map. Notice that the Oregon Trail also began in Independence, Missouri. From there it wound 2,000 miles toward the Northwest. It crossed the Great Plains and passed over the Rocky Mountains through the South Pass. Going through a **pass,** or a low point in the mountains, made the trip easier. After crossing through South Pass, travelers could continue to what is now Oregon.

Remind students that the Santa Fe Trail opened in 1821 and closed in 1880. Have students do research to find out what new mode of transportation replaced it. *(Santa Fe Railroad)*

A wagon train usually consisted of 100 prairie schooners. The pioneers met in early spring near the Missouri River. They then formed a company, elected officers, employed guides, and collected essential supplies while awaiting the mild May weather. Before departing, companies discussed their strategies for dealing with river and mountain crossings and possible Indian attacks.

Wagon trains were so named because they looked like trains. Between 1864 and 1869, the wagons on the Santa Fe Trail were sometimes attacked by Indians. To protect themselves, the pioneers traveled in parallel columns. If they were attacked, they could quickly form a circle for defense.

## The Western Trails

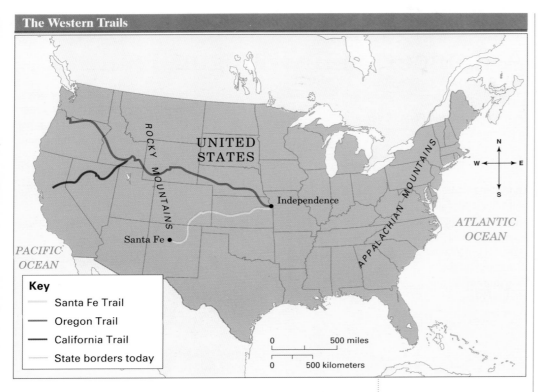

**Key**
— Santa Fe Trail
— Oregon Trail
— California Trail
— State borders today

UNITED STATES

ROCKY MOUNTAINS

APPALACHIAN MOUNTAINS

Independence

Santa Fe

PACIFIC OCEAN

ATLANTIC OCEAN

0    500 miles
0    500 kilometers

Some people on the Oregon Trail were heading to California. They hoped to find gold there. Those travelers could turn south from the Oregon Trail onto the California Trail.

Pioneer families traveled the Oregon Trail in **wagon trains.** As many as one hundred families would move along the trail in a long line of wagons pulled by oxen and mules. A scout, or guide, traveled with the wagon train. The scout knew where food, water, and good stopping places were.

Travelers on the Oregon Trail had to keep moving. It took four to six months to get to the end of the trail. They had to get through the Rocky Mountains before winter came, or snow and ice might trap them in the mountains. A wagon train usually moved no farther than 15 miles each day and stopped only at noon and at nightfall. Breakdowns or accidents might also force them to stop. The Moment in Time on the next page takes a look at a pioneer during one of these stops.

### How Do We Know?

*Pioneers on the Oregon Trail sometimes stopped at Independence Rock in Wyoming. Travelers would scratch their names in the rock there. We know this because their names are still there on the rock today.*

149

**Note:** You may wish to use this Moment in Time after discussing the rest of the lesson to deepen students' understanding of pioneer life.

## CULTURE

### Visual Learning

Read and discuss the captions. Ask students to use the information to infer what a typical day "on the road" would be like for pioneer children on the Oregon Trail. List some of the chores students mention on the board. *(fishing, helping prepare meals, gathering fuel and tending fires, caring for livestock, etc.)* Have students compare this list with a list of chores they do at home.

**More About Clothing** Clothing was hard to acquire on the frontier. Fabric for clothes was expensive, and spinning fabric was a long and difficult job. Shoes and boots were also a precious commodity. When the ones the pioneers brought with them wore out, they went barefoot or made shoepacks, which were similar to moccasins. Shoepacks covered the ankles and had heavy soles.

---

A MOMENT IN TIME

# A Pioneer on the Oregon Trail

*4:50 P.M. May 7, 1843*
*On the banks of the Platte River*
*in central Nebraska*

**Shawl**
This woman's mother wore this colorful shawl when she traveled to America from Ireland. Now it is making another long journey as this pioneer crosses America.

**Firewood**
Cottonwood branches make a great fire, and this woman plans to keep it going for several hours. After dinner, her new friends will join her family around the fire to talk about their plans to settle in Oregon.

**Flint**
Striking the rock in her pocket against a metal bar will make sparks to start a cooking fire. Tonight's dinner will be fresh fish from the Platte River.

**Dress**
Brand new at the start of the journey, this dress is now covered with prairie dust. The woman hopes that soon the wagon train will stop in one place long enough for her to wash it. The other dresses packed in her wagon are too fancy to wear on the trail.

**Shoes**
Before she left her farm in Ohio, this woman bought these tough leather shoes. The salesman who sold them to her said that they would hold up well on the rough, rocky trails of the mountains.

150

---

### Visual Learning

Have students draw modern equivalents of the pioneer items shown on this page. Have students put the modern equivalents next to the items on the page and compare and contrast them.

### Role-Playing

Have groups of about six students role-play the woman in the picture getting together with her friends that evening. Students can make up names for characters and improvise dialogue in which they talk about the day and their plans for settling in Oregon.

### Making a Model

Students might work in small groups to make models of covered wagons. Have students bring shoeboxes, wheels from old toys, fabric, and wire or plastic straws. When the models are done, students might like to display them in a long line as a wagon train.

◄ *This is one of the few photographs taken of people on the Oregon Trail.*

▼ *This box holds medicine made from herbs. Pioneers brought medicine on the trail to help sick or injured travelers.*

The trip west on the Oregon Trail was difficult for travelers. Food, water, and firewood were hard to find along the trail. Sometimes Indians would help pioneers by giving them directions or trading with them. However, not all Indians were friendly. Some Indians felt that they were being forced off their land by the settlers. These Indians would sometimes attack a wagon train. Pioneers were also killed by accidents and sickness during their journey.

The days of pioneer travel were long and hard, but the wagon trains moved on. The pioneers looked forward to starting new lives in the West. ■

■ *Life on the Oregon Trail was difficult because food, water, and firewood were scarce; Indians sometimes attacked; and pioneers died from sickness and accidents.*

■ *What was life like on the Oregon Trail?*

## R E V I E W

1. **FOCUS** Why did people travel on the Oregon Trail and the Santa Fe Trail?
2. **CONNECT** How was the journey of the Pilgrims on the *Mayflower* like the journey of the pioneers heading west on the trails? How was it different?
3. **CRITICAL THINKING** What do you think was one of the most difficult parts of a pioneer's life? What was the most exciting part? Explain.
4. **WRITING ACTIVITY** Imagine that you and a group of friends are going west a hundred years ago. You need to find a scout to guide your wagon train. Write a short paragraph that tells what kind of person you are looking for.

## C L O S E

Check students' understanding of the lesson by discussing the focus question. You may wish to use the Graphic Overview to summarize or to reteach the lesson.

## Answers to Review Questions

1. They traveled these trails to move farther west. Traders traveled the Santa Fe Trail. Families heading west to set up farms and build homes traveled the Oregon Trail. People also moved west to become miners.
2. The journeys were similar in that they were long, food was scarce, and many people died from sickness. They were different in that the Pilgrims traveled on water and the pioneers traveled on land. On land, the pioneers had more resources available to them.
3. Students may mention the scarcity of food and water or the threat of Indian attacks as the most difficult. They may mention seeing new lands as the most exciting.
4. Students' paragraphs might include that the scout should be experienced, resourceful, brave, and capable of leading people.

## Homework Options

Remind students that once the pioneers arrived in Oregon, new challenges awaited them. Have students list four things the pioneers had to do soon after they arrived. (*find land, clear land, build a house, find sources of food and water*)

**Study Guide:** page 27

## DECISION-MAKING PROCESS

1. Recognize the need for a decision
2. Define the goals and values involved
3. Acquire and evaluate necessary information
4. Identify and analyze possible alternatives
5. Choose the best alternative

This Making Decisions lesson, Packing Your Wagon for Oregon, uses steps 1, 4, and 5 of the decision-making process.

MAKING DECISIONS

# Packing Your Wagon for Oregon

## Here's Why

Imagine that it is the year 1840. You and your family are going to move west. The trip will take four to six months. Everything you take will have to be packed in a covered wagon. You will have to pack some food and a few necessary items, such as pots and pans. The inside of the wagon is very small, about 16 feet long and 5 feet wide. What will you choose to take?

## Objectives

1. Analyze essential and nonessential items to take in a covered wagon. (History 3; Critical Thinking 1, 2)
2. Choose essential items to take in a covered wagon. (History 3; Critical Thinking 3)

## Activity

Divide students into groups of six or eight students each. Have each group make a composite list of what items to take on the move west. Then call on two volunteers to choose the five items they each feel are most essential. Have the volunteers debate in front of the other members of the group about these items, each defending his or her own choices.

## Here's How

Think about the things a pioneer family needed. Look at the items pictured on this page and on page 152 to get some ideas. What other things would you want to take in your wagon? Think about reasons for taking them.

## Try It

Work with a partner. Make a list of all the things you would like to pack in your wagon. List those things that you must take. Also, list things that would be nice to take if there is room for them.

## Apply It

If you had room in your wagon for only five items, which five would you choose to take? Tell why you would take each one.

153

## Critical Thinking

Tell students that most of the early pioneers in Oregon planned to farm the rich land there. Because there were no stores in which to buy supplies, early settlers took what they needed with them. Ask students what they would take to plant their first crops. *(axes to clear the trees, a plow to break the ground, seeds to plant)* Ask students what they would take to build their log cabins. *(axes, saws, and other hand tools)* Finally, ask what items they would need to hunt and fish for food. *(guns and fishing equipment)*

For "Try It," suggest that students make two lists with the headings *Things I Must Take* and *Other Things I'd Like to Take.*

153

## Answers to Try It

The list of things that must be taken might include food, water, animal feed, pots, pans, guns, axes, knives, extra wagon wheels, and blankets. Students might list other everyday items as well as their favorite possessions as being nice to take, if there is room.

## Answers to Apply It

Accept all answers that students can explain. The five items might be food, water, animal feed, guns, and blankets. Without food and water, people would die. Without animal feed, the pack animals would die. A gun would be necessary for protection and for shooting animals for food. Blankets would be necessary for warmth at night.

## Collaborative Strategy

For recommended strategies for collaborative learning, see pages T34–T35.

## INTRODUCE

Tell students that "Fresh Water to Drink" is a chapter from *Little House on the Prairie*, a novel based on the author's childhood in a pioneer family. Explain that the story is written from the point of view of the young pioneer girl.

## READ AND RESPOND

Explain that Pa Ingalls has built a log cabin on the prairie and that all the furniture in the house—beds, tables, and chairs—will also be built by him. Suggest that, as students listen to the story, they imagine how they would have felt in Laura's place.

**pegged** fastened with a wooden pin

**pillow shams** coverings for pillows

➤ Remind students that they have learned that there are streams or rivers that run underground. Ask what Pa expected to find by digging a well. *(an underground stream)*

**153A**

## Thematic Connections

Social Studies: Pioneer life

Houghton Mifflin Literary Readers: Learning Lessons

# LITERATURE

# Fresh Water to Drink

### Chapter 12 *from* Little House on the Prairie
### *by Laura Ingalls Wilder*

Pa had made the bedstead. He had smoothed the oak slabs till there was not a splinter on them. Then he pegged them firmly together. Four slabs made a box to hold the straw-tick. Across the bottom of it Pa stretched a rope, zigzagged from side to side and pulled tight.

One end of the bedstead Pa pegged solidly to the wall, in a corner of the house. Only one corner of the bed was not against a wall. At this corner, Pa set up a tall slab. He pegged it to the bedstead. As high up as he could reach, he pegged two strips of oak to the walls and to the tall slab. Then he climbed up on them, and pegged the top of the tall slab solidly to a rafter. And on the strips of oak he laid a shelf, above the bed.

"There you are, Caroline!" he said.

"I can't wait to see it made up," said Ma. "Help me bring in the straw-tick."

She had filled the straw-tick that morning. There was no straw on the High Prairie, so she had filled it with dry, clean, dead grass. It was hot from the sunshine and it had a grassy, sweet smell. Pa helped her bring it into the house and lay it in the bedstead. She tucked the sheets in, and spread her prettiest patchwork quilt over them. At the head of the bed she set up the goose-feather pillows, and spread the pillow-shams against them. On each white pillow-sham two little birds were outlined with red thread.

Then Pa and Ma and Laura and Mary stood and looked at the bed. It was a very nice bed. The zigzag rope was softer than the floor to sleep on. The straw-tick was plump with the sweet-smelling grass, the quilt lay smooth, and the pretty pillow shams stood up crisply. The shelf was a good place to store things. The whole house had quite an air, with such a bed in it.

That night when Ma went to bed, she settled into the crackling straw-tick and said to Pa, "I declare, I'm so comfortable it's almost sinful."

Mary and Laura still slept on the floor, but Pa would make a little bed for them as soon as he could. He had made the big bed, and he had made a stout cupboard and padlocked it, so the Indians could not take all the cornmeal if they came again. Now he had only to dig a well, and then he would make that trip to town. He must dig the well first, so that Ma could have water while he was gone.

Next morning he marked a large circle in the grass near the corner of the house. With his spade he cut the sod inside the circle, and lifted it up in large pieces. Then he began to shovel out the earth, digging himself deeper and deeper down.

Mary and Laura must not go near the well while Pa was digging. Even when they couldn't see his head any more, shovelfuls of earth came flying up. At last the spade flew up and fell in the grass. Then Pa jumped. His hands caught hold of the sod, then one elbow gripped it, and then the other elbow, and with a heave Pa came rolling out. "I can't throw the dirt out from any deeper," he said.

He had to have help, now. So he took his gun and rode away on Patty. When he came back he brought a plump rabbit, and he had traded work with Mr. Scott. Mr. Scott would help him dig this well, and then he would help dig Mr. Scott's well.

Ma and Laura and Mary had not seen Mr. and Mrs. Scott. Their house was hidden somewhere in a little valley on the prairie. Laura had seen the smoke rising up from it, and that was all.

At sunup next morning Mr. Scott came. He was short and stout. His hair was bleached by the sun and his skin was bright red and scaly. He did not tan; he peeled.

"It's this blasted sun and wind," he said. "Beg your pardon, ma'am, but it's enough to make a saint use strong language. I might as well be a snake, the way I keep on shedding my skin in this country."

Laura liked him. Every morning, as soon as the dishes were washed and the beds made, she ran out to watch Mr. Scott and Pa working at the well. The sunshine was blistering, even the winds were hot, and the prairie grasses were turning yellow. Mary preferred to stay in the house and sew on her patchwork quilt. But Laura liked the fierce light and the sun and the wind, and she couldn't stay away from the well. But she was not allowed to go near its edge.

Pa and Mr. Scott had made a stout windlass. It stood over the well, and two buckets hung from it on the ends of a rope. When the windlass was turned, one bucket went down into the well and the other bucket came up. In the morning Mr. Scott slid down the rope and dug. He filled the buckets with earth, almost as fast as Pa could haul them up and empty them. After dinner, Pa slid down the rope into the well, and Mr. Scott hauled up the buckets.

Every morning, before Pa would let Mr. Scott go down the rope, he set a candle in a bucket and lighted it and lowered it to the bottom. Once Laura peeped over the edge and she saw the candle brightly burning, far down in the dark hole in the ground.

Then Pa would say, "Seems to be all right," and he would pull up the bucket and blow out the candle.

"That's all foolishness, Ingalls," Mr. Scott said. "The well was all right yesterday."

"You can't ever tell," Pa replied. "Better be safe than sorry."

Laura did not know what danger Pa was looking for by that candle-light. She did not ask, because Pa and Mr. Scott were busy. She meant to ask later, but she forgot.

One morning Mr. Scott came while Pa was eating breakfast. They heard him shout: "Hi, Ingalls! It's sunup. Let's go!" Pa drank his coffee and went out.

The windlass began to creak and Pa began to whistle. Laura and Mary were washing the dishes and Ma was making the big bed, when Pa's whistling stopped. They heard him say, "Scott!" He shouted, "Scott! Scott!" Then he called: "Caroline! Come quick!"

Ma ran out of the house. Laura ran after her.

"Scott's fainted, or something, down there," Pa said. "I've got to go down after him."

"Did you send down the candle?" Ma asked.

"No. I thought he had. I asked him if it was all right, and he said it was." Pa cut the empty bucket off the rope and tied the rope firmly to the windlass.

"Charles, you can't. You mustn't," Ma said.

*windlass* a lifting machine consisting of a cylinder wound with rope and turned by a crank

153B

## Background

Laura Ingalls Wilder was born in 1867 in a Wisconsin log cabin. As a child, she traveled with her family by covered wagon through Kansas, Minnesota, and the Dakota territory from 1867–1889. Later she wrote a series of nine novels, called the Little House books, based on her childhood experiences.

"Caroline, I've got to."

"You can't. Oh, Charles, no!"

"I'll make it all right. I won't breathe till I get out. We can't let him die down there."

Ma said, fiercely: "Laura, keep back!" So Laura kept back. She stood against the house and shivered.

"No, no, Charles! I can't let you," Ma said. "Get on Patty and go for help."

"There isn't time."

"Charles, if I can't pull you up—if you keel over down there and I can't pull you up—"

"Caroline, I've got to," Pa said. He swung into the well. His head slid out of sight, down the rope.

Ma crouched and shaded her eyes, staring down into the well.

All over the prairie meadowlarks were rising, singing, flying straight up into the sky. The wind was blowing warmer, but Laura was cold.

Suddenly Ma jumped up and seized the handle of the windlass. She tugged at it with all her might. The rope strained and the windlass creaked. Laura thought that Pa had keeled over, down in the dark bottom of the well, and Ma couldn't pull him up. But the windlass turned a little, and then a little more.

Pa's hand came up, holding to the rope. His other hand reached above it and took hold of the rope. Then Pa's head came up. His arm held onto the windlass. Then somehow he got to the ground and sat there.

The windlass whirled around and there was a thud deep down in the well. Pa struggled to get up and Ma said: "Sit still, Charles! Laura, get some water. Quick!"

Laura ran. She came hurrying back, lugging the pail of water. Pa and Ma were both turning the windlass. The rope slowly wound itself up, and the bucket came up out of the well, and tied to the bucket and the rope was Mr. Scott. His arms and his legs and his head hung and wobbled, his mouth was partly open and his eyes half shut.

Pa tugged him onto the grass. Pa rolled him over and he flopped where he was rolled. Pa felt his wrist and listened at his chest, and then Pa lay down beside him.

"He's breathing," Pa said. "He'll be all right, in the air. I'm all right, Caroline. I'm plumb tuckered out, is all."

"Well!" Ma scolded. "I should think you would be! Of all the senseless performances! My goodness gracious! scaring a body to death, all for want of a little reasonable care! My goodness! I—" She covered her face with her apron and burst out crying.

That was a terrible day.

"I don't want a well," Ma sobbed. "It isn't worth it. I won't have you running such risks!"

Mr. Scott had breathed a kind of gas that stays deep in the ground. It stays at the bottom of wells because it is heavier than the air. It cannot be seen or smelled, but no one can breathe it very long and live. Pa had gone down into that gas to tie Mr. Scott to the rope, so that he could be pulled up out of the gas.

When Mr. Scott was able, he went home. Before he went he said to Pa: "You were right about that candle business, Ingalls. I thought it was all foolishness and I would not bother with it, but I've found out my mistake."

"Well," said Pa, "where a light can't live, I know I can't. And I like to be safe when I can be. But all's well that ends well."

Pa rested awhile. He had breathed a little of the gas and he felt like resting. But that afternoon he raveled a thread from a tow sack, and he took a little powder from his powder-horn. He tied the powder in a piece of cloth with one end of the tow string in the powder.

"Come along, Laura," he said, "and I'll show you something."

They went to the well. Pa lighted the end of the string and waited till the spark was crawling quickly along it. Then he dropped the little bundle into the well.

In a minute they heard a muffled bang! and a puff of smoke came out of the well. "That will bring the gas," Pa said.

When the smoke was all gone, he let Laura light the candle and stand beside him while he let it down. All the way down in the dark hole the little candle kept on burning like a star.

So next day Pa and Mr. Scott went on digging the well. But they always sent the candle down every morning.

There began to be a little water in the well, but it was not enough. The buckets came up full of mud, and Pa and Mr. Scott worked every day in deeper mud. In the mornings when the candle went down, it lighted oozing-wet walls, and candlelight sparkled in rings over the water when the bucket struck bottom.

Pa stood knee deep in water and bailed out bucketfuls before he could begin digging in the mud.

One day when he was digging, a loud shout came echoing up. Ma ran out of the house and Laura ran to the well. "Pull, Scott! Pull!" Pa yelled. A swishing, gurgling sound echoed down there. Mr. Scott turned the windlass as fast as he could, and Pa came up climbing hand over hand up the rope.

"I'm blamed if that's not quicksand!" Pa gasped, as he stepped onto the ground, muddy and dripping. "I was pushing down hard on the spade, when all of a sudden it went down, the whole length of the handle. And water came pouring up all around me."

"A good six feet of this rope's wet," Mr. Scott said, winding it up. The bucket was full of water. "You showed sense in getting out of that hand over hand, Ingalls. That water came up faster than I could pull you out." Then Mr. Scott slapped his thigh and shouted, "I'm blasted if you didn't bring up the spade!"

Sure enough, Pa had saved his spade.

In a little while the well was almost full of water. A circle of blue sky lay not far down in the ground, and when Laura looked at it, a little girl's head looked up at her. When she waved her hand, a hand on the water's surface waved, too.

The water was clear and cold and good. Laura thought she had never tasted anything so good as those long, cold drinks of water. Pa hauled no more stale, warm water from the creek. He built a solid platform over the well, and a heavy cover for the hole that let the water bucket through. Laura must never touch that cover. But whenever she or Mary was thirsty, Ma lifted the cover and drew a dripping bucket of cold, fresh water from that well.

*quicksand* loose, wet sand that tends to suck down objects

## EXTEND

Have students write a paragraph or draw a picture describing what impresses them most about pioneer life.

**153D**

## Making a Paper Quilt

Provide colored construction paper, scissors, and paste. Have each student cut out a four-inch square and decorate it by cutting shapes out of other paper and pasting them on the square. Then combine all the students' squares to make a class patchwork "quilt."

## INTRODUCE

Ask what the pioneers did on the Oregon Trail for entertainment when they camped for the night. *(storytelling, singing, etc.)* If you know the tune or can obtain the notes from a music teacher, lead students in singing "The Old Chisholm Trail" on this page. Explain that cowboys sang this song as they drove cattle across the prairies. Ask what students know about cowboys.

Select a volunteer to read the lesson title and Thinking Focus. Suggest that students read to find answers to the focus question.

### Key Terms

Vocabulary strategies: T36–T37
**population**—the number of people
**trade center**—a place to do business

---

LESSON 3

# An Early Prairie Town

### THINKING FOCUS

*Why was Abilene known as a cattle town?*

### Key Terms

- population
- trade center

➤ *Nat Love was a famous cowboy who drove cattle across the prairies for nearly 20 years.*

Cowboys often sang as they moved cattle across the prairie. This song, "The Old Chisholm (*CHIHZ uhm*) Trail," was one of their favorites:

Oh come along, boys, and listen to my tale,
I'll tell you all my troubles on the ol' Chis'm trail.

Chorus: Come a-ti yi youpy youpy ya youpy yay,
    Come a-ti yi youpy youpy yay.

On a ten-dollar horse and
a forty-dollar saddle,
I was ridin' and a-punchin'
Texas cattle.

(Chorus)

I'm up in the mornin'
afore daylight,
An' afore I sleep
the moon shines bright.

(Chorus)

It's bacon and beans
most every day,
I'd as soon be eatin'
prairie hay.

(Chorus)

154

---

## Objectives

1. Identify reasons for the growth of prairie towns.
2. Explain why Abilene, Kansas, grew into a busy trade center.
3. List reasons for Abilene's decline as a cattle town.

## Graphic Overview

**GROWTH AND DECLINE OF ABILENE**

| Cause | | Effect |
|---|---|---|
| Railroad and Chisholm Trail meet in Abilene. | ➡ | Abilene becomes busy trade center. |
| Diseased cattle; more railroads built. | ➡ | Cattle business leaves Abilene. |
| Cattle business leaves Abilene. | ➡ | Abilene becomes quiet prairie town again. |

## Western Communities

Cowboys sang songs such as "The Old Chisholm Trail" to pass the time and to calm their herds. Cowboys were among the first people from the East to come to the prairies. But as the **population,** or number of people, in the United States grew in the 1860s, more and more people moved west.

The railroad brought many people to the prairies of Illinois, Missouri, and Kansas. Towns sprang up along the railroad line. Many people moved west to set up farms or to start businesses to serve the growing population already living there. The railroad also gave ranchers in the West a way to get cattle to markets in the East. ■

■ *Why did towns start springing up on the prairies?*

▲ *This picture shows Abilene, Kansas, during its peak as a cattle town.*

## The Growth of Abilene

One of the fastest-growing prairie towns was Abilene, Kansas. The Chisholm Trail stretched from San Antonio, Texas, to Abilene. This was the main trail for driving cattle out of Texas during the late 1860s. The railroad was also very important to Abilene's growth. For a few years,

## Map and Globe Skills

Have students trace the railroad lines from Abilene through Chicago. Inform students that this map shows only the railroad route to Abilene. Many other railroad lines also ran through Chicago. Ask students how this fact might have affected the growth of Chicago. (*Just as the railroad brought many people and businesses to Abilene, the many railroad lines through Chicago caused the growth of its population and businesses.*)

## Critical Thinking

Note that the population of Abilene increased rapidly. Discuss the relationship between an increased population and the increased need for goods and services.

■ *Abilene grew quickly because cowboys drove cattle there to be shipped east. The town grew to meet the needs of the cowboys.*

**156**

**Routes to Abilene**

Key
++++ Railroad
—— Chisholm Trail
—— State borders today

Chicago
to eastern cities
Abilene
Illinois
Kansas
Missouri
to eastern cities
Texas
San Antonio

0        250 miles
0        250 kilometers

---

### Across Time & Space

*Cowboys are now called cowhands. Life for many cowboys has changed. Today some cowhands use helicopters to look for missing cattle. They may move cattle from place to place in trucks.*

■ *Why did Abilene grow so quickly?*

156

the railroad ended in Abilene. Abilene's location at the end of the Chisholm Trail and at the end of the railroad made it an important western town.

People in the East needed beef. Cowboys drove cattle from Texas north along the Chisholm Trail to Abilene. From there, cattle were loaded onto trains and shipped to Chicago where they were prepared to be sold as meat in the East. Use the map to trace the routes used to move cattle from San Antonio to eastern cities.

Visitors to Abilene one hundred years ago could see in a minute that it was a cattle town. Cowboys and cattle were everywhere! Cowboys, happy to be done with a long cattle drive, wandered the streets. Cattle rattled pens and clattered up loading ramps onto trains.

Many businesses moved to Abilene. It quickly grew from a small prairie town into a busy **trade center,** or place to do business. Farmers near the town sold food to the cowboys. Hotels, stores, and other businesses provided cowboys with places to eat, sleep, and buy goods. ■

---

## Study Skills

Tell students that each piece of a cowboy's clothing served a useful purpose. Have students work individually or cooperatively to research the names for the clothing and equipment a cowboy used and the function each served. Suggest that students draw pictures of their findings and label the items for classroom display.

## Cultural Context

The cowboys of the middle 1800s had to be skillful with lariats, spurs, and branding irons. Eight to twelve cowboys usually managed a herd of about 2,500 cattle. In autumn the cowboys rounded up cattle and branded them, and in winter cowboys kept watch over the cattle. In spring the cattle were driven to the nearest railroad town. After selling the cattle, cowboys enjoyed a brief respite before the next season began.

## The Cowboys Move On

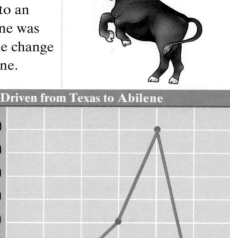

In 1871, Abilene's Texas cattle business came to an end. People and businesses started leaving. Abilene was no longer a busy trade center. This graph shows the change in the number of cattle that passed through Abilene.

Abilene's cattle business stopped for many reasons. Some settlers around Abilene were unfriendly to the cowboys. Also, Texas cattle were no longer allowed into areas of Kansas near Abilene. They carried a sickness that made cattle raised on the northern plains very ill. Texas ranchers did not like this new law against their cattle.

The most important reason that Abilene lost cattle business was that new railroads were built. They led to cities that were closer to Texas where cattle were raised than Abilene was. Cowboys no longer had to drive cattle as far as Abilene to reach railroad lines.

Today, visitors come to Abilene to learn about its colorful past. Many people must find it hard to believe that once the streets there were crowded with cowboys. ■

**Cattle Driven from Texas to Abilene**

Cattle (in thousands) / Year: 1868, 1869, 1870, 1871, 1872

■ Why did Abilene's cattle business come to an end?

---

### R E V I E W

1. **FOCUS** Why was Abilene known as a cattle town?
2. **CONNECT** Use the map on page 149 and the map on page 156 to find the Santa Fe Trail, the Oregon Trail, and the Chisholm Trail. Which trail crosses the most states?
3. **CRITICAL THINKING** What kinds of businesses do you think were harmed when cowboys stopped coming to Abilene?
4. **ACTIVITY** Draw a picture that shows some of the things you might have seen in Abilene in 1870. Then draw a picture that shows how the population and businesses had changed by 1872.

## Visual Learning

Note that cities and towns often thrive and/or grow smaller because of their location at a particular time in history. Direct attention to the graph and the change it shows in the number of cattle driven from Texas to Abilene. Ask students how they think a graph of Abilene's population during the same years would compare to this graph. (*The curve of the line would be similar since Abilene's population grew as its cattle business grew. It became smaller as the cattle business became smaller. The population graph would not end at zero, however, since Abilene still exists today.*)

■ *The cattle business stopped because some settlers around Abilene were unfriendly to cowboys, diseased cattle were no longer allowed near Abilene, and more railroads were built closer to Texas.*

### C L O S E

Discuss answers to the focus question and have students describe the reasons for Abilene's loss of the cattle business. You may wish to use the Graphic Overview to reteach the important ideas in the lesson.

---

## Answers to Review Questions

1. Abilene was an ideal spot to load cattle from Texas for shipment to Eastern cities because the Chisholm Trail and the railroad met there. Abilene became known as a cattle town due to the number of cowboys and cattle there.
2. The Oregon Trail
3. Answers should focus on those businesses that were mainly supported by cowboys, such as restaurants, hotels, saddle shops, etc.
4. The 1870 pictures might include cowboys, cattle, the railroad line, and busy streets with many people and businesses. The 1872 pictures might show boarded up businesses and nearly deserted streets.

## Homework Options

Have each student write two paragraphs, one describing life in Abilene at its peak and one describing life in Abilene after its loss of the cattle business.

**Study Guide:** page 28

## UNDERSTANDING MAPS

This skills feature uses a map of Kansas to teach students how to use a grid. It uses a world map to teach that the equator and the prime meridian are important grid lines.

## Study Skills

Tell students that many atlases include grids. To find a certain city on a map, students would look up its name in the index and find the page number of the map and the letter and number of the section in which the city is found on the map. Demonstrate this process for students.

---

## UNDERSTANDING MAPS

# Using Grids

**Here's Why** You can use a map to locate any place on the earth. Suppose you want to find Wichita, Kansas. You may search on a map of Kansas until you find it. But there is a better, faster way. You can use a grid.

**Here's How** A grid is made of columns and rows that cross one another. Here is a grid on a map of Kansas. The columns on this grid have numbers. The rows have letters.

Use the grid to find Wichita. First, find row C. Then find column 5. Move your finger across row C until you come to column 5. Wichita is located in that area.

Can you locate Dodge City on the map of Kansas? It is in the C3 area. What city is located at B6 on the map? In which area of the map is Topeka located?

**Kansas**

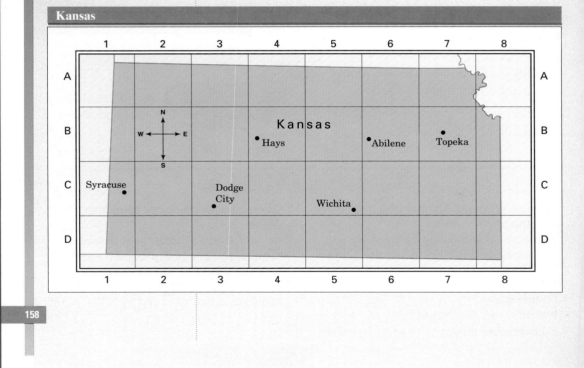

---

## Objectives

1. Use a map grid. (Map and Globe Skills 2)
2. Identify the equator and the prime meridian on a map and a globe. (Map and Globe Skills 2)
3. Locate places relative to the equator and to the prime meridian. (Map and Globe Skills 2)

## Using Grid Locations

Label the seats in your classroom with numbers and letters like the grid on a map. Call on students to give a clue about the identity of another student without naming the other student. The rest of the class then guesses the student described by giving the grid location of that student's seat.

## Using an Atlas

If you have a classroom set of atlases, have students take turns finding the names of cities in the index and locating each city on a map using its grid coordinates.

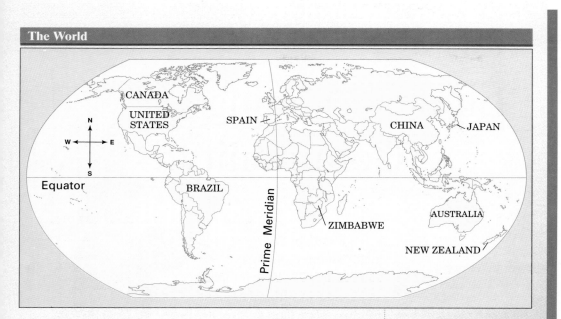

Many lines can be drawn on maps and globes to make grids. One of these lines goes around the globe halfway between the North Pole and the South Pole. It is called the equator. Another line goes from the North Pole to the South Pole. It is called the prime meridian. These are the two most important grid lines on maps and globes.

Look at the world map on this page. Find the United States. Is it north or south of the equator? Is the United States east or west of the prime meridian?

**Try It** Work with a partner. Use the world map on this page. Take turns naming places. Have the other person say whether your place is north or south of the equator and east or west of the prime meridian.

**Apply It** Use the world map on pages 232–233. Make a list of three countries that the equator runs through. List three countries that the prime meridian runs through.

159

## GEOGRAPHY
## Map and Globe Skills

The globe on this page shows where the equator and the prime meridian are. If you have a globe in the classroom, ask students to show where these two lines are located. Note that the equator extends all the way around the globe, but the prime meridian does not. Be sure students understand that the United States is north of the equator and west of the prime meridian.

## Answers to Try It

You may want to check on pairs of students at random to make sure they understand the "Try It" assignment.

## Answers to Apply It

Students' answers might include any of the following countries: equator—Ecuador, Colombia, Brazil, Gabon, Congo, Zaire, Uganda, Kenya, Singapore, Indonesia; prime meridian—Ghana, Togo, Burkina Faso, Mali, Algeria, Spain, France, United Kingdom.

## Map and Globe Skills

Have students work in groups of three or four to plan an around-the-world trip that begins at home and includes stops at the following places: two places south of the equator and west of the prime meridian; two south of the equator and east of the prime meridian; three north of the equator and east of the prime meridian.

Read the lesson title and have students tell what they know about mining. Help students recall the rise and fall of one type of western community—the cattle town of Abilene, Kansas. Explain that mining communities went through similar rises and falls. Have students read the Thinking Focus and predict what might cause the rise and fall of a mining community. Suggest that students read the lesson to confirm or reject their predictions.

### Key Terms

Vocabulary strategies: T36–T37
**vein**—a strip of a mineral
**mineral**—a material such as gold or silver found in the earth
**boom town**—a town that grows and becomes wealthy quickly

LESSON 4

# Life in a Mining Community

THINKING
**FOCUS**

*Why was Leadville known as a boom town?*

### Key Terms

- vein
- mineral
- boom town

"We're rich! We're rich!" shouted the two miners in 1878. They jumped up and down with excitement.

Just a few days before, the two men had walked into a store in Leadville, Colorado. Their clothes were ragged, and they had everything they owned with them. They had come to Leadville hoping to find silver.

The two men asked the owner of the store for supplies. They had no money, so they agreed to give the store owner one-third of any silver they found.

Then the two men went off into the hills. Since it was a warm day, they began digging in a shady spot. A few days later, after digging down 27 feet, the men struck a large **vein,** or strip, of silver. If they had dug a little farther away in any direction, they would have missed the silver completely.

Now the two men—who had started out in rags—were as rich as kings. And there was a very happy store owner in Leadville!

160

## Objectives

1. Identify reasons for the growth of towns in the Rocky Mountain region.
2. Describe Leadville, Colorado, as a boom town.
3. List the reasons for Leadville's decline.

## Graphic Overview

**LEADVILLE, COLORADO**

| Cause | | Effect |
|---|---|---|
| Silver is discovered. | → | The population increases. |
| Other minerals are discovered. | → | Business and population continue to grow. |
| Silver prices drop; less silver to mine. | → | Many miners and business owners move. |

## Wealth of the Rockies

Leadville was not the only spot in the Rocky Mountains where gold and silver were found. The map below shows that valuable minerals were found in many places in the West. **Minerals** are materials such as gold and silver that are found in the earth. When news of the discoveries spread, people from all over the country came to the area.

Towns started wherever the mines were. The population of these mining towns grew even more rapidly when the railroad was built through the mountains. The railroad brought in miners, business people, and heavy machines needed in the mines. These mining towns were the first real settlements in the Rockies. ■

▼ *Leadville, Colorado, was one of many mining towns in the Rocky Mountains. This picture was taken in 1901.*

■ *Why did many towns spring up in the Rocky Mountains?*

### Gold and Silver in the West

N W E S

ROCKY MOUNTAINS

Leadville•

UNITED STATES

PACIFIC OCEAN

Key
- Gold
- Silver
- ▨ Gold and silver
- — State borders today

0   500 miles
0   500 kilometers

161

Read the introductory narrative on page 160. Then have students find Leadville on the map on this page. Explain that Leadville is in the Rocky Mountains and that it was like many towns where silver or other valuable minerals were found.

To help students focus on the cause-and-effect relationships in the text, start the Graphic Overview on the board. Have students fill in causes and effects as they read.

■ *The discovery of minerals and the building of the railroad contributed to the development of many cities.*

### HISTORY
#### Critical Thinking

Have students identify the two main factors that contributed to the growth of mining towns. *(the discovery of minerals and the railroad)* Explain that gold rushes contributed to California's growth in the middle 1800s. Draw an analogy between farmers who took the Oregon Trail and miners who took the railroad.

### Access Strategy

Direct attention to the pick and spade on page 160. Discuss how the tools relate to minerals. *(They are used to dig.)* Ask what silver was and is used for, and list its uses on the board. *(money, utensils, jewelry, etc.)* Tell students that silver was discovered in Leadville in the 1800s. Have students locate Leadville on the map on this page and study the photograph of Leadville.

Remind students of Abilene and introduce the concept of a boom town by making a booming sound. Then elicit descriptions of a boom. Focus on the startling and sudden quality of the sound. Explain that Leadville, like Abilene, suddenly became a rich, crowded boom town in the course of one year. Preview the lesson by having a volunteer read the lesson headings.

### Access Activity

Display a variety of rocks, explaining that some rocks contain such minerals as gold, silver, copper, and diamonds. Have students go through catalogs and cut out pictures of products made from minerals. Students might use the pictures to make a collage. Point out that mountains are made largely of rocks and often contain valuable minerals.

GEOGRAPHY
## Critical Thinking

Emphasize that in just one year Leadville's population rose from 300 to 5,000. Stress the fact that Leadville's geographic location in the mountains made it an undesirable location to live for many years but the discovery of silver changed that. Discuss what type of people made up the population of 5,000. *(miners, business people, workers)* Ask how such a sudden boom in population affected daily life in Leadville. *(made it much busier and more crowded)*

■ *Miners and business people went to Leadville when it was a boom town.*

▼ *Silver from places like Leadville was used to make many beautiful things. This silver cup was bought for a young child named Richard.*

■ *What kind of people came to Leadville when it was known as a boom town?*

➤ *At this Leadville company, silver was melted and made into bars. Later, the silver could be made into coins, platters, cups, or other silver items.*

## A Boom Town

At the time that the two miners discovered silver, Leadville was a boom town. A **boom town** is a town that grows and becomes wealthy very quickly. News of the silver veins had spread quickly, and people poured into Leadville. Some people came hoping to find silver. Others came to earn money by working in mines owned by others. Business people came to open stores, hotels, and theaters for the new residents. In just one year, the population of Leadville rose from 300 people to 5,000 people!

Several silver veins were found near Leadville. Within one year, there were at least 12 silver mines in the area. People also mined gold, copper, and other valuable minerals. At one time, there were more than 240 mines around Leadville.

The rich residents of Leadville lived well, but not everyone made a lot of money. Many of the people who came to Leadville never found silver or any other valuable mineral. They often worked in mines for little money. ■

162

## Study Skills

Have each student write two descriptive paragraphs about Leadville. One paragraph should describe the town at the height of its boom. The other should describe Leadville several years later. Suggest that students think about the sights, sounds, and smells in a busy place versus those in a less busy place.

## Historical Context

Leadville got its name from the large quantities of lead ore that are found in the area. Silver, gold, iron, copper, manganese, tungsten, and zinc are also found there. Leadville is often referred to as Cloud City because it is 10,200 feet above sea level.

## The Silver Runs Out

The boom in Leadville did not last. As the chart on this page shows, by 1916 Leadville had lost much of its population. One reason people left Leadville was that silver had become less valuable. Because mine owners were not making as much money selling silver as they had before, they could not pay their workers as much. The workers moved on to better paying jobs in other places.

People also left Leadville because most of the silver there had been removed from the earth and there were few new discoveries. People went to other places to look for minerals or to work in other mines. Many businesses closed because their customers were gone.

Leadville did not disappear, but its days as a boom town were over. It still attracts many visitors, though. They go to Leadville to enjoy the mountains and to learn about the interesting history of western mining towns. ■

| Population of Leadville | |
| --- | --- |
| Year | Population |
| 1877 | 300 |
| 1878 | 5,000 |
| 1879 | 30,000 |
| 1900 | 12,500 |
| 1916 | 4,500 |
| Present | 4,000 |

▼ *The home of Horace Tabor still stands in Leadville today. Visitors can learn about this man who made a fortune from silver mines around Leadville during the 1800s.*

■ *What caused Leadville to go from a boom town to a quiet mountain town?*

## R E V I E W

1. **FOCUS** Why was Leadville known as a boom town?
2. **CONNECT** Compare the way businesses changed in Abilene, Kansas, and in Leadville, Colorado.
3. **CRITICAL THINKING** Pretend you have just arrived in Leadville and you want to be a miner. What questions would you ask the people in the town about Leadville and about mining?
4. **ACTIVITY** Pretend you are living in the East in 1879. You have heard about Leadville and its silver mines, and you have been given a free railroad ticket to go there. Will you use the ticket? Discuss your answer with your classmates.

### ECONOMICS

#### Critical Thinking

Have students predict the chain of events that might occur when a product such as silver is no longer popular. (*People buy less silver. Production of silver slows down. Workers lose their jobs, or wages are lowered. Workers have less money to spend. If workers buy less, then other workers have less work to do. Many workers have to find new jobs, and many leave to find work.*)

■ *The price of silver dropped and less silver was being found. Workers and businesses left*

### CLOSE

To assess students' comprehension of the lesson, ask the focus question. Discuss the factors that led to Leadville's rise and fall.

If necessary, use the Graphic Overview to reteach the lesson.

### Answers to Review Questions

1. Leadville was known as a boom town because silver was discovered there. Leadville grew and became wealthy quickly.
2. Both grew rapidly and then declined. Abilene's growth was based on the cattle business; Leadville's was based on mining.
3. Possible questions include: Where is a hotel? Where is a good place to eat? Where do miners buy supplies? Who knows the most about mines around Leadville?
4. Encourage students to consider the pros and cons of moving to Leadville. Pros: possibility of making more money, adventure. Cons: difficulty of starting over, town probably has problems due to unplanned growth.

### Homework Options

Have each student write two diary entries, one describing what life was like for a wealthy miner or merchant and one describing what life was like for a poor mine worker. Then have students read and discuss their entries.

**Study Guide:** page 30

**Answers to Reviewing Key Terms**
**A.**
1. pass
2. mineral
3. vein
4. pioneers
5. population
6. wagon trains
7. trade center
8. blazed
9. boom town

**Answers to Exploring Concepts**
1. Kentucky—cheaper land, rich soil
   Leadville—to mine silver, to provide goods/services for miners
   Oregon—to start farms and build homes on cheaper land
   Santa Fe—to find land (Traders went to Santa Fe to buy and sell goods.)
2. Daniel Boone blazed the trail and his men followed, clearing away underbrush and cutting down trees so that settlers could use the trail.
3. Scarcity of food, water, and firewood; attacks by Indians that felt threatened; wagon breakdowns
4. For a while, the end of the railroad and the end of the Chisholm Trail met in Abilene. It became an important cattle town and grew as businesses started to provide goods and services to the cowboys who were leading cattle to the end of the railroad line.

# Chapter Review

## Reviewing Key Terms

blaze (p. 136)
boom town (p. 162)
mineral (p. 161)
pass (p. 148)
pioneer (p. 135)
population (p. 155)
trade center (p. 156)
wagon train (p. 149)
vein (p. 160)

**A.** Choose the word that best completes the sentence.
1. Pioneers went through a (pass, vein) to get across a steep mountain.
2. A (mineral, population) is usually found in the earth.
3. A (pioneer, vein) is a long strip of a mineral.
4. (Sailors, Pioneers) left settled places and moved to the wilderness.
5. After most of the silver was mined, the (population, pass) of Leadville got smaller.
6. Pioneers traveled along the Oregon Trail in (boats, wagon trains).
7. People buy and sell goods at a (wagon train, trade center).
8. Daniel Boone (closed, blazed) a trail from Virginia to Kentucky.
9. A (mineral, boom town) grows quickly.

## Exploring Concepts

1. Pioneers moved to Kentucky and other places for different reasons. Copy and complete the chart to show why they moved.
2. Explain why Daniel Boone's work on the Wilderness Trail was important to the pioneers who moved west.
3. List three problems that pioneers on the Oregon Trail had.
4. How did the railroad help the town of Abilene grow?

| Where pioneers moved | Why they moved there |
|---|---|
| Kentucky | |
| Leadville | |
| Oregon | |
| Santa Fe | |

## Reviewing Skills

1. Look at the map of New Mexico on the right. Using the grid, tell what area Santa Fe is in. Locate Gallup. Where is Hobbs?

2. Use the political map on pages 232–233 to name two countries south of the equator.

3. Look at the map on page 156. What direction do you travel if you go from Abilene to San Antonio?

New Mexico

## Using Critical Thinking

1. Sometimes a wagon broke down on the rough trails and could not be fixed. What do you think pioneers did when their wagons broke down?

2. When most of the minerals were dug up in Leadville, miners had no jobs and many people had to move away. Where do you think those people moved to? What do you think they did to earn a living?

## Preparing for Citizenship

1. **ART ACTIVITY** Pretend you traveled on the Chisholm Trail. Draw a picture of something you saw on the trail. Put your picture with those of your classmates to make a long mural.

2. **COLLABORATIVE LEARNING** As a class project, do a live news report about crossing the mountains in a wagon train. Three students should be the TV reporters. The rest of the students should tell the reporters what happened to them on their trip across the mountains.

165

UNIT
## OVERVIEW

Read the unit title and introductory paragraph. Have students name some of the natural resources we take from the land. *(soil, trees, water, minerals, etc.)* Explain that some of these resources cannot be replaced, so we must be careful not to use them all up; other resources, such as trees, can be replaced, so we must replace the ones we cut down.

Ask students how the painting relates to honoring the land. *(It shows the American flag on the land, which is a reminder to honor the land.)*

### Looking Back

Remind students that in the last unit they saw how European settlers took over the land as they moved progressively farther west from one sea to the other.

### Looking Forward

The United States of today is the topic of the next three chapters:

**166**

*Unit 4*

# The Land Today

The United States is a land of plenty with vast resources stretching from sea to sea. Today, its people and cities use many of the same resources that fed, clothed, and sheltered the American Indians and pioneers of long ago. New ways of farming, making products, and moving goods to market help provide what today's growing population needs to live. These resources, however, cannot last forever. If we want to protect the beauty and the resources of our country, we must care for our land and all that it stands for.

166

*Kinuko Y. Craft. Watercolor and oil. Shown at Stars and Stripes exhibit at the American Institute of Graphic Arts, San Francisco.*

## BIBLIOGRAPHY

**Books for Students**
Cowcher, Helen. *Rain Forest*. New York: Farrar, Straus & Giroux, 1989. The animals of the rain forest sense the threat of something more powerful than Jaguar—the arrival of man and machines.

Madden, Don. *The Wartville Wizard.*

New York: Macmillan, 1986. A tidy old man is given the power to return litter to its owner.

Miles, Betty. *Save the Earth*. New York: Alfred A. Knopf, 1974. An ecology handbook for children.

Peet, Bill. *Farewell to Shady Glade*. Boston: Houghton Mifflin, 1981. A community of animals is uprooted from their homes by spreading urban blight. The story has a happy ending, but reminds children that our wildlife neighbors have rights, too.

**Books to Read Aloud**
Giono, Jean. *The Man Who Planted Trees*. Post Mills, VT: Chelsea Green, 1987. A story of what one person can do for the environment.

Selden, George. *The Old Meadow*. New York: Farrar, Straus & Giroux, 1987. Chester Cricket and the animals of the meadow join forces to save Mr. Budd and his dog Dubber from eviction.

## Notes on the Painting

This watercolor and oil painting was created by Kinuko Yamabe Craft, an artist who was born and educated in Japan. In 1964, Ms. Craft came to the United States to study art at the School of the Art Institute of Chicago. This painting is Ms. Craft's personal interpretation of the U.S. flag.

**Book for Teachers**
Murphy, Wendy. *The Future World of Agriculture*. New York: Franklin Watts, 1984. The future is the present in Walt Disney's EPCOT Center, which grows and serves its own food.

## Other Resources

**Visual Media**
*Our Environment (Set D)*. New York: Random House, 1982. Four sound filmstrips.

*Waste Is Waste*. Toronto: Mead Audiovisual, 1987. Filmstrip, cassette.

**Recordings**
*Hug the Earth*. Seattle: Tickle Tune Typhoon, 1985. Cassette.

*The Reason for a Flower*. New Rochelle, NY: Spoken Arts, 1989. Read-along cassette.

**Computer Software**
*Lunar Greenhouse*. St. Paul: Minnesota Educational Computing, 1989. Apple II family.

HOUGHTON MIFFLIN SOCIAL STUDIES

## Bookshelf

Peet, Bill. *The Wump World*. Boston: Houghton Mifflin, 1981. The Pollutions from Pollutus invade the Wump World.

Patent, Dorothy Hinshaw. *Where the Bald Eagles Gather*. New York: Clarion, 1984. Describes the autumn gathering of bald eagles in Glacier National Park.

**CHAPTER ORGANIZER**

# Chapter 9 *The Land of Plenty*

## CHAPTER PLANNING CHART

| Pupil's Edition | Teacher's Edition | Ancillaries |
|---|---|---|
| **Lesson 1: Farming in the San Joaquin Valley (4–5 days)**<br><br>Objective 1: Locate the San Joaquin Valley on a map. (Geography 1; Map and Globe Skills 2)*<br>Objective 2: Explain why crops grow so well in the San Joaquin Valley. (Geography 2, 3)<br>Objective 3: Explain how irrigation, fertilizers, and chemicals increase crop production in the San Joaquin Valley. (Geography 3; Economics 3)<br>Objective 4: Describe how crops are harvested in the San Joaquin Valley. (Geography 3; Economics 3) | • Graphic Overview (170)<br>• Access Strategy (171)<br>• Access Activity (171)<br>Historical Context (172)<br>Collaborative Learning (172) | Home Involvement (4)<br>• Poster (7)<br>Study Guide (31)<br>• Transparency (6) |
| **Making Decisions: Getting Farm Products to Stores**<br><br>Objective 1: Analyze the advantages and disadvantages of various means of transporting crops. (Economics 3; Critical Thinking 2)<br>Objective 2: Choose the best method of transporting each of three crops. (Economics 3; Critical Thinking 3) | | Discovery Journal (23)<br>• Poster (8) |
| **Understanding Number Information: Using Tables**<br><br>Objective: Read a table. (Visual Learning 2) | | Study Guide (32) |
| **Lesson 2: Steel In Pittsburgh (3–4 days)**<br><br>Objective 1: Explain how Pittsburgh's location contributed to its development as a steel city. (Geography 2)<br>Objective 2: Describe how the steel industry helped Pittsburgh grow. (Economics 1)<br>Objective 3: Identify problems resulting from the steel industry. (Geography 3)<br>Objective 4: Describe how Pittsburgh is recovering from the decline of the steel industry. (History 6) | • Graphic Overview (178)<br>• Access Strategy (179)<br>• Access Activity (179)<br>Art Connection (180) | Map Activity (10)<br>Study Guide (33) |
| **Lesson 3: Moving by Rail (4–5 days)**<br><br>Objective 1: Describe the role of railroads in our country's history. (History 5, 6)<br>Objective 2: Explain how other means of transportation affected business on the railroad. (Economics 1, 3)<br>Objective 3: Describe how railroads are used today. (Economics 1, 3) | • Graphic Overview (182)<br>• Access Strategy (183)<br>• Access Activity (183)<br>Historical Context (184)<br>Music Connection (184)<br>Research (185) | Discovery Journal (24)<br>Study Guide (34) |
| **Understanding Trade: Trade Among Countries**<br><br>Objective 1: Define international trade, import, and export. (Economics 4)<br>Objective 2: Identify some goods that the United States trades with other countries. (Economics 4) | | Study Guide (35) |
| **Chapter Review** | Answers (188–189) | Chapter 9 Test |

\* Objectives are correlated to the strands and goals in the program scope and sequence on pages T41–T48.

• LEP appropriate resources. (For additional strategies, see pages T32–T33.)

This chapter is the first in a unit that examines the United States today. Chapter 9 focuses on our current use of the land to meet our needs. Specifically, the chapter deals with agriculture, industry, and transportation.

**Lesson 1** examines the San Joaquin Valley in California, which produces one half of the fresh fruits, nuts, and vegetables that Americans consume. The San Joaquin Valley demonstrates how modern technology is used to produce huge amounts of food.

**Lesson 2** focuses on Pittsburgh, Pennsylvania, as an example of an industrial city. We chose Pittsburgh for several reasons. One reason is that the steel industry, which is often represented by Pittsburgh, occupies an important place in the industrial history of this country. Another reason is that Pittsburgh's geographic location influenced its growth as an industrial giant. Finally, Pittsburgh's economic history reflects various periods in the economic development of our nation.

**Lesson 3** focuses on transportation, specifically freight and passenger trains. We chose to examine railroads because of their prominent place in United States history. Lesson 3 examines the railroad's popularity and its advantages and disadvantages in relation to other modes of transportation over time.

The feature Understanding Trade follows Lesson 3. This feature extends the economic concepts introduced in this chapter to include international trade.

Chapter 9 examines how we use the land to meet our needs and wants and prepares students for Chapter 10, which discusses the necessity of taking care of our land.

### Bulletin Board

Title the bulletin board *The United States Today.* For Chapter 9, divide the board into three sections and label them *Farming, Industry,* and *Transportation.* Have students bring in appropriate pictures and clippings from newspapers and magazines to display on the board. As you move to chapters 10 and 11, change the section titles to fit the topics of those chapters and again have students bring in pictures and clippings.

### LEP: Making a Map

After reading Lesson 1, refer students to the chart on page 172. Using the fruits, nuts, vegetables, and field crops listed, have pairs of students choose several crops and plan a farm allotting one or more plots of land to each crop. Direct students to draw maps of their farms.

### Challenge: Writing a News Story

After reading Lesson 2, have students write brief accounts of the changes that have occurred in Pittsburgh since 1946. Tell students to use the *who, what, where, when,* and *why*

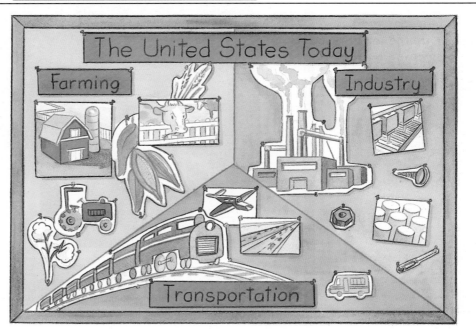

format, and to write in complete sentences. Suggest that students use a title such as *The New Pittsburgh.*

### Investigation

After concluding Lesson 3, have students investigate the railroads that service their community. Tell students to begin by looking under *Railroads* in the Yellow Pages of the telephone book to get the names and numbers of these railroads. Students can then call the railroads to obtain such information as routes, frequency, and use (passenger or freight or both). If you live in a large city, you may want to help students select one or two railroads to investigate.

CHAPTER
PREVIEW

H ave a volunteer read the chapter title. Invite speculation about the meaning of this title. Then read the introductory paragraph. Discuss how the way we meet our needs today differs from the ways the Indians and pioneers met their needs. *(Indians and pioneers had to make or grow almost everything they needed; today, other people make things that we buy in stores.)* As students look at the visuals and read the captions, locate Pittsburgh and the San Joaquin Valley on a wall map of the United States.

## Looking Forward

Farming, industry, and transportation are the topics of the next three lessons: Farming in the San Joaquin Valley, Steel in Pittsburgh, and Moving by Rail.

# Chapter 9

# *The Land of Plenty*

*Can you imagine having to grow your own food and build your own home? The Indians and pioneers had to do this to survive. Today we can depend on other people to farm the land and make building materials. Modern farms and businesses produce goods that are shipped across the country to people who need them. Our land of plenty provides all that we need to live.*

Pittsburgh, Pennsylvania, is built near three rivers and large amounts of coal. This location helped it become a major producer of the world's steel.

Train engines can pull many rail cars at the same time. Trains carry all kinds of goods from livestock to food to automobiles.

168

## BACKGROUND

The great productivity of U.S. agriculture and industry is largely a result of science and technology. Technology has greatly changed the work that Americans do. For example, although half of the produce in the United States is grown in the San Joaquin Valley, only a small percentage of the population of California works in agriculture.

Machines have taken over many jobs. For example, many people used to be needed to plant seeds using hand tools. Now a tractor-driven machine called a seed drill cuts furrows, drops seeds into the furrows, and then covers the seeds. It can plant many rows of seeds at a time. This means that just one person driving the seed drill can plant as much as several workers used to plant.

Agriculture is not the only area in which jobs have been eliminated by machines. In industry, for example, robots are taking over many jobs on the assembly line. Robots do such routine tasks as welding, drilling, and painting automobile parts. Advanced robots are being used now for higher-level jobs, such as inspecting an automobile part to make sure that it is the right size before putting the part into the car. Many assembly-line workers used to do these jobs in automobile plants.

An important source of jobs today is the growing service industry in the United States.

## Understanding the Visuals

The photographs on these pages represent the three lessons in this chapter and three essential elements of the United States economy: agriculture, industry, and transportation.

The San Joaquin (SAN waw KEEN) Valley produces half of the fruits and vegetables eaten in the United States. This valley also produces crops such as the cotton shown above.

All farmers in the San Joaquin Valley depend on water brought in from other areas to water their crops.

Education, health care, recreation, and business services are a few categories of service industries. About two-thirds of American workers are employed in service industries today.

170

## INTRODUCE

Read aloud the lesson title and have students tell what they know about farming. Stress the fact that almost everything we eat is grown on farms. Ask a volunteer to read the Thinking Focus. Point to the San Joaquin Valley on the map on page 171.

### Key Terms

Vocabulary strategies: T36–T37
**agriculture**—the business of farming
**irrigation**—the process of bringing water to dry land
**fertilizer**—chemicals that make plants grow stronger and more quickly

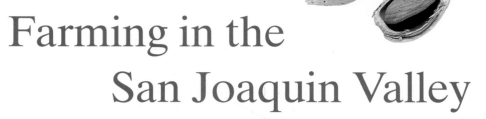

LESSON 1

# Farming in the San Joaquin Valley

### THINKING FOCUS

*What kinds of crops grow in the San Joaquin Valley, and why do they grow so well?*

### Key Terms

- agriculture
- irrigation
- fertilizer

➤ *This machine shakes almond trees so that the nuts fall to the ground. Later, the outer layer of the almonds will be peeled away. When the nuts are sent to stores, they look like the ones above.*

170

**P**edro Cruz struggled to hold the heavy bag of almonds. "Here, let me help you," offered his older sister Rosa. "No, no," said Pedro. "I'm fine."

Rosa smiled, knowing that Pedro was excited. Both children were on their way to Mexico to see their uncle. Pedro wanted to give him the almonds himself.

The Cruzes had left Mexico to become citizens of the United States. At first Pedro and Rosa's parents moved from state to state picking crops. Now the family lived and worked all year on a farm near Bakersfield, California.

"There it is!" shouted Pedro, pointing to the bus that would take them from Bakersfield to Mexico. He lifted his bag of almonds high, trying to control his excitement!

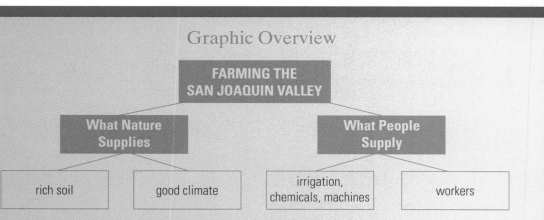

### Objectives

1. Locate the San Joaquin Valley on a map.
2. Explain why crops grow so well in the San Joaquin Valley.
3. Explain how irrigation, fertilizers, and chemicals increase crop production in the San Joaquin Valley.
4. Describe how crops are harvested in the San Joaquin Valley.

### Graphic Overview

**FARMING THE SAN JOAQUIN VALLEY**

**What Nature Supplies**

| rich soil | good climate |

**What People Supply**

| irrigation, chemicals, machines | workers |

## Rich Soil

Workers like the Cruzes harvest many different crops grown near Bakersfield. One half of the fresh fruits, nuts, and vegetables that are grown in the United States comes from the area known as the San Joaquin Valley. This land is north of Bakersfield in the central part of California.

Find the San Joaquin Valley on the map. Notice that the San Joaquin River runs through this land. Between which two rows of mountains does the San Joaquin Valley lie?

What makes the San Joaquin Valley so good for growing crops? The soil is good for plants. For thousands of years, streams and rivers from nearby mountains have carried rich soil down to the valley. Also, whenever rivers in the area overflowed, they added new soil to the land. Plants grow very well in this rich soil.

More than just rich soil makes the San Joaquin Valley good for **agriculture,** which is the business of farming. The valley also has a good climate in which to grow crops. The spring and fall are warm, and the summer is hot but dry. Winter is cool and wet. Temperatures rarely drop below freezing. With enough water, crops can grow all year in this climate.

Look at the lists on page 172. They show the four kinds of agricultural products that come from the San Joaquin Valley. What are these products? ■

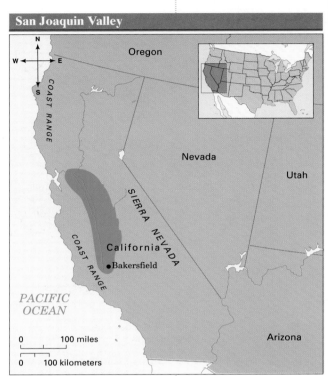

San Joaquin Valley

■ *What makes the San Joaquin Valley a good place for farming?*

171

**Livestock**

cattle

chickens

turkeys

**Fruits and Nuts**

| | |
|---|---|
| almonds | melons |
| apricots | olives |
| dates | peaches |
| figs | pistachios |
| grapes | plums |
| lemons | tomatoes |
| limes | walnuts |

**Field Crops**

alfalfa

barley

cotton

rice

wheat

**Vegetables**

carrots

lettuce

potatoes

► *The San Joaquin Valley produces everything from wheat that can be made into cereal for breakfast to cotton that can be made into clothes.*

## ECONOMICS
### Critical Thinking

Have students tell why irrigation is important in the San Joaquin Valley. *(Irrigation brings water to places that do not get enough rain.)* Explain that the California Aqueduct, which is a large human-made canal, provides much of the water for the valley. Then explain that, for thousands of years, people have put natural materials such as ground bones, wood ash, dried blood, and fish into the soil to fertilize it. These materials in the soil help plants grow. Now people also use chemicals to fertilize soil. These chemicals are not natural materials, but they have helped grow more crops faster.

### Across Time & Space

*Irrigation is not new. Over 1,000 years ago, Indians used ditches to bring water to huge areas of land in central Arizona.*

## Working the Land

Are rich soil and a good climate enough to produce such big crops? No. Plants also need lots of water. However, almost half of the San Joaquin Valley is desert. You remember that few plants grow well in deserts because there is not much rain. In the summer, the most important growing season, the San Joaquin Valley gets almost no rain.

How can the farmers in the San Joaquin Valley grow crops in such a dry place? They bring in water from other parts of California. Much of this water comes from the mountains in parts of northern and eastern California. The water is carried from the mountains to the valley through pipes, ditches, or canals. Bringing water to dry land is called **irrigation.**

Rich soil, a good climate, and irrigation help grow strong plants. Farmers also help plants grow by adding fertilizers to the soil. **Fertilizers** are chemicals that feed plants and make them grow stronger and more quickly.

### Visual Learning

Tell students that people have figured out how much each acre of farmland in the United States produces, on the average. The number is based on the total amounts of all types of farm products. Have students graph the following data on the overall increase in production, labeling the axes *Year* and *Amount*: 1900—146, 1925—143, 1950—213, and 1975—440.

### Historical Context

For most people, farming was once the main way of life. In the 1700s and early 1800s, for example, most American families lived on a farm and raised all they needed. As late as 1850, an average U.S. farmer produced only enough food for four people. Scientific and technological advances have changed the number of people farming. Now only 4 percent of Americans live on farms. Today, the average farmer produces enough food to feed almost 80 people.

### Collaborative Learning

Have students work in small groups to investigate different types of farms, such as field crop farms; vegetable farms; fruit and nut farms; flower farms; beef cattle, hog, and sheep farms; dairy farms; and poultry farms. Allow time for groups to present their findings in class, and encourage the use of visuals. If possible, arrange field trips to local farms of different types to give students first-hand knowledge of their operations.

Many farmers spray crops with chemicals that attack weeds and insects. These chemicals help farmers keep crops healthy and free from weeds. Some chemicals that farmers use are dangerous to people and animals, so many farmers try to use those that are safest. ∎

## Harvesting the Crops

Once crops are grown, they are harvested. Some crops are harvested by machines, which make the job quick and easy. However, large machines can damage certain crops. Therefore, some crops, like grapes, melons, and lemons, must be carefully harvested by people.

When the crops are ready, families like the Cruzes gather in an area and begin the hard job of harvesting. Thousands of farm workers are hired to pick the crops. The work is long and hard. Often, the living conditions near fields are poor.

After the crops are picked, they are packed and placed on trucks and trains. Products from the San Joaquin Valley are then sent to people throughout the country. ∎

■ *How do chemicals and irrigation help farmers?*

▼ *California produces more lemons than any other state in the United States.*

■ *How are farmers able to harvest so many crops?*

### REVIEW

1. **FOCUS** What kinds of crops grow in the San Joaquin Valley, and why do they grow so well?
2. **CONNECT** Compare how people use the land of the San Joaquin Valley with the way the Kwakiutl used the land.
3. **CRITICAL THINKING** Why do you think people in many states might worry if insects destroyed crops in the San Joaquin Valley?
4. **ACTIVITY** Look at the lists on page 172. Make your own list of products you have eaten recently that might have come from the San Joaquin Valley.

173

■ *Chemicals are used to make plants grow faster and to kill insects; irrigation brings water to plants.*

**ECONOMICS**
### Study Skills

Help students summarize the two methods farmers in the San Joaquin Valley use to harvest their crops and the reasons for each. (*Machines and workers—machines enable farmers to harvest huge quantities of certain items quickly, but delicate fruits and other produce must be picked by hand.*)

■ *Farmers use machinery or hire thousands of workers to harvest crops.*

### CLOSE

Check students' comprehension of the lesson by discussing the focus question. If necessary, use the chart on page 172 and the Graphic Overview to reteach the lesson.

173

## Answers to Review Questions

1. Answers will include chicken, cattle, and other livestock; cotton, wheat, and other field crops; grapes, citrus fruit, almonds, tomatoes, lettuce, melons, and other nuts, fruits, and vegetables. These crops grow well there because of the rich soil and good climate and because the farmers irrigate and use chemicals to help plants grow and to control insects and weeds.
2. People in the San Joaquin Valley farm the land. They bring water to the naturally rich soil and use the land to raise crops. The Kwakiutl gathered food from their surroundings rather than raise crops.
3. Since the valley produces half of our country's produce, crops destroyed by insects would cause severe shortages of food throughout the United States.
4. Students will have most likely eaten meat from chickens or cattle, eaten food products made of rice or wheat, and eaten a variety of fruits and vegetables.

## Homework Options

Have each student make a chart of the produce in the San Joaquin Valley and indicate with a symbol which products could be harvested by machine and which by hand.

**Study Guide:** page 31

## DECISION-MAKING PROCESS

1. Recognize the need for a decision
2. Define the goals and values involved
3. Acquire and evaluate necessary information
4. Identify and analyze possible alternatives
5. Choose the best alternative

This Making Decisions lesson, Getting Farm Products to Stores, uses steps 3, 4, and 5 of the decision-making process.

### GEOGRAPHY
### Critical Thinking

On a map of the United States, have students locate the San Joaquin Valley that stretches between Stockton and Bakersfield in central California. On the same map, have students locate East Coast cities such as Boston, New York, and Washington, D.C. Establish that crops from the San Joaquin Valley have to be shipped over 3,000 miles to be sold in these East Coast cities.

**Note:** Most crops do not go directly from farm to store. They must be processed or packaged first.

·MAKING DECISIONS

# Getting Farm Products to Stores

**Y**ou know that many different crops are grown in the San Joaquin Valley of California. You know why they grow so well there. You also know how they are harvested. But do you know how they get from a farm to stores across the country? Let's think about that a little bit.

## Here's Why

Suppose you grow almonds, tomatoes, and carrots on a farm in the San Joaquin Valley. You want to send them to cities in the United States and then to stores within the cities. You have to decide how to get your crops to the stores at the lowest cost before they spoil or rot. How will you send each of them?

### Objectives

1. Analyze the advantages and disadvantages of various means of transporting crops. (Economics 3; Critical Thinking 2)
2. Choose the best method of transporting each of three crops. (Economics 3; Critical Thinking 3)

### Activity

Assign groups of students to interview the produce managers at local supermarkets. Have students find out where the store's fruits and vegetables were grown and how they were transported to the store. Ask each group to report their findings to the class.

## Here's How

Your crops can be shipped by truck, airplane, or train. You may have to use more than one method of transportation. Use the chart below to help you decide how to ship your crops.

### Comparing Ways of Moving Farm Products

**Airplane**
Travels faster than trucks or trains.
Costs more than trucks or trains.
Cannot carry products directly to stores.

**Truck**
Costs less than airplanes or trains.
Can carry products directly to stores.
Travels slower than airplanes and trains.

**Train**
Can carry more than airplanes or trucks.
Costs more than trucks.
Cannot carry products directly to stores.

## Try It

Work with a partner. Discuss how to get your three crops to stores where you now live. Write four or more questions that you must answer before you can decide. One question might be: How much will it cost?

## Apply It

Now, make your decision. Write a report that tells how you will get each of your three crops to stores. Tell why you made your decision.

175

UNDERSTANDING
NUMBER INFORMATION

This skills feature uses a grain production table to teach students how to read a table.

ECONOMICS

## Visual Learning

Stress the need to use columns and rows together to find information in a table. If students find it difficult to keep their places, suggest that they use both hands. Show students how to place the right hand next to the appropriate column while they use the index finger of the left hand to move across the row.

Point out the first number in the table, 24. Write *24 million* on the chalkboard. Elicit that this number is 24,000,000 when written entirely in numerals.

**176**

UNDERSTANDING NUMBER INFORMATION

# Using Tables

**Here's Why**  You know that half of our country's fruits and vegetables come from the San Joaquin Valley in California. But what about grain crops, such as the wheat in the picture below? How much grain does California produce? How does its grain production compare with other states? One way you could find this information is to look at a table.

**Here's How**  A table is one way to organize number information so that it can be understood easily. Look at the table on the next page. It gives grain production from five states for the year 1986. What are the five states? Four grain crops are listed in the table. What are the four crops? Notice that each number shows how many millions of bushels are produced. One million is a large number: 1,000,000.

How can you find out how much of each crop a state produced in 1986? Find the name of the state on the left. Find the name of the crop at the top. Move your finger across the page until you come to the column for the crop you want. For example, to find how much corn was grown in California, go across the California row until you come to the corn column. The number in that space is the number of millions of bushels of corn grown in California in 1986. What is that number?

176

## Objective

Read a table. (Visual Learning 2)

| Grain Production in Millions of Bushels — 1986 | | | | |
|---|---|---|---|---|
| **States** | **Barley** | **Corn** | **Oats** | **Wheat** |
| California | 24 | 38 | 3 | 52 |
| Colorado | 21 | 99 | 3 | 96 |
| Kansas | 10 | 182 | 11 | 433 |
| Ohio | 1 | 476 | 12 | 48 |
| Texas | 2 | 149 | 8 | 120 |

**Try It** Use the table to compare states. For example, if you look at the column of numbers under *wheat*, you can see that Kansas grew the most wheat of these five states. How many millions of bushels of wheat did Kansas grow? Which of these five states grew the smallest amount of wheat? How many millions of bushels of wheat did that state grow?

**Apply It** Write three questions that can be answered from the table. Then work with a partner. Ask your partner to find the information in the table that answers your questions. Find the information that answers your partner's three questions.

## Visual Learning

Ask students how they could use this chart to determine which state has the highest grain production. *(Add the numbers across each row and compare the totals.)* Ask which state has the highest grain production *(Kansas)* and which has the lowest *(California).*

## Answers to Try It

Kansas grew 433,000,000 bushels. Ohio grew the smallest amount of wheat—48,000,000 bushels.

## Visual Learning

Survey the students to find out in which months their birthdays fall. List the 12 months of the year on the board, and as you go around the room asking for the month of birth, have a volunteer use tick marks at the chalkboard to tally the answers. Then ask each student to create a formal table showing the results of the survey.

## INTRODUCE

Read aloud the lesson title and have students tell what they know about steel, what it's used for, and how it's made. Have a volunteer read the Thinking Focus. Help students recall what they learned about the importance of location to the farming industry in the San Joaquin Valley. Suggest that they read to find out more about how Pittsburgh's location helped it become a steel-making center.

### Key Terms

Vocabulary strategies: T36–T37
**location**—where something is found
**steel mill**—factory that makes steel
**industry**—business
**services**—businesses that provide people with what they need or want

➤ *Steel mills probably sound very noisy because there are large machines and many people working.*

178

---

LESSON 2

# Steel in Pittsburgh

### THINKING FOCUS

*Why is Pittsburgh in a good location for making steel?*

### Key Terms

- location
- steel mills
- industry
- services

➤ *In 1930, Thomas Hart Benton painted* Steel. *It shows the inside of a steel mill. What do you think working in a mill would sound like?*

178

People like to invent tall tales about their heros. In Pittsburgh, Pennsylvania, a city famous for making steel, people tell stories about Joe Magarac. They say he was the greatest steel worker of all.

Joe Magarac was seven feet of solid steel from head to toe. He worked in a factory, mixing and pouring gallons of bubbling hot steel into big tubs. He stopped only to eat five or six meals a day. Joe stirred the red-hot steel with his bare hands. He would scoop it up and make eight long railroad rails at the same time. He'd squeeze them out from between his fingers, four from each hand.

Joe Magarac wasn't real, of course, but the tale of Joe Magarac shows that steelworkers are American heros.

---

## Objectives

1. Explain how Pittsburgh's location contributed to its development as a steel city.
2. Describe how the steel industry helped Pittsburgh grow.
3. Identify problems resulting from the steel industry.
4. Describe how Pittsburgh is recovering from the decline of the steel industry.

## Graphic Overview

### PITTSBURGH, THE "STEEL CITY"

| Location | Problems | Solutions |
|----------|----------|-----------|
| on three rivers | dirty air | air cleaned up |
| close to coal and iron | closing steel mills | new industries started |

## Steel City

Steel is a very strong metal. It is so strong that people use it to make cars, airplanes, trains, bridges, buildings, and all kinds of machines we use every day. The city that became best known for making steel is Pittsburgh. It is still called "Steel City."

One reason Pittsburgh became Steel City is that it is in a good location for making steel. The place where something is found is its **location.** Pittsburgh's location is good because it is close to natural resources that people use to make steel.

The most important natural resources near Pittsburgh are its rivers and its coal and iron. Find Pittsburgh's three rivers on the map. Miners dig the coal and iron from the earth nearby. These are then shipped on the rivers to Pittsburgh. Here, people who work in **steel mills,** which are factories that make steel, use the coal and iron to make steel. The steel is then shipped out to the world by ships or by trains. ∎

*▼ By 1904 there were over 30 steel mills. In the 1970s more steel was produced than ever before. But in the 1980s the number of mills dropped down to three.*

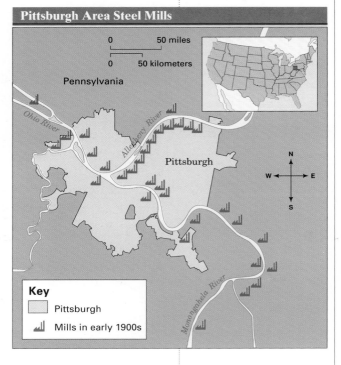

**Pittsburgh Area Steel Mills**

Pennsylvania

Ohio River

Allegheny River

Pittsburgh

Monongahela River

0       50 miles
0       50 kilometers

N W E S

**Key**

Pittsburgh

Mills in early 1900s

■ *How did Pittsburgh's location by three rivers help its steel industry?*

## Pittsburgh Grows

The steel **industry,** or business, helped make Pittsburgh great. Many people moved to Pittsburgh during the early 1900s to get jobs working in the steel industry. Because the steelworkers needed food, clothing, houses, and other goods, more people came to Pittsburgh to provide these things. For years, the city grew and grew.

179

GEOGRAPHY
## Visual Learning

Have students examine the photographs of Pittsburgh before and after the air pollution problem was solved. Tell students that Pittsburgh's air, before legislation, was so smoky, sooty, and dark that the city street lamps had to be kept on during the day so that people could see where they were going.

➤ *People began a smoke-control program in 1946 and had clean air by 1960.*

■ *The steel industry caused tremendous air pollution in Pittsburgh. Another problem was that other countries could make steel more cheaply so most steel mills closed down.*

➤ *This view of Pittsburgh in 1911 shows smoky air from the steel mills.*

▼ *This photograph shows a clear view of Pittsburgh today. What made the difference?*

■ *What problems did the steel industry cause?*

Over time, the amount of steel produced in Pittsburgh grew. With so many mills, there also came problems.

One problem was dirty air. To make steel, coal is burned. Burning coal sends off smoke. Pittsburgh used to have air filled with smoke. People didn't like living in smoky air. So in 1946, Pittsburgh began a smoke-control program. By 1960, the city had clean air again.

However, Pittsburgh faced another problem in the 1980s. Factories in other parts of the world also made steel. Other countries could make steel cheaper, so most of the steel mills in Steel City closed down. ■

## New Beginnings

The people of Pittsburgh went to work to solve this problem, too. They rebuilt the machines in their mills and found new ways to make steel more cheaply. People also started new industries in Pittsburgh, such as computer

## Visual Learning

To illustrate what pollution is made of and where it exists, have students spread a layer of petroleum jelly on small pieces of cardboard. Have students tape the cards to different places outside, such as a tree, a window sill, or a busy corner. After 24 hours, examine the amount of dirt on the cards and discuss where and why the pollution was the greatest.

## Art Connection

Have students make a collage using pictures of steel products cut out from magazines. You might want to have the class list a few of the products made from steel—such as automobiles, train rails, structural beams, etc.—to help students start thinking of what to look for.

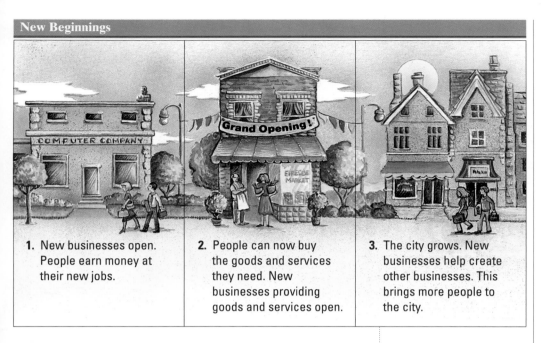

1. New businesses open. People earn money at their new jobs.

2. People can now buy the goods and services they need. New businesses providing goods and services open.

3. The city grows. New businesses help create other businesses. This brings more people to the city.

companies. Soon, more people got jobs in these new businesses.

The chart above shows how new businesses help a city grow. When new businesses open, people move nearby to work. With more people living in an area, more new businesses are needed to serve these people. **Services**—stores, schools, restaurants, gas stations—are businesses that provide people with what they need to live.

In this way, Pittsburgh has been able to keep growing. Some people think that Pittsburgh is one of the best cities in the United States in which to live. Joe Magarac would be proud of this city and how it has grown. ■

■ *In what ways has Pittsburgh kept growing?*

## R E V I E W

1. **FOCUS** Why is Pittsburgh in a good location for making steel?
2. **CONNECT** How does the workplace of a steelworker in Pittsburgh differ from the workplace of a farm worker in the San Joaquin Valley?
3. **CRITICAL THINKING** Why is it important for people in a city to try to make the air

clean and safe?
4. **WRITING ACTIVITY** Make a list of people you have seen working in services, such as bank tellers and secretaries. Next to it, write the businesses that they would work in, such as banks and offices.

181

### HISTORY
## Visual Learning

Focus attention on the process diagram. Point out that, in addition to the new computer industry, Pittsburgh attracted 150 research laboratories, which do scientific experiments, and industries that produce glass and electrical equipment. Then direct attention to the center panel, and ask students to name businesses that meet their needs and wants. *(Answers might include a variety of businesses, such as those that provide food, clothing, furniture, toys, videos, etc.)*

■ *Pittsburgh has attracted new industries, which attract more workers. More businesses open to provide goods and services*

## C L O S E

To assess students' understanding of the lesson, discuss the focus question. Then have students describe Pittsburgh's air pollution problem, what was done about it, and what happened to the steel industry in Pittsburgh. If necessary, use the Graphic Overview to reteach the lesson.

181

## Answers to Review Questions

1. Pittsburgh is close to coal and iron, which are used to make steel. It is also near three rivers, which are used to transport coal, iron, and finished steel products.
2. Steel workers work inside factories called steel mills. The factories are probably hot and noisy. Farm workers in the San Joaquin Valley work outside in fields, which are probably warm and quiet.
3. Clean and safe air is healthy air; dirty air causes people to become ill.

4. Students should list people and places of various services, including stores, restaurants, police and fire departments, schools, and so on.

## Homework Options

Have each student write a paragraph comparing Pittsburgh with Abilene or Leadville. Advise students to include why the cities grew and why people left the cities.

**Study Guide:** page 33

## INTRODUCE

Read aloud the poem on this page and discuss any experiences students have had riding trains. Have a volunteer read aloud the Thinking Focus. Ask students to recall the significant role the railroad played in the history and economy of Abilene and Leadville. Suggest that, by reading, students will learn more about the history and importance of trains.

### Key Terms

Vocabulary strategies: T36–T37
**freight**—goods
**trade**—buying and selling goods
**transportation**—ways of moving things or people

LESSON 3

# Moving by Rail

### THINKING FOCUS

*How do trains help move goods and people across America?*

### Key Terms

- freight
- trade
- transportation

## Travel

The railroad track is
    miles away,
And the day is loud
    with voices speaking,
Yet there isn't a train
    goes by all day
But I hear its whistle
    shrieking.

All night there isn't a
    train goes by,
Though the night is still
    for sleep and dreaming,
But I see its cinders red
    on the sky,
And hear its engine
    steaming.

My heart is warm with
    the friends I make,
And better friends I'll not
    be knowing;
Yet there isn't a train I
    wouldn't take,
No matter where it's going.

Edna St. Vincent Millay

This poem captures a good feeling that Americans have about trains. Trains remind us of faraway places that we'd like to visit. However, trains are useful to us in ways that are practical, too.

182

## Objectives

1. Describe the role of railroads in our country's history.
2. Explain how other means of transportation affected business on the railroad.
3. Describe how railroads are used today.

## Graphic Overview

### RAILROADS

| Types | Long Ago | Now |
|---|---|---|
| **Freight Trains** | carried goods across country | piggybacking; work with ships and trucks |
| **Passenger Trains** | made traveling much faster | used less than cars and planes |

## Trains and Other Ways to Travel

In this chapter you read about farming in the San Joaquin Valley and making steel in Pittsburgh. How do products like farm goods and steel get from where they are grown or made to where people use them?

Many things people need are shipped by train. Trains that carry **freight**—that is, goods like steel and almonds—are called freight trains. Trains that carry people when they travel are called passenger trains. A passenger is a person who rides from place to place.

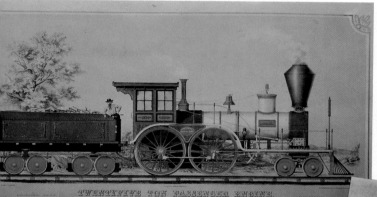

*This engine got its power from steam. It burned wood or coal to boil water. The steam from the boiling water ran the engine.*

*This advertisement for the St. Louis and San Francisco railroad line shows a brother and sister waiting in the station, ready for a journey by train.*

People have been using freight and passenger trains since the late 1860s, when railroads first crossed the nation from coast to coast. Trains became popular because they made traveling much faster. For example, in the 1880s a trip from Chicago to Denver in a horse-drawn buggy could take 49 days. The same trip by train took only six days, and it was a lot less bumpy!

By the 1920s, however, a new invention became popular, the automobile. Many Americans bought cars so they could travel wherever they wanted. They did not have to take trains, which went only to certain places.

Have students preview the lesson by reading the headings. You may wish to start the Graphic Overview on the board and have students complete it as they read the lesson.

### HISTORY
### Critical Thinking

Point out that trains were much faster and could carry much more than horses and wagons. They were once more important for transporting both freight and people. Then discuss the advantages—such as comfort, convenience, and time efficiency—that automobile travel offered Americans in the 1920s.

## Access Strategy

Explain that this lesson focuses on the development of America's railroad from 1860 to the present. You might subtract the dates to underscore the passage of over 130 years. Then define *freight* and write it on the board. Ask students for examples of freight transported to or from Abilene, Leadville, Pittsburgh, and the San Joaquin Valley.

Next, give students copies of an outline map of the United States. Explain that almonds from the San Joaquin Valley are being transported to Texas and Massachusetts. Have students use colored markers to draw on their maps train tracks to San Antonio and to Boston. Suggest that, by reading, students will learn more about the railroad and how businesses and passengers have depended on it.

## Access Activity

Have available a model train. Ask students to draw pictures of products that could be transported from Abilene, Leadville, Pittsburgh, and the San Joaquin Valley on the train.

■ *The railroad's business suffered because cars, trucks, buses, and planes traveled faster and more directly.*

■ *How did cars, trucks, buses, and airplanes affect business on the railroad?*

▼ *This is a freight yard. These cars are waiting to be loaded and hooked up to engines so their goods can be delivered across the country.*

In the 1950s, many people started to travel by airplane because it was even faster. At that time, a person could fly in a plane from New York to Los Angeles in 18 hours. The same trip by train would take three to four days. ■

## Railroads Today

Trains aren't as fast as planes and can't go everywhere that cars and trucks do, but they are still used because they cost less and can carry more. Trains move many of the goods people buy and sell. Buying and selling goods is called **trade.** Trains, ships, trucks, and airplanes help trade. These forms of **transportation,** or ways of moving things, take goods from place to place. Trains help trade between distant states in the United States.

Today, people use what is called "piggybacking" to load freight. Workers can load a box full of goods onto a train car, then stack another box, piggyback, on top of that one. This way, trains are even more useful since twice as many loads can be carried at the same time.

Ships, trains, and trucks work together to move freight. At a seaport, you might see boxes of tuna fish being unloaded from a ship. Those boxes might be put on a freight train and taken to a distant city. Then, they might be loaded on a truck to be delivered to a store near you.

On the next page, you can read more about freight trains—how they move and what they carry.

**ECONOMICS**
### Critical Thinking

While some freight, such as perishable items, is more likely to be transported directly by truck, other freight is moved mostly by train. Bulky raw materials, such as coal, timber, and iron ore, are most easily transported by railroad. Tell students that the railroad is often the most economical and practical mode of transport for these products.

184

## Social Participation

Divide the class into three groups. Have each group pick a destination (over 300 hundred miles away) for a four-day trip. Assign one mode of transportation—either car, train, or plane—to each group. Have students discuss and list positive and negative aspects of their assigned modes of transportation.

## Historical Context

The first trains were pulled by horses. In 1830 a famous race was held between a steam locomotive, the *Tom Thumb*, and a horse to convince the owners of the Baltimore and Ohio Railroad to switch from horses to steam-powered engines. At first *Tom Thumb* led the race, but then its engine belt slipped and the horse won. Despite this, steam engines became widespread. During the 1950s, most railroads switched to diesel-electric trains.

# A Freight Train

*Modern freight trains have many cars that are used for different purposes. These cars are used to move everything from tanks of liquids to livestock to coal.*

**Stacked three high,** this car carries up to 18 automobiles. Today, freight trains move six out of every ten new automobiles made in the United States.

**Piggyback boxcars** carry peaches from factories where they were canned to cities where they will be sold. A boxcar is a closed train car that carries almost anything.

**An engine leads the way!** It has the power to pull all the cars. This modern engine runs on diesel *(DEE zuhl),* a form of oil. The engineer controls how fast the train goes.

**More About the Tri-Level Auto Car** This freight car can carry 12 full-size cars or 18 subcompact cars. These multi-level auto cars have significantly reduced the cost of transporting cars from factories to dealers. New vertical auto cars that can carry up to 30 small cars are also coming into use.

## Visual Learning

Direct attention to the boxcar carrying peaches. Remind students that it would cost more to transport these canned peaches by truck or air than by train.

185

## Research

Have students research how trains are used for mass transit in cities. Mention that two very important means of transportation in many large cities are subways and commuter trains.

Have students share their findings with their classmates. Encourage them to include visuals in their reports.

## Visual Learning

Have students use an encyclopedia to find pictures of different kinds of rail cars, such as tank cars, piggyback flatcars, and open-top hoppers. Have students draw a mural of an imaginary engine pulling different types of rail cars across the country. Have students make up a name for their railroad and label the types of cars and their contents.

➤ *79 mph compared to 21 mph, or 58 mph faster*

### Visual Learning

Refer students to the graph on this page. Suggest that they are traveling from New York City to Bar Harbor, Maine (a distance of 550 miles). Elicit that the trip would take an hour by air. Note that the same trip would take about seven hours by train. *(550 mi. ÷ 79 mph = 6.96 or 7 hours)* Ask students if they would rather ride in a plane for one hour or a train for seven hours.

➤ *The TGV goes 89 mph faster than a U.S. train, or more than twice as fast.*

■ *Railroads help businesses today by transporting freight quickly and economically and by providing transportation for workers.*

### CLOSE

To check students' understanding of the lesson, ask the focus question. Then discuss with students how new forms of transportation have affected railroads. If necessary, use the Graphic Overview to reteach the lesson.

**186**

➤ *This chart compares travel by steam train and horse before 1929 and between modern trains and airplanes. How many miles per hour can a modern train go compared to a steam-powered train?*

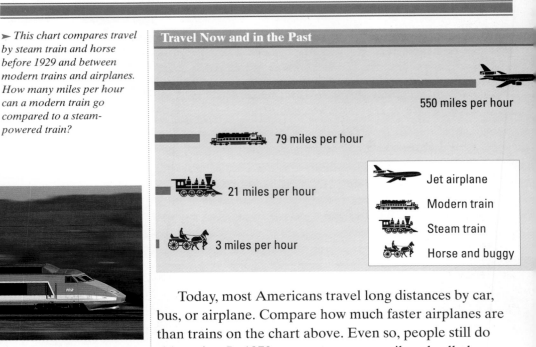

▲ *The TGV is a bullet train that travels from Paris to Lyon, France. Its name means "great speed" in French because it can travel 168 miles per hour. How much faster is that than U.S. trains?*

■ *How are railroads helping businesses today?*

**Travel Now and in the Past**

550 miles per hour

79 miles per hour

21 miles per hour

3 miles per hour

Jet airplane
Modern train
Steam train
Horse and buggy

Today, most Americans travel long distances by car, bus, or airplane. Compare how much faster airplanes are than trains on the chart above. Even so, people still do ride trains. In 1970, a new passenger railroad called Amtrak began. The name "Amtrak" comes from "**Am**erica," "**tra**vel," and "**tra**ck." Thousands ride Amtrak for short trips, often to get to and from work.

People are inventing new kinds of trains, too. One type of new train, called a bullet train, can travel very fast. In the future, bullet trains may carry people to jobs far away from their homes. Because the trains are so fast, people will be able to get to and from work more quickly than ever. ■

### REVIEW

1. **FOCUS** How do trains help move goods and people across the United States?
2. **CONNECT** How might very fast freight trains be helpful to farmers in the San Joaquin Valley?
3. **CRITICAL THINKING** What do you think would happen to the transportation industry if someone invented a faster and cheaper way of moving goods?
4. **ACTIVITY** Work with a group. Make a model freight train out of shoeboxes. Draw on a shoebox to make it look like a certain type of train car. Load your train car with freight. Decide where it is going and then tell the class.

## Homework Options

Ask students to imagine traveling cross-country in the sleeping car of a passenger train. Have each student write a journal entry describing what he or she sees, hears, feels, and smells on the journey.

**Study Guide:** page 34

## Answers to Review Questions

1. Freight trains are used, together with ships and trucks, to move goods from one place to another. Passenger trains transport workers and travelers.
2. Very fast trains would help farmers in the San Joaquin Valley by getting fresh produce to markets far away quickly and inexpensively.
3. People would use the new method of transportation. The older way of moving goods might lose business. Prices of goods

could possibly decrease.
4. Students may choose to make models of an old locomotive or of a modern freight train. Train cars might include flatcars that carry boxcars, tank cars, auto cars, and so on.

## UNDERSTANDING TRADE

# Trade Among Countries

Some food grown in California is sold to other states. Some of it is sold to other countries. The United States buys products from other countries, too. The buying and selling of products among countries is called international trade.

Products that a country sells to another country are called exports. Products that a country buys from another country are called imports. Exports go out. Imports come in.

The United States trades with many countries around the world. Canada is the largest trade partner of the United States. In fact, Canada and the United States sell more products to each other than do any other two countries in the world. Some of these products are shown on the map below.

International trade is important to most countries. When countries export products, they earn money. When they import products, they get things they need.

**Trade Between the United States and Canada**

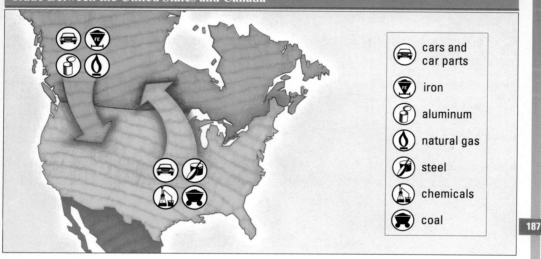

| | |
|---|---|
| cars and car parts | |
| iron | |
| aluminum | |
| natural gas | |
| steel | |
| chemicals | |
| coal | |

187

**Answers to Reviewing Key Terms**

A.
1. location
2. services
3. agriculture
4. freight
5. steel mills
6. fertilizer
7. trade
8. industry
9. transportation
10. irrigation

**Answers to Exploring Concepts**

A. trains—1860s, cars—1920s, airplanes—1950s

B.
1. Crops can grow in the San Joaquin Valley because the land is irrigated.
2. The city will grow as new people come to provide goods and services to the people already there. A city with plenty of jobs for people is a good place to live because there is enough money in the area to provide extra things like recreational facilities.
3. Freight is moved on trains to a city where it is loaded on a truck and then delivered to a store or other business.

---

# Chapter Review

## Reviewing Key Terms

agriculture (p. 171)  location (p. 179)
fertilizer (p. 172)  services (p. 181)
freight (p. 183)  steel mills (p. 179)
industry (p. 179)  trade (p. 184)
irrigation (p. 172)  transportation (p. 184)

**A.** Write the key term for each meaning.
1. where something is found
2. businesses that perform work or provide people with what they need to live

3. the business of farming
4. materials that are carried by train, ship, truck, or plane
5. factories that make steel
6. chemicals that make plants grow strong and more quickly
7. the buying and selling of goods
8. a business that makes things to sell
9. a way of moving goods or passengers
10. the bringing of water to dry land

## Exploring Concepts

**A.** Copy the timeline below. On your timeline, show when trains, automobiles, and airplanes began to be used a lot for travel. Draw a picture for each of the three dates.

**B.** Answer each question at the right with one or two sentences.

1. How can crops grow in dry areas like the San Joaquin Valley?
2. Usually a city grows and is a good place to live if there are plenty of jobs for people. Why do you think this is true?
3. Explain how trains and trucks work together to move freight.

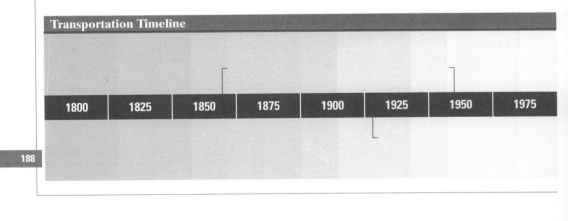

**Transportation Timeline**

| 1800 | 1825 | 1850 | 1875 | 1900 | 1925 | 1950 | 1975 |

## Reviewing Skills

1. The table below shows the amount of land used to grow the main agricultural crops in three states. Write three sentences about what the table shows.

2. Look at the physical map on pages 238–239. What physical features are in Alabama?

| State | Thousands of Acres |
|---|---|
| California | 4,922 |
| Alabama | 2,267 |
| Arizona | 738 |

## Using Critical Thinking

1. Many crops are grown in California and shipped to other states. Why do you think strawberries are not shipped the same way as cotton? How do you think strawberries and cotton are each shipped?

2. In big cities, the air is made dirty by automobile engines. What would you suggest to help solve this problem?

## Preparing for Citizenship

1. COLLECTING INFORMATION Work with a partner. Prepare a scrapbook of pictures of goods made of steel. Look through old magazines to find as many pictures as you can.

2. COLLABORATIVE LEARNING Many tall-tale characters are heroes to certain industries. For example, Joe Magarac is a hero to steelmakers, John Henry is a hero to railroaders, and Paul Bunyan is a hero to lumberjacks. Make up your own classroom tall-tale hero. Brainstorm the kinds of things your hero would do. Work in small groups to write stories. Put all the stories together to make a classroom book. Vote on a title for your book. Choose someone to draw a cover.

189

**CHAPTER ORGANIZER**

# Chapter 10 *Taking Care of Our Land*

## CHAPTER PLANNING CHART

| Pupil's Edition | Teacher's Edition | Ancillaries |
|---|---|---|
| **Literature Selection: *Once There Was a Tree*** | | Discovery Journal (25, 26) |
| **Lesson 1: Saving Our Land (4–5 days)**<br><br>   Objective 1:  Explain the reasons for conserving natural resources. (Economics 1; Geography 3)*<br>   Objective 2:  Identify ways to conserve natural resources. (Citizenship 1, 2) | • Graphic Overview (198)<br>• Access Strategy (199)<br>• Access Activity (199)<br>  Debate (200)<br>  Writing a Paragraph (201)<br>  Writing Letters (202) | Map Activity (11)<br>Study Guide (36)<br>• Study Print (12) |
| **Lesson 2: Protecting Our Resources (4–5 days)**<br><br>   Objective 1:  Identify the main sources of air, water, and soil pollution. (Geography 3)<br>   Objective 2:  Explain why pollution is harmful. (Geography 3)<br>   Objective 3:  Describe ways to reduce air, water, and soil pollution. (Political Systems 1; Citizenship 1, 2) | • Graphic Overview (204)<br>• Access Strategy (205)<br>• Access Activity (205)<br>  Political Context (206) | Study Guide (37) |
| **Lesson 3: Recycling to Save Our Resources (4–5 days)**<br><br>   Objective 1:  Identify the major source of trash. (Geography 3; Economics 1)<br>   Objective 2:  Explain the importance of recycling. (Geography 3; Economics 1)<br>   Objective 3:  Identify ways that people can help solve the trash problem. (Citizenship 1, 2) | • Graphic Overview (208)<br>• Access Strategy (209)<br>• Access Activity (209)<br>  Economic Context (210)<br>  Social Context (210) | Study Guide (38) |
| **Understanding Group Activities: Recycling Products**<br><br>   Objective:  Participate in a group project. (Social Participation 2) | | Study Guide (39) |
| **Chapter Review** | Answers  (214–215) | Chapter 10 Test |

\* Objectives are correlated to the strands and goals in the program
  scope and sequence on pages T41–T48.

• LEP appropriate resources. (For
  additional strategies, see pages
  T32–T33.)

This chapter is the second of three chapters that examine the United States today. The previous chapter introduced ways in which people use the land for agriculture, industry, and transportation. Chapter 10 focuses on some of the consequences of our use of natural resources. By concentrating on how we can work together to solve environmental problems, this chapter prepares the way for Chapter 11, which deals with our national heritage.

We chose to focus this chapter on the quality of the environment because it is an urgent issue. The topic is also a vital part of any discussion of our use of the land today. We divide environmental issues into three main categories: conservation of natural resources, cleaning up pollution, and recycling.

Chapter 10 opens with the literature selection *Once There Was a Tree,* which examines the question of natural resource ownership. This selection builds the understanding that the earth is a shared home.

**Lesson 1** discusses ways to conserve forests, soil, and water—three vital natural resources. The feature A Closer Look: National Parks displays the beauty and diversity of our national parks—wilderness lands that have been set aside and protected.

**Lesson 2** examines air, water, and soil pollution. The lesson looks at the causes and results of pollution. It also describes how people are working to clean up the environment and prevent further pollution.

**Lesson 3** discusses recycling as an essential approach to solving the environmental problem of waste disposal. The skill feature Understanding Group Activities suggests a group recycling project, giving students a concrete way to help take care of our land.

Chapter 10 prepares students for the next and final chapter, which focuses on our national pride and heritage.

### LEP: Making a Poster

After concluding Lesson 1, have students make posters showing ways to conserve various resources and urging people to use these conservation methods.

### Challenge: Writing a Travel Brochure

After reading Lesson 1, have students write and design travel brochures for a national park of their choice. Provide sample travel brochures. Have students use a folded piece of 8 1/2-by-11-inch paper. Suggest that the name of the park and an illustration appear on the cover and a list of park features, animals, and activities appear on the inside.

### Oral Report

After reading Lesson 2, tell students to gather clippings from current magazines that address air, soil, and water pollution. Have students summarize the information in the articles in oral reports for the class.

### Illustrating

After concluding Lesson 3, have pairs of students make a drawing titled *If They Recycled, So Can We.* Using the information in Across Time and Space on page 211, have students draw a line through the middle of a large piece of paper. In the upper half, have them illustrate pioneers recycling cloth and grease, and in the lower half have them illustrate two ways in which they can recycle.

Chapter 10

# Taking Care of Our Land

*Our country is a land of great natural beauty. But today we are using resources rapidly and producing large amounts of trash and poisons that harm our land. To protect the beauty of our land, many people are working to clean up our environment and to find ways to use resources wisely.*

Every year, more and more people in the United States are saving old newspapers and other kinds of trash that can be used again or made into something new.

These stacks of old boxes will be made into new cardboard items and used again. That means fewer trees will be cut down to make new cardboard.

190

ronmental issues to public attention.

One early conservationist was John Muir, a naturalist who founded the Sierra Club in 1892. Muir wanted to protect the giant redwood forests and the wilderness areas of the California Sierra Nevadas. Today, the Sierra Club works throughout the United States to protect the environment, wilderness areas, and endangered wildlife species.

The conservation movement gained momentum in the early 1900s. One enthusiastic advocate was the 26th President of the United States, Theodore Roosevelt. He

helped establish the first wildlife refuge, increased the total acreage of our national forests, and influenced the creation of many conservation projects and state agencies.

One person who helped extend our appreciation of the resources of the world's oceans is Jacques Cousteau. Since 1951, Cousteau has been traveling the seas, exploring and documenting the life that thrives in the ocean's depths. By writing books and making films and television series, he has educated people about these wonders and about the potential threats that modern

The photographs and illustration on these pages represent the topics covered in the three lessons of this chapter: conservation, pollution control, and recycling.

If we all work together to clean up our resources, more areas can become as clean and beautiful as this protected land in one of our many national parks.

Every day we use clean water in our homes. If we try to use less water each time, we are helping to save our clean water resources.

industrial nations pose to ocean plant and animal life.

In 1961 the World Wildlife Fund was established to save endangered species of wildlife and their habitats across the world. This fund helps educate people about animals that are disappearing from the earth, such as the African elephant, which is hunted for its ivory tusks. The fund also works to save threatened areas where many species of plants and animals live, such as the world's rain forests.

Even though many organizations now work to promote conservation efforts, much still needs to be done on a global scale to preserve our wildlife, oceans, forests, and other resources.

## INTRODUCE

Remind students that throughout this book they have learned how people have used the natural resources of the earth. Explain that this selection looks at how people think about the land and its resources.

## READ AND RESPOND

You may wish to read this selection aloud. After reading the introductory paragraph, have students answer the question posed. Then suggest that, as you read, they listen to check their predictions.

**maggot** the wormlike form of a newly hatched insect

192

*A tree stump is a home to insects, a scratching post for bears, and a place where people can rest. So who really owns the tree stump? Read a story that answers this question about the land.*

LITERATURE

# ONCE THERE WAS A TREE

**Written by Natalia Romanova**

**Adapted by Anne Schwartz**

**Illustrated by Gennady Spirin**

Once there was a tree. It had grown for many years and now it was growing old.

Dark clouds swept across the sky. Rain fell, thunder roared, and a lightning bolt split the tree in two.

A woodsman came upon the broken tree and sawed it down so that only the stump remained. Soon a bark beetle with long feelers settled in. The beetle loved the stump and laid her eggs under its bark.

The eggs hatched and tiny maggots emerged. All summer long they gnawed tunnels in the bark. Winter came and they slept. When they awoke in the spring with long feelers of their own, it was time to fly away.

## Thematic Connections

Social Studies: How people interact with the land

Houghton Mifflin Literary Readers: Changes

## Background

*Once There Was a Tree* was first published in the Soviet Union in 1983. Its author, Natalia Romanova, was born and raised in Leningrad, Russia. Ms. Romanova published her first children's book in 1961. She has since published eight other children's books and many screenplays. *Once There Was a Tree* is the only book of hers that has been translated into English.

But the tree stump was not deserted for long. With all the entrances and exits the maggots had made, here was the perfect place for ants to live. One ant brought a leaf, another a twig, and another a grain of sand. They cleared out the tunnels and made the stump their home.

A bear approached the tree stump, sniffed at it, and sharpened her claws on the bark. The stump was hers, like everything else around. Even the ants in the stump were hers, and no other bear would dare disturb them.

194

A titmouse flew down and landed on the stump. She spotted an ant dragging a caterpillar and pecked at it. Now the caterpillar was hers. The ants were hers, too, and so was the tree stump. No other birds would come near.

One rainy day a frog found shelter in a hole in the tree stump. Time and weather had dug these holes, which would protect others who also passed by.

The warm sun dried the tree stump, and soon a new occupant had moved in— an earwig. Liking nothing better than the shade, he crept under the bark to sleep.

*titmouse*  a type of bird

*earwig*  a type of insect

195

196

A man was walking in the woods and saw the tree stump. He sat down on it to rest, and now the tree stump was his.

The man thought he owned the forest—and the earth—so why not the tree stump?

But who really owns the tree stump? The bark beetle that gnaws tunnels inside it? The ants that travel through the tunnels? The earwig that sleeps under its bark? Or the bear that uses it to sharpen her claws?

Does it belong to the titmouse that flies down upon it? The frog that finds shelter in one of its holes? Or the man who believes he owns the forest?

## Interviewing

Invite a professional landscape designer or a speaker from an arboretum to talk to the class about the life cycle and care of trees, including how long it takes a tree to grow and how they are protected. Before the speaker arrives, work with students to generate a list of questions to be asked.

To extend the activity, have students write thank-you notes in which they summarize one or two facts they learned.

Maybe the tree stump belongs to all—the beetle and the ants, the bear and the titmouse, the frog, the earwig, and even the man. All must live together.

Meanwhile the tree stump gets older and older. The sun warms it; the rain cools it. Soon it begins to rot. Night comes, and the forest is cast in moonlight. What remains of the tree stump glows in the dark.

Now the tree stump is gone. A new tree has grown in its place. A titmouse is perched in its branches—it is her tree. An ant crawls up high—on her tree. A bear lumbers by and sharpens his claws on the bark. A man lies down to rest in its shade. The tree belongs to all, because it grows from the earth that is home for all.

◄ Some students may be curious about what causes the rotting stump to glow in the dark. Explain that the glowing light is caused by certain bacteria and plants growing on the decaying stump. Students may be familiar with fireflies, insects that give off light.

## EXTEND

Help students cut out a large circle from mural paper. Have them work together to plan and create a mural illustrating the life cycle of the tree from seed to seedling to grown tree to stump. Students can also show the interdependence of the tree and other living things by showing animals that eat the berries, seeds, or bark and that make their homes in the tree.

## Role-Playing

Divide the class into small groups. Designate one student in each group as the old tree and have the remaining students take on the roles of the living things that visited the tree. Have students role-play an imaginary dialogue that might go on if all these living things were to meet at the old tree. Encourage students to try to capture the change in point of view expressed in this selection from an initially selfish attitude to one in which the characters recognize that the tree belongs to all who depend upon it.

## Further Reading

You may want to have your students look for more books to read on this topic in the school or local library.

## INTRODUCE

Help students recall that the tree in *Once There Was a Tree* belongs to us all because it grows from the earth that is home for us all. Then read aloud the lesson title and introductory material. Invite students to describe any experiences they may have had with dust storms or other kinds of severe storms. Explain that such storms can damage the land, which is an important natural resource. Help students recall other important natural resources.

Have a volunteer read aloud the Thinking Focus. Ask students to predict ways they can conserve natural resources. Suggest that students read to confirm their predictions and to learn additional conservation methods.

### Key Terms

Vocabulary strategies: T36–T37
**topsoil**—the top layer of soil
**conservation**—protecting natural resources
**environment**—everything that surrounds us, including air, water, and land

198

---

LESSON 1

# Saving Our Land

*How can we conserve our natural resources?*

➤ *This picture shows a dust storm that took place in Hugoton, Kansas, in 1937.*

198

"Mother, what is that?" asks Ellie, pointing to a dark cloud moving toward the house.

"It's a dust storm!" shouts Mother. "Quick! Shut the door!"

Ellie bolts the door and helps her mother close the windows. Just as the last one is latched, the storm hits.

The afternoon becomes dark as dust blocks the sun. Outside, it is almost impossible to see or breathe. Even inside the small farmhouse, dust begins to form layers.

The next morning, all is quiet. Ellie opens the door a crack and looks outside. Dust still falls slowly from the sky. A layer of dust covers the barn, the fence, and even the clothesline. It lies like a thick blanket over the land.

---

## Objectives

1. Explain the reasons for conserving natural resources.
2. Identify ways to conserve natural resources.

## Graphic Overview

SAVING OUR LAND

Reasons for Conserving      Ways of Conserving

## The Need to Protect Land

In the 1930s, strong winds swept across much of the Great Plains. The winds picked up soil from the dry earth, creating huge clouds of dust. The map shows where these storms were. This area was known as the Dust Bowl.

Dust storms wear away the top layer of soil, called **topsoil.** These storms usually happen when land is very dry and when there are not enough plants to hold topsoil in place. Dusty, loose soil can be swept away by strong winds.

Land and water are important natural resources. Events like the storms that took place in the Dust Bowl called attention to the need to conserve these resources.

### Conservation Efforts

When the early settlers spread out across the United States, they were amazed by the richness of the land. They saw forests that spread out for miles and miles. The prairies they traveled seemed to be endless.

Today, however, we know that our resources are not endless and that we need to protect them. Protecting our natural resources is called **conservation.**

There are many different ways of protecting our resources. Over a hundred years ago, the leaders of our country began to conserve some wilderness areas. Some of these are called national parks. The land there is protected from changes. On the next pages, you will read about some of these national parks. ■

**The Dust Bowl**

**Key**
- Area of the Dust Bowl
- Areas damaged by later dust storms

▲ *The darker orange area on the map shows the Dust Bowl. Why do you think it was called a bowl?*

■ *Why do we need to protect our land?*

199

**DEVELOP**

Have students preview the lesson by reading the headings and looking at the visuals. You may wish to start the Graphic Overview on the board and have students complete it as they read and discuss the lesson.

**ECONOMICS**
### Critical Thinking

Point out that topsoil is essential to every living thing on earth. Stress the idea of ecological interdependence by asking: How do animals rely on fertile soil? *(Fertile soil feeds the plants that provide animals with food.)* Could people survive without fertile soil? *(no)* How do people rely on trees? *(Trees provide people with wood for products, with foods such as fruits and nuts, and with oxygen to breathe.)*

◄ *because it was shaped like a bowl*

■ *We need to protect our land because some natural resources are limited, and we do not want to exhaust our natural resources and destroy life on earth.*

199

### Access Strategy

Write *Saving Our Land* on the board (and all the italicized words that follow). Explain that in 1872, the United States government set aside certain *wilderness* areas that would be protected and, therefore, not changed by people. Focus students' attention on Mt. McKinley on page 201. Ask who would like to go there and why. Elicit that the *land, trees,* and *water* make it a beautiful wilderness.

Next, focus on how students can save or protect trees and water. Remind them that most paper products are made from trees. Ask students to point out all paper products in the classroom. Check the wastebasket for reusable paper. Explain to students that they can save trees by using paper economically. Ask students how they might protect the earth's water supply. Suggest that in this lesson students will learn how people can save the land, water, and trees.

### Access Activity

Discuss wasteful practices with students, such as overwatering lawns, lengthy showers, etc. Have students brainstorm others. Then have each student draw a picture of a wasteful practice that he or she might help eliminate.

## Visual Learning

Explain to students that our national park system preserves some of our land in its natural state. Have students read the captions and identify the locations of the three national parks shown. *(Wyoming, Idaho, Montana, Alaska, Hawaii)* Help students locate these states on the map of the United States and tell which state is closest to their state. Invite volunteers to tell which park they would like to visit most and why.

**More About Geysers** People from all over the world go to Yellowstone National Park to see the famous geyser, "Old Faithful." It erupts approximately every 65 minutes. Each eruption lasts about four minutes. Water from this geyser reaches heights of 120 to 150 feet.

**200**

A CLOSER LOOK

# National Parks

*In 1872, the United States government began to set aside certain wilderness areas that would not be changed by people. Since plant and animal life in these areas is protected, visitors can enjoy the land's natural beauty.*

**U.S. National Parks**

Denali National Park

Yellowstone National Park

Hawaii Volcanoes National Park

PACIFIC OCEAN

ATLANTIC OCEAN

Gulf of Mexico

**Planning a vacation?** This map shows national parks across the United States. Use it to find the three national parks pictured on these two pages. Which of these three parks is nearest you?

200

**The first national park in the United States** was Yellowstone National Park in Wyoming, Idaho, and Montana. It has thousands of hot springs. Some springs are so hot the water boils. Others shoot water and steam from deep in the ground a hundred feet into the air. These fountains of hot water are called geysers *(GY zuhrz)*.

## Visual Learning

Provide students with old nature magazines. Have them cut out pictures of unspoiled landscapes to create an environmental collage. Ask students to title the collage.

## Debate

Draw attention to the picture of Mt. McKinley on page 201. Tell students to pretend that this is not a protected national park and that they will determine its future. Divide the class into two groups. Have one group represent an environmental/protectionist point of view and the other group represent skiing/resort developers. Provide time for students to prepare their arguments and to present their debate. Explain to students that ideally we need to balance our use of resources and our protection of them. We cannot preserve *all* places as they are.

The highest peak in North America, Mount McKinley, stands in Denali National Park in Alaska. There are also many other mountains in the park. Moose, deer, and other wildlife roam the land there.

Red-hot lava spouts from Kilauea (kee low AY uh). It is a volcano in Hawaii Volcanoes National Park.

This rock was formed when hot lava, which is melted rock from inside the earth, poured from a volcano, cooled, and hardened.

201

## Critical Thinking

Ask students to predict what might happen to the natural beauty of national parks if they were not protected by the government. Discuss how people change the land. Note, however, that national parks have been changed to a certain extent also. They have roads, hiking trails, campgrounds, etc.

**More About Kilauea** Kilauea is the largest active volcanic crater in the world. A crater is a bowl-shaped area where molten rock escapes. Kilauea lies along the side of a larger volcano called Mauna Loa on the island of Hawaii. Kilauea is two miles wide and 400 feet deep.

## Writing a Paragraph

Explain to students that park rangers teach people about the features in national parks. They also enforce park rules that apply to tourists and campers; they protect the animals from poachers and the forest from fires. Have each student write a short paragraph about why he or she would or would not like such a job.

## Visual Learning

Create a large outline shape of a tree from used paper grocery bags. Attach it to a bulletin board and title it *Save This Tree*. Then have students brainstorm a list of things they can do to save paper and trees. Have students write their ideas on pieces of the paper bags, which they can color and cut into the shape of leaves and attach to the tree shape.

GEOGRAPHY

## Visual Learning

Ask students why conserving topsoil is so important. *(It is needed to grow food for people and animals.)* Then direct attention to the diagram and have students tell how each method shown helps conserve topsoil. *(The windbreaks slow the wind to help prevent it from carrying away topsoil. Plowing across hills helps keep water from running downhill and eroding the soil. Leaving parts of plants in the ground helps hold the soil in place. Planting in strips helps keep water from washing soil away.)*

## Conserving Our Resources

We must conserve all of our natural resources. For example, we need rich topsoil to grow food for people and livestock. Plants grow very well in areas with rich topsoil. That is why farmers are so concerned with soil conservation. Look at the chart below to learn ways that farmers conserve topsoil on farmland.

**Four Ways That Farmers Conserve Soil**

Farmers plant rows of trees, called windbreaks, along the edge of fields. The trees slow the wind so it doesn't cause dust storms.

Farmers plow across hills so that plowed soil forms ridges. The ridges catch the water so it doesn't run downhill and erode the soil.

Farmers cut off a crop and leave the lower part of the plants behind. The roots of these plants hold the soil in place so that rain cannot wash it away.

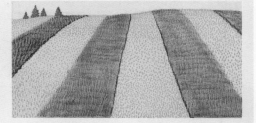

Farmers plant crops in strips. A crop that holds water well is placed next to a crop that does not. The plants that hold water keep the water from washing soil away.

The conservation of our forests is also important. Forests give us wood for lumber, paper, and much more. They also provide homes for many animals. We can help conserve forests by limiting how many trees are cut. We can also plant new trees where they have been cut down.

## Social Participation

Have students work in small groups to create "Save Our Water" checklists. Their lists should include tightly turning off water faucets; fixing drips and leaks; never letting water continue to run while brushing one's teeth; and using less water for showers and baths. Have the groups share lists and then compile a composite class list.

## Writing Letters

Have small groups of students compose letters to the Environmental Protection Agency, Waterside Mall, 401 M Street, S.W., Washington, D.C. 20460. Each group can write to request different information, such as a list of EPA agencies and their locations; information about what the EPA does; pamphlets about air pollution; brochures about how to start a recyling center; or information about a specific problem in the students' own community. Have students share the information they get with the class.

You can help conserve forests by using paper wisely. Use paper plates and cups only when you have to. Write on both sides of a piece of notebook paper before throwing it away.

Water is another important resource. People, plants, and animals need water to live. What can you do to conserve water? Try not to waste it. Take shorter showers and turn off the water while you brush your teeth.

Conserving soil, trees, and water helps to create a healthy environment. All the things that surround us — air, water, and land— are a part of our **environment.** We must do more than conserve our natural resources. We must also try to clean those resources that have become too dirty to use. In the next lesson, you will read about what you can do to keep our environment clean. ■

■ *List three natural resources and tell what people can do to conserve them.*

◄ *National forests are areas that are taken care of by the United States government. Trees in national forests can be cut down, but the government makes sure that new trees are planted to replace them.*

■ *Soil: plant windbreaks, plow across hills, leave plant stalks when harvesting, plant crops in strips. Trees: use fewer paper plates and cups, write on both sides of paper. Water: take shorter showers, turn off water while brushing teeth.*

## R E V I E W

1. **FOCUS** How can we conserve our natural resources?
2. **CONNECT** How does farming in the San Joaquin Valley depend on natural resources?
3. **CRITICAL THINKING** How would your life be different if the place where you live had very little water?
4. **ACTIVITY** Work with a partner. List some of the kinds of plants that need topsoil. Then make a list of the things that can be made from these plants. Finally, tell why topsoil is important.

203

## INTRODUCE

Remind students that in the last lesson they learned about ways to conserve wilderness areas, trees, soil, and water. In this lesson, they will learn about pollution of our air, water, and soil and about ways of reducing pollution. Have a volunteer read the lesson title and the Thinking Focus. List students' answers to the focus question on the chalkboard and have them read to check their predictions.

### Key Terms

Vocabulary strategies: T36–T37
**pollution**—something in the air, water, or soil that makes it unhealthy
**waste**—things people do not need and want to throw away, such as garbage and harmful chemicals

204

LESSON 2

# Protecting Our Resources

*Why is it important to lower the amount of pollution?*

### Key Terms

- pollution
- waste

➤ *This animal rescue worker is holding a sea otter that was once covered with oil.*

204

In the spring of 1989, rescue teams rushed to Alaska. A ship had accidentally spilled millions of gallons of oil into the ocean, harming the plant and animal life there.

Many rescue workers were worried about sea otters. Otters have thick fur that keeps them warm in cold water. When their fur gets oily, however, otters can no longer stay warm. Otters also lick their fur clean. The oil that otters were swallowing was poisoning them.

First, the workers had to catch the otters. Then they washed off the oil with dish detergent. The teams worked hard to save the otters. Many otters died, but thanks to the workers, many healthy otters returned to the sea.

## Objectives

1. Identify the main sources of air, water, and soil pollution.
2. Explain why pollution is harmful.
3. Describe ways to reduce air, water, and soil pollution.

## Graphic Overview

**POLLUTION**

| Problems | → | Solutions |

## Pollution

In the last lesson, you read about conserving our natural resources. An important part of conservation is keeping our environment clean. Oil spills like the one in Alaska cause pollution. When harmful chemicals make the air, water, or soil unhealthy or poisonous, it is called **pollution.** Besides accidental oil spills, there are other types of pollution that happen every day.

Cars and factories create air pollution. When car engines burn gasoline, they give off poisons that make the air dirty. Some of the smoke that comes from factories also pollutes the air. This type of pollution is harmful to plants and animals, including people.

Air pollution makes the air hard to breathe. It can hurt our lungs and sting our eyes. Sometimes pollution can weaken or kill trees and other plants. It can even wear away the stone in buildings. If this pollution gets into the water of lakes and streams, it can harm animal and plant life there.

Other kinds of water pollution can be caused by communities or factories dumping waste into oceans, rivers, and lakes. **Waste** includes things we don't need anymore and want to throw away, such as garbage and harmful chemicals. Water pollution can kill plant and animal life and can make drinking water unsafe.

◄ *Often, the pollution in air cannot be seen, but it can be harmful enough to eat away stone, as on the arm of this statue. You can also see from this leaf how pollution that gets into rain water can harm trees.*

205

205

## Cleaning Waste Water

The water most people use goes down a drain, through pipes and tunnels, to a place where it is cleaned.

A screen stops big pieces of waste.

Water moves slowly in a tank, so pieces of waste sink to the bottom.

The water moves even more slowly in the next tank. Smaller bits of waste sink to the bottom.

---

■ *Air pollution: car exhaust and factory smoke. Water pollution: communities or factories dumping wastes into water. Soil pollution: harmful chemicals from wastes that are dumped on the ground.*

■ *What are some of the causes of pollution?*

People use water for many things, for cooking, washing, or drinking. No matter what we use it for, it becomes waste water and has to be cleaned before we can reuse it in our homes. Notice the pipe on the diagram above that carries waste water from a house. Some communities do not clean their waste. They may empty waste water directly into lakes, rivers, or the ocean.

Waste can also pollute the soil. If people don't get rid of home or factory wastes properly, the harmful chemicals can leak into the ground and poison our soil. ■

## What We Can Do

The problems of air, water, and soil pollution are not easy to solve. Many people are trying to find answers.

Scientists are working on ways to cut back air pollution. They are inventing new car engines and new types of fuel that produce cleaner air.

There are ways for factories to make less air pollution. Some harmful materials can be replaced with less harmful ones. Factories that must use dangerous materials can use filters. Filters are like nets. They can catch the poisons before they get into the air. ■

---

### POLITICAL SYSTEMS
### Social Participation

Tell students that cooperation between many people is required to solve the problems of pollution. Government agencies, scientists, business people, and individuals must all work together. All of us contribute to, and are affected by, pollution.

### Visual Learning

Have students draw individual pictures showing the effects of pollution. When they are done, ask each student to come to the front of the room, display his or her picture and describe the pollution, its causes, and its effects. Post the pictures on the classroom wall.

### Political Context

In the early 1900s, New York's Hudson River was a clean and healthy river. Then factories dumped garbage, sewage, and industrial wastes into it. By the 1960s, the Hudson was foul and polluted. A group of citizens became concerned and banded together, working to clean up the Hudson. They also built a boat, called *Clearwater,* which sails the Hudson carrying schoolchildren from towns on the river. While on this ship, which is modeled on sloops of 100 years ago, children learn how to monitor water pollution. Gradually, the Hudson is being cleaned up, and some fish are returning to the river.

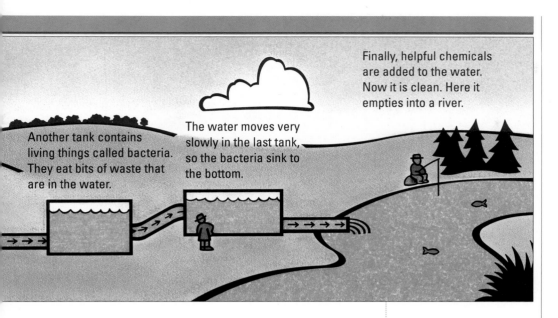

Another tank contains living things called bacteria. They eat bits of waste that are in the water.

The water moves very slowly in the last tank, so the bacteria sink to the bottom.

Finally, helpful chemicals are added to the water. Now it is clean. Here it empties into a river.

Communities and factories can also help stop water pollution. They can stop pouring waste water into lakes, rivers, and oceans. As the diagram shows, waste water needs to be cleaned before it is put back into nature, just as it is cleaned before we can use it again at home.

Dangerous wastes from communities and factories don't have to be dumped on the ground. They can be destroyed, made harmless, or cleaned and used again. If they must be stored underground, they can be sealed in special boxes, so they don't leak into the soil.

You can help solve pollution problems, too. You can encourage your family to walk instead of using the car when it is possible. You may choose to write to people who make laws and tell them to work for clean air and water. What other ways can you think of? ■

■ *What can we do to cut down on soil, water, and air pollution?*

## REVIEW

1. **FOCUS** Why is it important to lower the amount of pollution?
2. **CONNECT** Some problems can be caused by chemicals used in farming and by smoke from steel mills. What natural resources can these pollute?
3. **CRITICAL THINKING** Think of three ways that you can get people more interested in pollution.
4. **ACTIVITY** Make posters that show ways people can lower pollution. Display them for others to see.

207

## INTRODUCE

Read aloud the lesson title and have students tell what they know about recycling. Then read the Thinking Focus and ask students to name the pollution problem they will be reading about. *(garbage)* Have students predict how recycling can reduce this problem. Suggest that students read to check their predictions.

### Key Terms

Vocabulary strategies: T36–T37
**decompose**—rot
**recycling**—turning a used product into something that can be used again

LESSON 3

# Recycling to Save Our Resources

### THINKING FOCUS

*How does recycling help to make our garbage problem smaller?*

### Key Terms

- decompose
- recycling

In March of 1987, this boat left New York. It was taking a load of garbage to North Carolina. When the boat arrived in North Carolina, however, it was not allowed to unload. The people there would not take the garbage.

The boat left North Carolina and went to ports in other states and in other countries to try to get rid of its load. The people in these places would not take the garbage either. Finally, after months of traveling from place to place, the boat returned to New York where the garbage was burned.

208

## Objectives

1. Identify the major source of trash.
2. Explain the importance of recycling.
3. Identify ways that people can help solve the trash problem.

## Graphic Overview

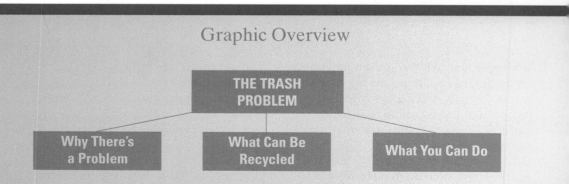

## The Garbage Problem

Some people say that by the year 2000, each person in the United States will throw away about six pounds of garbage a day. Why will we have so much garbage? Half of our garbage is packages that hold items we buy and use.

Think about your garbage. Do you throw away a lot of packages? Americans expect products they buy to be well wrapped. Toothpaste, for example, comes in a plastic tube *and* a cardboard container. Crackers are wrapped in plastic *and* put in a cardboard box. When we use the products, we throw the packages away. We must have a place to put this garbage.

Some of our packages harm the environment because they **decompose,** or rot, very slowly. Plastic, metal, and glass, for example, take many years to decompose. People are trying to find ways of solving the problem. ■

■ *What makes up much of our garbage?*

◄ *These children are doing their part to help the environment. What can you and your friends do?*

## Recycling

We throw away so much garbage that we are running out of places to dump it all. How can we throw away less garbage? One way is to turn it into something new that can be used again. This is called **recycling.**

209

### DEVELOP

Have students find the headings *The Garbage Problem, Recycling,* and *You Can Help*. Help students realize that the lesson is divided into parts that name the problem, tell how it can be solved or made better, and suggest ways they can help. You may wish to start the Graphic Overview on the board and have students complete it as they read and discuss the lesson.

■ *Packages make up half of our garbage.*

### ECONOMICS
#### Critical Thinking

Tell students to notice how much packaging they throw away when they use groceries at home.

209

### Access Strategy

Write *recycling* on the chalkboard. Explain that recycling is "using things over again so they complete a cycle." The graphic below illustrates the process:

Preview with students the chart and graph shown on page 210. Discuss why the United States has been slow to recycle waste. Help students see that since we have so much more land than Japan or Western European nations, the problem did not become apparent to us as early as it did to those countries. Also point out that as a nation with plentiful resources, it was unfortunately easy to develop a wasteful attitude.

### Access Activity

Discuss with students the problem of excessive packaging of products. For example, many food items are packaged in a closed box, and then the box is wrapped in paper, which is sometimes unnecessary for food preservation. Have students bring in examples of items with excessive packaging, and explain how these items could be packaged less wastefully.

## Critical Thinking

Have students find Japan on a world map. Point out that Japan is one of the most heavily populated countries in the world. Explain that Japan's small size and large population make recycling a necessity. Tell students that Japan leads the world in recycling. All the Japanese must take part in a strict recycling program. Last year the Japanese recycled 50% of their paper, 55% of their glass, and 66% of their cans. Ask students what lesson the United States can learn from Japan's example.

➤ *Develop more recycling programs. Encourage legislators to pass laws requiring recycling. Make it easy and convenient for people to become involved in recycling.*

■ *Recycling results in less trash. This is important because we are running out of places to dump trash and because some trash harms the environment.*

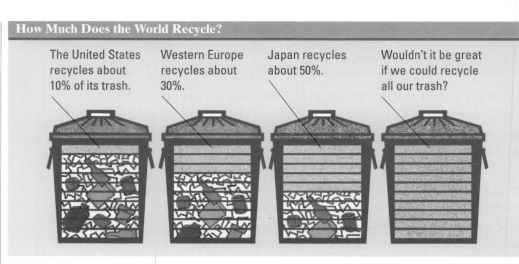

**How Much Does the World Recycle?**

The United States recycles about 10% of its trash.

Western Europe recycles about 30%.

Japan recycles about 50%.

Wouldn't it be great if we could recycle all our trash?

▲ *What are some ways to encourage people in the United States to recycle their garbage?*

■ *Why is recycling important?*

▼ *This chart shows that much of the waste in U.S. homes is made up of materials that can be recycled.*

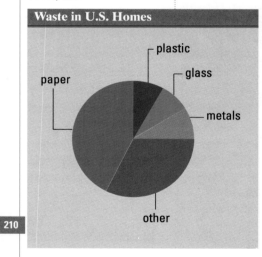

**Waste in U.S. Homes**

- plastic
- glass
- metals
- other
- paper

210

Some garbage can be recycled into things we need. Old newspapers can be made into new paper or building materials. Plastic bottles can be made into other plastic products. Glass can be made into new glass. Aluminum cans can be made into new cans. These materials and others can be recycled and used again. Recycling helps us make less garbage. ■

## You Can Help

Protecting the environment is a big job, but we can all do our part. Planning ahead is a good way to start. We can carefully think about what products to buy before we buy them. This will help us plan what to do with our garbage.

Many communities have recycling centers. Is there a center where you live? If so, can you think of ways to recycle the garbage from your own home? Maybe you could start by sorting your garbage. You could separate cans, plastic, paper, and glass from the rest of your family's garbage. Then take these items to the recycling center. From there, your garbage will be shipped to places where it can be made into new products.

## Social Participation

Organize a field trip to a recycling center or invite a guest speaker from the community to speak on how the community disposes of paper, glass, cans, and plastic. Have students discuss with these environmental experts what they can do to help alleviate the waste disposal problem.

## Economic Context

Recycling not only helps reduce pollution, but also provides low-cost materials for manufacturing without depleting natural resources. Aluminum from recycled cans can be used to make other aluminum products, such as aluminum foil. Recycled paper can be used to make insulation, roofing, plasterboard, and other construction materials. Recycled glass can be used to make materials for building roads.

## Social Context

As the problem of where to dispose of garbage heightens, many towns across America have made recycling garbage a law. Community members must separate paper, glass, cans, and food garbage into separate bags so that recycling can occur efficiently and quickly. In a few years, recycling laws may be enforced nationwide.

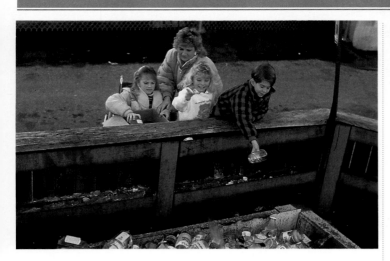

◄ *Recycling centers like this one help us to use much of our trash again.*

Does your school have a recycling program? If not, can you think of ways to get one started?

Many communities also have programs to make it easy for people to recycle. For example, in some areas people are given containers in which to place newspapers, plastics, and glass. Then on certain days, trucks pick up these items at people's homes.

If you live in an area that does not have a recycling program or recycling centers, there is still something you can do to help protect our natural resources. You may want to write letters to lawmakers and ask them to try to bring recycling centers to your area. You can ask your teacher to give you the names and addresses of the people who make the laws where you live.

Each year, more and more people are becoming interested in recycling. We all must work together to conserve our resources. ■

### Across Time & Space

*Pioneers recycled things that many of us throw away today. For example, they made old clothing into quilts and used cooking grease to make soap or medicine.*

■ *How can people help solve our trash problem?*

### R E V I E W

1. **FOCUS** How does recycling help to make our garbage problem smaller?
2. **CONNECT** How can conservation and recycling help us protect our forest land?
3. **CRITICAL THINKING** Why is it important that

people start to recycle their garbage now?

4. **ACTIVITY** Make something useful from an empty package. For example, a juice can can be made into a pencil holder. Share your idea with friends.

211

## UNDERSTANDING GROUP ACTIVITIES

This skills feature uses a recycling center plan to help students learn about participation in a group project.

### CITIZENSHIP

#### Social Participation

Have students sequence the steps to follow to establish a recycling center and discuss the importance of having everyone work together to accomplish the goal.

*Sample steps might include:*

- *gather or build separate containers for glass, plastic, aluminum, and paper*
- *decorate and label containers*
- *collect materials for determined period of time*
- *determine which recycling center to take materials to*
- *bundle, load, and take materials to center*

### Objective

Participate in a group project. (Social Participation 2)

---

UNDERSTANDING GROUP ACTIVITIES

# Recycling Products

**Here's Why**   You have seen how important recycling is to our environment. Recycling helps to save our natural resources. It also helps solve the problem of getting rid of trash.

Suppose you wanted to recycle products. Where would you start?

**Here's How**   You could start by setting up a recycling center in your school or classroom. Your class can work together on the project.

First, decide on the products you are going to recycle. Choose paper, glass, aluminum, plastics, or any combination of products. Then divide your class into small groups. Each group can collect one kind of trash.

Find containers for each type of trash you plan to recycle. If you use plastic bags, be sure they are the kind that can be recycled. The box they come in will tell you if they can be recycled.

You might want to have a theme for your recycling center. Work in groups to draw pictures and make up names for "monsters" that might eat a particular type of waste. For example, children in Toledo, Ohio, feed their glass bottles into the mouth of "Chewbottle." Aluminum cans go into a crusher named "Jaws."

**Try It**   Each day for a week, pick up trash around your school. Put each kind of trash into its recycling container. Do not mix different kinds of trash in one container. At the end of the week, arrange to have the trash taken to a community recycling center.

**Apply It**   Set up a recycling center in your home. Work with your family to recycle paper, cans, and other trash. Put each kind of trash in its own container. Help your family take the trash to a community recycling center.

## Answers to Try It

At the end of each week, have the students in each group hold a round-table discussion about how the recycling center is working and what can be done to make it more efficient. At this time, you may wish to evaluate the group's progress and have the group discuss ways to continue their achievements and to improve problem areas.

## Social Participation

Ask each student to write a short essay on what it takes to work well together in a group. Have them describe the types of people who help make a group function effectively and the personality qualities they have. Allow time for the essays to be read aloud and discussed.

**Answers to Reviewing Key Terms**
**A.**
1. pollution
2. decompose
3. topsoil
4. recycling
5. conservation
6. waste
7. environment

**Answers to Exploring Concepts**
**A.** Sample answers:
   Plastic forks—use in an art project; wash and reuse
   Metal cans—decorate and use as pencil holder; take to recycling center
   Newspapers—use for papier-mâché; take to recycling center
   Glass jars—use for kitchen storage or craft project; take to recycling center
**B.** Sample answers:
1. Farmers can plant windbreaks along the edge of fields.
2. Cars and factories cause air pollution. Oil spills and dumping wastes into oceans, lakes, and rivers cause water pollution.

# Chapter Review

## Reviewing Key Terms

conservation (p. 199)   recycling (p.209)
decompose (p. 209)      topsoil (p. 199)
environment (p. 203)    waste (p. 205)
pollution (p. 205)

**A.** Write the key term that best completes each sentence.
1.  Harmful chemicals and waste in the air, water, or soil cause _____.
2.  Some plastic bags may hurt our environment because they do not _____ easily.
3.  _____ is blown away in a windstorm when there are no plants to hold it in place.
4.  Turning garbage into something that can be used again is called _____.
5.  _____ is taking good care of our natural resources.
6.  Trash, garbage, and things we often throw away are _____.
7.  Our _____ is the air, water, and land around us.

## Exploring Concepts

**A.** The chart below shows some of the many things we throw away. Copy the chart. In the second column, list one or more ways that each thing can be recycled. Try to think of some ideas of your own for ways to recycle.

**B.** Write one or two sentences to answer each question.
1.  What can farmers do to keep from losing topsoil in dust storms?
2.  What are some of the things that cause pollution?

| Things we throw away | Ways to recycle |
| --- | --- |
| Plastic forks | |
| Metal cans | |
| Newspapers | |
| Glass jars | |

## Reviewing Skills

1. Sometimes you outgrow your clothes and they no longer fit. For a group project, bring some of your outgrown clothes to school. Sort and fold the clothes. Then put them in paper bags. Give your clothes to a group or an organization that gives clothing to people who need it.

2. Write two "If . . . then" statements that tell what might happen if more people learn about the problems of pollution.

## Using Critical Thinking

1. What might happen in our cities if we do not try to reduce air pollution?

2. Farmers use chemicals to make crops grow better and to kill insects that eat plants. Do you think the use of such chemicals is good or bad? Why?

3. If we had no national parks, what would our country be like?

## Preparing for Citizenship

1. **ART ACTIVITY** Work in small groups. Use waste materials such as plastics, packaging, newspaper, and string to make a model of a national park.

2. **COLLABORATIVE LEARNING** Have a class trial for someone who is accused of throwing trash in the park. Choose a judge, twelve jury members, witnesses, and the person who is accused of the crime. Have the witnesses tell the judge why they think the person is innocent or guilty. Then, the jury should meet and decide if the accused person is innocent or guilty. If the accused person is guilty, the jury should decide what the punishment will be.

215

215

## CHAPTER ORGANIZER

# Chapter 11 Our Holidays and Symbols

## CHAPTER PLANNING CHART

| Pupil's Edition | Teacher's Edition | Ancillaries |
|---|---|---|
| **Lesson 1: Celebrating Our Land (3–4 days)**<br><br>Objective 1: Explain the significance of Arbor Day. (National Identity 3)*<br>Objective 2: Identify some national holidays and their significance. (National Identity 3) | • Graphic Overview (218)<br>• Access Strategy (219)<br>• Access Activity (219)<br> Historical Context (220)<br> Interviewing (221)<br> Writing a Letter (222)<br> Interviewing (222) | Discovery Journal (27, 2<br>Map Activity (12)<br>• Poster (10)<br> Study Guide (40) |
| **Understanding a Summary: Using Main Ideas**<br><br>Objective: Write a summary. (Study Skills 2) | | Study Guide (41) |
| **Lesson 2: National Symbols (3–4 days)**<br><br>Objective 1: Tell why we have national symbols. (National Identity 3)<br>Objective 2: Identify the meaning of the following national symbols: eagle, Liberty Bell, flag. (National Identity 3; Visual Learning 4) | • Graphic Overview (225)<br>• Access Activity (226)<br>• Access Strategy (226)<br> Language Arts Connection (227)<br> Music Connection (227) | Study Guide (42) |
| **Chapter Review** | Answers (229–230) | Chapter 11 Test |

* Objectives are correlated to the strands and goals in the program scope and sequence on pages T41–T48.

• LEP appropriate resources. (For additional strategies, see pages T32–T33.)

Chapter 11, the final chapter in this book, focuses on the heritage of our country, specifically our national holidays and symbols. We chose these topics to encourage students to view our land, which they have learned so much about, with pride. We also want students to understand the threads that hold us together as a nation and that help form our national identity.

**Lesson 1** examines Arbor Day and some of our national holidays. It includes the feature A Moment in Time: An Immigrant on July 4, which shows a proud young immigrant at a Fourth of July celebration. The discussion of national holidays helps students see that we have many reasons to celebrate our good fortune as a nation.

**Lesson 2** focuses on national symbols. Special attention is given to the history of our flag. The discussion helps reinforce the idea that the 50 states make up one nation.

By the time students conclude this book, they should have a general understanding of our country's land, people, and history.

## ACTIVITIES & PROJECTS

### LEP: Interviewing

After reading Lesson 2, have pairs of students interview each other, asking what their favorite holiday is and how they celebrate it.

### Challenge: Writing a Play

After concluding Lesson 1, have students write a one-act play with two or three scenes. The theme of the play should be why we celebrate a particu-

lar holiday. Allow students to choose a holiday from the list on page 221. The play might involve explaining a holiday to someone who doesn't know or understand the holiday, such as a young child or a recent immigrant.

### Writing a Narrative

After concluding Lesson 1, have students read the captions included in A Moment in Time: An Immigrant on July 4 on page 222. Ask each student to write a brief story describing how the girl spent the rest of her day celebrating the Fourth of July.

### Designing a Symbol

After reading Lesson 2, have pairs of students pick a national holiday from a grab bag. Then have them either draw or make a model of a symbol for that holiday.

# Chapter 11

# *Our Holidays and Symbols*

*We the people of the United States of America are proud of our country. We set aside holidays that celebrate important events from our history and honor special people. We choose symbols that remind us that we are a nation of people who are free and proud of our land.*

These children are celebrating Arbor Day by wearing evergreen tree hats. On this day we plant trees to show our pride in the beauty of the land.

**216**

The flag is a national symbol that shows some of the history of our nation. Each stripe stands for one of the first 13 colonies. The 50 stars stand for the 50 states that today make up the United States.

To help students understand the emotional power of symbols, have students look at the flag as the entire class sings "America the Beautiful." Ask students to describe how they feel about the flag.

The bald eagle is also a symbol of the United States. This strong, proud bird shows our courage, our respect for the land, and our love of freedom.

The Washington Monument is a national symbol that honors George Washington, our first president. It stands in our country's capital, Washington, D.C.

217

Because of this, it is often called the "Gateway to the West." The Arch, made of steel and concrete, is 630 feet tall (63 stories high) and weighs 43,000 tons. Construction of the Arch began in 1963 and was completed in 1965. Today, visitors can ride small trams to the top of the Arch, where they can view the city from an observation area.

LESSON 1

# Celebrating Our Land

### THINKING FOCUS

*Why do Americans celebrate state and national holidays?*

### Key Term

- national holiday

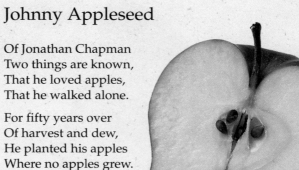

## Johnny Appleseed

Of Jonathan Chapman
Two things are known,
That he loved apples,
That he walked alone.

For fifty years over
Of harvest and dew,
He planted his apples
Where no apples grew.

Why did he do it?
We do not know.
He wished that apples
might root and grow.

Rosemary Carr and Stephen Vincent Benet

## Arbor Day

Many poems and tales have been written about Johnny Appleseed. Most of these are a mix of truth and imagination. The stories are based on a real man named John Chapman. He lived during the late 1700s and early 1800s. For forty years, he traveled from Pennsylvania to Illinois planting apple trees.

Few apple trees grew where John Chapman traveled so he planted apple trees from the East as he went. He would also give apple trees and apple seeds to settlers he met. People began to call him Johnny Appleseed.

218

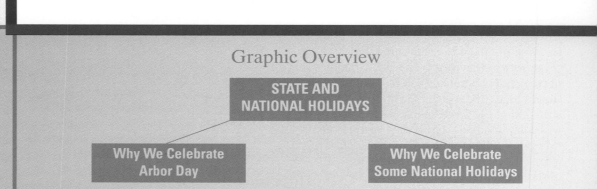

◄ *Settlers said that Johnny Appleseed traveled barefooted through the wilderness giving apple seeds or small apple trees to every person he met along the way.*

Some people remember Johnny Appleseed and his trees on Arbor Day. This is a holiday that is set aside for planting trees. It is called Arbor Day because an arbor is a place that is shaded by trees.

Arbor Day was started by J. Sterling Morton, who worked with lawmakers in Nebraska. Because Nebraska is part of the dry plains of the United States, few trees grow there naturally. Morton saw that trees were needed to provide wood for the people who were moving to Nebraska. Trees would also protect the land. The plains received very little rain. Tree roots would help keep the soil in place and hold water. They would also slow the wind during dust storms and snow storms.

## Across Time & Space

*J. Sterling Morton's Arbor Day was not the first time trees were planted on a special day. Hundreds of years ago, a group of people that lived in Mexico planted a tree whenever a child was born.*

◄ *Today some people in the United States celebrate Arbor Day by planting trees.*

Have students preview the lesson by reading the headings and looking at the visuals. Explain that Arbor Day is an example of a state holiday.

You may wish to start the Graphic Overview on the board and have students complete it as they read the lesson.

### ECONOMICS
## Critical Thinking

Remind students that they have already learned how planting trees helps control soil erosion. *(Trees keep the wind from blowing the soil away, and their roots keep moisture in the ground.)* Point out that planting trees on Arbor Day is good for the environment.

219

## Access Strategy

Direct attention to the illustration of Johnny Appleseed on this page. Read the caption aloud. Then ask students to describe the location and Johnny's feelings. Ask what he might be saying or singing. Explain that Johnny Appleseed was really John Chapman, who gave apple seeds to settlers from Pennsylvania to Illinois nearly 200 years ago.

Introduce the word *arbor* (related to the Spanish *arbol*, meaning "tree") by writing it and its definition on the board. (An arbor is a shaded shelter in a garden.) Then introduce Arbor Day. Tell students that on Arbor Day some people remember Johnny Appleseed's efforts to plant trees.

Explain that in some states Arbor Day is an official state holiday. Suggest that, by reading, students will learn about how it came to be a state holiday and what some of America's national holidays are.

## Access Activity

Have students use a calendar to find the dates on which the national holidays listed on page 221 are celebrated. Discuss the reasons for celebrating each holiday.

### HISTORY
#### Study Skills

Help students summarize how Arbor Day got started and what role J. Sterling Morton played in it. *(J. Sterling Morton recognized how important trees could be to Nebraska, a plains state with few trees. Trees helped beautify the landscape, provided shade and wood, and helped conserve soil. Morton worked with lawmakers in Nebraska to declare Arbor Day a state holiday that people would celebrate by planting trees.)*

■ *They plant trees.*

▲ *This 1932 painting by Grant Wood is called* Arbor Day. *It shows a teacher and students planting a tree in front of their school on Arbor Day.*

■ *On Arbor Day, how do people show that they care for the land?*

220

J. Sterling Morton planned a tree-planting day. That day, April 10, 1872, was the first Arbor Day. The whole state of Nebraska celebrated by planting trees. As news of Arbor Day spread, more and more states began to celebrate this special day.

Arbor Day is still a holiday in Nebraska, though it is now celebrated on April 22. This day was Morton's birthday. Different states celebrate this holiday on different days of the year, but it is celebrated throughout most of the United States and in some parts of Canada. Other countries also set aside days and even weeks as a time to plant trees.

Celebrating Arbor Day gives people the chance to give back to the land some of the things that are taken from it. It also reminds us that it is important to protect our natural resources, especially the land. ■

## Visual Learning

Discuss how the painting on this page shows schoolchildren celebrating a state holiday. Then have students name some holidays they celebrate at school. Have students pick holidays and draw pictures of themselves celebrating their chosen holidays. Display the pictures in groups by holiday.

## Historical Context

John Chapman (1774–1845) was born in Leominster, Massachusetts, and died in Indiana. Little is known of his childhood. From the time he was 23 to 48 years old, Chapman journeyed through Pennsylvania, Ohio, Indiana, and Illinois. He planted orchards as settlers moved farther west. Contrary to the tales told about him, John Chapman was not poor; he was a shrewd businessman. He owned 1,200 acres of planted land.

Chapman became a folk hero because of the many stories and poems that developed about him. Many of them were probably imaginary. They told about his cheerfulness, love of animals, and odd appearance. (He was said to have worn an old coffee sack, no shoes, and a cooking pot on his head.)

# National Holidays

Arbor Day became a Nebraska holiday when lawmakers there decided the state would celebrate it each year. Other states celebrate Arbor Day, too. In the United States, each state can choose different holidays that its citizens will celebrate.

Some holidays are celebrated by every state in our country. Holidays that are called by the national government and that honor our country and its people are called **national holidays.** The chart on this page shows some of the national holidays that we celebrate.

| National Holidays | | |
| --- | --- | --- |
| **Holiday** | **Date** | **What We Honor** |
| Martin L. King, Jr., Day | Third Monday in January | Martin L. King, Jr.'s, birthday |
| Presidents' Day | Third Monday in February | George Washington's and Abraham Lincoln's birthdays |
| Memorial Day | Last Monday in May | U.S. soldiers killed in war |
| Independence Day | July 4 | Independence from England |
| Labor Day | First Monday in September | Working people |
| Columbus Day | Second Monday in October | European discovery of America |
| Veterans' Day | November 11 | U.S. soldiers who fought in wars |
| Thanksgiving Day | Fourth Thursday in November | Pilgrims' first harvest |

Some national holidays celebrate famous events in history. On Thanksgiving Day, for example, we remember how the Pilgrims thanked God for their harvest and celebrated with the Wampanoag, who had helped them. On Independence Day, we remember July 4, 1776, the day early leaders of America stated that the United States was free from England. Today on July 4, we also celebrate the freedoms that American citizens have. Each year, new citizens, like the one on the next page, join the United States to enjoy the rights and freedoms of our country.

## Critical Thinking

Direct attention to the chart, and have students note its organization. Discuss the significance of each holiday listed.

## Interviewing

Have students role-play the parts of Johnny Appleseed, Christopher Columbus, and Martin Luther King, Jr. Have other students role-play talk-show hosts who interview these celebrity guests by asking such questions as: What is your name? What did you do? Why did you do it? What are you most proud of accomplishing? How would you like to see your holiday celebrated?

## Study Skills

Have each student compose a survey to ask people what holiday they would like to see made a national holiday and how they would like to celebrate the holiday. Have students poll their friends, parents, or students in another class and summarize the results.

**Note:** You may wish to use this Moment in Time after completing the rest of the lesson to emphasize the personal meaning of some national holidays.

## NATIONAL IDENTITY

### Visual Learning

Have students identify the national symbol the girl is holding and read the caption relating to it. Then have students identify the state symbol the girl is wearing and read the caption relating to it.

Explain that the Fourth of July celebrates our gaining our freedom from England over 200 years ago. Discuss how proud the girl probably feels about celebrating her first Fourth of July as a citizen of the United States. Then have students tell how they celebrate the Fourth of July and how it makes them feel.

**More About Guatemala** The girl is a new immigrant from Guatemala, a Spanish-speaking country in Central America. Guatemala is known for its high-quality woven cloth. Each section of the country has special designs that it is famous for.

## A MOMENT IN TIME

# An Immigrant on July 4

*1:15 P.M., July 4, 1991
At an Independence Day parade
in Corpus Christi, Texas*

**Flag**
This young immigrant happily tells everyone she meets that she is now a citizen of the United States. Waving the flag is another way for her to say that she is proud of her new country.

**Lone Star Button**
For her, living in the United States also means living in Texas. This button shows a star, the symbol of Texas. She plans to pin it on her uncle when he moves to the United States next year.

**Camera**
The pictures she takes of today's celebration will be a wonderful surprise for her friend Tina in Guatemala. The two girls write to each other each week. Tina hopes to visit the United States someday.

**Purse**
She was given this purse for her ninth birthday. The colorful Guatemalan fabric was woven by hand by her grandmother.

222

### Visual Learning

Have students find pictures of the Statue of Liberty in a reference book. Ask what holiday is usually associated with the statue. (*Independence Day*) Then have students draw the statue, labeling different parts and what they symbolize (*torch and crown—light of liberty; tablet—date of Declaration of Independence; broken chain—end of unjust rule*)

### Writing a Letter

Have each student compose a short letter that the girl in the Moment in Time would enclose with the pictures she will send to her friend Tina in Guatemala. Suggest that students describe the parade and its significance. Students might also include descriptions of how they feel about being citizens of the United States now.

### Interviewing

Invite a recently naturalized citizen or a representative of the Immigration and Naturalization Service (see the blue pages in your telephone book) to class to talk to students about the requirements for becoming citizens.

Two of our national holidays honor well-known citizens of our country. We honor George Washington and Abraham Lincoln on Presidents' Day. On Martin Luther King, Jr., Day, we remember this man who fought for freedom for all people.

Some national holidays honor many of our citizens. On Labor Day, we honor all people who work, or labor, to provide things we need. On Veterans' Day, we remember Americans who have fought to keep our country free. Memorial Day is a holiday when we remember soldiers who have died during wars. All of these holidays remind us of the ideas and the beliefs that make our land great. ■

■ *What kinds of people and events do our national holidays celebrate?*

◄ *For many people national holidays are a time to remember our country and all that it gives us.*

### Critical Thinking

Tell students that George Washington (1732–1799) is known as "The Father of Our Country" because he was an important general in the war for independence and the first President of the new nation. Abraham Lincoln (1809–1865) was President during the Civil War and was instrumental in abolishing slavery. Martin Luther King, Jr., (1929–1968) was a leader of the civil rights movement of the 1950s and 1960s. He won the Nobel Peace Prize in 1964 for leading non-violent protests against racial discrimination. Have students nominate other important Americans they should honor and tell why.

■ *Some national holidays celebrate famous events in history; some honor famous citizens; and others honor groups of citizens.*

## CLOSE

Check students' understanding of the lesson by asking the focus question. If necessary, use the Graphic Overview and the chart on page 221 to reteach the lesson.

## REVIEW

1. **FOCUS** Why do Americans celebrate state and national holidays?
2. **CONNECT** How do stories about men like Johnny Appleseed and Joe Magarac help us remember good things about our country?
3. **CRITICAL THINKING** Think of a person or an event that is important enough to be honored as a national holiday. Write a paragraph telling why.
4. **ACTIVITY** Choose two holidays that you know. Draw a picture that shows what we honor on these days. Make a holiday book that contains your picture and your classmates' pictures.

223

## Answers to Review Questions

1. Americans celebrate state holidays to honor special people or events important to the state just as national holidays honor our country and its people. Some holidays celebrate famous events. Some honor famous citizens, and other holidays honor groups of citizens.
2. Stories about Johnny Appleseed and Joe Magarac tell about ordinary people working hard and becoming heroes. These stories remind us that ordinary people helped build our country.
3. Students may also choose a group of people, such as firefighters, police, or nurses, who should be honored.
4. Encourage students to explain their pictures.

## Homework Options

Have each student categorize the national holidays by what they celebrate: Special Events (*Independence Day, Thanksgiving*); Famous People (*Martin Luther King, Jr., Day, Presidents' Day, Columbus Day*); Groups of Citizens (*Memorial Day, Labor Day, Veterans' Day*).

**Study Guide:** page 40

## UNDERSTANDING A SUMMARY

This skills feature uses the main ideas from the Arbor Day lesson to teach students to write a summary.

### CULTURE

### Study Skills

Summarize the lesson by writing the following on the board:
To write a summary,
- tell only main ideas, not details
- use as few words as possible
- use your own words

224

UNDERSTANDING A SUMMARY

# Using Main Ideas

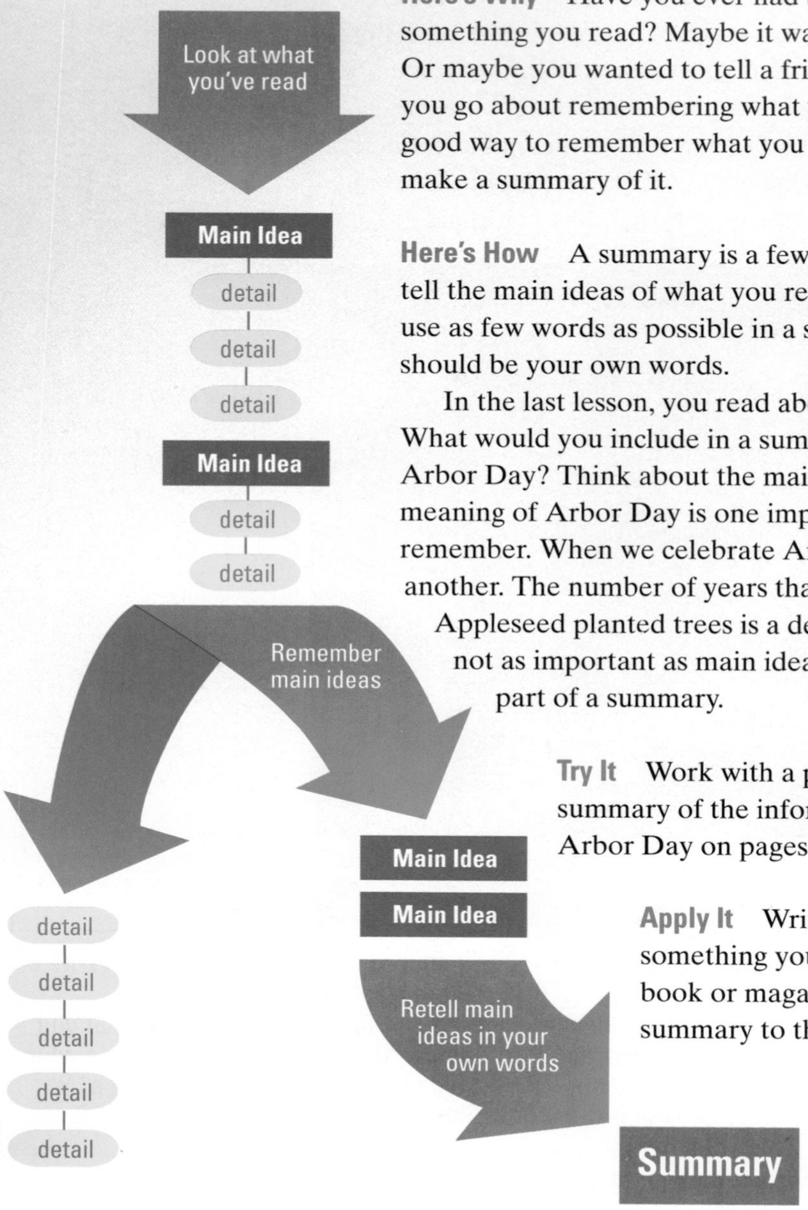

**Look at what you've read**

**Main Idea**
- detail
- detail
- detail

**Main Idea**
- detail
- detail

**Remember main ideas**

- detail
- detail
- detail
- detail
- detail

224

**Main Idea**

**Main Idea**

**Retell main ideas in your own words**

**Summary**

**Here's Why**   Have you ever had to remember something you read? Maybe it was for a test. Or maybe you wanted to tell a friend. How do you go about remembering what you read? A good way to remember what you read is to make a summary of it.

**Here's How**   A summary is a few sentences that tell the main ideas of what you read. You should use as few words as possible in a summary. They should be your own words.

In the last lesson, you read about Arbor Day. What would you include in a summary about Arbor Day? Think about the main ideas. The meaning of Arbor Day is one important idea to remember. When we celebrate Arbor Day is another. The number of years that Johnny Appleseed planted trees is a detail. Details are not as important as main ideas. They are not part of a summary.

**Try It**   Work with a partner. Write a summary of the information about Arbor Day on pages 219 and 220.

**Apply It**   Write a summary of something you have read in a book or magazine. Read your summary to the class.

## Objective

Write a summary.  (Study Skills 2)

## Writing a Summary

Have each student write a brief summary of an article in a newspaper. Then call on volunteers to read their summaries aloud.

## Answers to Try It

Arbor Day is a state holiday that is celebrated on different days in different states. People plant trees on Arbor Day. The holiday reminds people to protect natural resources, especially the land.

LESSON 2

# National Symbols

W hat would you think if a wild turkey were our national symbol? Over 200 years ago, Benjamin Franklin suggested that the turkey be chosen to stand for the United States. Franklin didn't much like the eagle. He thought that the turkey was a wise and clever bird. He also knew that it had played a role in the history of our nation. The wild turkey was an important food for early settlers.

Other people thought the eagle was a better symbol for the freedom and power of our nation. The bald eagle has great strength. With its huge wings, it flies high and free above the land. An eagle's eye can see movement below from hundreds of feet in the air. For all these reasons, the bald eagle became our national symbol.

Today the eagle is on some of our coins. Look at the coins above. One of them is what a quarter might look like if Benjamin Franklin had gotten his way. Which bird do you think is the best symbol of the United States?

### THINKING FOCUS

*Why do we have national symbols?*

### Key Terms

- liberty
- monument

---

## DEVELOP

Have students preview the lesson by reading the headings and looking at the visuals. Then begin the Graphic Overview on the board and have students complete it as they discuss the lesson.

### CULTURE
Study Skills

Emphasize that our national symbols reflect our pride in our country. Write the words *turkey* and *eagle* on the board. Then as you read each of the following words aloud, have students tell you under which animal to write the word: *soaring, plodding, proud, strong.* Add any other adjectives the students can contribute. Conclude that Americans value the qualities associated with eagles.

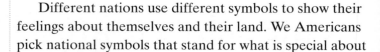

## Symbols Show Pride

▼ *The Liberty Bell has been cracked twice. It hasn't been rung since 1835, the second time it broke.*

### How Do We Know?

*How do we know that eagles are in danger? The U.S. Fish and Wildlife Service sends out teams of people to study bald eagles and keep track of how many new ones are born each year. The teams usually watch the birds with binoculars from a distance. That way, the eagles aren't frightened.*

Different nations use different symbols to show their feelings about themselves and their land. We Americans pick national symbols that stand for what is special about our country. Our symbols stand for our pride and good feelings about the United States.

For example, the Liberty Bell is a symbol of the **liberty,** or freedom, that Americans believe in. The Liberty Bell was rung in 1776 when the United States declared its independence from England. Today it hangs in Philadelphia, Pennsylvania.

Other cities have monuments that are national symbols. A **monument** is a building that honors a person or an event. If you were to visit our nation's capital, Washington, D.C., you could see the tall Washington Monument. It was built to honor George Washington. The Gateway Arch stands west of the Mississippi River in St. Louis, Missouri. This stainless steel monument honors the pioneers who moved West to settle the land.

### Preserving Our Symbols

These symbols are special because they remind us of important ideas and beliefs about our country and our land. That is why we should try to preserve them.

Today the bald eagle is so rare that it is in danger of dying out. Pollution and hunting have put the bald eagle in danger. Changes to the land have made it hard for the eagle to find food to eat and places to build nests.

226

## Access Activity

Have students choose and draw an animal other than an eagle to represent the United States. Tell students to list the animal's qualities that make it a fitting symbol for our country.

## Access Strategy

Begin by drawing several symbols (heart—love; oak tree—strength; smiling face—happiness, etc.) on the board. Elicit what they symbolize. Have volunteers draw other symbols and explain their meanings.

Ask what is the best known symbol of the United States. *(the flag)* Have students look at the flag on page 227. Ask what the 50 stars and 13 stripes stand for. *(the 50 states and the original 13 colonies)*

*An important reason the bald eagle was chosen as a national symbol was that it lived only in North America. The bald eagle has been seen in each of the United States, except Hawaii.*

If we work together to care for bald eagles, however, we can help them become plentiful again. As long as they are not hunted and have trees, clean food, and clean land to live on, they will be safe. ■

■ *Why is the eagle a good symbol of the United States?*

## Old Glory

The best-known symbol of the United States is our flag. Sometimes it is called "Old Glory." The flag is a symbol of the idea that we are one nation made up of separate states.

Look at the flag on this stamp. It has 50 stars. Each star stands for one state in our country. The 50 stars mean our nation has 50 states. Our flag also has 13 stripes. Each stripe stands for one of the 13 English colonies that were settled in America.

Our flag is a symbol both of our history and of our nation today, but it has not always looked as it does now. The postage stamps we use to mail letters all over the country have shown a history of our flag. On the next page you can see some of the forms our flag has taken.

*This 1988 stamp shows "Old Glory" as it looks today. The U.S. Postal Service makes sure that it has an up-to-date flag stamp at all times.*

▼ *What is wrong with this can of asparagus? It's against the law to use the flag to advertise or sell products.*

227

■ *The eagle has great strength, a huge wing span, keen eyesight, and the ability to fly high. It lives only in North America and has been found in all 49 of the states on the continent.*

227

## Our Flag's History in Postage Stamps

This 1775 flag shows a snake warning enemies not to tread, or step, on it. It was the first flag to be flown on U.S. Navy ships.

The first Congress decided to use this flag in 1777. Its 13 stripes and stars stand for the original colonies and states. This flag is called the "Stars and Stripes."

This flag is the "Star Spangled Banner." Our national anthem was written about this flag with 15 stars and stripes. It was our country's flag from 1795 to 1818.

In 1959 the flag had 48 stars, as this one does. Two more stars were added later that year when Alaska and Hawaii became our 49th and 50th states.

■ *Our history is reflected in the 13 stripes symbolizing the original 13 colonies. The 50 states that we have today are represented by the 50 stars.*

■ *How does the flag symbolize our history, as well as our nation today?*

As you can see, the flag has changed from the time before we won our independence from England to today. As states joined the union, stars were added to the flag. Whatever form the flag took, it has always stood for a single nation that believes in "liberty and justice for all." ■

### CLOSE

Check students' understanding of the lesson by asking the focus question. Review the Graphic Overview, discussing how the various symbols stand for the nation's proud feelings about freedom, strength, and unity.

### R E V I E W

1. **FOCUS** Why do we have national symbols?
2. **CONNECT** How was the flag changed as our nation moved West?
3. **CRITICAL THINKING** Name other things that might be used as a national symbol.

4. **ACTIVITY** Create your own flag. Choose designs that remind you of the land and people that you learned about in this book. Let these be the symbols on your flag. Display and discuss your design with your classmates.

228

## Homework Options

Have students write personal essays about what the United States means to them.

**Study Guide:** page 42

## Answers to Review Questions

1. National symbols show our feelings about our country and remind us of important ideas and beliefs about our country.
2. As settlers moved to the West, our nation became larger. Eventually more states were added to the United States and stars were added to the flag to represent those new states.

3. Students may suggest various animals, such as bears or buffaloes, or other objects, such as trees or hearts. Students should be able to explain what each symbol would stand for.
4. Encourage creativity of design and ask students to explain what the symbols they used tell about our country.

# Chapter Review

## Reviewing Key Terms

liberty (p. 226)
national holiday (p. 221)
monument (p. 226)

**A.** Write *true* or *false* for each sentence. If a sentence is false, rewrite it to make it true.

1. A national holiday celebrates a famous event in our history or honors people of our country.
2. A place to hold indoor games is called a monument.
3. Liberty is freedom from control by others.

**B.** Write the correct key term for each numbered blank.

Presidents' Day is a __1__ when people throughout the country honor the past presidents of the United States. In Washington, D.C., people may visit a __2__ that honors Abraham Lincoln. Our presidents must work for __3__ and justice for all.

## Exploring Concepts

**A.** The bald eagle is our national symbol. Copy the chart. Fill in the second column to show what the early Indians might have chosen for their symbols.

| Indian people | Symbol |
|---|---|
| Kwakiutl | |
| Cheyenne | |
| Navajo | |

**B.** Long ago the bald eagle was chosen to be our national symbol. Write two reasons why you think that was a good choice.



**Answers to Reviewing Key Terms**

**A.**
1. True
2. False. A building that honors a person or an event is called a monument.
3. True

**B.**
1. national holiday
2. monument
3. liberty

**Answers to Exploring Concepts**

**A.** Sample answers:
Kwakiutl—salmon, cedar tree
Cheyenne—buffalo, cottonwood tree
Navajo—corn, sheep

**B.** Sample answers:
The bald eagle was a good choice because it is a very strong bird. The bald eagle flying free in the sky stands for our freedom.

## Reviewing Skills

1. Read the second paragraph on page 219 again. In one or two sentences, write a summary of the paragraph in your own words.

2. Draw a map to show that Johnny Appleseed walked ten miles in one day from one town to another. Use a scale of one inch for one mile.

## Using Critical Thinking

1. The Wampanoag and the Delaware helped the Pilgrims and the early settlers survive in the wilderness. Do you think monuments should be built in their honor? If so, where?

2. The picture shows children planting trees on Arbor Day many years ago. Today, some towns celebrate Arbor Day and hold tree-planting ceremonies. Do you think Arbor Day should be a national holiday? Why?

## Preparing for Citizenship

1. **ART ACTIVITY** The Liberty Bell is a symbol of our liberty and freedom. Draw a picture of something else that you think would be a good symbol of our liberty. Show your picture to the class. Tell them why it is a good symbol of liberty.

2. **COLLABORATIVE LEARNING** Divide the class into four groups. Each group should prepare a short skit, song, or poem about someone who did something special for our country. Perform your skits, songs, or poems for other classes in your school.

230

# Time/Space Databank

## WORLD: *Political*

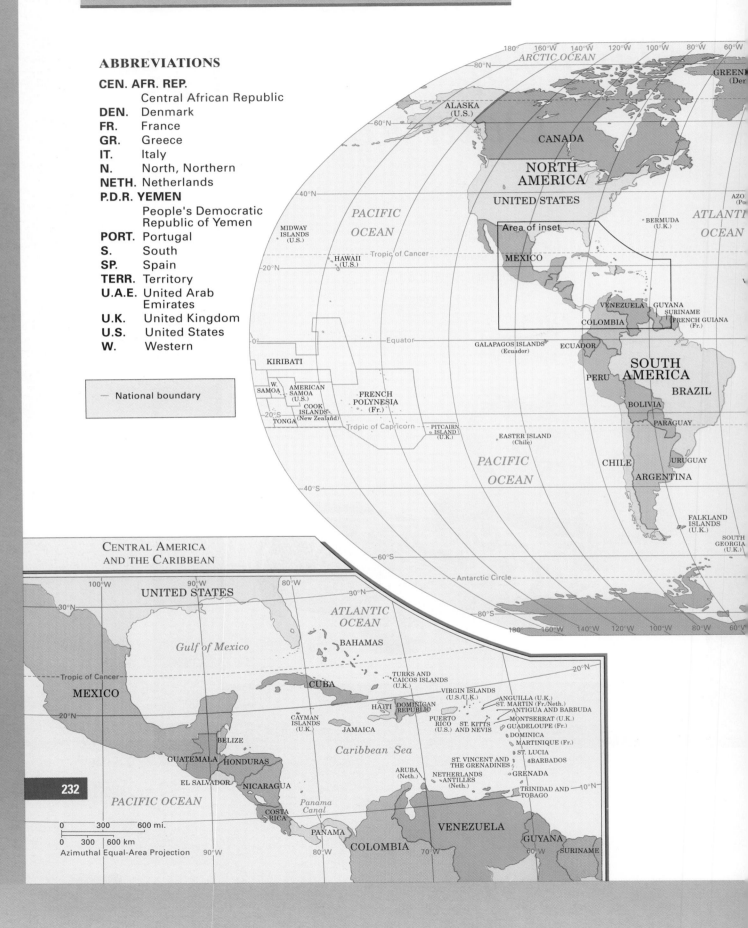

**ABBREVIATIONS**

**CEN. AFR. REP.**
    Central African Republic
**DEN.**  Denmark
**FR.**  France
**GR.**  Greece
**IT.**  Italy
**N.**  North, Northern
**NETH.** Netherlands
**P.D.R. YEMEN**
    People's Democratic
    Republic of Yemen
**PORT.** Portugal
**S.**  South
**SP.**  Spain
**TERR.** Territory
**U.A.E.** United Arab
    Emirates
**U.K.**  United Kingdom
**U.S.**  United States
**W.**  Western

—  National boundary

**232**

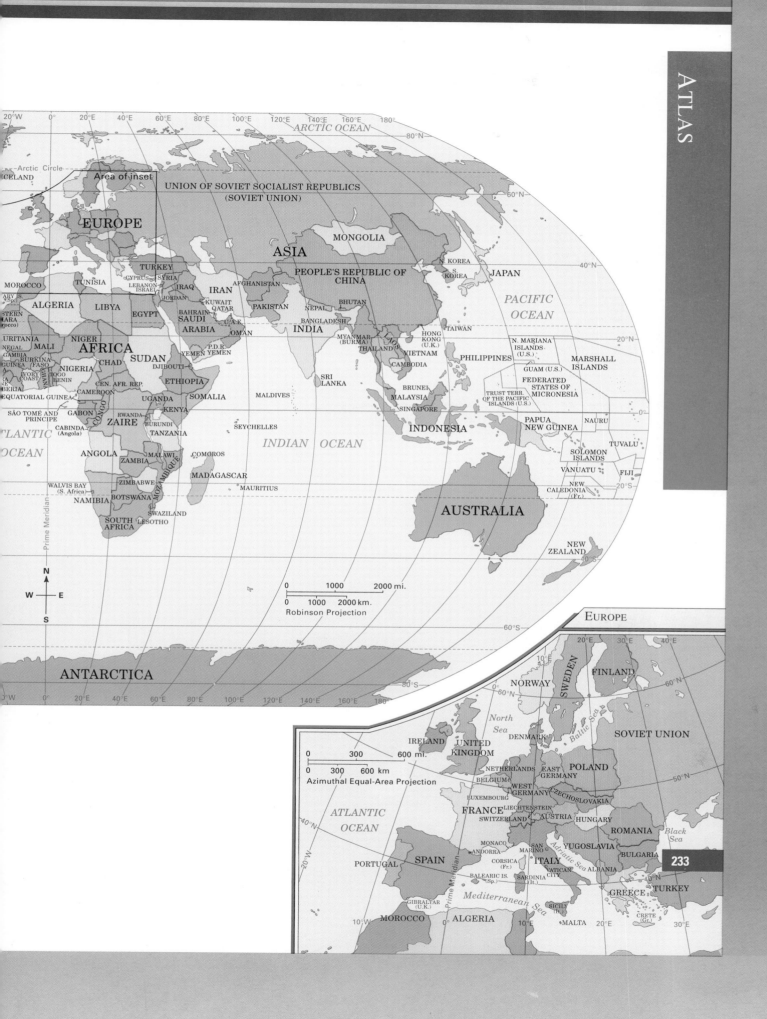

ARCTIC OCEAN
80°N

Arctic Circle
ICELAND
Area of inset
UNION OF SOVIET SOCIALIST REPUBLICS
(SOVIET UNION)
60°N

EUROPE
MONGOLIA
ASIA
N. KOREA
S. KOREA
JAPAN
40°N
PEOPLE'S REPUBLIC OF CHINA
TURKEY
CYPRUS SYRIA
LEBANON
ISRAEL
IRAQ
IRAN
AFGHANISTAN
PACIFIC OCEAN
MOROCCO
TUNISIA
JORDAN
KUWAIT
QATAR
PAKISTAN
P.D.R.
BHUTAN
ARY IS.
(Sp.)
ALGERIA
LIBYA
EGYPT
BAHRAIN
SAUDI
ARABIA
U.A.E.
OMAN
NEPAL
BANGLADESH
INDIA
TAIWAN
HONG
KONG
(U.K.)
20°N
WESTERN
SAHARA
(Morocco)
URITANIA
MALI
NIGER
AFRICA
CHAD
SUDAN
YEMEN YEMEN
DJIBOUTI
MYANMAR
(BURMA)
THAILAND
LAOS
VIETNAM
N. MARIANA
ISLANDS
(U.S.)
MARSHALL
ISLANDS
NEGAL
GAMBIA
GUINEA
BURKINA
FASO
IVORY
COAST
TOGO
BENIN
NIGERIA
CEN. AFR. REP.
ETHIOPIA
SRI
LANKA
CAMBODIA
GUAM (U.S.)
BERIA
EQUATORIAL GUINEA
CAMEROON
UGANDA
SOMALIA
MALDIVES
BRUNEI
MALAYSIA
FEDERATED
STATES OF
MICRONESIA
SÃO TOMÉ AND
PRINCIPE
GABON
CONGO
ZAIRE
RWANDA
BURUNDI
KENYA
TANZANIA
SEYCHELLES
SINGAPORE
TRUST TERR.
OF THE PACIFIC
ISLANDS (U.S.)
PAPUA
NEW GUINEA
NAURU
0°
TLANTIC
OCEAN
ANGOLA
MALAWI
ZAMBIA
COMOROS
INDIAN OCEAN
INDONESIA
SOLOMON
ISLANDS
TUVALU
CABINDA
(Angola)
ZIMBABWE
MOZAMBIQUE
MADAGASCAR
VANUATU
FIJI
20°S
WALVIS BAY
(S. Africa)
BOTSWANA
MAURITIUS
NEW
CALEDONIA
(Fr.)
NAMIBIA
SWAZILAND
AUSTRALIA
SOUTH
AFRICA
LESOTHO

N
W E
S

0    1000    2000 mi.
0  1000  2000 km.
Robinson Projection

NEW
ZEALAND
40°S

60°S

ANTARCTICA
80°S

0°W    0°    20°E    40°E    60°E    80°E    100°E    120°E    140°E    160°E    180°

20°W    0°    20°E    40°E    60°E    80°E    100°E    120°E    140°E    160°E    180°

Prime Meridian

EUROPE

20°E    30°E    40°E
10°E
NORWAY
SWEDEN
FINLAND
60°N
North
Sea
DENMARK
SOVIET UNION
IRELAND
UNITED
KINGDOM
NETHERLANDS
EAST
GERMANY
POLAND
BELGIUM
WEST
GERMANY
CZECHOSLOVAKIA
50°N
LUXEMBOURG
LIECHTENSTEIN
FRANCE
SWITZERLAND
AUSTRIA
HUNGARY
ROMANIA
Black
Sea
MONACO
SAN
MARINO
YUGOSLAVIA
ANDORRA
BULGARIA
CORSICA
(Fr.)
ITALY
VATICAN
CITY
ALBANIA
PORTUGAL
SPAIN
SARDINIA
(It.)
BALEARIC IS.
(Sp.)
GREECE
TURKEY
GIBRALTAR
(U.K.)
Mediterranean Sea
SICILY
(It.)
CRETE
(Gr.)
MOROCCO
ALGERIA
MALTA
10°E
20°E
30°E

ATLANTIC
OCEAN
40°N

0    300    600 mi.
0  300  600 km.
Azimuthal Equal-Area Projection

Baltic Sea
Adriatic Sea

10°W    0°    Prime Meridian

233

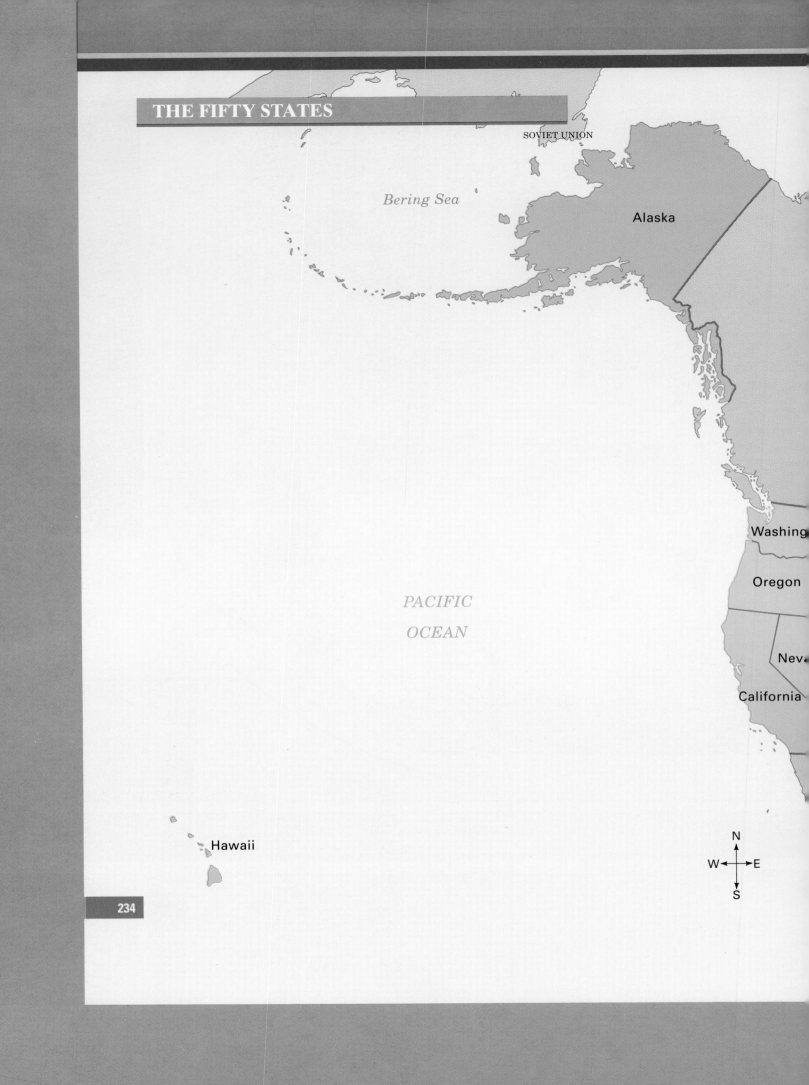

SOVIET UNION

*Bering Sea*

Alaska

*PACIFIC*

*OCEAN*

Washing

Oregon

Nev

California

Hawaii

N

W ← → E

S

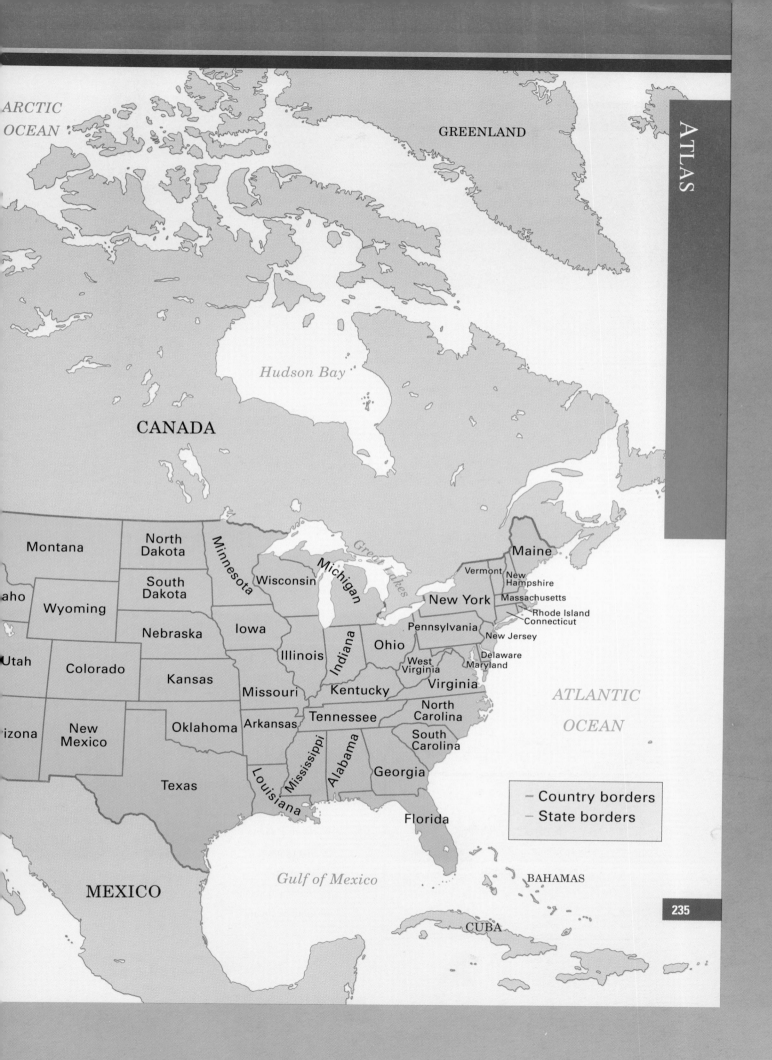

ARCTIC
OCEAN

GREENLAND

Hudson Bay

CANADA

Montana

North
Dakota

Minnesota

Michigan

Great Lakes

Maine

aho

South
Dakota

Wisconsin

Vermont

New
Hampshire

Wyoming

New York

Massachusetts

Rhode Island
Connecticut

Utah

Nebraska

Iowa

Pennsylvania

New Jersey

Colorado

Illinois

Indiana

Ohio

Delaware
Maryland

izona

Kansas

Missouri

Kentucky

West
Virginia

Virginia

ATLANTIC

OCEAN

New
Mexico

Oklahoma

Arkansas

Tennessee

North
Carolina

South
Carolina

Texas

Louisiana

Mississippi

Alabama

Georgia

Florida

Country borders
State borders

MEXICO

Gulf of Mexico

BAHAMAS

235

CUBA

# UNITED STATES: *Political*

ALASKA

U.S.S.R.

ARCTIC OCEAN

Arctic Circle

Yukon River

0   300   600 mi.
0   300   600 km

Alaska

Fairbanks

CANADA

Anchorage

Juneau

ALEUTIAN   ISLANDS

PACIFIC

OCEAN

HAWAII

KAUAI

NIIHAU

OAHU

Honolulu

PACIFIC

LANAI

MOLOKAI

MAUI

KAHOOLAWE

OCEAN   Hawaii

HAWAII   Hilo

0   100   200 mi.
0   100   200 km

236

Seattle

Washington

Olympia

Columbia River

Portland

Salem

Oregon

Idaho

Boise

Helena   Montana

Billings

Wyomin

Snake River

Pocatello

Casper

Nevada

Salt Lake City

Chey

Provo

San
Francisco

Sacramento

Carson City

Utah

Den

Colorad

California   Las Vegas

Colorado River

P

Los Angeles

Santa Fe

Albuquerque

San Diego

Arizona

New Mexic

Phoenix

Tucson

⊛  National capital

★  State capital

•  Major city

—  National boundary

—  State boundary

MEXIC

CANADA

North Dakota
Bismarck ★
Fargo ●

Minnesota

South Dakota
Pierre ★
Sioux Falls ●

Minneapolis ★
St. Paul ★

Wisconsin

Lake Superior

Michigan

Lake Huron

Lake Michigan

Milwaukee ★
Madison ★

Lansing ★

Lake Erie

Lake Ontario

Maine
Augusta ★

Vermont
Burlington ●
Montpelier ★
New Hampshire
Portland ●
Concord ★

Iowa
Sioux City ●
Omaha ●
Des Moines ★

Nebraska
Platte River
Lincoln ★

Missouri River

Detroit ●
Chicago ●

Illinois
Springfield ★

Indiana
Indianapolis ★

Ohio
Cleveland ●
Columbus ★

Albany ★
New York

Massachusetts
Boston ★
Hartford ★
New Haven ●

Providence ★
Rhode Island
Connecticut

Pennsylvania
Harrisburg ★
Pittsburgh ●

New Jersey
Trenton ★
New York ●

Philadelphia ●
Wilmington ●
Dover ★
Delaware

Kansas
Topeka ★
Wichita ●

Kansas City ●
St. Louis ●
Jefferson City ★

Missouri

Louisville ●
Frankfort ★
Evansville ●
Kentucky

West Virginia
Charleston ★

Virginia
Richmond ★

Baltimore ●
Washington ●
Annapolis ★
Maryland

Norfolk ●

Arkansas River

Oklahoma
Oklahoma City ★
Tulsa ●
Fort Smith ●
Little Rock ★

Arkansas

Tennessee
Nashville ★
Memphis ●

North Carolina
Raleigh ★
Charlotte ●

ATLANTIC OCEAN

Red River

Texas
Dallas ●
Austin ★
Houston ●

Mississippi River

Greenville ●

Alabama
Birmingham ●
Montgomery ★

Georgia
Atlanta ★

South Carolina
Columbia ★
Charleston ●

Savannah ●

Louisiana
Jackson ★
Mississippi
Baton Rouge ★
New Orleans ●

Tallahassee ★

Florida
Tampa ●

BAHAMAS

Rio Grande

Gulf of Mexico

N
W    E
S

Miami ●

0    200    400 mi.
0    200    400 km
Albers Equal-Area Projection

CUBA

237

# UNITED STATES: *Physical*

## ALASKA

ARCTIC OCEAN

U.S.S.R.

BROOKS RANGE

Arctic Circle

SEWARD PEN.

Bering Strait

70°N

65°N

60°N

CANADA

Mt. McKinley
20,320 ft.
6,194 m

ALASKA RANGE

ALEUTIAN ISLANDS

KODIAK

170°E    180

170°W    160°W    150°W    140°W    130°W

0    300    600 mi.
0    300    600 km

50°N

55°N

PACIFIC OCEAN

40°N

35°N

30°N

25°N

CANADA

RANGE

Mt. Rainier
14,410 ft.
4,392 m

Mt. St. Helens
8,364 ft.
2,549 m

Mt. Hood
11,239 ft.
3,426 m

CASCADE RANGE

COASTAL RANGES

COLUMBIA PLATEAU

BITTERROOT RANGE

ROCKY MOUNTAINS

BIG HORN MTS.

Missouri River

Yellowstone

Mt. Shasta
14,162 ft.
4,317 m

CENTRAL VALLEY

SIERRA NEVADA

Great Salt Lake

WASATCH RANGE

UINTA MTS.

CONTINENTAL DIVIDE

GREAT BASIN

San Francisco Bay

Mt. Whitney
14,494 ft.
4,418 m

DEATH VALLEY

MOJAVE DESERT

GRAND CANYON

PAINTED DESERT

Pike
14,
4,

SAC. MTS.

Rio Grande

CHANNEL ISLANDS

MEXI

## HAWAIIAN ISLANDS

160°W    155°W

KAUAI

NIIHAU

OAHU

MOLOKAI

LANAI    MAUI

KAHOOLAWE

PACIFIC OCEAN

HAWAII

20°N

0    100    200 mi.
0    100    200 km

238

## Land Elevation

| Feet | Meters |
|------|--------|
| 13,120 | 4,000 |
| 6,560 | 2,000 |
| 1,640 | 500 |
| 656 | 200 |
| 0 | 0 |
| Below sea level | Below sea level |

Ice-covered land

▲ Mountain Peak

130°W    125°W    120°W    115°W    110°W    105°W

145°W    140°W    135°W    130°W    125°W    120°W    115°W    110°W

50°N    55°N    45°N

CANADA

Lake of
the Woods

MESABI
RANGE

Lake Superior

Lake
Huron

Lake
Michigan

Lake Ontario

Lake Erie

WHITE
MTS.

▲ Mt. Washington
6,288 ft.
1,917 m

ADIRONDACK
MTS.

CATSKILL
MTS.

NANTUCKET

MARTHA'S
VINEYARD

LONG ISLAND

Red River

Mississippi

Des Moines

River

Missouri
River

SAND HILLS

Platte

River

P L A I N S

CENTRAL PLAINS

River

Wabash

River

Ohio
River

Susquehanna
River

ALLEGHENY
PLATEAU

Delaware

Delaware
Bay

Chesapeake Bay

40°N

OZARK
PLATEAU

CUMBERLAND PLATEAU

Tennessee
River

BLUE

RIDGE MTS.

▲ Mt. Mitchell
6,684 ft.
2,037 m

VA

FALL

LINE

35°N

ATLANTIC

OCEAN

70°W

ansas River

Arkansas

River

Mississippi

OUACHITA
MOUNTAINS

Red

River

KY

APPALACHIAN

MOUNTAINS

SC

ATLANTIC COASTAL PLAIN

LANO
ACADO

EDWARDS
PLATEAU

Red

River

Brazos

River

Sabine

River

Colorado

River

Tombigbee

River

Alabama

River

Pearl River

GA

Savannah R.

30°N

Chattahoochee

Altamaha
R.

GULF COASTAL PLAIN

Galveston
Bay

Mobile
Bay

Pensacola
Bay

N
W    E
S

Tampa
Bay

Lake
Okeechobee

BAHAMAS

25°N

Gulf of Mexico

EVERGLADES

FLORIDA KEYS

CUBA

20°N

0        200        400 mi.
0    200    400 km
Albers Equal-Area Projection

239

100°W    95°W    90°W    85°W    80°W    75°W    70°W    55°N    65°W    60°W

50°N

45°N

100°W    95°W    90°W    85°W    80°W    75°W

This gazetteer will help you locate many of the places discussed in this book. The page number tells you where to find each place on a map.

## A

**Abilene** Prairie town in Kansas. It became a booming cattle town in the 1860s. (p. 156)

**Africa** The earth's second largest continent. It lies between the Atlantic and Indian oceans. (pp. 232–233)

**Alabama** Southeastern state on the Gulf of Mexico. Its capital is Montgomery. (pp. 236–237)

**Alaska** State farthest north of all states. Its capital is Juneau. (pp. 236–237)

**Allegheny River** River in eastern United States. It joins the Monongahela River at Pittsburgh to form the Ohio River. (p. 179)

**Appalachian Mountains** Mountain range in eastern North America. It extends about 1,600 miles from southern Canada to Alabama. (p. 122)

**Arizona** Southwestern state on the Mexican border. Its capital is Phoenix. (pp. 236–237)

**Arkansas** South central state. Its capital is Little Rock. (pp. 236–237)

**Asia** The earth's largest continent. It is separated from Europe by the Ural Mountains. (pp. 232–233)

**Atlantic Ocean** The earth's second largest body of water. It borders the eastern coast of the United States. (p. 5)

## B

**Bakersfield** City in south central California at the southern end of the San Joaquin Valley. (p. 171)

**Boonesboro** Pioneer settlement in central Kentucky. Named after Daniel Boone. (p. 135)

## C

**California** Western state on the Pacific coast. Its capital is Sacramento. (pp. 236–237)

**California Trail** Southern branch of the Oregon Trail. It was used by pioneers traveling to California. (p. 149)

**Canada** Country to the north of the United States. Its capital is Ottawa. (pp. 232–233)

**Chicago** City in northeastern Illinois on the shore of Lake Michigan. (p. 156)

**Chisholm Trail** Main trail for cattle drives out of Texas in the 1860s. It extended from San Antonio, Texas, to Abilene, Kansas. (p. 156)

**Colorado** Western state. Its capital is Denver. (pp. 236–237)

**Colorado River** River in southwestern United States. It begins in the mountains of Colorado and flows into the Gulf of California. (p. 21)

**Connecticut** Northeastern state. Its capital is Hartford. (pp. 236–237)

**Cumberland Gap** A pass through the Appalachian Mountains where Kentucky, Virginia, and Tennessee join. (p. 135)

## D

**Delaware** Eastern state on the Atlantic coast. Its capital is Dover. (pp. 236–237)

**Denver** City in north central Colorado. (pp. 236–237)

**Dodge City** City in southwestern Kansas. (p. 158)

## E

**England** The southern part of the island of Great Britain. People from England started many colonies in North America. (p. 117)

**Europe** The earth's second smallest continent. It extends west from the Ural Mountains. (pp. 232–233)

## F

**Florida** Southeastern state on the Atlantic coast. Its capital is Tallahassee. (pp. 236–237)

**France** Country in western Europe. People from France settled in North America beginning in the 1600s. (p. 233)

## G

**Georgia** Southeastern state on the Atlantic coast. Its capital is Atlanta. (pp. 236–237)

**Germany** Former country in Europe, now divided into two countries. German people came to settle eastern North America in the early 1700s. (p. 233)

**Grand Canyon** Canyon of the Colorado River in northwestern Arizona. It is 217 miles long and 4 to 18 miles wide. (p. 20)

**Great Lakes** Group of five lakes between Canada and the United States, including Lakes Superior, Huron, Erie, Ontario, and Michigan. (p. 49)

**Guatemala** Country in Central America. (p. 232)

**Gulf of Mexico** Part of the Atlantic Ocean that borders the southern part of the United States and the eastern part of Mexico. (p. 49)

## H

**Harrodsburg** One of two pioneer towns in central Kentucky (with Boonesboro) at which branches of the Wilderness Trail ended. (p. 135)

**Hawaii** State and island group in the central Pacific Ocean. Its capital is Honolulu. (pp. 236–237)

**Holston River** River in northeastern Tennessee and southwestern Virginia. The Wilderness Road began there. (p. 135)

**Hudson River** River in New York. It begins in the mountains of northern New York and flows into the Atlantic Ocean at New York City. (p. 19)

## I

**Idaho** Northwestern state. Its capital is Boise. (pp. 236–237)

**Illinois** North central state. Its capital is Springfield. (pp. 236–237)

**Independence** City in western Missouri. In pioneer days, it was the starting point for travelers using the Oregon and Santa Fe Trails. (p. 149)

**Indiana** North central state. Its capital is Indianapolis. (pp. 236–237)

**Iowa** North central state. Its capital is Des Moines. (pp. 236–237)

**Ireland** Small country in the British Isles. People from Ireland settled in eastern North America in the early 1700s. (p. 233)

## K

**Kansas** Central state. Its capital is Topeka. (pp. 236–237)

**Kentucky** Southeastern state. Its capital is Frankfort. (pp. 236–237)

**Kilauea** One of two volcanoes in Hawaii Volcanoes National Park. (p. 201)

## L

**Lake Ontario** One of the five Great Lakes, which lie between the United States and Canada. (p. 49)

**Leadville** Town in central Colorado. It became a boom town of silver mining during the 1870s. (p. 161)

**Los Angeles** City in southern California on the Pacific coast. In pioneer days, it became the end of the Santa Fe Trail. (pp. 236–237)

**Louisiana** Southeastern state on the Gulf of Mexico. Its capital is Baton Rouge. (pp. 236–237)

## M

**Maine** Northeastern state on the Atlantic coast. Its capital is Augusta. pp. (236–237)

**Maryland** Eastern state on the Atlantic coast. Its capital is Annapolis. (pp. 236–237)

**Massachusetts** Northeastern state on the Atlantic coast. Its capital is Boston. pp. (236–237)

**Mauna Loa** One of two volcanoes in Hawaii Volcanoes National Park. (p. 201)

**Mexico** Country to the south of and bordering the United States. Its capital is Mexico City. (p. 21)

**Michigan** North central state. Its capital is Lansing. (pp. 236–237)

**Minnesota** North central state. Its capital is St. Paul. (pp. 236–237)

**Mississippi** Southern state on the Gulf of Mexico. Its capital is Jackson. (pp. 236–237)

**Mississippi River** Second longest river in the United States. It begins in northern Minnesota and flows into the Gulf of Mexico at New Orleans. (p. 49)

**Missouri** Central state. Its capital is Jefferson City. (pp. 236–237)

**Missouri River** Longest river in the United States. It begins in western Montana and flows into the Mississippi River near St. Louis. (pp. 236–237)

**Monongahela River** River in eastern United States. It joins the Allegheny River at Pittsburgh to form the Ohio River. (p. 179)

**Montana** Northwestern state. Its capital is Helena. (pp. 236–237)

**Mount McKinley** Mountain peak in south central Alaska. It is the highest peak in North America at 20,320 feet. (pp. 238–239)

## N

**Nebraska** North central state in the Great Plains. Its capital is Lincoln. (pp. 236–237)

**Nevada** Western state. Its capital is Carson City. (pp. 236–237)

**New Hampshire** Northeastern state on the Atlantic coast. Its capital is Concord. (pp. 236–237)

**New Jersey** Northeastern state on the Atlantic coast. Its capital is Trenton. (pp. 236–237)

**New Mexico** Southwestern state on the Mexican border. Its capital is Santa Fe. (pp. 236–237)

**New York** Northeastern state. Its capital is Albany. (pp. 236–237)

**New York City** City in New York at the mouth of the Hudson River. It is the largest city in the United States. (p. 122)

**North America** The third largest continent. It includes the countries of the United States, Canada, Mexico, and those of Central America. (pp. 232–233)

**North Carolina** Southeastern state on the Atlantic coast. Its capital is Raleigh. (pp. 236–237)

**North Dakota** North central state. Its capital is Bismarck. (pp. 236–237)

**North Pole** The most northern point of the earth. (p. 159)

## O

**Ohio** North central state. Its capital is Columbus. (pp. 236–237)

**Ohio River** River formed in Pennsylvania where the Allegheny and the Monongahela rivers join. It flows into the Mississippi River in Illinois. (p. 179)

**Oklahoma** Southwestern state. Its capital is Oklahoma City. (pp. 236–237)

**Oregon** Northwestern state on the Pacific coast. Its capital is Salem. (pp. 236–237)

**Oregon Trail** Pioneer route from Independence, Missouri, to the West. (p. 149)

## P

**Pacific Ocean** The earth's largest body of water. It borders the western coast of the United States. (p. 5)

**Pennsylvania** Northeastern state. Its capital is Harrisburg. (pp. 236–237)

**Philadelphia** City in southeastern Pennsylvania on the Delaware River. (p. 122)

**Pittsburgh** City in southwestern Pennsylvania at the place where the Allegheny and Monongahela rivers meet to form the Ohio River. (p. 179)

**Platte River** Most important river in Nebraska. Its two branches begin in the mountains of Colorado. (pp. 236–237)

**Plymouth** Harbor town in southeastern Massachusetts. (p. 117)

**Plymouth Colony** Second English settlement in America. It was founded by Pilgrims in 1620. (p. 117)

## R

**Rhode Island** Northeastern state on the Atlantic coast. Its capital is Providence. (pp. 236–237)

**Rocky Mountains** Longest mountain range in North America. It extends more than 3,000 miles from northern Alaska to northern New Mexico. (pp. 238–239)

## S

**St. Louis** City in eastern Missouri on the Mississippi River. (pp. 236–237)

**San Antonio** City in southern Texas. It was the beginning of the Chisholm Trail during the 1860s. (p. 156)

**San Joaquin Valley** Rich farming area in central California. The San Joaquin River runs through this land. (p. 171)

**Santa Fe** City in north central New Mexico. It is the capital of New Mexico. In pioneer days, it was an important stop on the Santa Fe Trail. (p. 149)

**Santa Fe Trail** Pioneer route from Independence, Missouri, to Santa Fe, New Mexico. It was extended later to Los Angeles, California. (p. 149)

**Scotland** Northern part of the island of Great Britain. People from Scotland settled in the eastern part of North America in the early 1700s. (p. 233)

**Sonoran Desert** Desert in southwestern United States and northwestern Mexico. (p. 52)

**South America** The earth's fourth largest continent. It lies between the Atlantic Ocean and the Pacific Ocean. (pp. 232–233)

**South Carolina**  Southeastern state on the Atlantic coast. Its capital is Columbia. (pp. 236–237)

**South Dakota**  North central state. Its capital is Pierre. (pp. 236–237)

**South Pole**  The most southern point of the earth. (p. 159)

**Spain**  Country in southwestern Europe. People from Spain came to North America to start colonies. (p. 233)

## T

**Tennessee**  Southeastern state. Its capital is Nashville. (pp. 236–237)

**Teton Mountains**  Range of the Rocky Mountains in northwestern Wyoming and southeastern Idaho. Grand Teton is the highest peak in the range. (pp. 238–239)

**Texas**  South central state on the Gulf of Mexico coast. Its capital is Austin. (pp. 236–237)

## U

**United States**  Country of central and northwestern North America. It is made up of 50 states. Its capital is Washington, D.C. Its abbreviation is U.S. (pp. 232–233)

**Utah**  Western state. Its capital is Salt Lake City. (pp. 236–237)

## V

**Vermont**  Northeastern state. Its capital is Montpelier. (pp. 236–237)

**Virginia**  Southeastern state on the Atlantic coast. Its capital is Richmond. (pp. 236–237)

**Virginia Colony**  First English colony in North America, made up of several settlements. (p. 117)

## W

**Washington**  Northwestern state on the Pacific coast. Its capital is Olympia. (pp. 236–237)

**Washington, D.C.**  Eastern city on the Potomac River. It is the capital of the United States. (pp. 236–237)

**West Virginia**  East central state. Its capital is Charleston. (pp. 236–237)

**Wichita**  City in south central Kansas. (p. 158)

**Wilderness Road**  Pioneer road from Virginia to Kentucky through the Cumberland Mountains. Daniel Boone led the men who cut the trail for the road. (p. 135)

**Wisconsin**  North central state. Its capital is Madison. (pp. 236–237)

**Wyoming**  Western state. Its capital is Cheyenne. (pp. 236–237)

## Y

**Yellowstone National Park**  Oldest and largest United States national park. Most of it is in northwestern Wyoming. It is famous for its hot springs. (p. 200)

**mountain**
a steeply raised mass of land, much higher than the surrounding country

**ocean**
a salty body of water covering a large area of the earth (also, **sea**)

**tree line**
on a mountain, the area above which no trees grow

**mountain range**
a row of mountains

**valley**
low land between hills or mountains

**highland**
land that is higher than most of the surrounding land

**forest**
a large area of land where many trees grow

**hill**
a raised mass of land, smaller than a mountain

**prairie**
a large, level area of grassland without trees

**desert**
a dry area where few plants grow

**plain**
a broad, flat area of land

244

**harbor**
a protected body of water where ships can safely stop

**sea level**
the level of the surface of the ocean

**coast**
the land next to the ocean

**bay**
part of a lake or ocean extending into the land

**river**
a large stream of water that runs into a lake, ocean, or another river

**island**
a body of land with water all around it

**shore**
the land along the edge of a lake, sea, or ocean

**lowland**
land that is lower than most of the surrounding land

**lake**
a body of water with land all around it

245

# GLOSSARY

## Pronunciation Key

| Spellings | Symbol | Spellings | Symbol | Spellings | Symbol |
|---|---|---|---|---|---|
| pat | ă | kick, cat, pique | k | thin | th |
| pay | ā | lid, needle | l | this | *th* |
| care | âr | mum | m | cut | ŭ |
| father | ä | no, sudden | n | urge, term, firm, | ûr |
| bib | b | thing | ng | word, heard | |
| church | ch | pot, horrid | ŏ | valve | v |
| deed, milled | d | toe | ō | with | w |
| pet | ĕ | caught, paw, for | ô | yes | y |
| bee | ē | noise | oi | zebra, xylem | z |
| life, phase, rough | f | took | o͞o | vision, pleasure, | zh |
| gag | g | boot | o͞o | garage | |
| hat | h | out | ou | about, item, edible, | ə |
| which | hw | pop | p | gallop, circus | |
| pit | ĭ | roar | r | butter | ər |
| pie, by | ī | sauce | s | | |
| pier | îr | ship, dish | sh | Primary stress ´ | |
| judge | j | tight, stopped | t | Secondary stress ´ | |

## A

**adaptation** (ăd´āp-tā´shən)  A change in the way of life of people, animals, or plants in order to fit the surroundings in which they live.  (p. 101)

**agriculture** (ăg´rĭ-kŭl´chər)  The business of working the soil, growing crops, and raising livestock.  (p. 171)

## B

**blaze** (blāz)  To mark a trail by cutting bark from a tree.  (p. 136)

**boom town** (bo͞om´ toun´)  A town that grows and becomes wealthy very quickly.  (p. 162)

## C

**cedar** (sē´dər)  A type of evergreen tree whose wood is often reddish in color. (p. 66)

**ceremony** (sĕr´ə-mō´nē)  An act that is performed in honor of an important event. People may sing, dance, tell stories, or make speeches during a ceremony.  (p. 72)

**chant** (chănt)  A song that is sung on the same note or on a few notes, often as a form of prayer.  (p. 103)

**climate** (klī´mĭt)  The weather, including amount of rain, snow, wind, and the degree of coldness or hotness of an area over a long time.  (p. 54)

**coast** (kōst)  The land beside a sea.  (p. 5)

**colony** (kŏl´ə-nē) An area that is settled by people from a faraway country and ruled by that home country. (p. 117)

**conservation** (kŏn´sûr-vā´shən) The protection or wise use of things found in nature that are useful to people. (p. 199)

## D

**decompose** (dē´kəm-pōz´) To rot or fall apart slowly. (p. 209)

**desert** (dĕz´ərt) A dry, sandy area that gets very little rain. (p. 51)

## E

**environment** (ĕn-vī´rən-mənt) The surroundings in which animals, people, and plants live. (p. 203)

**erosion** (ĭ-rō´zhən) The slow wearing away of land. (p. 5)

## F

**fertilizer** (fûr´tl-ī´zēr) Chemicals that are added to soil to make plants grow healthier and more quickly. (p. 172)

**flood** (flŭd) Water that overflows its banks and covers land that is normally dry. (p. 23)

**forest** (fôr´ĭst) A large area of land that is covered with trees and other plants. (p. 28)

**freight** (frāt) Materials that are carried by train, ship, truck, or airplane. (p. 183)

## G

**goods** (gŏŏdz) Things that people buy and sell. (p. 122)

## H

**hogan** (hō´gän´) A one-room Navajo house made of logs covered with mud. Mud kept hogans warm in summer and cool in winter. (p. 99)

**humus** (hyōō´məs) The brown or black matter that is found in soil and made up of rotting plants or animals. (p. 30)

## I

**industry** (ĭn´də-strē) A business that makes things to sell or that provides services. (p. 179)

**inland** (ĭn´lənd) Away from the coast. (p. 121)

**irrigation** (ĭr´ĭ-gā´shən) To bring water to dry land through the use of ditches, canals, or pipes. (p. 172)

## L

**lake** (lāk) A large body of water with land all around it. (p. 19)

**liberty** (lĭb´ər-tē) Freedom from control by others. (p. 226)

**livestock** (līv´stŏk´) Animals, such as sheep or horses, that are raised for home use or to be sold. (p. 101)

**location** (lō-kā´shən) The place where something could be or is found. (p. 179)

**long house** (lông´ hōus´) A house up to 60 feet long that was used by Eastern and Western North American Indians. This type of house was built with logs that were split into thin boards. (p. 67)

## M

**mineral** (mĭn´ər-əl) A naturally occurring material, such as gold or iron, that is found in the earth. (p. 161)

**monument** (mŏn´yə-mənt) A statue or building that honors a person or an event. (p. 226)

**mountain** (mōun´tən) Land that has steep sides and a rounded or pointed peak, and that stands much higher than the land around it. (p. 45)

**myth** (mĭth) A story that explains something in nature or the beliefs that a group of people share. (p. 87)

## N

**national holiday** (năsh´ə-nəl hŏl´ĭ-dā´) A holiday that is set aside by the national government to honor a country and its people. (p. 221)

**natural resource** (năch´ər-əl rē´sôrs´) Anything that is found in nature that people can use. (p. 81)

## O

**ocean** (ō´shən) A large body of salt water. Oceans cover much of the earth's surface. The three largest oceans of the world are the Pacific, the Atlantic, and the Indian. The Pacific is the largest of the three. (p. 5)

## P

**pass** (păs) A narrow passage at a low point between mountain peaks. (p. 148)

**physical feature** (fĭz´ĭ-kəl fē´chər) A natural part of the earth's surface. (p. 45)

**pioneer** (pī´ə-nîr´) A person who is the first to settle in a wilderness area, leading the way for others to follow. (p. 135)

**pollution** (pə-lōō´shən) Harmful material that makes the air, water, or soil dirty. (p. 205)

**population** (pŏp´yə-lā´shən) The number of people that live in an area. (p. 155)

**prairie** (prâr´ē) A large area of flat or hilly land covered by grasses. (p. 34)

**predator** (prĕd´ə-tər) An animal that lives by hunting other animals for food. (p. 35)

## R

**recycling** (rē-sī´klĭng) The process of treating trash so that it can be used again. (p. 209)

**river** (rĭv´ər) A large moving stream of water that flows into an ocean, lake, or other body of water. (p. 18)

## S

**salmon** (săm´ən) A type of fish that usually lives in salt water but swims up a river to lay its eggs. (p. 65)

**sand painting** (sănd´ pān´tĭng) A picture that is made by Navajo Indians with bits of crushed rock, plants, and other dry materials. A sand painting tells a story about nature and spirits. (p. 104)

**services** (sûr´vĭs-əz) Businesses that perform work or provide help for people. (p. 181)

**steel mills** (stēl´ mĭlz´) Factories that make steel. (p. 179)

**survive** (sər-vīv´) To stay alive. (p. 117)

**symbol** (sĭm´bəl) Something that stands for something else. (p. 88)

## T

**temperature** (tĕm´pər-ə-chŏor´) The degree of coldness or hotness of something. (p. 45)

**timberline** (tĭm´bər-līn´) The limit of height on a mountain above which trees do not grow. (p. 45)

**tipi** (tē´pē) A cone-shaped tent made of animal skins or bark used by some North American Indians. (p. 81)

**topsoil** (tŏp´soĭl´) The top layer of soil, usually darker and richer than the soil beneath it. (p. 199)

**totem pole** (tō´təm pōl´) A wooden pole that Northwest Coast Indians decorated with carved figures that may help show a family's history. (p. 71)

**trade** (trād) The business of buying and selling goods. (p. 184)

**trade center** (trād´ sĕn´tər) A town or city where people take part in buying and selling goods and services. (p. 156)

**transportation** (trăns´pər-tā´shən) A system or way of moving passengers or things that people buy and sell. (p. 184)

## V

**vein** (vān) A long strip of mineral found in rock. (p. 160)

## W

**wagon train** (wăg´ən trān´) A line of wagons pulled by oxen, mules, or horses that was used to transport people and goods across the country. (p. 149)

**waste** (wāst) Materials that are no longer useful and are thrown away. (p. 205)

**wilderness** (wĭl´dər-nĭs) Land that has not been changed by people or their actions. (p. 122)

# ACKNOWLEDGMENTS

### Text (continued from page iv)

**96–97** Reprinted with permission of Charles Scribner's Sons, an imprint of Macmillan Publishing Company from *The Desert Is Theirs* by Byrd Baylor, illustrated by Peter Parnall. Text copyright © 1975 Byrd Baylor. Illustrations copyright © 1975 Peter Parnall. **98** untitled Navajo poem, Copyright © 1978 by Richard Erdoes. Reprinted by permission of Sterling Publishing Co., Inc., 387 Park Ave. S., New York, NY 10016. **138–45 (xvi–xvii)** Chapters 1 and 2 from *Wagon Wheels* by Barbara Brenner, illustrated by Don Bolognese. Text Copyright © 1978 by Barbara Brenner. Illustrations Copyright © 1978 by Don Bolognese. Reprinted by permission of Harper & Row, Publishers, Inc. **154** "The Old Chisolm Trail", Copyright © 1939 by Kansas State Historical Society. Reprinted by permission of Kansas State Historical Society. **182** "Travel" by Edna St. Vincent Millay. From *Collected Poems*, Harper & Row. Copyright 1921, 1948 by Edna St. Vincent Millay. Reprinted by permission. **192–97** (text) *Once There Was a Tree* by Natalia Romanova, adapted by Anne Schwarz. Copyright © 1985 by K. Thienemanns Verlag, Stuttgart. English translation © 1985 by Dial Books for Young Readers. Reprinted by permission of the publisher, Dial Books for Young Readers. (illustrations) *Once There Was a Tree* by Natalia Romanova, adapted by Anne Schwarz, pictures by Gennady Spirin. Copyright © 1985 by K. Thienemanns Verlag, Stuttgart. Reproduced by permission of the publisher, Dial Books for Young Readers, and VAAP on behalf of the artist. **218** From "Johnny Appleseed" from *A Book of Americans*, Rosemary and Stephen Vincent Benet. Copyright 1933 by Rosemary & Stephen Vincent Benet. Copyright renewed © 1961 by Rosemary Carr Benet. Reprinted by permission of Brandt & Brandt Literary Agents, Inc. **246** Pronunciation key copyright © 1985 by Houghton Mifflin Company. Adapted and reprinted by permission from *The American Heritage Dictionary*, Second College Edition.

### Illustrations

Literature border design by Peggy Skycraft.

**Ligature** 35, 37. **Brian Battles** 68, 69, 107. **Howard Berelson** 53, 74, 150, 222. **Chris Bjornberg, Photo Researchers** 2–3, 26, 42. **Jeanni Brunnick** 82, 83. **Randy Chewning** 45, 47, 119. **Susan David** 6, 22. **Roger Dondis** 105, 106(r). **Ebet Dudley** 48. **Randall Fleck** 70, 98, 106(l). **Mark Langeneckert** 32, 56, 85. **Joe LeMonnier** 5, 109. **Al Lorenz** 67, 124. **Laura Lydecker** 36. **Kathy Mitchell** 89, 101, 181. **James Needham** 29, 202. **Ed Parker** 9, 120, 126–127, 172, 225. **Judy Reed** 157. **Gary Toressi** 244, 245. **Cindy Wrobel** 186, 187, 191, 206–7, 210. **Oliver Yourke** 185. **Other: 104** Source of painting: *Navajo Sandpainting Art* by Eugene Baatsoslanii Joe and Mark Bahti, Copyright © 1978, Treasure Chest Publications.

### Maps

**Ligature** 59, 111, 165. **R. R. Donnelley & Sons Company Cartographic Services** Back Cover, 232–33, 234–35, 236–37, 238–39. **JAK Graphics** 19, 21, 35, 49, 52, 81, 100, 117, 122, 131, 135, 149, 156, 158, 159, 161, 171, 179, 199, 200.

### Photographs

GH—Grant Heilman Photography; LC—Library of Congress; MA—Museum of the American Indian; NYPL—New York Public Library; PH—Photographic Resources; PR—Photo Researchers, Inc.; RBC—Royal British Columbia Museum, Victoria, BC, Canada; RR—Root Resources; SK—Stephen Kennedy; TBM—The Thomas Burke Memorial Washington State Museum; TIB—The Image Bank; TS—Tom Stack & Associates; TSW—TSW—Click/Chicago Ltd.

**Front cover** Peter Bosey, Missouri School for the Blind. **xviii–1** © David Muench. **2** © Jeff Apoian, Nawrocki Stock Photo (tl,br); © Geraldo Corsi, TS (c). **3** © Grant Heilman, GH. **4** SK (t,bl,br); © Lawrence Migdale, PR (b). **5** © Brian Parker, TS. **7** SK (t); © Four By Five, Inc. (l); © Eric Simmons, Stock Boston (cr). **8–9** SK. **18** © L. L. T. Rhodes, TSW (tr); © Frank Oberle, PH (c). **19** © Jim Appleyard. **20** © Fred McConnaughey, PR (tl); © Alain Thomas, PR (b). **20–21** SK. **21** Smithsonian Institution (tl); Dennis Hamm, National Park Service (br). **22** © Thomas G. Rampton, GH. **23** © Steve Proehl, TIB. **25** Thomas G. Rampton, GH (t); Steve Prochl, TIB. **26** © Ruth Dixon (tl); © Diana L. Stratton, TS (c). **26–27** © Grant Heilman, GH. **27** © Hugh Spencer, PR (tr); © Bob McKeever, TS (br). **28** © Steve Maslowski, PR (t); © Tom Mareschal, TIB (b). **30** SK (tl,tr,bl,br); © John Kaprielian, PR (tc).

**31** SK (tl,cr); © Steve Maslowski, PR (tc); © Jeff Lapore, PR (c). **33** The Thomas Gilcrease Institute of American History and Art, Tulsa, OK (l); SK (r). **34** Grant Heilman, GH. **35** © Diana L. Stratton, TS. **36** SK; © Rod Planck, PR (l); © Leonard Lee Rue III, PR (r). **37** © Brian Parker, TS (l); © Larry P. Brock, PR (r). **38** SK. **39** SK. **42** © J. H. Robinson, PR (r); ©Joe McDonald, TS (b). **42–43** © Bob Firth. **43** © Kenneth W. Fink, RR. **44** © David Stoecklein, The Stock Market (tr); SK (r); © Don Murie, Meyers Photo-Art (b). **46** © Leonard Lee Rue III, TSW. **50** © Frank Oberle, PH (t); © Frank Siteman, PH (b). **51** © G. C. Kelley, PR. **52** © Grant Heilman, GH. **54** © Milton Rand, TS (t); © Stephen Krasemann, PR (b). **55** SK (tl); © John Cancalosi, TS (tr); © Bob McKeever, TS(b). **56–57** SK. **60–61** © Werner Forman Archive/Private Collection, NY. **62** © Chris Speedie, Image Finders (l); RBC (r). **62–63** Edward Curtis, LC. **63** Eduardo Calderon, TBM. **64** RBC (l); Edward Curtis, University of Washington Libraries (detail) (r). **65** © Werner Forman Archive. **66** Eduardo Calderon, TBM (t); TBM (b). **71** LC (bl); © Dan Fivehouse, Image Finders (br). **72** TBM (bl); LC (br). **73** © Werner Forman Archive/Provincial Museum, Victoria, BC, Canada (t); H. I. Smith, American Museum of Natural History (b). **75** TBM. **78** © Brian Parker, TS (l); Philbrook Museum of Art, University of Tulsa Collection (r). **79** © Paul Conklin (t); Smithsonian Institution (b). **80** © Native American Images. **81** Museum of the Great Plains. **82** © Brian Parker, TS. **82–83** SK. **83** MA (c). **84** Smithsonian Institution. **86** Field Museum of Natural History. **87** USDA-NFS. **88** MA (l); Field Museum of Natural History (c). **90** Mesa Verde National Park (l); PR (b). **91** SK (r): NYPL; The Denver Art Museum; Peter Kaplan; Philadelphia Museum of Art; Georgia Historical Society; MA; Reader's Digest; SK (b): Holmes & Meier Publishers; MA. **94** © Mark Bahti (l); © Lois Moulton, TSW (c). **94–95** © Marcia Keegan. **95** Philbrook Art Center, Tulsa, OK (b). **98** © Craig Aurness, West Light. **99** SK (t,b); © Roger Wolken, TSW (cr). **102** Grant Heilman, GH. **103** © Terry Eiler, Stock Boston. **104** © Mark Bahti. **105** © Terry Eiler, Stock Boston. **107** SK. **112–13** Nebraska State Historical Society. **114** © UPI/ Bettman Newsphoto. **114–15** Malcolm Varon, Metropolitan Life. **115** © Jeff Apoian, PR (tr); New York State Historical Assn. (br). **116** NYPL (t); Plymouth, Pilgrim Society (b). **118** © UPI/Bettman Newsphoto. **121** SK. **123** © North Wind Picture Archives. **125** NYPL (t); The Farmer's Museum, NY (r). **126** SK. **128** SK, St. Louis Public Library (l); Missouri Historical Society (b). **129** SK, Jane Knirr Archive. **132** © Esto Photographics (l); Private Collection (c). **132–33** The Kansas State Historical Society, Topeka; © Time-Life, Henry Beville, Anne and Madison Grant. **134** © David Muench. **135** © David Muench. **136** © William Strode. **137** Joshua Shaw, Museum of Science and Industry, Chicago. **146** © L. E. Schaefer, RR. **147** The Granger Collection. **148** Elmer Fryer, Kathy Spangler Archive. **151** Denver Public Library (t); from *The Old West: The Pioneers*, Harald Sund © 1974 Time-Life Books, Inc. (b). **152** USDA (t); © Mary Root, RR. **153** National Archives. **154** © William Loren Katz Collection. **155** NYPL. **160** © North Wind Picture Archives. **161** LC. **162** Yale University Art Gallery (t); W. H. Jackson, Culver Pictures, Inc. (b). **163** Jack Parsons, The Stock Broker. **166–67** © 1987 Kinuko Y. Craft. **168** © Tony Schanuel, PH (l); Greater Pittsburgh Office of Promotion (r). **168–69** © Grant Heilman, GH. **169** © John Livzey. **170** SK(t,l); © GH (b). **173** SK (t); © Grant Heilman, GH (b). **174** © Lee Balterman, Gartman Agency. **174–75** SK. **175** © William J. Kennedy, TIB (t); © Hans Wendler, TIB (c); © Michael Melford, TIB (b). **176** © Simon Wilkinson, TIB. **178** © Collection of the Equitable Life Assurance Society of the United States. **180** © Detroit Publishing Co., LC. (tr); © Robert Colton, Black Star (bl). **182** © Bob Taylor, FPG International. **183** Coverdale & Colpitts (tl); LC (br). **184** © Dave Gleiter, FPG International. **185** SK(t); © Tom Tracy, FPG International (br). **186** © Chuck O'Rear, West Light. **190** © Dennis Stock, Magnum Photos (l); © Alvis Upitis, TIB (c); **190–91** USDA-NPS. **198** D. L. Kernodle for FSA, LC. **200** © Spencer Swanger, TS. **201** © John Buitenkant, PR (t); © Greg Vaughn, TS (b). **203** USDA-FS Bauermeister (l); USDA-FS Frank Erickson (r). **204** © Mike Mathers, Black Star. **205** © Mike Andrews, Animals, Animals/Earth Scenes (l); © Roger J. Cheng (tr). **208** © Dennis Capolongo, Black Star. **209** Rick Benkof. **211** SK. **212** SK. **213** © John Fong. **215** SK. **216** © Brent Jones. **216–17** © Raphael Macia, PR (b); © John G. Herron, Stock Boston (t); **217** © Grant Spencer, PR. **218** SK. **219** John Chapman, The Granger Collection (tl); SK (tr); © John Lei, Stock Boston (b). **220** Grant Wood, © Associated American Artists, NY. **223** © COMSTOCK. **226** © Minardi, Uniphoto Picture Agency. **227** © T. Kitchin, TS (t); SK, U. S. Postal Service (cl); © Pentagram (br); **227–28** SK, U. S. Postal Service. **230** Grantwood, © Associated American Artists, NY.

Picture research assistance by Carousel Research, Inc. and Meyers Photo-Art.

254